THE TV COMPANION
COOKBOOK
2011

THE TV COMPANION
COOKBOOK
2011

BY THE EDITORS AT
AMERICA'S TEST KITCHEN

ILLUSTRATIONS BY
JOHN BURGOYNE

PHOTOGRAPHY BY
DANIEL J. VAN ACKERE
CARL TREMBLAY

AMERICA'S TEST KITCHEN
BROOKLINE, MASSACHUSETTS

AMERICA'S TEST KITCHEN
17 Station Street, Brookline, MA 02445

Library of Congress Cataloging-in-Publication Data
The Editors at America's Test Kitchen

AMERICA'S TEST KITCHEN: THE TV COMPANION COOKBOOK 2011
1st Edition

ISBN-10: 1-933615-72-9   ISBN-13: 978-1-933615-72-1
Hardcover: $34.95 US
1. Cooking. 1. Title
2010

Manufactured in the United States of America

10 9 8 7 6 5 4 3 2 1

Distributed by America's Test Kitchen
17 Station Street, Brookline, MA 02445

EDITORIAL DIRECTOR: Jack Bishop
EXECUTIVE EDITOR: Elizabeth Carduff
SENIOR EDITOR: Lori Galvin
ASSOCIATE EDITOR: Kate Hartke
EDITORIAL ASSISTANT: Alyssa King
DESIGN DIRECTOR: Amy Klee
ART DIRECTOR: Greg Galvan
ASSOCIATE ART DIRECTOR: Matthew Warnick
DESIGNER: Beverly Hsu
STAFF PHOTOGRAPHER: Daniel J. van Ackere
FOOD STYLISTS: Marie Piraino and Mary Jane Sawyer
PRODUCTION DIRECTOR: Guy Rochford
SENIOR PRODUCTION MANAGER: Jessica Lindheimer Quirk
SENIOR PROJECT MANAGER: Alice Carpenter
TRAFFIC AND PRODUCTION COORDINATOR: Kate Hux
COLOR AND IMAGING SPECIALIST: Andrew Mannone
PRODUCTION AND IMAGING SPECIALISTS: Judy Blomquist and Lauren Pettapiece
COPYEDITOR: Cheryl Redmond
PROOFREADER: Debra Hudak
INDEXER: Elizabeth Parson

CONTENTS

PREFACE

INSTEAD OF CALLING THIS VOLUME A COMPANION cookbook to our America's Test Kitchen TV show, we should have simply called it *The Best of Cook's Illustrated Magazine 2011* since we select the best recipes from that year's magazine when we choose the episodes for our show. It is much like an animated, live-video version of the magazine—you can actually watch us cook through every issue of *Cook's,* cover to cover, picking out the best of the best.

My family's farm is situated in a small valley, nestled in a large uninhabited area, as wild as when the first settlers founded Vermont in the 18th century. Hiking up into the mountains above the homestead, I am always surprised by what still lies undetected. On a recent horseback ride, I almost ran into a black bear. I've seen large flocks of wild turkeys, a buck appearing out of the smoky twilight on the last day of the season, bobcats, porcupines, herons, hawks, a bald eagle, coyotes, and tracks that looked a whole lot like a cougar to me. Uncovering secrets is about time and patience, about going back, again and again, to discover what you have missed the first 100 times around.

That sounds a great deal like the philosophy of our test kitchen. When I founded *Cook's Magazine* 30 years ago, in 1980, I often wondered if we would run out of things to investigate, as if cooking were some finite universe of recipes and techniques. Of course that hasn't happened—it turns out that a new day in the test kitchen is much like a new day in the woods. You never know what to expect.

Some of our test kitchen discoveries sound simple enough—how to produce a world-class old-fashioned pot roast—but, yet, the most basic procedures are often the most difficult to deconstruct. How do you get a great baked apple without that mealy texture or an apple that is half cooked and half crunchy? This book solves that age-old problem. Similar seemingly simple recipes include Pan-Seared Scallops, Steak Frites, Best Beef Stew, and Hearty Minestrone. In recent years, we have tended to look farther afield as well, bringing new recipes into the American repertoire such as Greek-Style Shrimp with Tomatoes and Feta or Chicken Canzanese. Of course we also pull out all

the stops to make the very best versions of classics such as chicken pot pie, chocolate cupcakes, banana bread (one of my personal favorites), and homemade focaccia.

Years ago, I was standing by our narrow brook and heard a low humming sound. I looked up and saw a black swarm of honeybees about 8 feet off the ground and 10 feet high, floating above the field and up into the woods. I tried to run and keep up with the swarm but soon lost them in the half-light of the dark woods. It reminded me of a story from *Old Squire's Farm,* a series of short stories about six young orphaned children who were sent to live with their grandparents on a Maine farm after the Civil War. On one occasion, they set out to hive a wild swarm of bees after church. They found them in a tree but, before they could get at them, the swarm took off towards a horse pasture. One of the kids threw a coat at the swarm and managed to trap the queen but this only enraged the bees, which then attacked the colts. The horses proceeded to run helter-skelter towards a swamp, two of them getting bogged down in the muck. After much hauling on ropes by neighbors, the horses were recovered, although badly stung, and the children returned home, "our faces disfigured…our clothes torn, and we were plastered from head to foot with mud."

That is much like a good day at the test kitchen. We set out to do something simple and then end up surprised and exhausted by the unexpected turn of events. You just never know where a day of test cooking is going to take you.

We hope that this volume of recipes offers you this same promise—minus the misadventures. We guarantee that the prize is always worth the trouble, whether it is a bucket of honey or the perfect bowl of beef stew. All you need is a good guide (this cookbook!), some enthusiasm for the culinary arts, and an hour or so of your precious time. We are confident that your stay in the kitchen will be considered time well spent.

Christopher Kimball
Founder and Editor, *Cook's Illustrated* and *Cook's Country*
Host, *America's Test Kitchen* and
Cook's Country from America's Test Kitchen

WELCOME TO AMERICA'S TEST KITCHEN

THIS BOOK HAS BEEN TESTED, WRITTEN, AND EDITED by the folks at America's Test Kitchen, a very real 2,500-square-foot kitchen located just outside of Boston. It is the home of *Cook's Illustrated* magazine and *Cook's Country* magazine and is the Monday-through-Friday destination for more than three dozen test cooks, editors, food scientists, tasters, and cookware specialists. Our mission is to test recipes over and over again until we understand how and why they work and until we arrive at the "best" version.

Our television show highlights the best recipes developed in the test kitchen during the past year—those recipes that our test kitchen staff makes at home time and time again. These recipes are accompanied by our most exhaustive equipment tests and our most interesting food tastings.

Christopher Kimball, the founder and editor of *Cook's Illustrated* magazine, is host of the show and asks the questions you might ask. It's the job of our chefs, Julia Collin Davison, Bridget Lancaster, Rebecca Hays, and Yvonne Ruperti to demonstrate our recipes. The chefs show Chris what works and what doesn't, and they explain why. In the process, they discuss (and show you) the best examples from our development process as well as the worst.

Adam Ried, our equipment guru, and Lisa McManus, our gadget guru, share the highlights from our detailed testing process in Equipment Corner segments. They bring with them our favorite (and least favorite) gadgets and tools.

Jack Bishop is our ingredient expert. He has Chris taste our favorite (and least favorite) brands of common food products. Chris may not always enjoy these exercises (jarred horseradish and vegetable oil aren't always a whole lot of fun to taste), but he usually learns something as Jack explains what makes one brand superior to another.

Although just nine cooks and editors appear on the television show, another 50 people worked to make the show a reality. Executive Producer Melissa Baldino conceived and developed each episode and Associate Producer Stephanie Stender organized many aspects of filming to ensure that taping would run smoothly. Meg Ragland assisted with all the historical recipe research. Guy Crosby, our science expert on the show, also researched the science behind the recipes. Along with the on-air crew, executive chefs Erin McMurrer and Keith Dresser helped plan and organize the 26 television episodes shot in May 2010 and ran the "back kitchen," where all the food that appeared on camera originated. Meredith Butcher and Tai Sierra organized the tasting and equipment segments.

During filming, chefs Andrew Janjigian, Jennifer Lalime, Dan Souza, Chris O'Connor, Matthew Herron, Suzannah McFerran, Bryan Roof, Andrea Geary, and interns Dan Cellucci, Theary So, Seth Diamond, Dan Jablow, and Kevin Warren cooked all the food needed on set. Additional cooks worked on set developing recipes for our magazines and books—Cali Rich, Eva Katz, Lynn Clark, Sarah Wilson, Kelly Price, Diane Unger, Sarah Gabriel, Carolynn Purpura, Lisa McManus, and Meredith Butcher. Test Kitchen Manager Gina Nistico, Consultant Nadia Domeq, and Senior Kitchen Assistant Leah Rovner

were charged with making sure all the ingredients we needed were on hand. Kitchen Assistants Maria Elena Delgado, Ena Gudiel, and Edward Tundidor also worked long hours. Chefs Adelaide Parker, Yvonne Ruperti, Dan Zuccarello, Christie Morrison, and Rebeccah Marsters helped coordinate the efforts of the kitchen with the television set by readying props, equipment, and food. Christine Smith led all tours of the test kitchen during filming.

The staff of A La Carte Communications turned our recipes, tastings, testings, and science experiments into a lively television show. Special thanks to director and editor Herb Sevush and director of photography Jan Maliszewski.

We also appreciate the hard work of the video production team, including Stephen Hussar, Michael McEachern, Peter Dingle, Ken Fraser, Roger Macie, Gilles Morin, Brenda Coffey, Elena Battista, Michael Andrus, Aaron Frutman, Leah Strahm, and Ariana Johnston. Thanks also to Peter Tannenbaum, the second unit videographer.

We also would like to thank Christina Regan, Nancy Bocchino, and Bara Levin at WGBH Station Relations, and the team at American Public Television that presents the show: Cynthia Fenneman, Chris Funkhouser, Judy Barlow, and Tom Davison. Thanks also for production support from DGA Productions, Boston, and Zebra Productions, New York.

DCS by Fisher & Paykel, Kohler Company, Woodbridge by Robert Mondavi, Diamond Crystal Kosher Salt, and Cooking.com helped underwrite the show and we thank them for their support. We also thank Marcy McCreary, Ann Naya, and Bailey Vatalaro for handling underwriter relations and Deborah Broide for managing publicity.

Meat was provided by Scott Brueggeman of DiLuigi Sausage Company of Danvers, Massachusetts. Fish was supplied by Ian Davison of Constitution Seafood of Boston, Massachusetts. Live plants and garden items for the show were furnished by Mark Cutler at Mahoney's Garden Center of Brighton, Massachusetts. Aprons for Christopher Kimball were made by Nicole Romano and staff aprons were made by Crooked Brook. Props were designed and developed by Jay Layman, Christine Vo, and Erica Lee and Foam Props of Woburn, Massachusetts.

AMERICA'S TEST KITCHEN

THE TV COMPANION COOKBOOK 2011

WEEKNIGHT
Workhorses

Boneless country-style spare ribs, which are cut from the loin, make tender, juicy cutlets.

DO MOST OF US TURN TO PAN-SEARING WHEN WE REALLY WANT TO wow those around the dinner table? Probably not. Quick sautés, such as pan-seared chicken breasts and sautéed pork cutlets, are usually reserved for those nights when the cook is harried and food is about fuel, not flavor. A boneless, skinless chicken breast, as convenient as it is, doesn't have the bone and skin to protect it from the intensity of a hot pan. Inevitably, it emerges moist in the middle and dry at the edges, with an exterior that's leathery and tough. We wanted a pan-seared chicken breast as moist and juicy as its skin-on, bone-in counterpart.

As for pork cutlets, they may be conveniently packaged at the supermarket but the contents, ragged slices cut from lean center-cut pork loin, typically cook up dry and chewy. We wanted to find a more flavorful, tender cut for cutlets. And because we wanted our dish to still be quick and easy, we didn't want to spend a lot of time on prep. Join us as we improve upon weeknight workhorses—we think the results may just prompt you to add them to your Saturday night rotation.

PAN-SEARED CHICKEN BREASTS

✔ **WHY THIS RECIPE WORKS:** For chicken breasts with flavorful, moist, and tender meat, we gently parcooked boneless, skinless breasts in the oven and then seared them on the stovetop. Salting the chicken breasts first helped retain their moisture. We also turned to a Chinese technique called "velveting," which involves dipping the partially cooked chicken in a protective coating of oil and cornstarch. This step gave our chicken a crisp crust and helped keep the meat juicy.

WHAT COOK DESPERATE FOR A QUICK DINNER HASN'T thrown a boneless, skinless chicken breast into a hot pan, keeping fingers crossed for edible results? The fact is, pan-searing is a surefire way to ruin this cut. Unlike a split chicken breast, which has the bone and skin to help keep the meat moist and juicy, a boneless, skinless breast is fully exposed to the intensity of the hot pan, so by the time the interior has cooked through, the exterior has dried out. But there's no denying the appeal of a cut that requires no butchering—plus even when chicken is served with skin, most people push it to the side of the plate. What would it take to get a pan-seared boneless, skinless breast every bit as flavorful, moist, and tender as its skin-on counterpart?

We weren't the only ones to question the typical sear-cover-and-cook approach. The problem is that the center of a thick chicken breast takes a long time to reach 165 degrees. Meanwhile, the outer layers are busy overcooking, losing moisture, and turning stringy and tough. One unconventional recipe called for parcooking the chicken in water before searing. In theory, the idea was sound: Poaching would cook the breasts gently and evenly, and the parcooked, warm chicken should take much less time to develop a flavorful brown crust than straight-from-the-fridge meat. The chicken was juicy and brown, all right—but also flavorless, since much of

the chicken's juices seeped into the cooking liquid and subsequently got poured down the drain.

Moving on, we tried ditching the water bath in favor of the oven, still keeping the same gently-parcook-then-sear order, a technique we've used successfully in the test kitchen with thick-cut steaks. We placed four chicken breasts in a baking pan, cooked them in a 275-degree oven until they hit 150 degrees, and then seared them. They browned quickly and beautifully, but while the meat was moist enough on the inside, the exterior had so dehydrated that we practically needed a steak knife to saw through it.

What about salting? Like brining, salting changes the structure of meat proteins, helping them to retain more moisture as they cook. Ideally, chicken should be salted for at least six hours to ensure full penetration and juiciness. But boneless, skinless breasts are supposed to be quick and easy, so we weren't willing to commit more than 30 extra minutes to the process. We found that poking holes into the meat with a fork created channels for the salt to reach the interior of the chicken, maximizing the short salting time. This made the interior even juicier, but the exterior was still too dried out.

If the issue was really the chicken's exterior, should it be somehow protected from the oven's dry heat? We tried the exact same method, this time placing the breasts in a baking dish that we wrapped tightly in foil before heating. Bingo! In this enclosed environment, any moisture released by the chicken stayed trapped under the foil, keeping the exterior from drying out without becoming so overtly wet that it couldn't brown quickly. In fact, this cover-and-cook method proved so effective that we could combine the 30-minute salting step with the roasting step.

We now had chicken breasts that were supremely moist and tender on the inside with a flavorful, browned exterior—a big improvement over the leathery hides of most pan-seared breasts. With a little more effort, could we do better still? To protect thin cutlets from the heat of the pan and encourage faster browning, many recipes dredge them in flour. Raw breasts are malleable,

PAN-SEARED CHICKEN BREASTS WITH LEMON AND CHIVE PAN SAUCE

which means they make good contact with the pan. The parcooked breasts, on the other hand, had already firmed up slightly, so only some of the flour was able to come in contact with the hot oil in the pan, leading to spotty browning.

Simple dredging was out, and we definitely didn't want to go the full breading route. The only other thing we could think of was a technique from Chinese cooking called velveting. Here the meat is dipped in a mixture of oil and cornstarch, which provides a thin, protective layer that keeps the protein moist and tender even when exposed to the ultra-high heat of stir-frying. Though we'd never heard of using this method on large pieces of meat like breasts, we saw no reason it wouldn't work here. We brushed our parcooked chicken with a mixture of 2 tablespoons melted butter (which would contribute more flavor than oil) and a heaping tablespoon of cornstarch before searing it.

As soon as we put the breasts in the pan, we noticed that the buttery slurry helped the chicken make better contact with the hot skillet, and as we flipped the pieces, we were happy to see an even, golden-brown crust. However, tasters reported that the cornstarch, annoyingly, was leaving a slightly pasty residue. Replacing the cornstarch with flour didn't work; the protein in flour

produced a crust that was tough and bready instead of light and crisp. It turned out that achieving the exact right amount of protein and starch in the coating was the key. A mixture of 3 parts flour to 1 part cornstarch created a thin, browned, crisp coating that kept the breast's exterior as moist as the interior—some tasters thought it was even better than real chicken skin itself.

Served on its own or with a simple pan sauce, this tender, crisp-coated chicken far surpassed any other pan-seared breasts we've ever made. Start to finish, they did take a little longer to cook than the fastest methods, but the hands-on time was almost the same as for breasts you just throw into the skillet—and the great results made the time completely worthwhile.

Pan-Seared Boneless, Skinless Chicken Breasts
SERVES 4

For the best results, buy similarly sized chicken breasts. If your breasts have the tenderloin attached, leave it in place and follow the upper range of baking time in step 1. For optimal texture, sear the chicken immediately after removing it from the oven.

4   (6 to 8-ounce) boneless, skinless chicken breasts, trimmed (see note)
1   teaspoon table salt
1   tablespoon vegetable oil
2   tablespoons unsalted butter, melted
1   tablespoon unbleached all-purpose flour
1   teaspoon cornstarch
½   teaspoon ground black pepper
1   recipe pan sauce (optional; recipes follow)

1. Adjust an oven rack to the lower-middle position and heat the oven to 275 degrees. Use a fork to poke the thickest half of each breast five to six times, then sprinkle each breast with ¼ teaspoon salt. Place the chicken, skinned side down, in a 13 by 9-inch baking dish and cover tightly with aluminum foil. Bake until the chicken registers 145 to 150 degrees on an instant-read thermometer, 30 to 40 minutes.

2. Remove the chicken from the oven and transfer, skinned side up, to a paper towel–lined plate and pat dry with paper towels. Heat the oil in a 12-inch skillet over medium-high heat until smoking. While the pan is heating, whisk the butter, flour, cornstarch, and pepper together in a small bowl. Lightly brush the tops of the chicken with half of the butter mixture. Place the chicken in the skillet, coated side down, and cook until browned, 3 to 4 minutes. While the chicken browns, brush the second side with the remaining butter mixture. Using tongs, flip the chicken, reduce the heat to medium, and cook until the second side is browned and the chicken registers 160 to 165 degrees, 3 to 4 minutes. Transfer the chicken to a platter and let rest while preparing the pan sauce (if not making the pan sauce, let the chicken rest 5 minutes before serving).

Lemon and Chive Pan Sauce
MAKES ABOUT ¾ CUP

- 1 **medium shallot, minced (about 3 tablespoons)**
- 1 **teaspoon unbleached all-purpose flour**
- 1 **cup low-sodium chicken broth**
- 1 **tablespoon juice from 1 lemon**
- 1 **tablespoon minced fresh chives**
- 1 **tablespoon unsalted butter, chilled**
  Table salt and ground black pepper

Add the shallot to the empty skillet and cook over medium heat until softened, about 2 minutes. Add the flour and cook, stirring constantly, 30 seconds. Add the broth, increase the heat to medium-high, and bring to a simmer, scraping the pan bottom to loosen the browned bits. Simmer rapidly until reduced to ¾ cup, 3 to 5 minutes. Stir in any accumulated chicken juices, return to a simmer, and cook 30 seconds. Off the heat, whisk in the lemon juice, chives, and butter; season with salt and pepper to taste. Spoon over the chicken and serve immediately.

NOTES FROM THE TEST KITCHEN

SECRETS TO BETTER PAN-SEARED CHICKEN BREASTS

1. Poke the thicker part of the breasts with the tines of a fork before salting to allow the salt to penetrate the meat more quickly, which results in juicy interiors in a minimum of time.

2. Bake the chicken at a low temperature in a foil-covered dish to ensure even cooking and to keep the exterior from drying out.

3. Brush the butter, flour, and cornstarch onto the breasts to create a "skin" to protect the meat during searing.

4. Briefly sear the parcooked coated breasts to keep them moist and create crisp exteriors.

Bourbon and Cranberry Pan Sauce

MAKES ABOUT ¾ CUP

- 1 **medium shallot, minced (about 3 tablespoons)**
- 1 **teaspoon unbleached all-purpose flour**
- ¾ **cup low-sodium chicken broth**
- ½ **cup bourbon**
- ⅓ **cup dried cranberries**
- ½ **teaspoon minced fresh thyme leaves**
- 1 **tablespoon unsalted butter**
- 1 **teaspoon red wine vinegar**
- **Table salt and ground black pepper**

Add the shallot to the empty skillet and cook over medium heat until softened, about 2 minutes. Add the flour and cook, stirring constantly, 30 seconds. Remove the pan from the heat and add the broth, bourbon, cranberries, and thyme. Return the pan to medium-high and bring to a simmer, scraping the pan bottom to loosen the browned bits. Simmer rapidly until reduced to ¾ cup, 3 to 5 minutes. Stir in any accumulated chicken juices; return to a simmer and cook 30 seconds. Off the heat, whisk in the butter and vinegar; season with salt and pepper to taste. Spoon over the chicken and serve immediately.

Fennel and Mustard Pan Sauce

MAKES ABOUT ¾ CUP

- 1 **medium shallot, minced (about 3 tablespoons)**
- 1 **teaspoon fennel seeds**
- 1 **teaspoon unbleached all-purpose flour**
- ¾ **cup low-sodium chicken broth**
- ½ **cup dry vermouth or white wine**
- 2 **tablespoons whole-grain mustard**
- 1 **tablespoon unsalted butter**
- 1 **teaspoon chopped fresh tarragon leaves**
- **Table salt and ground black pepper**

Add the shallot and fennel seeds to the empty skillet and cook over medium heat, stirring often, until softened and browned around the edges, 2 to 3 minutes. Add the flour and cook, stirring constantly, 30 seconds. Add the broth and vermouth, increase the heat to medium-high, and bring to a simmer, scraping the pan bottom to loosen any browned bits. Simmer rapidly until reduced to ¾ cup, 3 to 5 minutes. Stir in any accumulated chicken juices; return to a simmer and cook 30 seconds. Off the heat, whisk in the mustard, butter, and tarragon; season with salt and pepper to taste. Spoon over the chicken and serve immediately.

RATING FIRE EXTINGUISHERS

According to the National Fire Protection Association, cooking mishaps are the number one cause of home fires and home fire injuries, so it pays to have an extinguisher you can use easily and effectively when seconds count. Under the supervision of firefighters, we tested nine fire extinguishers on burning vegetable oil and cotton dish towels. Six were traditional ABC extinguishers designed to fight the three most common types of fires that can break out in the home: combustible material (A), flammable liquid (B), and electrical (C). We also tested two extinguishers in small aerosol cans and another "designer" canister. The ABC, or "multipurpose," extinguishers are filled with monoammonium phosphate, which forms a barrier between the fuel and oxygen, but it also scars appliance surfaces. The BC extinguishers (for flammable liquid and electrical fires) contain nondamaging sodium bicarbonate, a pressurized spray of baking soda, which coats the fuel to similarly cut off its supply of oxygen. The three nontraditional models used proprietary water-based formulas; these did not impress us. Our top two models (both traditional) finished neck-and-neck, but because one was a nondamaging BC-type model, that made it our top pick. In extinguishers that bear the UL mark, ratings have been tested and confirmed by Underwriters Laboratories, an independent product safety and compliance certification firm. The number indicates the approximate square feet of coverage and the letters represent the types of fires it is designed to put out. Brands are listed in order of preference. See www.americastestkitchen.com for updates to this testing.

HIGHLY RECOMMENDED

KIDDE Kitchen Fire Extinguisher
(model #21005753/FX10K)
PRICE: $18.97 **UL RATING:** 10-B:C
EXTINGUISHING AGENT: Dry chemical
(sodium bicarbonate)
FIREFIGHTING ABILITY: ★★★ **EASE OF USE:** ★★★
COMMENTS: Extremely fast, powerful, well-directed spray that quickly extinguished grease fire and burning dish towels.

KIDDE ABC Dry Chemical Fire Extinguisher
(model #466142; also known as FA110)
PRICE: $19.99 **UL RATING:** 1-A:10-B:C
EXTINGUISHING AGENT: Dry chemical
(monoammonium phosphate)
FIREFIGHTING ABILITY: ★★★ **EASE OF USE:** ★★★
COMMENTS: Big, focused spray with spot-on aim that took only a few seconds to put out grease and towel fires.

RECOMMENDED

FIRST ALERT Kitchen Fire Extinguisher
(model #KFE2S5)
PRICE: $22.34 **UL RATING:** 5-B:C
EXTINGUISHING AGENT: Dry chemical
(sodium bicarbonate)
FIREFIGHTING ABILITY: ★★★ **EASE OF USE:** ★★
COMMENTS: Pulling off this model's odd plastic cap seemed an unnecessary extra step that cost valuable seconds. Effective once in use.

RECOMMENDED *(cont.)*

FIRST ALERT Multipurpose Fire Extinguisher
(model #FE1A10GO)
PRICE: $21.99 **UL RATING:** 1-A:10-B:C
EXTINGUISHING AGENT: Dry chemical
(monoammonium phosphate)
FIREFIGHTING ABILITY: ★★★ **EASE OF USE:** ★★
COMMENTS: The pin on this device was so hard to pull out that it was necessary to put the canister down and use both hands. Effective at putting out grease fire; powerful spray extinguished the dish towel and blew it off the heat source.

RECOMMENDED WITH RESERVATIONS

FIRST ALERT Tundra Fire Extinguishing Spray
(model #AF-400)
PRICE: $14.97 **UL RATING:** None
EXTINGUISHING AGENT: Liquid (proprietary formula)
FIREFIGHTING ABILITY: ★★ **EASE OF USE:** ★★★
COMMENTS: This can was as easy to use as a can of Reddi-wip. Extinguished the grease fire but left the dish towel slightly smoldering.

BUCKEYE Multipurpose Dry Chemical Fire Extinguisher (model #2.5 SA ABC)
PRICE: $29.90 **UL RATING:** 1-A:10-B:C
EXTINGUISHING AGENT: Dry chemical
(monoammonium phosphate)
FIREFIGHTING ABILITY: ★★★ **EASE OF USE:** ★★
COMMENTS: Very direct, narrow spray easily extinguished both types of fires. But the quality was inconsistent: The pin slid out too easily on one sample and got stuck on another.

SAUTÉED PORK CUTLETS WITH MUSTARD-CIDER SAUCE

SAUTÉED PORK CUTLETS

✔ **WHY THIS RECIPE WORKS:** Choosing meaty boneless country-style spare ribs was our first step to achieving pork cutlets with great flavor. Because the ribs are sold in small pieces, they require little work to be fashioned into cutlets. A quick brine, enhanced with sugar, yielded cutlets with a golden brown exterior. And cooking the cutlets in a combination of olive oil and butter further ensured a browned, flavorful crust.

ON PAPER, A PACKAGE OF SUPERMARKET PORK CUTLETS offers everything the time-pressed cook could want in a weeknight meal: thrift, almost no preparation, and dinner on the table in minutes. But on your plate, these advantages don't mean a thing. Unlike more uniformly shaped chicken cutlets, which turn out moist and tender (provided they're cooked right), prepackaged center-cut pork loin is usually poorly butchered into ragged and uneven slabs, for predictably dry, stringy results. We didn't need to work through more than one batch of cutlets to confirm our fears: By the time the cutlets took on any color (lean pork is notoriously flavorless without proper browning), not a drop of moisture was left in them, and all semblance of tenderness had evaporated as well. We wanted scaloppini that had it all—moist, tender meat, and a flavorful crust.

If the bulk of our problems revolved around dry meat, brining or salting (aka dry-brining) was a must. Both methods alter the shape of the muscle proteins, making the meat less prone to squeezing out water as it cooks. Because salting requires that the moisture first be drawn out of the meat before the salt can dissolve and be absorbed, this approach takes longer to have an impact. Since time was of the essence, we opted for brining. A 30-minute soak was enough to give these ¼-inch-thick cutlets the moisture boost they needed, as well as seasoning them throughout for better flavor.

The only problem? Brining actually worked too effectively. The retained moisture kept the meat so wet that it steamed, and the cutlets were cooked all the way through before they even had a prayer of browning. What we needed was some way to trigger browning while the meat's exterior was still wet. In our recipe for Pan-Roasted Thick-Cut Fish Fillets (page 75), the solution to this very problem was to sprinkle sugar over the moist surface of the fish before we put it in the pan. Sugar caramelizes at a lower temperature than protein, about 200 degrees versus the 300 degrees it takes for a good sear to develop on meat. But instead of sprinkling the sugar on the cutlets, could we mix it into the brine? Just 1½ teaspoons added to the brining liquid did the trick, helping the cutlets develop a more golden brown crust without turning them into candy. Could we get the meat to go darker still?

The only other element to play with was the cooking fat. We'd been using olive oil, but if we included some butter, its sugars and milk proteins would allow for better browning on the exterior of the meat and boost flavor at the same time. (Butter alone wouldn't be feasible. With its low smoke point, it would burn too easily over the relatively high heat we needed for searing.) Half a tablespoon of butter heated in the pan with a tablespoon of oil not only deepened the browning on the cutlets, but left us enough flavorful browned bits in the pan (the fond) for a pan sauce.

Still, perfectly cooked though they were, our cutlets lacked one critical thing: deep meaty taste. Maybe we were asking too much of the ultra-lean loin. We soon found ourselves back at the supermarket, scanning the butcher's case for something that would give us richer pork flavor.

Determined as we were to find a more flavorful cut, our options for pork scaloppini were limited. We needed another relatively large cut that would slice neatly, cook quickly, and maintain tenderness. Tenderloin—the thin, tapered muscle that runs along the opposite side of the spine from the larger loin muscle—was one option. But while its texture is more supple than the loin's (no surprise, given the name), this cut has even less flavor.

Frustrated, we did more research and stumbled across a scaloppini recipe calling for an unusual cut: pork leg. Little known in the United States but common in Canadian butcher shops, this cut comes from the larger muscles in the upper hind leg of the pig—the same

joint cured and smoked to produce ham. These powerful muscles are packed with flavor. Could scaloppini fashioned from this odd Canadian cut be the solution to our problem? To our disappointment, we discovered fresh ham is packed with more than just flavor: It's also full of connective tissue, awkwardly shaped bones, and thick fat deposits that needed to be removed before we could create cutlets. Sure, they were flavorful in the end, but there was no way our "quick" weeknight dinner was going to start with half an hour of butchering.

Observing the deep red meat of the ham gave us another idea. When buying pork chops, if you ask the butcher for a blade-end cut (the end closest to the front of the pig), you get a chop with a small eye of pale meat from the lean loin and plenty of flavorful darker red meat from the hog's fattier shoulder. This was the meat

we were after. Cutting scaloppini from a whole blade-end roast was one option, but an easier (albeit unusual) option also occurred to us: boneless country-style spare ribs. A common choice for braising, smoking, or grilling, these meaty ribs combine a large portion of the flavorful shoulder meat with minimal connective tissue and only a bit of bland loin (and occasionally none at all).

Even better, because the ribs are sold portioned into relatively small pieces, they required little work to be fashioned into cutlets. It was a simple matter of trimming each rib of external fat, slicing it lengthwise into two or three pieces about ⅜ inch wide, and gently pounding each of them into ¼-inch-thick cutlets. Even though these ribs were fattier than meat from the loin, pork these days is still bred to be lean, and we found 30 minutes in a sweetened brine was still necessary for the best flavor and browning. (Ditto on the oil-butter combo for the cooking fat.) After just four minutes total in a hot skillet, these cutlets cooked up exactly as we'd hoped: tender, juicy, and flavorful on the inside, with a deep brown crust.

All that was left was to whip up a couple of pan sauces. We first homed in on a variation made with mustard and cider (both great complements to pork). As the pork brined, we reduced a flour-thickened mixture of cider and stock flavored with dry mustard, shallots, and sage. After removing the cooked cutlets from the pan, we

deglazed the fond-crusted skillet with our reduction, then swirled in coarse mustard and butter for a rich, glossy sauce that coated our tender, browned cutlets beautifully. No longer was this dish just a pedestrian effort for a weeknight repertoire. Meaty pork cutlets dressed up this nicely are snazzy enough for serving company.

NOTES FROM THE TEST KITCHEN

TURNING RIBS INTO CUTLETS
Rather than settle for raggedy prepackaged cutlets, we cut our own from boneless country-style ribs.

START WITH A BONELESS RIB

CUT INTO TWO OR THREE PIECES

POUND INTO THIN CUTLETS

Sautéed Pork Cutlets with Mustard-Cider Sauce
SERVES 4

We prefer natural to enhanced pork (pork that has been injected with a salt solution to increase moistness and flavor). If the pork is enhanced, do not brine. Look for ribs that are about 3 to 5 inches long. Cut ribs over 5 inches in half crosswise before slicing them lengthwise to make pounding more manageable.

> Table salt
> 1½ teaspoons sugar
> 1½ pounds boneless country-style pork spareribs, trimmed (see note)
> 1½ tablespoons unsalted butter, cut into 6 equal pieces
> 1 small shallot, minced (about 1 tablespoon)
> 1 teaspoon unbleached all-purpose flour
> 1 teaspoon dry mustard
> ½ cup low-sodium beef or chicken broth
> ¼ cup apple cider
> ½ teaspoon minced fresh sage
> Ground black pepper
> 1 tablespoon olive oil
> 2 teaspoons whole-grain mustard

1. Dissolve 1 tablespoon salt and sugar in 2 cups water in a medium bowl. Cut each pork rib lengthwise into 2 or 3 cutlets about ⅜ inch wide. Gently pound the cutlets to ¼-inch thickness between two layers of plastic wrap. Submerge the cutlets in the brine, cover with plastic wrap, and refrigerate for 30 minutes. (Do not overbrine.)

2. Meanwhile, melt 2 pieces of the butter in a small saucepan over medium heat. Add the shallot and cook until softened, about 1½ minutes. Stir in the flour and dry mustard and cook for 30 seconds. Gradually whisk in the broth, smoothing out any lumps. Stir in the cider and sage, bring to a boil, then reduce to a gentle simmer and cook for 5 minutes. Remove the pan from the heat, cover, and set aside.

3. Adjust an oven rack to the middle position and heat the oven to 200 degrees. Remove the cutlets from the brine, dry thoroughly with paper towels, and season with pepper. Heat the oil in a 12-inch skillet over medium-high heat until just smoking. Add 1 piece more butter, let it melt, then quickly lay half of the cutlets in the skillet. Cook until browned on the first side, 1 to 2 minutes.

4. Using tongs, flip the cutlets and continue to cook until browned on the second side, 1 to 2 minutes. Transfer the cutlets to a large plate and keep warm in the oven. Repeat with the remaining cutlets and 1 piece more butter.

5. Return the empty skillet to medium heat, add the reserved broth mixture, and bring to a simmer. Cook, scraping up the browned bits, until the sauce is slightly thickened and has reduced to about ½ cup, about 2 minutes. Stir in any accumulated pork juices and simmer for 30 seconds longer.

6. Off the heat, whisk in the whole-grain mustard and remaining 2 pieces butter. Season the sauce with salt and pepper to taste, spoon it over the cutlets, and serve immediately.

VARIATION

Sautéed Pork Cutlets with Lemon-Caper Sauce
Follow the recipe for Sautéed Pork Cutlets with Mustard-Cider Sauce, substituting ¼ cup white wine for the cider, 2 teaspoons lemon juice for the sage, and 2 tablespoons rinsed capers, 1 teaspoon minced fresh parsley, and 1 teaspoon finely grated lemon zest for the mustard.

NOTES FROM THE TEST KITCHEN

COMMON (AND UNCOMMON) CUTS FOR PORK CUTLETS

We rejected two of the most popular cuts for pork cutlets that come from the whole loin—the center-cut loin and tenderloin—in favor of an unusual but far more flavorful choice: boneless country-style ribs.

OUR CHOICE: COUNTRY-STYLE RIBS
Individual ribs cut from the blade (front) end of the loin, containing mostly dark meat from the fatty, flavorful shoulder.
PROS: Exceptionally flavorful
CONS: None

RUNNER-UP: CENTER-CUT LOIN
Cut from the large muscle that runs through the loin section. Most common choice for packaged supermarket cutlets.
PROS: Relatively tender
CONS: Extremely lean and prone to drying out

RUNNER-UP: TENDERLOIN
Small, tapering muscle located inside the rib cage about halfway down the spine.
PROS: Most tender part of the pig; easily fashioned into uniform cutlets
CONS: Lean, with only moderate flavor

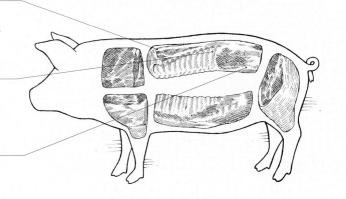

RATING MEAT POUNDERS

The key to quick-cooking pork or chicken cutlets is a uniformly thin piece of meat—and the way to accomplish this is to use a meat pounder. We recently tested five different meat pounders in two different styles: three that have an offset handle, and two that have a vertical handle. While in the past we've like offset-handled pounders, we noticed that the heel of the disk on this style can occasionally cut into the meat. Overall, we found we preferred the models with vertical handles, as they offered better leverage and control. We also favored models that were heavier (approaching 2 pounds) and had larger surface areas. Brands are listed in order of preference. See www.americastestkitchen.com for updates to this testing.

HIGHLY RECOMMENDED

NORPRO Grip-EZ Meat Pounder (model #7033)
PRICE: $17.50
AVERAGE STROKES NEEDED TO FLATTEN CUTLET: 12
WEIGHT: 1.75 lbs
COMMENTS: The shape and heft of this vertical-style model provided the right combination of control and force to produce nearly flawless cutlets.

RECOMMENDED

LEIFHEIT Pro Line Reversible Meat Tenderizer (model #23014)
PRICE: $20.99
AVERAGE STROKES NEEDED TO FLATTEN CUTLET: 13
WEIGHT: 1.8 lbs
COMMENTS: We got comparable results to our winner's with this vertical-style pounder, though some testers found the thick handle awkward. The pounding disk, which detaches from the handle, has a reversible spiked side for tenderizing tougher cuts.

WÜSTHOF Classic Meat Pounder (model #4702)
PRICE: $179.99
AVERAGE STROKES NEEDED TO FLATTEN CUTLET: 7
WEIGHT: 2.95 lbs
COMMENTS: This offset-handled heavy hitter was more efficient than our winner—with twice the surface area and almost twice the weight, it required half as many strokes to pound a perfect cutlet—but it costs 10 times as much.

RECOMMENDED WITH RESERVATIONS

NORPRO Meat/Veal Pounder (model #6211)
PRICE: $17.99
AVERAGE STROKES NEEDED TO FLATTEN CUTLET: 17
WEIGHT: 1.65 lbs
COMMENTS: When pitted against heavier models, the flaws of this offset-handled pounder became apparent. Shorter testers, pounding at a less optimal angle, found that the heel of the disk often dug into and tore the meat.

NOT RECOMMENDED

RÖSLE Stainless Steel Meat Pounder (model #12819)
PRICE: $39.95
AVERAGE STROKES NEEDED TO FLATTEN CUTLET: 20
WEIGHT: 1.6 lbs
COMMENTS: The lightest of the bunch, this offset-handled model had the look—and effectiveness—of a cookie spatula. Furthermore, testers struggled to prevent the heel of the disk from digging into the meat.

DUTCH OVEN
Classics

Browning the beef in two batches and then adding the onions and carrots are just a few key steps to beef stew with out-of-this-world flavor.

A DUTCH OVEN IS THE GO-TO POT FOR A VARIETY OF DISHES IN THE test kitchen, but none more so than for soups and stews. Its ample size and heavy construction make it the perfect vessel for the gentle, even simmering that these dishes require.

One of our favorite ways to make the onset of winter more bearable is to pull out our Dutch oven and prepare beef stew. Nothing tastes better or is more satisfying than chunks of tender beef in a rich gravy. But admittedly, some recipes yield meat that isn't as tender or as beefy-tasting as we'd like. And gravies can turn out weak and thin or just plain lackluster. We wanted to devise a method for extraordinary beef stew, one packed with beefy flavor—from juicy, fork-tender chunks of meat to an intensely rich, velvety gravy.

For those who prefer chicken to beef, chicken and dumplings is the order of the day. While rib-sticking-rich chicken and dumplings has their place, we wanted a version that was lighter and a bit more refined. Equally important, we wanted airy dumplings that floated in the broth and didn't sink to the bottom of the pot.

Dust off your Dutch oven if you haven't used it lately; we'll show you two reasons why you should be cooking with it more often.

BEST BEEF STEW

✔ **WHY THIS RECIPE WORKS:** The key to great beef stew is to maximize flavor at every step. To begin, we chose a tasty cut of beef—chuck—and browned it properly, taking care not to crowd the meat in the pan. Adding ingredients rich in glutamates (compounds that give food a savory taste), such as tomato paste, salt pork, and anchovies, deepened the flavor of our stew. And adding both flour and gelatin gave our beef stew a satisfying thickness.

AS BEEF STEW SIMMERS, IT EMITS A RICH AROMA, BUT, in our opinion, the taste is never as complex as the scent. It's not that it's bad, but it's nowhere near good enough to merit the several hours of waiting this cold-weather dish typically requires. Of the dozen or so recipes we have tried, from quick-and-easy versions with canned beef broth, heavy thickeners, and tiny pieces of beef to better (but still disappointing) four-hour versions, the only one that delivered truly satisfying flavor came from the famed Michelin-starred chef Thomas Keller. The problem? It required four days, a dozen dirty pots and pans, and nearly 50 ingredients. The results were fit for royalty, but it was hardly the approachable, home-cooked meal we were aiming for. There had to be a compromise, and we set out to find it.

The basic process for beef stew is straightforward: Brown chunks of beef in a Dutch oven, add aromatics and thickener, cover with liquid, and simmer until everything is tender and the flavors meld. The key to developing complexity is to maximize flavor in every step. American beef stew is first and foremost about the beef, so picking the right cut is essential. Supermarket "stew meat" was a nonstarter; the jumble of bits and chunks was impossible to cook evenly. Cuts like tenderloin, strip, and rib eye, while great for searing or grilling, turned mealy with prolonged cooking. Cuts like hanger or skirt steak offered great flavor, but their texture was stringy. While well-marbled blade steaks and short ribs (favored by Keller) worked well, in the end they were no better than chuck-eye roast. It's one of the cheapest, beefiest cuts in the supermarket, and it turns meltingly tender when properly cooked.

The first key to rich, meaty flavor is proper browning, which meant searing the meat in two batches for a big pot of stew. Then we caramelized the usual choices of onions and carrots (rather than just adding them raw to the broth, as many recipes suggest). Though at first we planned to remove the meat while sautéing the vegetables, we found that when we left it in the pot, its residual heat helped the onions and carrots cook faster and more evenly. We quickly sautéed crushed garlic before adding ¼ cup of flour to lightly thicken the stew. Next we deglazed the pan with 2 cups of red wine and simmered the liquid to reduce it and to let its raw flavor dissipate. We then added 2 cups of chicken broth (favored over tinny canned beef broth) and let the stew simmer for 2½ hours in the oven (which provides a more even heat than the stovetop).

The stew was bare bones, but we'd worry about additions later. For now, we needed to focus on the flavor of the broth, which was not developing very well. Our stew still lacked real meatiness. We decided to attack the problem in a more scientific manner.

We've long known that ingredients rich in glutamates—compounds that give foods a savory, meaty

SCIENCE DESK

FISHING FOR MEATIER FLAVOR

To boost meaty flavor in food, we often add ingredients high in glutamate. This common amino acid is the building block for MSG and occurs naturally in a variety of foods, from mushrooms to cheese, tomatoes, and fish. Thus it wasn't exactly a surprise that the addition of two such glutamate-rich ingredients—tomato paste and salt pork—to our beef stew intensified its savory taste. But when we added a third glutamate-packed ingredient, anchovies, the beefy flavor seemed to increase exponentially. Evidence published recently in *Proceedings of the National Academy of Sciences* explains why: Besides glutamate, anchovies contain the compound inosinate. Scientists have found that inosinate has a synergistic effect on glutamate, heightening its meaty taste by up to fifteenfold.

BEST BEEF STEW

taste—can enhance the flavor of a dish. Tomatoes are one such ingredient. We experimented with various canned tomato products, finally landing on tomato paste, which lent the right background note.

Thinking of other glutamate-rich ingredients, we wondered about cured meats that have a super-concentrated flavor. Bacon was too smoky, but salt pork worked well, adding a subtle depth to both broth and beef. Then we remembered another salted product that's packed with glutamates: anchovies. We mashed one up and incorporated it with the garlic and tomato paste. It was a smashing success. We found we could add up to four fillets with increasingly better results before the fishiness revealed itself. Finally, our stew was packed with meaty depth. But one problem remained: texture.

Keller's stew starts with homemade veal stock. As it cooks, collagen in the veal bones is transformed into gelatin, which gives the final stew a luxurious, mouth-coating texture—something that our flour-thickened broth lacked. Theoretically, powdered gelatin should work as well, but once we removed the flour, we needed to add nearly ½ cup of gelatin powder to thicken the stew sufficiently. What about a combination of flour and gelatin? We made the stew with ¼ cup of flour just as before but added a single packet of bloomed gelatin after removing the stew from the oven. After just three minutes of simmering on the stovetop, the liquid developed a rich, glossy sheen that looked (and tasted) every bit as rich as the veal stock–based version.

The rest of the recipe was simple: we added frozen pearl onions toward the end of cooking along with frozen peas. Starchy russets broke down too easily, but medium-starch Yukon Golds added halfway through cooking were a success. As we ladled ourselves bowls of the supremely meaty and satisfying stew, we couldn't help but appreciate that sometimes the little things really do matter.

Best Beef Stew

SERVES 6 TO 8

Use a good-quality medium-bodied wine, such as a Côtes du Rhône or Pinot Noir, for this stew. Try to find beef that is well marbled with white veins of fat. Meat that is too lean will come out slightly dry. Four pounds of blade steaks, trimmed of gristle and silver skin, can be substituted for the chuck-eye roast. While the blade steak will yield slightly thinner pieces after trimming, it should still be cut into 1½-inch pieces. Look for salt pork that looks meaty and is roughly 75 percent lean.

- 2 medium garlic cloves, minced or pressed through a garlic press (about 2 teaspoons)
- 4 anchovy fillets, minced fine (about 2 teaspoons)
- 1 tablespoon tomato paste
- 1 (4-pound) boneless beef chuck-eye roast, trimmed and cut into 1½-inch pieces
- 2 tablespoons vegetable oil
- 1 large onion, halved and sliced ⅛ inch thick
- 4 carrots, peeled and cut into 1-inch pieces
- ¼ cup unbleached all-purpose flour
- 2 cups red wine (see note)
- 2 cups low-sodium chicken broth
- 4 ounces salt pork (see note), rinsed of excess salt
- 2 bay leaves
- 4 sprigs fresh thyme
- 1 pound Yukon Gold potatoes, scrubbed and cut into 1-inch pieces
- 1½ cups frozen pearl onions, thawed
- 2 teaspoons (about 1 packet) unflavored powdered gelatin
- ½ cup water
- 1 cup frozen peas, thawed
  Table salt and ground black pepper

1. Adjust an oven rack to the lower-middle position and heat the oven to 300 degrees. Combine the garlic and anchovies in a small bowl and press the mixture with the back of a fork to form a paste. Stir in the tomato paste and set the mixture aside.

2. Pat the meat dry with paper towels (do not season the meat). Heat 1 tablespoon of the vegetable oil in a large Dutch oven over high heat until just starting to smoke. Add half of the beef and cook until well browned on all sides, about 8 minutes total, reducing the heat if the oil begins to smoke or the fond begins to burn. Transfer the beef to a large plate. Repeat with the remaining 1 tablespoon vegetable oil and remaining beef, leaving the second batch of meat in the pot after browning.

3. Reduce the heat to medium and return the first batch of beef to the pot. Add the onion and carrots to the pot and stir to combine with the beef. Cook, scraping the bottom of the pan to loosen any browned bits, until the onion is softened, 1 to 2 minutes. Add the garlic mixture and cook, stirring constantly, until fragrant, about 30 seconds. Add the flour and cook, stirring constantly, until no dry flour remains, about 30 seconds.

4. Slowly add the wine, scraping the bottom of the pan to loosen any browned bits. Increase the heat to high and allow the wine to simmer until thickened and slightly reduced, about 2 minutes. Stir in the broth, salt pork, bay leaves, and thyme. Bring to a simmer, cover, transfer to the oven, and cook for 1½ hours.

5. Remove the pot from the oven. Remove and discard the bay leaves and salt pork. Stir in the potatoes, cover, return the pot to the oven, and cook until the potatoes are almost tender, about 45 minutes.

6. Using a large spoon, skim any excess fat from the surface of the stew. Stir in the pearl onions. Cook over medium heat until the potatoes and onions are cooked through and the meat offers little resistance when poked with a fork (the meat should not be falling apart), about 15 minutes. Meanwhile, sprinkle the gelatin over the water in a small bowl and allow to soften for 5 minutes.

7. Increase the heat to high and stir in the softened gelatin mixture and the peas. Simmer until the gelatin is fully dissolved and the stew is thickened, about 3 minutes. Season with salt and pepper to taste. Serve. (The stew can be cooled, covered tightly, and refrigerated for up to 2 days. Reheat it gently before serving.)

RATING BEEF BROTH

Historically, we've found commercial beef broth to be light on beefy flavor—and so we've avoided it at all costs. Wanting to find out if supermarket offerings had improved, we gathered 13 top-selling beef broths, stocks, and bases and rated them on beef flavor, aroma, saltiness, and overall appeal. The top eight brands were then tasted in gravy and French onion soup (five were eliminated). Ultimately, our top two broths delivered on rich, beefy flavor—but using very different ingredients. The runner-up, College Inn, relies on beef, beef derivatives, and glutamate-rich additives (such as yeast extract and tomato paste) for flavor, and other additives for body. The winning brand, Rachael Ray, has a shorter but less foreign ingredient list that starts with concentrated beef stock, which means this stock has more fresh, real meat than the other samples. Brands are listed in order of preference. See www.americastestkitchen.com for updates to this testing.

RECOMMENDED

RACHAEL RAY Stock-in-a-Box All-Natural Beef Flavored Stock (Made by Colavita)
PRICE: $4.95 for 32 oz
SODIUM: 480 mg per cup
COMMENTS: "Steak-y" and "rich" with "gelatin-like body," this was the only product to achieve truly beefy flavor without a slew of processed additives. Its primary ingredient—concentrated beef stock—contains twice as much meat as regular beef stock.

COLLEGE INN Bold Stock Tender Beef Flavor
PRICE: $3.99 for 32 oz
SODIUM: 730 mg per cup
COMMENTS: Praised for its "strong aroma of roasted bones" and "robust" flavor, this broth—full of beef derivatives and flavor-boosting additives—tasted "nicely beefy," though some tasters noted it became "very salty" when reduced in gravy.

RECOMMENDED WITH RESERVATIONS

SWANSON Cooking Stock, Beef
PRICE: $2.99 for 26 oz
SODIUM: 500 mg per cup
COMMENTS: Despite scoring high in the gravy test with "decent beef flavor" and "sweet," "onion" notes, slightly "sour" and "bitter" flavors were detected in the plain tasting as well as in the soup.

PROGRESSO 100% Natural Beef Broth Flavored
PRICE: $3.29 for 32 oz
SODIUM: 850 mg per cup
COMMENTS: More than 25 adjectives were used to describe this high-salt broth (several of them favorably); however, "beefy" was used sparingly. (No surprise since water is the first ingredient.)

RECOMMENDED WITH RESERVATIONS *(cont.)*

REDI-BASE Beef Base
PRICE: $7.95 for 8 oz (makes 2½ gallons)
SODIUM: 690 mg per cup
COMMENTS: In 2006, this brand topped our rankings, our only complaint being that many tasters "found the gravy salty." This time they were less forgiving: this brand had few flavors besides salt, save for a faint "roasted," "beefy flavor."

NOT RECOMMENDED

WOLFGANG PUCK Organic Beef Flavored Broth
PRICE: $3.42 for 32 oz
SODIUM: 660 mg per cup
COMMENTS: "Sweet," "mild," "vegetal," "boring." This broth steered clear of yeast extract, and tomato paste is listed last. As a result, the broth was watery, lacking character and flavor.

IMAGINE Organic Beef Flavored Cooking Stock
PRICE: $3.87 for 32 oz
SODIUM: 630 mg per cup
COMMENTS: In our plain tasting this broth was described as "sweet," vegetal," "sugary," and "light in color and flavor." "Is there even beef broth in here?" one taster asked.

PACIFIC Organic Beef Broth
PRICE: $3.99 for 32 oz
SODIUM: 570 mg per cup
COMMENTS: Recommended in our last tasting, Pacific was comparatively "vegetal" this time.

STREAMLINED CHICKEN AND DUMPLINGS

✔ WHY THIS RECIPE WORKS: For a broth full of clean, concentrated chicken flavor, we found that browning thighs and simmering them in chicken broth (rather than water) produced the most flavorful mixture. Adding chicken wings (which are rich in collagen) later on gave the stew body. For light, but sturdy dumplings, we came up with a formula that employed buttermilk for flavor and eliminated baking powder, which was making the dumplings too fragile. An egg white prevented the dumplings from turning mushy. And wrapping the lid of the Dutch oven in a kitchen towel prevented the stew's moisture from saturating our light-as-air dumplings.

DATING BACK TO THE EARLY 17TH CENTURY, CHICKEN and dumplings is as classic as American food gets. Although the dish has taken on distinct regional differences—Northerners typically like their broth thick and their dumplings fluffy, while down South the broth is usually more soup-like, with flat, square dumplings—a general rule applies to the chicken. The more mature the bird, the better the flavor. Generations ago, an egg hen or rooster several years old would be simmered for four or even six hours until falling off the bone, producing a rich broth. The simple addition of dumplings made it a flavorful, thrifty meal.

Chickens sold in supermarkets today are usually no more than seven weeks old, and a few tests proved conventional wisdom right: No matter how long you cook them, whole young chickens yield unimpressive broth. To coax old-fashioned, full flavor from supermarket birds—and create dumplings that would please both Northern and Southern palates—it was time for some modern adjustments.

Great chicken broth needs two things: flavor and body. Would a particular part of a younger bird produce a flavorful broth? We made a series of broths with thighs, drumsticks, and breasts, both skin-on and skin-off. With or without skin, the stock made with just white meat was thin and flavorless, the meat dry and bland. Drumsticks performed better, but the skin-on thighs were a clear winner, with the most deeply flavored broth of the lot and meat that stayed tender.

To further boost flavor, we used a few proven test kitchen tricks. First, we replaced water with broth. Though store-bought broth can taste thin on its own, when cooked with real chicken parts, it turns decidedly richer. Second, we browned the meat before adding the liquid. Finally, we browned aromatics in the fond from the chicken and added alcohol. Carrots, celery, and onions introduced sweetness, while ¼ cup of dry sherry—preferred by tasters over white wine and vermouth—added acidity and depth.

Now we had to resolve the North-South debate about body. Northerners thicken with flour, while Southerners tend to leave well enough alone. We prepared two versions: The first batch we left plain, the other we thickened with ½ cup of flour (the amount typical in many Yankee versions) just before deglazing with the sherry. Tasters deemed the straight broth too thin, and they rejected the sludgy consistency of the thickened broth. Knocking the flour down to ¼ cup produced broth with just the right amount of body, but all agreed it muted the chicken flavor. Cutting the flour to 2 tablespoons still masked chicken essence. Switching to cornstarch had the same effect.

Looking for an alternative, we recalled that several hours of boiling converts the connective tissue in a chicken carcass to gelatin and thickens the broth. We didn't want our broth cooking for hours, but then we realized we'd left something out of our initial broth testing: wings. Because of their multiple joints, wings contain far more connective tissue than legs or breasts. If we added plenty of wings (a half dozen seemed right) with the thighs, could we extract enough gelatin to thicken the broth? This turned out to be just what was needed. Time to move on to the dumplings.

In the South, dumplings are made of dough rolled out to about ¼ inch thick and cut into squares that are then added to the pot. It's a tedious and messy process that yields dense, doughy dumplings. The Yankee approach

STREAMLINED CHICKEN AND DUMPLINGS

is far simpler, resulting in fluffier dumplings made just like drop biscuits. You simply mix flour and leavener in one bowl and fat and a liquid in another, combine the two mixtures rapidly, and drop biscuit-sized balls into the broth.

Given the differences in technique, we weren't disappointed when (except for two holdouts, from Kentucky and Alabama) our colleagues preferred the lighter Yankee dumplings. The problem was, they weren't all that light.

Since the Yankee dumplings are so closely related to oven-baked drop biscuits, we tried using our standard drop biscuit recipe (flour, salt, sugar, baking powder and soda, butter, and buttermilk). These dumplings had great tangy buttermilk flavor, and because they had more leavener and butter, they were far from leaden. In fact, they were so fragile they disintegrated into the broth.

The ideal dumpling should have all the lightness of our drop biscuits, but enough structure to hold together in the broth. Knowing that fat coats flour and weakens its structure, we tried gradually cutting down on the recipe's 8 tablespoons of butter. At 4 tablespoons, their structure improved somewhat; removing any more compromised flavor. Since they were cooking in a moist environment,

our next thought was cutting back the liquid. Reducing the amount of buttermilk from a full cup to ¾ cup was another improvement—but the dumplings were still far too delicate.

Perhaps the problem was too much leavener, which can lead to overrising and poor structure. Completely eliminating the baking powder (only baking soda remained) gave them just the right density in the center, but they were still mushy around the edges. While eggs are not traditional biscuit ingredients, we tried adding one, hoping that the extra protein would help the dumpling hold together. A whole egg created too much eggy flavor. A single egg white added just the right amount of structure without affecting flavor. We also waited to add the dumplings until the broth was simmering, reducing their time in the broth.

One last problem remained: Steam was condensing on the inside of the pot's lid and dripping onto the dumplings, turning their tops soggy. Wrapping a kitchen towel around the lid of the Dutch oven worked like a charm, trapping the moisture before it had a chance to drip down and saturate our light-as-air dumplings and flavor-packed broth.

Streamlined Chicken and Dumplings

SERVES 6

We strongly recommend buttermilk for the dumplings, but you can substitute ½ cup plain yogurt thinned with ¼ cup milk. If you want to include white meat (and don't mind losing a bit of flavor in the process), replace 2 chicken thighs with 2 boneless, skinless chicken breast halves (about 8 ounces each). Brown the chicken breasts along with the thighs and remove them from the stew once they reach an internal temperature of 160 degrees, 20 to 30 minutes. The collagen in the wings helps thicken the stew; do not omit or substitute. Since the wings yield only about 1 cup of meat, using their meat is optional.

STEW

- 2½ pounds bone-in, skin-on chicken thighs, trimmed
     Table salt and ground black pepper
- 2 teaspoons vegetable oil
- 2 small onions, minced
- 2 carrots, peeled and cut into ¾-inch pieces
- 1 celery rib, chopped fine
- ¼ cup dry sherry
- 6 cups low-sodium chicken broth
- 1 teaspoon minced fresh thyme leaves
- 1 pound chicken wings
- ¼ cup chopped fresh parsley leaves

DUMPLINGS

- 2 cups (10 ounces) unbleached all-purpose flour
- 1 teaspoon sugar
- 1 teaspoon table salt
- ½ teaspoon baking soda
- ¾ cup cold buttermilk (see note)
- 4 tablespoons (½ stick) unsalted butter, melted and cooled
- 1 large egg white

1. FOR THE STEW: Pat the chicken thighs dry with paper towels and season with 1 teaspoon salt and ¼ teaspoon pepper. Heat the oil in a large Dutch oven over medium-high heat until shimmering. Add the chicken thighs, skin side down, and cook until the skin is crisp and well browned, 5 to 7 minutes. Using tongs, turn the chicken pieces and brown the second side, 5 to 7 minutes longer; transfer to a large plate. Discard all but 1 teaspoon fat from the pot.

NOTES FROM THE TEST KITCHEN

KEY STEPS TO STREAMLINED CHICKEN AND DUMPLINGS

1. Adding an egg white helps develop light-as-air dumplings that don't disintegrate.

2. Waiting to add the dumplings until the broth is simmering sets the dumplings' bottoms and keeps them whole.

3. Wrapping the lid with a towel absorbs excess moisture that can turn the dumplings soggy.

2. Add the onions, carrots, and celery to the pot. Cook, stirring occasionally, until caramelized, 7 to 9 minutes. Stir in the sherry, scraping up any browned bits. Stir in the broth and thyme. Return the chicken thighs, along with any accumulated juices, to the pot and add the chicken wings. Bring to a simmer, cover, and cook until the thigh meat offers no resistance when poked with the tip of a paring knife but still clings to the bones, 45 to 55 minutes.

3. Remove the pot from the heat and transfer the chicken to a cutting board. Allow the broth to settle for 5 minutes, then skim the fat from the surface using a wide spoon or ladle. When cool enough to handle, remove and discard the skin from the chicken. Using your fingers or a fork, pull the meat from the chicken thighs (and wings, if desired) and cut into 1-inch pieces. Return the meat to the pot.

4. FOR THE DUMPLINGS: Whisk the flour, sugar, salt, and baking soda in a large bowl. Combine the buttermilk and melted butter in a medium bowl, stirring until the butter forms small clumps. Whisk in the egg white. Add the buttermilk mixture to the dry ingredients and stir with a rubber spatula until just incorporated and the batter pulls away from the sides of the bowl.

5. Return the stew to a simmer, stir in the parsley, and season with salt and pepper to taste. Using a greased tablespoon measure (or #60 portion scoop), scoop level amounts of batter and drop them into the stew, spacing the dumplings about ¼ inch apart (you should have about 24 dumplings). Wrap the lid of the Dutch oven with a clean kitchen towel (keeping the towel away from the heat source) and cover the pot. Simmer gently until the dumplings have doubled in size and a toothpick inserted into the center comes out clean, 13 to 16 minutes. Serve immediately. (The stew can be prepared through step 3 up to 2 days in advance; bring the stew back to a simmer before proceeding with the recipe.)

NOTES FROM THE TEST KITCHEN

BEST PARTS FOR BROTH

NATURAL THICKENER
The multiple joints in chicken wings contain lots of collagen that converts into gelatin during cooking—a better broth thickener than flour, which masks chicken flavor.

FULL OF FLAVOR
Pound for pound, chicken thighs impart richer flavor to broth than any other part of the bird. Plus, they require far less cooking time than it takes to coax the flavor out of a whole bird or carcass.

Old-Fashioned
SUNDAY DINNERS

*For our streamlined chicken
pot pie, we substitute an
easy-to-make savory crumble
topping for the usual pie crust.
Breaking the biscuitlike dough
into pieces helps the crumble
bake up extra-crunchy.*

AS MUCH AS WE LIKE EXPANDING OUR CULINARY REPERTOIRE, WE always have had a soft spot for the simple, but satisfying dishes we've come to associate with Sunday dinner: pot roast and chicken pot pie.

Pot roast is as simple as it gets—cook beef roast under cover, with or without vegetables, until tender. Or *is* it that simple? Inexpensive pot roast is tough by nature and, if cooked improperly, it can be bland, desiccated, and sinewy. We wanted to uncover the secrets to truly great pot roast—one with supremely tender meat, great beefy flavor, and a well-seasoned gravy.

Chicken pot pie, on the other hand, may hark back to simpler times, but its preparation is anything but. Cooking a chicken, building a gravy, prepping the vegetables, and *then,* the onerous task of mixing and rolling pie dough, remind us that our Sunday is far from a day of rest. We wanted a streamlined homemade pot pie that gave us a break—one with moist chunks of chicken, tender vegetables, a rich gravy, and a homemade (but fuss-free) pastry topping to cap it off.

OLD-FASHIONED POT ROAST

✔ **WHY THIS RECIPE WORKS:** To turn the tough bargain cut, chuck eye, into a meltingly tender roast sauced in savory, full-bodied gravy, we separated the roast into two lobes, which allowed us to remove the knobs of fat that stubbornly refused to render and also shortened the cooking time. Salting the roast improved flavor as did sautéing onion, celery, carrot, garlic before we added them to the pot. Beef broth and red wine yielded a gravy with rich flavor and sealing the pot with aluminum foil before securing the lid concentrates the steam for an even simmer and fork-tender meat.

THERE IS NO SHORTAGE OF WAYS TO POT A ROAST, typically a tough cut made tender after hours of cooking in a covered vessel. Italians favor a nice bottle of Barolo for the braising liquid. The French supplement the beef with veal and cognac-soaked salt pork. Central Europeans might turn to flavorings like beer and orange peel. Here in the United States, styles range from Tex-Mex, with chili powder and jalapeños in the mix, to teriyaki renditions flavored by dried red pepper and soy sauce.

These jazzed-up iterations have their place, but to us there's something equally appealing about the simplest approach: Throw the meat into a pot with liquid, a few basic seasonings, and some carrots and onions; cover and place in a low oven; then walk away until dinner. Our goal was to make this no-frills recipe the best it could be: a meltingly tender, sliceable roast sauced in a full-bodied gravy. We wanted it to be good enough for Sunday supper, of course—but also ready for prime-time Saturday night.

As we pulled together a file of recipes to try, we came across a strikingly minimalist take on the dish in *Mrs. Lincoln's Boston Cook Book* (1884), the precursor to *Fannie Farmer's Boston Cooking-School Cook Book*. The recipe listed just two ingredients: a large roast and a cup

of water. Bigger, clearer beef flavor was definitely one of our goals, so it couldn't hurt to try it. But one thing gave us pause: Mrs. Lincoln suggested either a rump or a round roast, but we knew these cuts from the back leg of the cow to be somewhat lean and lacking in flavor as well as the collagen that is key to turning a tough cut tender. Instead, we opted for a cut from the shoulder, the chuck eye. This well-marbled roast is full of collagen and particularly suited to braising, with a long, tapered shape that slices easily.

We followed the rest of her sparse instructions to the letter—sear the roast, cover tightly (we even sealed the Dutch oven with aluminum foil before adding the lid to trap as much liquid as possible), and place it "where it will just keep below the boiling point." For us, this meant the 350-degree oven specified in most modern pot roast recipes.

After 4½ hours of simmering, much of the collagen in the roast had broken down into gelatin, a stand-in for the moisture wrung out of the meat by the long cooking, turning it tender and thickening the braising liquid. This gravy, while not complex, was surprisingly beefy. Maybe Mrs. Lincoln was on to something with the scant 1 cup of liquid she added to the pot. Many recipes we found called for three times that amount; she must have realized the beef would contribute enough of its own juices to fill out a decent gravy.

But this bare-bones recipe could never give us the full-flavored dish we had in mind. To rectify that, we began by salting the meat before cooking. Salting draws moisture out of the meat, forming a shallow brine that, over time, migrates back into the meat to season it throughout rather than just on the exterior. With a large roast such as a turkey, we often advocate letting the salted meat rest overnight. Since our roast was much smaller—and we didn't want to turn this dish into a two-day affair—we tried just an hour. This proved enough time to noticeably amp up the beefiness.

We also wanted to do something about the pesky globs of interior fat that stubbornly refused to render, a common problem with pot roast. We opened the roast

OLD-FASHIONED POT ROAST

along its natural seam and trimmed away the excess. We were about to tie the two lobes together with string when we thought better of it: Why not just leave them as two separate roasts? When we double-checked with a follow-up test, the benefit was twofold: Using these smaller roasts shaved about an hour off the cooking time, from roughly 4½ hours down to 3½ hours. Plus, all that exposed surface area meant the salt penetrated even further in just an hour.

In the interest of more streamlining, we wondered if the initial sear called for not only in Mrs. Lincoln's recipe but every other pot roast recipe we found was really necessary. Browning meat, of course, sets off the Maillard reaction, creating literally thousands of new compounds that intensify flavor. But in another low-liquid braise we'd developed in the test kitchen, we found that the "dry" part of meat that stayed above the liquid eventually browned, even without searing. Since much of our roast sat well above the braising liquid, similar low-temperature browning should occur here as well. We prepared two roasts, one seared and one not. When we offered our colleagues a bite from each and nobody could pick out

the seared roast, we knew we'd found a way to make a simple recipe even simpler. (For more on this topic, see "Low-Temperature Browning" on page 34.)

It was time to think about the gravy. The first thing we did to beef up its flavor was to trade the water for a cup of beef broth. Some amount of red wine was also a given. Not only would it add needed depth to the braise, it is packed with glutamates that significantly enhance meaty flavor. We added a half cup to keep liquid to a minimum, along with a tablespoon of tomato paste, another glutamate-rich ingredient. A couple cloves of garlic and some herbs were obvious additions; we chose bay leaf and pungent thyme, both excellent flavorings in meaty dishes. The standard mirepoix trio of onions, carrots, and celery was also a must. We found that sautéing them in a few tablespoons of butter instead of oil brought extra richness.

By the time we pulled the roast out of the pot, the vegetables had broken down and started to thicken the gravy. We couldn't resist eking out every bit of their flavor, so we tossed them into the blender with the defatted cooking liquid, extra beef broth (to thin the consistency), balsamic vinegar, and a bit more wine for brightness. The resulting gravy was exceptionally rich and full-bodied, the perfect complement to ladle over the meat, which was now rested and sliceable.

By Mrs. Lincoln's standards, this pot roast might not qualify as the most basic. But we know of very few recipes that taste as good with so little effort.

Old-Fashioned Pot Roast

SERVES 6 TO 8

To separate the roast into two pieces, simply pull apart at the natural seam and then trim away any large knobs of fat. Our recommended beef broth is Rachael Ray Stock-in-a-Box All-Natural Beef Flavored Stock.

1 **boneless chuck-eye roast (3½ to 4 pounds), pulled into 2 pieces at the natural seam and fat trimmed (see note)**
  Table salt
2 **tablespoons unsalted butter**
2 **medium onions, halved and sliced thin (about 2 cups)**
1 **large carrot, chopped medium (about 1 cup)**
1 **celery rib, chopped medium (about ¾ cup)**
2 **medium garlic cloves, minced or pressed through a garlic press (about 2 teaspoons)**
1 **cup beef broth, plus 1 to 2 cups for the sauce (see note)**
½ **cup dry red wine, plus ¼ cup for the sauce**
1 **tablespoon tomato paste**
1 **bay leaf**
1 **sprig plus ¼ teaspoon chopped fresh thyme**
  Ground black pepper
1 **tablespoon balsamic vinegar**

1. Sprinkle the pieces of meat with 1½ teaspoons table salt, place on a wire rack set over a rimmed baking sheet and let stand at room temperature 1 hour.

2. Adjust an oven rack to the lower-middle position and heat the oven to 300 degrees. Heat the butter in a heavy-bottomed Dutch oven over medium heat. When the foaming subsides, add the onions and cook,

KEYS TO FLAVORFUL POT ROAST

SALT THE ROAST: Rubbing the roast halves with salt and resting 1 hour improves meaty flavor.

ADD (A LITTLE) LIQUID: Adding just a scant 1½ cups of liquid to the pot leads to a more intensely flavored gravy.

SEAL THE POT: Sealing the pot with foil before covering preserves valuable juices and ensures the roast has enough liquid for braising.

BULK UP THE GRAVY: Pureeing the pot roast's cooked onions, carrots, and celery and then combining them with the gravy adds body and flavor.

stirring occasionally, until softened and beginning to brown, 8 to 10 minutes. Add the carrot and celery and continue to cook, stirring occasionally, for 5 minutes longer. Add the garlic and cook until fragrant, about 30 seconds. Stir in 1 cup of the broth, ½ cup of the wine, the tomato paste, bay leaf, and thyme sprig; bring to a simmer.

3. Season the beef generously with pepper. Using three pieces of kitchen twine, tie each piece of meat into a loaf shape for even cooking.

4. Nestle the meat on top of the vegetables. Place a large piece of aluminum foil over the pot and cover tightly with the lid; transfer the pot to the oven. Cook the beef until fully tender and a sharp knife easily slips in and out of the meat, 3½ to 4 hours, turning the beef halfway through the cooking time.

5. Transfer the roasts to a carving board and tent loosely with foil. Strain the liquid through a fine-mesh strainer into a 4-cup liquid measuring cup. Discard the thyme sprig and bay leaf. Transfer the vegetables to a blender. Allow the liquid to settle 5 minutes, then skim any fat off the surface. Add the remaining beef broth as necessary to bring the liquid amount to 3 cups. Place the liquid in the blender with the vegetables and blend until smooth, about 2 minutes. Transfer the sauce to a medium saucepan and bring to a simmer over medium heat.

6. While the sauce heats, remove the twine from the roasts and slice against the grain into ½-inch-thick slices. Transfer the meat to a large serving platter. Stir the chopped thyme, remaining ¼ cup wine, and balsamic vinegar into the sauce and season to taste with salt and pepper. Serve immediately, passing the sauce separately.

SCIENCE DESK

LOW-TEMPERATURE BROWNING

When meat is seared at very high temperatures, the Maillard reaction rapidly kicks in, rendering the exterior deeply browned and flavorful. But can browning take place at lower temperatures in the moist, closed environment of a braise, where the temperature can never rise above the boiling point of water, 212 degrees?

THE EXPERIMENT

We cooked two pot roasts according to our recipe, one that we seared first before adding liquid to the pot; the other we placed directly in the pot without searing.

THE RESULTS

The dry part of the two roasts that rose above the liquid had a similar level of browning, and tasted virtually identical.

THE EXPLANATION

In the searing heat of a 500-degree pan, the Maillard reaction kicks in very rapidly to quickly produce countless new flavor compounds that improve flavor. But given enough time, browning can also occur at temperatures as low as 200 degrees. Our pot roast cooks for a good 3½ hours, ample time for lots of new flavor compounds to be created on the dry top part of the meat—and allowing us to skip the sear.

Old-Fashioned Pot Roast with Root Vegetables

Follow the recipe for Old-Fashioned Pot roast, adding 1 pound carrots, peeled and cut crosswise into 2-inch pieces, 1 pound parsnips, peeled and cut crosswise into 2-inch pieces, and 1½ pounds russet potatoes, peeled, halved lengthwise, and each half quartered, to the pot in step 4 after the roasts have cooked for 3 hours. Once the pot roast and vegetables are fully cooked, transfer the large pieces of carrot, parsnip, and potato to a serving platter using a slotted spoon, cover tightly with foil, and proceed with the recipe as directed.

Old-Fashioned Pot Roast with Mushroom and Prune Gravy

Follow the recipe for Old-Fashioned Pot Roast, substituting dark beer (porter or stout) for the red wine, omitting the tomato paste, and adding 1 ounce well-rinsed dried porcini mushrooms and ½ cup pitted prunes to the Dutch oven with the beef broth in step 2. While the roast cooks, heat 2 tablespoons unsalted butter in a 12-inch skillet over medium heat; when the foaming subsides add 1 pound thinly sliced cremini mushrooms and cook until all the liquid has evaporated and the mushrooms have started to brown, 7 to 10 minutes. Add the sautéed mushrooms to the pureed sauce in step 6 and omit the balsamic vinegar.

NOTES FROM THE TEST KITCHEN

IDENTICAL TWINS?

The roast on the left was seared before braising; the roast on the right was not. Both achieved similar levels of browning, and they tasted almost identical.

SEARED   **NOT SEARED**

CHICKEN POT PIE

✔ **WHY THIS RECIPE WORKS:** To streamline classic chicken pot pie, we poached chicken breasts and thighs (instead of roasting a whole chicken) then used the poaching liquid as the base of a flavorful sauce. To boost the flavor of the sauce further, we relied on a few foods rich in glutamates (naturally occurring flavor compounds that enhance meaty flavor), like sautéed mushrooms, soy sauce, and tomato paste. For our pot pie crust, we developed an easy-to-make savory crumble enriched with Parmesan cheese, and to ensure the topping baked up crisp and not soggy, we gave the crumble a head start by baking it separately before sprinkling it over our pie.

FEW DISHES CAN WHET THE TASTE BUDS LIKE CHICKEN pot pie. Those three little words conjure images of buttery, flaky crust set atop moist chicken enveloped by rich, creamy sauce and surrounded by sweet peas and tender carrots. Who wouldn't want to serve such soul-satisfying fare? But let's get real. As homey as it sounds, this dish is a production. You've got to cook and break down chicken, make a sauce, parcook vegetables, and all the while prepare, chill, and roll out pie crust. Then, after all that work, there's still no guarantee the chicken won't be dry, the vegetables overcooked, the sauce pasty, and the crust more soggy than flaky. Given the effort (and uncertainty) involved, we'd wager most people have never tasted a true, from-scratch version. Of course, some recipes shortcut the process with leftover chicken and prefab pastry. But these only up the chances of uninspiring results. Who ever raves about reheated chicken?

But our own fantasy of rich-tasting, completely homemade pie pot full of tender, juicy chicken and bright vegetables was too stirring to ignore. We vowed to streamline the dish and get it on the table in 90 minutes, tops.

The first step was to figure out how to cook the chicken. High-roasting or gently pot-roasting a whole bird—two of our favorite methods—would take too long. Poaching bone-in pieces was an obvious route to try, but between the cooking, cooling, and dismantling,

CHICKEN POT PIE WITH SAVORY CRUMBLE TOPPING

it also took the better part of an hour. Next we tried sautéing boneless, skinless thighs and breasts (either whole or diced), but they inevitably developed a crusty, browned exterior that tasters found unappealing in pot pie. Nobody enjoyed eating chicken "nubs."

But starting with skinless, boneless parts was definitely a time-saver, though it did mean doing away with two prime sources of a bird's flavor. We wondered if poaching the boneless, skinless parts might have potential. To help replace lost flavor, we used chicken broth instead of water as the poaching liquid. As it turned out, the pared-down breasts and thighs actually provided two benefits: First, the meat cooked in a fraction of the time: Even the thickest pieces were done in 12 minutes, at most. Second, these smaller pieces required less cooking liquid, which became the base of the velvety, relatively full-bodied sauce without the need for reducing. Plus, with the skin and bones already removed, the meat was easy to handle and shredded nicely into bite-sized morsels.

Now what to do about the vegetables? Our tasters clamored for a traditional medley of onions, carrots, celery, and peas, which sounded just right to us, too. Cooking the chicken together with the vegetables, while undeniably efficient, resulted in meat and sauce that tasted like vegetable soup base and vegetables that turned mushy and tasted like, well, nothing. Besides, who wants to eat poached onions? Cooking the two elements separately— the chicken in broth, the vegetables in a little oil—was the only way to bring out and maintain their distinct flavors and textures in the pie. We then brightened the filling with a squirt of fresh lemon juice and minced parsley and added the frozen peas right before transferring everything to the baking dish. The whole process turned out to be less fussy than we thought; during the five minutes or so that it took to sauté the vegetables, we could shred the chicken.

As for the sauce, stirred together from a butter-and-flour roux, the poaching liquid, and milk, it tasted clean and nicely chickeny. But without the benefit of a fond from dark, caramelized bits of roasted chicken as a flavor base or the deeply concentrated jus of a pot-roasted bird, it lacked a certain savory depth. What we needed were some powerhouse ingredients to give it a boost— and fortunately we had some test kitchen precedent to

fall back on. A few years ago, we challenged ourselves to make full-flavored beef soup in an hour, and the key to maximum flavor in a hurry turned out to be adding foods rich in glutamates—naturally occurring flavor compounds that enhance savory qualities. Many of these are pantry items that we tend to keep on hand—tomato paste, red wine, soy sauce, and anchovies—as well as mushrooms and Parmesan cheese. Red wine, of course, was out of the question, and the idea of salty little fish in our pie did not appeal. However, sautéed mushrooms were a no-brainer. We also cooked 1 teaspoon each of soy sauce and tomato paste in the pan until it browned and caramelized and we used this to start our sauce. Together, these three ingredients greatly enhanced the sauce's savory character. And because the amount of soy sauce and tomato paste was so tiny, no one even guessed they were in the mix.

It was time to put a lid on it—but exactly what sort of crust was not yet clear. Though we would miss cracking a fork through a rich, buttery seal, we could think of two reasons why traditional pie pastry wouldn't work: First, we were on the clock. Second, baking the pie long enough for the crust to finish would almost certainly wreak havoc on our carefully calibrated filling, drying out the chicken and turning the vegetables to mush.

NOTES FROM THE TEST KITCHEN

BUILDING A FLAVOR BASE IN HALF THE TIME

We cut time but not flavor, creating a fond from the browned, caramelized remainders of these three glutamate-rich ingredients to use as a base for the sauce.

MUSHROOMS
Sautéed mushrooms begin to build flavor.

TOMATO PASTE
Tomato paste added to the pan caramelizes to create more flavor.

SOY SAUCE
The sugars in soy sauce also brown, further boosting flavor.

ENSURING A CRISP TOPPING

We swapped the traditional labor-intensive crust for a simpler savory crumble topping on our pot pie. Prebaking the crumble before sprinkling it over the pie ensures it stays crisp.

Of the simpler from-scratch options, cream biscuits came to mind. These quick-cooking Yankee-style pastries came together in a jiffy, but most tasters felt that despite their nicely browned, craggy peaks, the soft, tender undersides offered too little textural contrast with the creamy filling. A chicken pie—even a speedy one—needs a crisp, buttery top.

Then a colleague mentioned a more rugged-textured topping she had stumbled across in a recipe from Boston chef Gordon Hamersley: a vegetable stew with a garlic-cheddar "crumble" crust. We flipped through the pages of his cookbook, *Bistro Cooking at Home,* until we found it. Not quite biscuit, not quite pie crust, this savory topping turned out to be a snap to prepare—just rub butter into flour, salt, and leavening; toss in some grated cheese, pepper, and minced garlic; bind the lot together with cream; and crumble it over the filling. It also boasted a lightly crunchy exterior and tender interior, plus an appealingly rough-hewn appearance. It wouldn't be traditional, but since expediency was our primary goal, it was worth a shot.

In fact, the crumble proved a huge hit, especially after some tweaking here and there: Out came the overly assertive garlic along with the cheddar, which we replaced with glutamate-rich Parmesan. We also changed how to marry the two components. Since the chicken filling was already fully cooked, we decided to prebake the crumble before scattering it over the casserole, so that a brief stint in the oven would be all the pie needed. Prebaking would also ensure the crumble didn't lose any of its wonderful crispness. There was nothing to it, really. Crumbling the mixture onto a sheet pan and baking it while we made the filling fit smoothly into our method. At that point, the topped casserole needed a mere 15 minutes to brown and start bubbling up the sides—just long enough for us to tidy up the dirty pots and utensils.

Time check? Not even 90 minutes. Homemade pot pie on the fly had seemed like a lofty goal, but it won over even the traditionalists among us. Instead of merely imagining pot pie's homey appeal, this was one they could really dig into.

Chicken Pot Pie with Savory Crumble Topping

SERVES 6

This recipe relies on two unusual ingredients: soy sauce and tomato paste. Do not omit them. They don't convey their distinct tastes but greatly deepen the savory flavor of the filling. When making the topping, do not substitute milk or half-and-half for the heavy cream.

FILLING

- 1½ pounds boneless, skinless chicken breasts and/or thighs
- 3 cups low-sodium chicken broth
- 2 tablespoons vegetable oil
- 1 medium onion, minced
- 3 medium carrots, peeled and cut crosswise into ¼-inch-thick slices (about 1 cup)
- 2 small celery ribs, chopped fine
  Table salt and ground black pepper
- 10 ounces cremini mushrooms, stems trimmed, caps wiped clean and sliced thin
- 1 teaspoon soy sauce
- 1 teaspoon tomato paste
- 4 tablespoons (½ stick) unsalted butter
- ½ cup unbleached all-purpose flour
- 1 cup whole milk
- 2 teaspoons juice from 1 lemon
- 3 tablespoons minced fresh parsley leaves
- ¾ cup frozen baby peas

CRUMBLE TOPPING

- 2 cups (10 ounces) unbleached all-purpose flour
- 2 teaspoons baking powder
- ¾ teaspoon table salt
- ½ teaspoon ground black pepper
- ⅛ teaspoon cayenne pepper
- 6 tablespoons (¾ stick) unsalted butter, cut into ½-inch cubes and chilled
- 1 ounce Parmesan cheese, grated fine (about ½ cup)
- ¾ cup plus 2 tablespoons heavy cream (see note)

1. FOR THE FILLING: Put the chicken and broth in a Dutch oven over medium heat. Cover and bring to

a simmer; simmer until the chicken is just done, 8 to 12 minutes. Transfer the cooked chicken to a large bowl. Pour the broth through a fine-mesh strainer into a liquid measuring cup and reserve. Do not wash the Dutch oven. Meanwhile, adjust an oven rack to the upper-middle position and heat the oven to 450 degrees.

2. FOR THE TOPPING: Line a rimmed baking sheet with parchment paper. Combine the flour, baking powder, salt, pepper, and cayenne in a large bowl. Sprinkle the butter pieces over the top of the flour. Using your fingers, rub the butter into the flour mixture until it resembles coarse cornmeal. Stir in the Parmesan. Add the cream and stir until just combined. Crumble the mixture into irregularly shaped pieces ranging from ¼ to ¾ inch onto the prepared baking sheet. Bake until fragrant and starting to brown, 10 to 13 minutes. Set aside.

3. Heat 1 tablespoon of the oil in the now-empty Dutch oven over medium heat until shimmering. Add

the onion, carrots, celery, ¼ teaspoon salt, and ¼ teaspoon pepper; cover and cook, stirring occasionally, until just tender, 5 to 7 minutes. While the vegetables are cooking, shred the meat into small bite-sized pieces. Transfer the cooked vegetables to the bowl with the chicken; set aside.

4. Heat the remaining 1 tablespoon oil in the again-empty Dutch oven over medium heat until shimmering. Add the mushrooms; cover and cook, stirring occasionally, until the mushrooms have released their juices, about 5 minutes. Remove the cover, stir in the soy sauce and tomato paste. Increase the heat to medium-high and cook, stirring frequently, until the liquid has evaporated, the mushrooms are well browned, and a dark fond begins to form on the surface of the pan, about 5 minutes. Transfer the mushrooms to the bowl with the chicken and vegetables. Set aside.

5. Heat the butter in the again-empty Dutch oven over medium heat. When the foaming subsides, add the flour and cook 1 minute. Slowly whisk in the reserved chicken broth, milk, and any accumulated chicken juices. Bring to a simmer, scraping the pan bottom with a wooden spoon to loosen the browned bits, then continue to simmer until the sauce fully thickens, about 1 minute. Season with salt and pepper to taste. Remove from the heat and stir in the lemon juice and 2 tablespoons of the parsley.

6. Stir the chicken and vegetable mixture and peas into the sauce. Pour the mixture into a 13 by 9-inch baking dish or casserole dish of similar size. Scatter the crumble topping evenly over the filling. Bake on a rimmed baking sheet until the filling is bubbling and the topping is well browned, 12 to 15 minutes. Sprinkle with the remaining 1 tablespoon parsley and serve.

RATING PLASTIC FOOD STORAGE CONTAINERS

Finding a good food storage container shouldn't take as much thought or effort as it often does. We selected eight BPA-free plastic food storage containers (research links BPA, bisphenol-A, to various health issues), choosing square or rectangular as close as possible to an 8-cup capacity, and tested each for leaking, durability, odor-retention, and design. We put them in the microwave, the freezer, and the refrigerator. We ran them through dozens of dishwasher cycles, submerged them in water, and dropped them to see how they held up. Brands are listed in order of preference. See www.americastestkitchen.com for updates to this testing.

HIGHLY RECOMMENDED

SNAPWARE MODS (model #98213 72915)
SIZE: Large rectangle, 8 cups
PRICE: $6.99
MATERIAL: Polypropylene with silicone gasket
DISHWASHER PLACEMENT: Lid on top rack only
LEAKS: ★★½ **ODORS:** ★★★
MICROWAVE: ★★★ **DURABILITY:** ★★★
COMMENTS: The simple snap-down lid sealed easily throughout testing. Though it allowed a few drops of water in during the first submersion test, after dishwashing, the seal was perfect. The flat, rectangular shape encourages quick cooling or heating and stacks easily, with the lid attaching to the bottom.

RECOMMENDED

LOCK & LOCK Classic Food Storage Container
(model #HPL818)
SIZE: Rectangle, 8 cups
PRICE: $7.49
MATERIAL: Polypropylene with silicone gasket
DISHWASHER PLACEMENT: Top rack only
LEAKS: ★★½ **ODORS:** ★★★
MICROWAVE: ★★ **DURABILITY:** ★★★
COMMENTS: Sturdy, with a secure seal. Performed dependably overall but leaked a few drops during the first submersion test—though the seal improved after dishwashing 50 times. It stained slightly and has a taller, deeper shape than preferred.

OXO Good Grips Top Container (model #1172700)
SIZE: Medium rectangle, 9.3 cups
PRICE: $7.99
MATERIAL: Polypropylene with silicone gasket
DISHWASHER PLACEMENT: Top rack only
LEAKS: ★★½ **ODORS:** ★★★
MICROWAVE: ★★ **DURABILITY:** ★★½
COMMENTS: When new, this container leaked when submerged, but after dishwashing 50 times, the seal improved. It stained slightly and has a taller, deeper shape than preferred.

FRESHVAC PRE Vacuum Food Storage
(model #1-2200S)
SIZE: Square, 9.3 cups
PRICE: $5.99
MATERIAL: Polypropylene
DISHWASHER PLACEMENT: Lid on top rack only
LEAKS: ★★★ **ODORS:** ★★★
MICROWAVE: ★★ **DURABILITY:** ★
COMMENTS: We struggled to achieve a perfect airtight seal after the dishwasher test. Its shape is low but too rounded and bulbous for efficient storage.

RECOMMENDED WITH RESERVATIONS

GLADWARE Deep Dish (model #12587 70045)
SIZE: Rectangle, 8 cups
PRICE: $5.97 for set of 3
MATERIAL: Polypropylene
DISHWASHER PLACEMENT: Top and bottom racks
LEAKS: ★★ **ODORS:** ★
MICROWAVE: ★ **DURABILITY:** ★
COMMENTS: Performed acceptably when new but became alarmingly soft in the microwave. After 50 dishwasher cycles, the seal leaked profusely, chili stained, and bad odors hung on. It's best for a potluck—it's cheap and you won't care if you don't get it back.

NOT RECOMMENDED

STERILITE Ultra-Seal (model #0322)
SIZE: Rectangle, 8.3 cups
PRICE: $6.49
MATERIAL: Polypropylene with silicone gasket
DISHWASHER PLACEMENT: Top rack only
LEAKS: ★ **ODORS:** ★★★
MICROWAVE: ★★ **DURABILITY:** ★
COMMENTS: The seal was uneven and because the lid lacked rigidity, the corners leaked badly even when new. The flap popped open during the drop test. Chili stained more than in other containers.

ZIPLOC Snap 'n Seal (model #10885)

SIZE: Large rectangle, 9.5 cups
PRICE: $4.55 for set of 2
MATERIAL: Polypropylene
DISHWASHER PLACEMENT: Top rack
LEAKS: ★ **ODORS:** ★★★
MICROWAVE: ★ **DURABILITY:** ★
COMMENTS: Despite being roomy, this model felt cheap and flimsy. It was extremely leaky, both before and after 50 dishwasher cycles. Not on par with better containers in the lineup. Its only virtue: a rock-bottom price.

RUBBERMAID Lock-its (model #7K95)
SIZE: Square, 9 cups
PRICE: $12.99
MATERIAL: Polypropylene
DISHWASHER PLACEMENT: Top and bottom racks
LEAKS: ★½ **ODORS:** ★★★
MICROWAVE: ★ **DURABILITY:** ★
COMMENTS: This usually dependable brand flopped—poorly made flap seals distorted in the microwave, popping back up when pressed down. The top flew off in our drop test.

SOUTHERN FARE,
Reinvented

Frying chicken doesn't need to make a mess of your stovetop—our hybrid method uses a lot less oil than traditional fried chicken recipes, freeing you from the usual post-fry cleanup.

UNLESS YOU CRAVE AUSTERITY—SAY NEW ENGLAND BOILED DINNER and brown bread—it's safe to say that Southerners have it over Northerners when it comes to irresistible, crave-worthy dishes. Two Southern favorites, barbecued pulled pork and fried chicken, are particular standouts in our book.

Pulled pork is so good that it's a shame most can't enjoy it year round. In colder climes, manning a grill for the hours it takes to cook this cut of meat until meltingly tender often requires pulling on a parka—a task most of us aren't up for. Cooking pulled pork indoors (essentially braising the meat in the oven) is an alternative, but the recipes we've tried result in meat that tastes steamed, not barbecued. The smoke flavor is nil and heaping on barbecue sauce simply doesn't make it barbecue. We wanted to devise an indoor method for pulled pork that delivered tender, smoky meat that easily pulls into shreds—pulled pork so good, we'd be satisfied all through the winter.

Most of us prefer to get our fried chicken fix by eating out rather than facing a potful of messy oil at home. But is there an easier way to make homemade fried chicken? Some resort to oven-fried chicken, but it just doesn't have the crunch and flavor of the real deal. We wanted to develop an easier method for making real fried chicken—one with juicy, well-seasoned meat and a crisp, craggy mahogany crust. Break out the sweet tea as we make Southern favorites accessible to everyone.

INDOOR PULLED PORK

✓ WHY THIS RECIPE WORKS: Indoor pulled pork requires a dual cooking method to keep the meat moist inside while developing a flavorful outer crust. Essentially, this translates to cooking the pork in the oven, covered (for moist, tender meat) and uncovered (to yield a flavorful crust, or bark). For smoky barbecued flavor, we found that liquid smoke, which we used both to brine and rub the meat, did the trick. A pulled pork recipe wouldn't be complete without at least one of the three authentically regional sauces we developed to moisten and flavor the meat.

NOT TO MINIMIZE ANYONE'S ACCOMPLISHMENTS, BUT when it comes to barbecue, professional pit masters have it made: A commercial smoker goes a long way toward getting great results. Even home cooks who live in temperate climates have a leg up, since (with proper technique) a kettle grill works almost as well as a pit. But here in New England, if you get a hankering for pulled pork in winter, you're in a bind. You either have to wait until spring, when the snow melts and the winds die down, or bring the operation indoors.

The phrase "indoor barbecue" is usually code for "braised in a Dutch oven with bottled barbecue sauce." This results in mushy, waterlogged meat and candy-sweet sauce—a far cry from what we were after. We wanted moist, tender, shreddable meat with deep smoke flavor all the way through, plus a dark, richly seasoned crust.

With any kind of barbecue, a good amount of fat is necessary for moisture and flavor. Well-marbled Boston butt (from the upper portion of the front leg of the pig) is a favorite for pulled pork because of its high level of marbling. Since we were shredding the meat anyway, we opted for the boneless version. We'd fine-tune our dry rub later, but for now, we applied a mixture of salt, pepper, and sugar to a 5-pound roast.

We considered our next key decision: oven temperature. On the grill, barbecue temperatures hover between 250 and 300 degrees. For the oven, we opted for 300 degrees, hoping to have our meat on the table as soon as possible.

We wanted supremely moist meat, so we brined the pork in salt water before placing it in the oven. Six hours later, the meat had developed a substantial black crust (or "bark"), but one taste revealed that this bark, while flavorful, was dry as a bone, and the meat underneath was tough and almost impossible to shred. Why should the standard five or six hours on a grill produce tender meat with a crisp yet moist crust, while the same time in an oven only delivered barely edible leather?

We knew for meat to become tender, its connective tissue must break down. This requires both heat and time. Meat needs to hold an internal temperature of around 200 degrees for at least an hour in order for collagen (a key protein component of connective tissue) to dissolve. Apparently, our meat was heating too slowly in the oven—though we wondered why, since 300 degrees was at the top end of the temperature scale for barbecue.

It soon dawned on us that there's a crucial difference between real barbecue and oven barbecue. On a grill, as moisture escapes from damp wood chips and steaming meat, it's trapped underneath the dome of the lid, creating a moist cooking environment. To create extra steam, some cooks even place a pan of water beside the coals. An oven, by contrast, is ventilated to remove any moisture that builds up inside. Since moist air transfers heat more effectively than dry air, an oven is less efficient than either a grill or a smoker.

Confident of our reasoning, we boosted the oven temperature to 325 degrees to jump-start collagen breakdown, then set a pan of water on the lowest oven rack, directly underneath the pork. No luck; our oven was still too dry. What if we trapped the moisture right up against the meat? But an aluminum foil shield did this too well. The meat came out moist and tender in only 4½ hours, but there was no bark.

We'd need to use a dual method: covering the pork for part of the time to speed up cooking and keep it moist, then uncovering it for the remainder to allow the meat to develop a crust. We experimented until we found the perfect balance: Three hours of covered cooking rendered the meat meltingly tender, while an hour and a half uncovered helped a nice crust to form. This bark was so good that our tasters pleaded for more, a request we accommodated by splitting the pork butt

INDOOR PULLED PORK WITH SWEET AND TANGY BARBECUE SAUCE

in half horizontally before cooking, greatly increasing its surface area. (Surprisingly, we found we still needed the same amount of cooking time to ensure tender meat.)

We'd achieved the right texture, now we needed to master the defining feature of barbecue: smoky flavor. We ignited wood chips in a foil packet on the stovetop and put them in the oven with the pork, but they extinguished quickly. We tried grinding the chips in a spice grinder, hoping they would stay lit longer. One ruined spice mill later, we were no better off. We used smoky Lapsang Souchong tea to impart smoky flavor to a previously developed recipe for oven-barbecued ribs but those ribs are exposed to smoke for a mere 30 minutes. After 4½ hours of tea smoke, our pork butt tasted too strongly of, well, tea.

There was another option: When developing our recipe for skillet barbecued pork chops, we learned that liquid smoke is a natural product derived from condensing the moist smoke of smoldering wood chips. Starting modestly because of its strength, we tried adding a teaspoon of liquid smoke to our gallon of brine. To our delight, the smoky flavor made its way into the meat without overwhelming it and tasted completely natural. Seeking deeper flavor, we ended up using a full 3 tablespoons in the brine; more than that made no further impact. But we thought our pork could still be a little smokier.

We were reminded that pulled pork can be cooked with a dry rub or a wet rub. What if we used both methods, thereby incorporating smoke flavor two ways? First, we fortified our dry rub with smoked paprika, then supplemented the dry rub with a wet rub of mustard mixed with a little more liquid smoke. Success! Our pork finally had a deep, well-developed smokiness.

All we needed now was a sauce. Not wanting to limit ourselves to just one barbecue region or style, we developed a classic sweet and tangy sauce, a vinegar sauce (Lexington, North Carolina, style), and a mustard sauce (South Carolina style). Since our pork emerged from the oven complete with flavorful drippings, we enriched each sauce with ½ cup of the defatted liquid. Our indoor barbecue may involve some degree of illusion—but we'd challenge any barbecue lover not to be taken in by the (liquid) smoke and mirrors.

Indoor Pulled Pork with Sweet and Tangy Barbecue Sauce

SERVES 6 TO 8

Sweet paprika may be substituted for smoked paprika. Covering the pork with parchment and then foil prevents the acidic mustard from eating holes in the foil. Serve the pork on hamburger rolls with pickle chips and thinly sliced onion. In place of the Sweet and Tangy Barbecue Sauce or the variations that follow, you can use 2 cups of your favorite barbecue sauce thinned with ½ cup of the defatted pork cooking liquid in step 5. The shredded and sauced pork can be cooled, tightly covered, and refrigerated for up to 2 days. Reheat it gently before serving.

PORK

- 1   cup plus 2 teaspoons table salt
- ½   cup plus 2 tablespoons sugar
- 3   tablespoons plus 2 teaspoons liquid smoke
- 1   (5-pound) boneless pork butt roast, cut in half horizontally
- ¼   cup yellow mustard
- 2   tablespoons ground black pepper
- 2   tablespoons smoked paprika (see note)
- 1   teaspoon cayenne pepper

SWEET AND TANGY BARBECUE SAUCE

- 1½   cups ketchup
- ¼   cup light or mild molasses
- 2   tablespoons Worcestershire sauce
- 1   tablespoon hot sauce
- ½   teaspoon table salt
- ½   teaspoon ground black pepper

1. FOR THE PORK: Dissolve 1 cup of the salt, ½ cup of the sugar, and 3 tablespoons of the liquid smoke in 1 gallon cold water in a large container. Submerge the pork in the brine, cover with plastic wrap, and refrigerate for 2 hours.

2. While the pork brines, combine the mustard and remaining 2 teaspoons liquid smoke in a small bowl; set aside. Combine the black pepper, paprika, remaining 2 tablespoons sugar, remaining 2 teaspoons salt, and cayenne in a second small bowl; set aside. Adjust an oven rack to the lower-middle position and heat the oven to 325 degrees.

NOTES FROM THE TEST KITCHEN

CUTTING A PORK BUTT IN HALF

Halving the pork increases its surface area, which creates more flavorful crust.

Holding your knife parallel to the cutting board, press one hand flat against the top of the pork butt while cutting horizontally.

GETTING SMOKE FLAVOR WITHOUT A FIRE

1. Add liquid smoke to the brine to draw smoky flavor deep into the meat.

2. Rub the pork with more liquid smoke to give the crust, or bark, a pronounced smoky flavor.

3. Add smoked paprika to the dry rub to bring in additional smokiness and help the bark develop its color.

Lexington Vinegar Barbecue Sauce

MAKES ABOUT 2½ CUPS

- 1 **cup cider vinegar**
- ½ **cup ketchup**
- ½ **cup water**
- 1 **tablespoon sugar**
- ¾ **teaspoon table salt**
- ¾ **teaspoon red pepper flakes**
- ½ **teaspoon ground black pepper**

Combine all the ingredients in a medium bowl with ½ cup defatted cooking liquid (in step 5) and whisk to combine.

South Carolina Mustard Barbecue Sauce

MAKES ABOUT 2½ CUPS

- 1 **cup yellow mustard**
- ½ **cup white vinegar**
- ¼ **cup packed light brown sugar**
- ¼ **cup Worcestershire sauce**
- 2 **tablespoons hot sauce**
- 1 **teaspoon table salt**
- 1 **teaspoon ground black pepper**

Combine all the ingredients in a medium bowl with ½ cup defatted cooking liquid (in step 5) and whisk to combine.

3. Remove the pork from the brine and dry thoroughly with paper towels. Rub the mustard mixture over the entire surface of each piece of pork. Sprinkle the entire surface of each piece with the spice mixture. Place the pork on a wire rack set over a foil-lined rimmed baking sheet. Place a piece of parchment paper over the pork, then cover with a sheet of aluminum foil, sealing the edges to prevent moisture from escaping. Roast the pork for 3 hours.

4. Remove the pork from the oven; remove and discard the foil and parchment. Carefully pour off the liquid in the bottom of the baking sheet into a fat separator and reserve for the sauce. Return the pork to the oven and cook, uncovered, until well browned, tender, and the center of the roast registers 200 degrees on an instant-read thermometer, about 1½ hours. Transfer the pork to a serving dish, tent loosely with foil, and let rest for 20 minutes.

5. FOR THE SAUCE: While the pork rests, pour ½ cup of the defatted cooking liquid from the fat separator into a medium bowl; whisk in the sauce ingredients.

6. TO SERVE: Using two forks, shred the pork into bite-sized pieces. Toss with 1 cup sauce and season with salt and pepper to taste. Serve, passing the remaining sauce separately.

NOTES FROM THE TEST KITCHEN

LIQUID SMOKE
Liquid smoke is an all-natural product that lends a deep, grill-smoked taste to our indoor recipe. Our favorite brand is Wright's Liquid Smoke ($2.99 for 3.5 ounces).

EASIER FRIED CHICKEN

✔ **WHY THIS RECIPE WORKS:** To fry up a batch of crackling-crisp, golden brown fried chicken without relying on a messy pot full of oil, we turned to a hybrid method. To start, we fry the chicken in a reduced amount of oil, then move the operation into the oven, where we place the chicken parts on a rack set over a baking sheet. Using a rack promotes air circulation around the chicken and helps ensure an evenly crisp crust. Soaking the chicken in well-seasoned buttermilk both enhances flavor and ensures that the chicken retains moisture as it cooks. And adding a little buttermilk to the dry ingredients of the coating creates irregular texture, which translates to extra crunch.

HERE'S ONE THING WE CAN ALL AGREE ON: FRIED chicken is great. Crackling crisp, golden brown, and juicy—what's not to love? And here's something else we can all agree on: Heating, and then cleaning up, more than a quart of fat on the stovetop is too much trouble for most home cooks. These two premises have spawned a slew of "oven-fried" chicken recipes designed to deliver one (the chicken) without the other (the hot fat). Using bread crumbs, crushed Melba toast, or even breakfast cereal, these versions certainly deliver crunch and can even boast moist, juicy meat. But they are at best a pale imitation and not a replica of the real deal.

With many such recipes, reducing fat is the overriding goal. Not for us. Fried chicken should be an occasional indulgence, and we're not going to settle for second-rate flavor for the sake of a few calories. Our goal was to achieve true fried chicken—golden brown and crisp with a buttermilk-and-flour-based coating—but without having to dispose of a pot full of fat.

Fried chicken recipes often call for soaking the chicken pieces in buttermilk—it has just enough acid to help tenderize the outer layers of the meat without turning them mushy—then dredging them in seasoned flour before deep-frying. Over the years, we've discovered a few other tricks to help ensure moist meat and an extra-crisp crust. They would make a good jumping-off point, we thought.

For our deep-fried chicken, we first heavily salt the buttermilk before soaking the chicken pieces, which turns the buttermilk into a brine and helps the meat retain moisture as it cooks. We also add baking powder to the seasoned dredging mixture. As the chicken fries, the baking powder releases carbon dioxide, leavening the crust and increasing its surface area, keeping it light and crisp. Finally, while traditional fried chicken recipes call for only dry ingredients in their dredging mixture, we've found that adding buttermilk to the dry ingredients before dredging the chicken creates small clumps of batter that become super crisp as they fry.

We figured we'd be better able to replicate deep-fat frying if we first reviewed what exactly it accomplishes: Just like any other high-heat cooking method, it facilitates the Maillard reaction and the creation of hundreds of new flavor compounds that are the hallmark of properly browned food. It also dehydrates. As the water in the coating reaches 212 degrees (its boiling point), it converts to steam and is expelled from the food (this is what causes the bubbles you see when food is dropped into hot fat). It is this dehydration, along with the hardening of the protein structure in the flour and chicken skin triggered by heat, that gives fried chicken its crisp crust. Last, deep-fat frying cooks the food; the trick when frying chicken is finding the right oil temperature to cook the meat through without burning the exterior.

An oven could obviously get hot enough to produce browning and cause dehydration. So could we get oven-fried chicken closer to the deep-fried original if we simply ditched the bread crumbs and crushed crackers as a coating and went with traditional flour-dredged pieces? The idea was a shot in the dark—and it totally missed. After an hour in the oven, the chicken was spotty brown, with some regions coated in raw flour and others nearly burnt. Biting into it revealed a powdery, brittle crust, not a moist, crisp one. There must be something else involved with deep-frying that we were missing.

The answer to the coating question lay in a discovery we made developing an easier method for French fries. It turns out that, contrary to popular belief, the higher

EASIER FRIED CHICKEN

the temperature of the frying fat, the more it is absorbed by the food being fried. So as a piece of chicken cooks at a relatively hot 300 to 350 degrees, almost all of the moisture in the coating is expelled and replaced with oil. That oil is essential to the flavor and texture of a really good crisp crust—and its absence in the breaded and baked chicken explained the dry, floury results. When the coating's moisture evaporated, there was nothing to replace it. The bottom line? At least some form of frying would be required.

Our standard fried chicken recipe calls for a full 5 cups of oil. To achieve a fully cooked chicken, we cover the Dutch oven for part of the time and carefully monitor the temperature throughout using a deep-fat thermometer. Perhaps the solution to easier fried chicken was as simple as reducing the volume of oil. We tested our way down to 1¾ cups—just enough oil that when we nestled the chicken pieces into it they would raise the level to help cook their sides. Then, all we'd have to do was flip them over to finish cooking once the first side was golden brown. Simple, right?

Wrong. If we'd been using 5 cups, the oil's temperature would have stayed roughly the same after the addition of the chicken. With only 1¾ cups, however, the temperature dropped dramatically as the chicken was added, to just over 200 degrees from 375. To get the oil back up to the optimal range, we had to crank the flame to high, which fueled a new problem: burnt patches on the parts of the chicken that had been in direct contact with the bottom of the pan (and without a full pot of oil to keep the chicken afloat, this meant a lot of the pieces). To avoid burning, the chicken couldn't stand much more than three or four minutes of frying per side, not enough time for it to cook through. Furthermore, much of the chicken never quite caught up after the big temperature drop; even after being flipped, it was still dead cold in the center and pale golden brown..

We began to wonder if we'd discounted the oven prematurely. Radiant, circulating heat might be just the ticket to replace the even heating of a deep, hot oil bath and allow our chicken to brown and cook through properly. We decided to try a hybrid method: we'd start by frying the chicken on the stovetop until it formed a light brown crust, then finish it in a hot oven (perched on a wire rack set in a sheet pan to prevent burnt spots and promote air circulation all around the meat) to both cook it through and deepen its color.

Our only question: Would there be enough fat left on the surface of the chicken after its initial fry to fully permeate the crust as it dehydrated, just as in traditionally fried chicken? In a word, yes. Fifteen minutes in the oven was all it took to give our shallow-fried chicken a golden brown crust that was crisp and craggy enough to make the Colonel blush.

When we tasted it side by side with fried chicken cooked in the usual quart-plus of oil, we couldn't tell the two batches apart. But their differences were very apparent when it came time to take care of the cooking fat. Oil crisis? Solved.

SCIENCE DESK

THE MAGIC OF A BUTTERMILK BRINE
In fried chicken recipes, soaking the chicken in buttermilk is a standard approach that helps tenderize the meat (mainly the outer layers). But is adding salt to the buttermilk really necessary to ensure meat that's also juicy?

THE EXPERIMENT
We cooked four batches of chicken side by side. Three of them were soaked for an hour, one in a solution of buttermilk and salt, one in only buttermilk, and one in a plain saltwater solution. The fourth was not soaked. All the chicken was dredged in flour before frying.

THE RESULTS
The unsoaked chicken was both dry and tough. The saltwater-soaked chicken was moist but a little bit rubbery. The chicken soaked in plain buttermilk, while quite tender lacked moisture. Only the chicken soaked in salted buttermilk came out both tender and moist.

THE EXPLANATION
Buttermilk and salt play equally important roles here. Buttermilk contains acids that, over time, can soften the proteins in the meat, leading to softer, more tender texture. Just as in a normal brine, salt helps change the protein structure of the meat so that it can retain more moisture as it cooks, producing noticeably juicier results.

Easier Fried Chicken

SERVES 4

A whole 4-pound chicken, cut into eight pieces, can be used instead of the chicken parts. Skinless chicken pieces are also an acceptable substitute, but the meat will come out slightly drier. A Dutch oven with a 10-inch diameter can be used in place of the straight-sided sauté pan.

1¼ cups buttermilk
   Table salt
3 teaspoons ground black pepper
1 teaspoon garlic powder
1 teaspoon paprika
   Cayenne pepper
   Dash of hot sauce
3½ pounds bone-in, skin-on chicken parts (breasts, thighs, and drumsticks or a mix, with breasts cut in half), trimmed of excess fat (see note)
2 cups unbleached all-purpose flour
2 teaspoons baking powder
1¾ cups vegetable oil

1. Whisk 1 cup of the buttermilk, 1 tablespoon salt, 1 teaspoon of the black pepper, ¼ teaspoon of the garlic powder, ¼ teaspoon of the paprika, pinch of cayenne, and the hot sauce, together in a large bowl. Add the chicken pieces and turn to coat. Refrigerate, covered, at least 1 hour or up to overnight.

2. Adjust an oven rack to the middle position and heat the oven to 400 degrees. Whisk the flour, baking powder, 1 teaspoon salt, and remaining 2 teaspoons black pepper, ¾ teaspoon garlic powder, ¾ teaspoon paprika, and ¼ teaspoon cayenne together in a large bowl. Add the remaining ¼ cup buttermilk to the flour mixture and mix with your fingers until combined and small clumps form. Working with one piece at a time, dredge the chicken pieces in the flour mixture, pressing the flour onto the pieces to form a thick, even coating. Place the dredged chicken on a large plate, skin side up.

3. Heat the oil in a 10-inch straight-sided sauté pan over medium-high heat to 375 degrees, about 5 minutes. Carefully place the chicken pieces in the pan, skin side down, and cook until golden brown, 3 to 5 minutes. Carefully flip the chicken pieces and continue to cook until golden brown on the second side, 2 to 4 minutes longer. Transfer the chicken to a wire rack set over a rimmed baking sheet. Bake the chicken until an instant-read thermometer inserted into the thickest part of the chicken registers 160 degrees for breasts and 175 for legs and thighs, 15 to 20 minutes. (Smaller pieces may cook faster than larger pieces. Remove the chicken pieces from the oven as they reach the correct temperature.) Transfer the chicken to a paper towel–lined plate and let rest 5 minutes before serving.

NOTES FROM THE TEST KITCHEN

OIL CONSERVATION
Properly frying chicken from start to finish using traditional methods requires lots of messy oil. Our hybrid stove-to-oven method cuts it way back.

TRADITIONAL WAY
5 cups oil

OUR WAY
1¾ cups oil

RATING ELECTRIC PRESSURE COOKERS

Pressure cookers cook faster than ordinary pots by creating pressure that raises the temperature of boiling water from 212 to 250 degrees. Tightly sealed, they require less cooking liquid, making flavors more concentrated and intense. In the past, pressure cookers were prone to over-pressurizing and exploding. Today's models offer better lid locks and release valves—and new electric models even promise to maintain pressure automatically. Plus, some electric models can multitask as rice cookers and slow cookers. We decided to test four electric models against our longtime favorite stovetop model, the Fagor Duo 8-Quart Pressure Cooker. Right off the bat, three electric models had ill-fitting gaskets, and we were nearly scorched by escaping steam as we struggled to lock them. Only one electric model locked easily and cooked beautifully. While this model could double as a rice cooker and slow cooker, its functions as a slow cooker were limited, and it cost about $30 more than the price of our stovetop favorite—which is still our winner. Brands are listed in order of preference. See www.americastestkitchen.com for updates to this testing.

RECOMMENDED

FAGOR Duo 8-Quart Pressure Cooker (model # 918060787)
PRICE: $89.95
SIZE: 8 quarts
COMMENTS: Simple and effective, this top-ranking model beat out the electric competition. A yellow valve pops up to indicate when it's reached high pressure, with no guesswork. The wide-bottomed cooking surface provides ample space for sautéing.

RECOMMENDED WITH RESERVATIONS

FAGOR Electric Multi-Cooker (model #670040230)
PRICE: $119.95
SIZE: 6 quarts
COMMENTS: Like its stovetop sibling, the lid and gasket fit snugly on the first try, eliminating any fear of pressure release. Although it also operates as a rice cooker and a slow cooker, its capabilities as a slow cooker are limited and it cost more than our stovetop model, so the extra functions are not really worth it.

CUISINART Electric Pressure Cooker (model #CPC-600)
PRICE: $133.95
SIZE: 6 quarts
COMMENTS: Unlike its competitors, this appliance only functions as a pressure cooker. It did take a few tries to get the gasket to lock into place (the first round released all the steam and burned our black beans). The removable cooking pot is dishwasher-safe.

NOT RECOMMENDED

DENI Electric Pressure Cooker (model #9780)
PRICE: $189.99
SIZE: 8.5 quarts
COMMENTS: While this model is generous in size, its performance did not meet expectations. The extremely heavy lid didn't latch properly, allowing steam to leak. Despite being big and heavy, the pan insert spun and wobbled while we were browning ingredients, making cooking challenging, and was cumbersome to clean, since it is not dishwasher-safe.

NESCO Professional Digital 3-in-1 Cooker (model #PC-6–25-30TPR)
PRICE: $109.99
SIZE: 6 quarts
COMMENTS: The lid gasket was a struggle to tighten, leaking hot steam as it cooked. Even when we finally sealed the pot, it reopened halfway through cooking. The cooking pot is not dishwasher-safe.

FALL *Favorites*

WHEN SUMMER'S AIR TURNS COOL AND CRISP, IT'S TIME TO PUT AWAY the grill and head indoors for great fall cooking. With no worries of overheating a summer kitchen, roasting a big cut of meat, like pork shoulder, is a terrific option. Unlike lean pork loin, pork shoulder is well-marbled and covered with a thick fat cap that bastes the meat as it renders, ensuring that it is supremely flavorful. We wanted to perfect a technique for roast pork shoulder—one that would yield juicy, tender meat and a well-seasoned crisp crust.

And what better dessert to serve following pork roast than old-fashioned baked apples? Baked apples can fill a kitchen with an inviting aroma. But the first bite reveals this simple dessert's shortcomings— weak flavor, a mushy texture, and an unremarkable filling. We wanted to develop a recipe for baked apples that would rival the best apple crisp or apple pie—one that boasted juicy, sweet-tart apples and a generous pocket of filling enriched with warm complementary spices.

For our baked apples, we peel the apple base to prevent the fruit from collapsing in the oven.

SLOW-ROASTED PORK

✔ WHY THIS RECIPE WORKS: Salting our roast, a Boston butt, and letting it rest overnight enhances juiciness and seasons the meat throughout. Taking a cue from Chinese barbecued pork, we added brown sugar to the salt rub. Our sugar-enhanced rub pulled moisture from the outer layers of the meat, drying out the exterior so it browned better. It also caramelized on the meat's surface to create a crackling-crisp, salty-sweet crust.

IT'S BEEN MORE THAN 20 YEARS SINCE THE NATIONAL Pork Board launched a campaign to persuade poultry-loving Americans to eat more pig—specifically the lean "other white meat" between the pig's shoulder and leg known as the loin—and producers began developing new breeds of slimmer pigs. Ever since, consumers have been flocking like lemmings to butcher cases to buy up the loin and then heading home to try everything under the sun to improve the almost-fat-free meat's bland flavor and stringy chew.

But this premise—cut the fat, then jump through hoops to make lean meat taste less dull—never made sense to us. We wanted to explore the glories of old-fashioned, better-tasting (read: less lean) pork. One such cut, the shoulder roast (also called "Boston butt" or "pork butt"), has seen new life in both restaurants and supermarket butcher cases. We decided to ditch the loin in favor of this cut, which is not only loaded with flavorful intramuscular fat but also boasts a thick fat cap that renders to a bronze, baconlike crust. A bonus: Pork butt is cheap. True, it would take several hours of roasting before the well-worked shoulder muscle broke down and became fork-tender. But the rewards of richly flavored, crisp-crusted roast would make it time well spent.

The rectangular slab known as pork butt—not to be confused with the cone-shaped, more sinewy "picnic" roast that comes from just below the shoulder blade—can be purchased either boneless or bone-in. Both have their advantages: Boneless cuts typically cook faster than bone-in and come partially butterflied, which leaves plenty of interior meat exposed and available for seasoning. Meanwhile, bone-in roasts take longer to cook and restrict seasoning to the exterior, but retain more moisture and cook more evenly. (See "Bone-In Pork Butt: Fatty, Moist, and Flavorful" on page 59.) Test kitchen precedent had us leaning toward the latter, and one side-by-side comparison was all we needed to confirm our decision.

To start, we used our basic knowledge of what it takes to roast large, tough cuts of meat to put together a basic working recipe. First, we salted the meat and left it to rest. We frequently use this technique to allow the seasoning to penetrate deep beneath the surface of a large, tough roast and break down its proteins for improved texture, not to mention bigger flavor. (When the meat has a high fat content, like pork butt, and dryness isn't a concern, we prefer salting to brining for the clearer flavor and less spongy texture it produces.) A few tests confirmed that an overnight rest (versus two, four, or even six hours) worked best. Then we set the oven to the same temperature we use to barbecue pork butt on the grill, 275 degrees, covered the roast with aluminum foil to trap the damp, collagen-melting heat, and let the meat go until the barest prick of a fork cleaved the roast into rough hunks along its seams. According to our timer, that was right around the seven-hour mark, and the results weren't bad for a first stab.

The pork was tender—our instant-read thermometer registered about 190 degrees. Just as with barbecue, slowly and gently taking the pork well beyond its 145-degree "done" stage not only melts fat, but also breaks down collagen and tenderizes the meat. Its flavor was also fuller than any loin roast we'd ever cooked. Yet for all the time this meat had spent in the oven, it actually tasted more steamed than roasted. And given the aluminum foil shield, the exterior was also pale and soggy.

First things first: we'd been eyeing that thick fat cap as crispy skin fodder, so the aluminum foil cover had to go. (Plus, with so much fat marbling, we figured the pork wouldn't dry out very quickly.) What's more, we needed to get our roast to taste like, well, a roast, so we spent our next several tests turning the oven dial up notch by notch to instill oven-concentrated, meaty flavor and boost browning. At 325 degrees we stopped. After about five hours, the meat's collagen had broken down and rendered the interior meltingly tender, yet sliceable.

The higher heat also crisped up the crust—though not quite as much as we'd hoped. And while decently rendered and copper-colored, the exterior fat was still not sufficiently crunchy and brittle. We wondered if we shouldn't be rubbing the roast's exterior with more than just a handful of salt. At this point, our thoughts turned to Chinese barbecue, in which the pigs are heavily seasoned with equal parts salt and sugar to encourage a crackly-crisp, salty-sweet crust. The idea seemed promising, so we rubbed sugar over the pork butt just before putting it in the oven. As we expected, the sugar caramelized and helped crisp the fat cap. We got even deeper browning when we rubbed ⅓ cup sugar on the meat together with the salt and left it to rest overnight. Because sugar is hygroscopic, over time it pulls water from the outer layers of the meat, drying out the exterior and boosting browning. But to ensure the meat didn't get too dark, we brushed off some of the sugar-salt rub before roasting. When we switched from white sugar to brown, tasters praised the crust's subtle molasses flavor and hints of caramel (and fellow Chinese barbecued pork fans immediately recognized its addictive "meat-candy" effect).

While the cooked pork rested for about an hour (a necessary step that allows the juices to redistribute in the meat), we noticed the roasting pan was coated with a nice layer of drippings. Ordinarily, we wouldn't think twice about scraping up these flavorful bits of fond and turning them into a quick sauce, but in this case we had reason to pause. The drippings from this particular roast burned quickly, thanks to their high sugar content. This was quickly fixed with a V-rack and a quart of water poured into the bottom of the pan. Once the roast was perched higher up, its fat dripped down and mixed with the water, all of which pooled into a significant jus, with no burning.

With just the pork, salt, sugar, heat, and time, we'd produced a roast that far outdid the fussier, less flavorful specimens we were used to preparing, so any sauce we made would have to be simple. Our first inclination: something fruity, with sweet and sour elements to cut the meat's richness. We combined ¼ cup of the defatted pork jus (this was potent stuff) with peaches, white wine, sugar, vinegar, and a couple of sprigs of fresh thyme and reduced the mixture to a thin syrup. To round out the sweetness, we finished it with a spoonful of whole-grain mustard.

This meat spoke for itself—particularly the fat responsible for its richness and twofold texture. (Each slice was at once meltingly tender within and almost like cracklings at the surface.) In fact, it was head and (pardon the pun) shoulders above any pork loin we'd ever tasted.

SLOW-ROASTED PORK SHOULDER WITH PEACH SAUCE

Slow-Roasted Pork Shoulder with Peach Sauce

SERVES 8 TO 12

We prefer natural pork to enhanced pork (pork that has been injected with a salt solution to increase moistness and flavor), though both will work in this recipe. Add more water to the roasting pan as necessary during the last hours of cooking to prevent the fond from burning.

PORK ROAST

- 1 (6 to 8-pound) bone-in pork butt roast (see note)
- ⅓ cup kosher salt
- ⅓ cup packed light brown sugar
- Ground black pepper

PEACH SAUCE

- 10 ounces frozen peaches, cut into 1-inch chunks (about 2 cups) or 2 fresh peaches cut into ½-inch wedges
- 2 cups dry white wine
- ½ cup granulated sugar
- ¼ cup plus 1 tablespoon unseasoned rice vinegar
- 2 sprigs fresh thyme
- 1 tablespoon whole-grain mustard

1. FOR THE ROAST: Using a sharp knife, cut slits in the fat cap of the roast, spaced 1 inch apart, in a crosshatch pattern, being careful not to cut into the meat. Combine the salt and brown sugar in a medium bowl. Rub the salt mixture over the entire pork shoulder and into the slits. Wrap the roast tightly in a double layer of plastic wrap, place on a rimmed baking sheet, and refrigerate for at least 12 hours or up to 24 hours.

2. One hour before cooking, unwrap the roast and brush off any excess salt mixture from the surface. Season the roast with pepper. Transfer the roast to a V-rack coated with vegetable oil spray set in a large roasting pan and add 1 quart water to the roasting pan. Meanwhile, adjust an oven rack to the lowest position and heat the oven to 325 degrees.

3. Cook the roast, basting twice during cooking, until the meat is extremely tender and an instant-read thermometer inserted into the roast near, but not touching, the bone registers 190 degrees, 5 to 6 hours. Transfer the

NOTES FROM THE TEST KITCHEN

THE IMPORTANCE OF TAKING THINGS SLOW

OVERNIGHT SALTY SWEET RUB: We rub our roast with a mixture of salt and sugar and let it rest overnight. The salt enhances juiciness and seasons the meat, while the sugar caramelizes to create a crackling-crisp, salty-sweet crust.

LOW OVEN: Cooking the pork at 325 degrees for 5 to 6 hours pushes the meat well beyond its "done" mark, encouraging intramuscular fat to melt, collagen to break down and tenderize the meat, and the fat cap to render and crisp.

BONE-IN PORK BUTT: FATTY, MOIST, AND FLAVORFUL

Instead of the lean center-cut loin, our choice for roasting is pork butt (also known as Boston butt). This shoulder roast packs plenty of intramuscular fat that melts and bastes the meat during cooking, and it's available with or without the bone. We prefer bone-in for two reasons: First, bone conducts heat poorly and acts as an insulator against heat. This means that the meat surrounding it stays cooler and the roast cooks at a slower, gentler pace. Second, bones have a large percentage of the meat's connective tissue attached to them, which eventually breaks down to gelatin and helps the roast retain moisture.

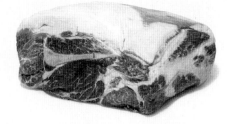

BETTER WITH THE BONE

roast to a carving board and let rest, loosely tented with foil, for 1 hour. Transfer the liquid in the roasting pan to a fat separator and let stand for 5 minutes. Pour off ¼ cup jus and discard any remaining jus and fat.

4. FOR THE SAUCE: Bring the peaches, wine, sugar, ¼ cup of the vinegar, ¼ cup defatted jus, and thyme to a simmer in a small saucepan; cook, stirring occasionally, until reduced to 2 cups, about 30 minutes. Stir in the remaining 1 tablespoon vinegar and the mustard. Remove the thyme sprigs, cover, and keep warm.

5. Using a sharp paring knife, cut around the inverted T-shaped bone, until it can be pulled free from the roast (use a clean kitchen towel to grasp the bone). Using a serrated knife, slice the roast. Serve, passing the sauce separately.

VARIATION

Slow-Roasted Pork Shoulder with Cherry Sauce

Follow the recipe for Slow-Roasted Pork Shoulder with Peach Sauce, substituting 10 ounces fresh or frozen pitted cherries for the peaches, red wine for the white wine, red wine vinegar for the rice vinegar, and adding ¼ cup ruby port along with the defatted jus. Increase the granulated sugar to ¾ cup, omit the thyme sprigs and mustard, and reduce the mixture to 1½ cups.

BAKED APPLES

✔️ **WHY THIS RECIPE WORKS:** Picking the right apples—Granny Smiths—was the first step to developing baked apples with good texture and flavor. Peeling the apples entirely prevented them from getting mushy in the oven, while sautéing their tops before stuffing them with a flavorful and rich dried fruit and nut filling gave the apples themselves an intense flavor. As the final step in our baked apple recipe, we used the slices we had lopped off of the tops of the apples as a natural covering, so the filling wouldn't burn.

THE CHARMS OF A FRESH APPLE AREN'T DIFFICULT TO grasp. Sweet with a touch of ripe tartness, the flesh bursts with all the crisp, juicy complexity of a young white wine. But slide that same fruit into the oven, and the dry heat makes quick work of killing off every ounce of apple appeal. The crunchy texture turns to mush. The skin becomes chewy as vinyl upholstery. The interior cells rupture, releasing a rush of moisture that dilutes the once-flavorful sugars and acids. The end result: a bland, squishy "dessert" that makes you wish you'd gone with the chocolate soufflé. Not that cookbooks don't try every trick for overcoming this dowdy dish's flaws, masking the flavor woes with sticky sauces and stuffing the hollowed-out center with toothsome ingredients. A nice idea—yet too many we tried came up short in the finesse department, with one-dimensional (read: achingly sweet) sauces and fillings with flavors that fell flat.

It didn't make sense. After all, few things are more delicious than a fresh-baked apple pie, where the fruit breaks down just enough to become tender and sweet but still maintain a firm bite. But without the flaky, buttery crust, was a cooked apple just a wan filling with delusions of grandeur? Previous pie testing has taught us that good apple cookery is as much about picking the right variety of fruit as it is about how you bake with it. Heading back to the test kitchen, we tried several of the most widely available apples—both sweet and tart—in a basic working recipe. We removed the cores with a paring knife, leaving 1-inch-diameter cavities, then placed

BEST BAKED APPLES WITH DRIED CRANBERRIES AND PECANS

the apples in a baking dish, stuffing them with a simple filling (raisins, toasted pecans, and brown sugar would do for the moment), and wetting the dishes with apple cider, which we hoped would cook down into a sauce. We baked them at 375 degrees until they were easily pierced with a paring knife, which took between 30 and 45 minutes, depending on the apple type.

To our surprise, the winner wasn't any of our favorites for eating out of hand, like the Jonagold or the Fuji. Even the flesh of a McIntosh, a variety prized for both snacking and baking, broke down under the oven's heat and turned to mush. The very qualities that made for a great snacking apple proved too delicate to survive a stint in the oven. Best in show was the Granny Smith—firm and nicely tart, yes, but only mildly fruity and sweet. They held up fairly well in the heat, and their acerbic bite balanced nicely with the sweetness of the filling and sauce.

SCIENCE DESK

PREVENTING APPLE BLOWOUTS
While developing our recipe for baked apples, we couldn't ignore a persistent problem: apples that "blew out" and collapsed in the oven. Could removing the skin solve the issue?

THE EXPERIMENT
We prepared two batches of six baked Granny Smith apples each, one skin-on, the other skin-off, using our placeholder filling and sauce (raisins, toasted pecans, and brown sugar for the filling; apple cider for the sauce). Then we baked each batch in a 13- by 9-inch baking dish in a 375-degree oven until the apples could be pierced easily with a knife.

THE RESULTS
To our surprise, all the skin-off apples held their shape, without a single blowout. Within the skin-on batch, half of the apples collapsed.

THE EXPLANATION
In nature, the peel protects an apple; in the oven, it traps moisture that's been transformed into steam. As the steam attempts to escape, its outward pressure ruptures cells and eventually bursts through the apple's skin, causing blowouts. Removing all the skin allows the steam to escape without damaging the fruit's structure.

But even the Grannies were prone to occasional collapse. We tried resolving the problem first by adjusting the cooking temperature (300 degrees, then 350, then 400)—to no avail. Perplexed, we consulted our science editor, who fingered trapped steam—from the extra moisture released by the breakdown of the interior cells—as the culprit, suggesting we remove some of the peel to create additional escape routes. (We'd already created one escape route by removing the core.) First, we tried poking the peel all over with a wooden skewer, but the results were uninspiring (and ugly). Removing a strip of skin from the top yielded a similar marginal improvement. Cutting multiple holes in the apple's surface—jack-o'-lantern style—seemed drastic.

Or was it? Maybe the problem was that pricking, poking, and peeling the skin here and there weren't drastic enough. It occurred to us that the apples for apple pies are always peeled, thus allowing moisture to evaporate through ventilation slits in the crust as the pie bakes. In contrast, even the best (relatively speaking) of the baked apples we'd tried sported unappealingly tough, chewy skin—so why keep the skin at all? Maybe peeling the entire apple would give the flesh a little breathing room—rather than letting it steam in its own jacket and turn to mush—and help the fruit retain the kind of tender-firm texture that it does in a good pie. To find out, we prepared a dish of skinned apples, set them in the oven, and crossed our fingers. As it turned out, there wasn't a bad apple in the bunch; and when we baked another batch, comparing skin-on with skin-off apples, we confirmed that this method was not only better but virtually foolproof. (To understand why, see "Preventing Apple Blowouts," at left.)

With the baking technique settled, we could concentrate on flavor—literally. Up until now, the apple cider we had poured into the bottom of the baking dishes was the only "sauce" to speak of; its flavor was sweet and bright but juicelike, lacking body and complexity. Reducing it with a viscous sweetener seemed like an easy fix—we tried corn syrup, honey, and maple syrup and found that the rich, nutty maple paired beautifully with tart fruit.

As for the filling, our initial raisin–brown sugar–pecan combo wasn't bad, but it definitely benefited from some finessing by way of cinnamon (for a touch of heat), orange zest (for freshness), and a knob of creamy butter. Even better, we swapped out the sweet raisins for tangy dried cranberries and bulked up the nuttiness with chewy rolled oats.

The filling was coming along so well that we wanted more of it. We decided to widen the cavity, trading a paring knife for a melon baller, which was easier to manipulate. After experimenting with various dimensions, we landed on 1½ inches as the optimal diameter (see "Making Enough Space for the Filling," on page 64)—a sprawling abyss compared to the 1-inch-wide cavity we'd started with. We took advantage of all the newfound room by bolstering the fruitiness of the filling with diced apple pieces.

And yet, the apple vessels themselves still lacked the concentrated, rich flavor of other cooked fruit desserts. Paging through our collection of apple dessert recipes, we came across the French classic tarte Tatin, and we realized the solution. For this popular Parisian bistro tart, peeled, sliced apples are sautéed in butter and sugar to coax an intense, candylike caramelized flavor from the fruit. It seemed to be just the missing flavor to send our baked apples over the top.

Of course, we couldn't slice the apples—but maybe we could create a flat surface that would caramelize on the stovetop. Setting aside the baking dish we'd been using, we melted a tablespoon of butter in a large nonstick skillet, sliced ½ inch off the top of our apples, and added

them top side down. It took about three minutes for them to turn golden brown over medium heat. We then flipped them and added the filling. Instead of transferring the stuffed fruit back to the baking dish, we simply added our sauce and transferred the entire skillet to the oven.

To our delight, the skillet turned out to be an ideal container, giving us ample room to baste during cooking and a handle to easily maneuver it. When we removed these apples from the oven, we knew we were on to something: Tasters who had originally told us they loathed baked apples were now leaving their plates spotless and returning for seconds and thirds.

The only outstanding issue was some slight burning on top of the fruit. At first we considered an aluminum foil cover, but then we realized we already had natural caps: the slices we had lopped off the apples. We made one final batch and knew we'd accomplished our goal. With just a little help from French cuisine, we had transformed the dowdiest of dishes into a rich, satisfying dessert.

Best Baked Apples with Dried Cranberries and Pecans

SERVES 6

If you don't have an ovenproof skillet, transfer the browned apples to a 13 by 9-inch baking dish and bake as directed. The recipe calls for seven apples; six are left whole and one is diced and added to the filling. Serve the apples with vanilla ice cream, if desired.

- **7** large (about 6 ounces each) Granny Smith apples (see note)
- **6** tablespoons (¾ stick) unsalted butter, softened
- **⅓** cup dried cranberries, chopped coarse
- **⅓** cup coarsely chopped pecans, toasted
- **¼** cup packed (1¾ ounces) brown sugar
- **3** tablespoons old-fashioned oats
- **1** teaspoon finely grated zest from 1 orange
- **½** teaspoon ground cinnamon
    Pinch table salt
- **⅓** cup maple syrup
- **⅓** cup plus 2 tablespoons apple cider

1. Adjust an oven rack to the middle position and heat the oven to 375 degrees. Peel, core, and cut 1 apple into ¼-inch dice. Combine 5 tablespoons of the butter, the cranberries, pecans, brown sugar, oats, orange zest, cinnamon, salt, and diced apple in a large bowl; set aside.

2. Shave a thin slice off the bottom (blossom end) of the remaining 6 apples to allow them to sit flat. Cut the top ½ inch off the stem end of the apples and reserve. Peel the apples and use a melon baller or small measuring spoon to remove a 1½-inch-diameter core, being careful not to cut through the bottom of the apple.

3. Melt the remaining 1 tablespoon butter in a 12-inch nonstick ovensafe skillet over medium heat. Once the foaming subsides, add the apples, stem side down, and cook until the cut surface is golden brown, about 3 minutes. Flip the apples, reduce the heat to low, and spoon the filling inside, mounding the excess filling over the cavities; top with the reserved apple caps. Add the maple syrup and ⅓ cup cider to the skillet. Transfer the skillet to the oven and bake until a skewer inserted into the apples meets little resistance, 35 to 40 minutes, basting every 10 minutes with the maple syrup mixture in the skillet.

4. Transfer the apples to a serving platter. Stir up to 2 tablespoons of the remaining cider into the sauce in the skillet to adjust the consistency. Pour the sauce over the apples and serve.

VARIATIONS

Best Baked Apples with Raisins and Walnuts

Follow the recipe for Best Baked Apples with Dried Cranberries and Pecans, substituting coarsely chopped raisins for the cranberries, coarsely chopped, toasted walnuts for the pecans, lemon zest for the orange zest, and ¼ teaspoon ground nutmeg for the cinnamon.

Best Baked Apples with Dried Figs and Macadamia Nuts

Follow the recipe for Best Baked Apples with Dried Cranberries and Pecans, substituting coarsely chopped dried figs for the cranberries, coarsely chopped, toasted macadamia nuts for the pecans, lemon zest for the orange zest, and ¼ teaspoon ground ginger for the cinnamon.

Best Baked Apples with Dried Cherries and Hazelnuts

Follow the recipe for Best Baked Apples with Dried Cranberries and Pecans, substituting coarsely chopped dried cherries for the cranberries, coarsely chopped, toasted hazelnuts for the pecans, and ½ teaspoon ground black pepper for the cinnamon.

Best Baked Apples with Dried Apricots and Almonds

Follow the recipe for Best Baked Apples with Dried Cranberries and Pecans, substituting coarsely chopped dried apricots for the cranberries, coarsely chopped, toasted almonds for the pecans, and 1 teaspoon vanilla extract for the cinnamon.

NOTES FROM THE TEST KITCHEN

MAKING ENOUGH SPACE FOR THE FILLING

Most recipes for baked apples call for tiny cavities, which hold a paltry amount of filling. Once we solved the structural problems and baked up a sturdier apple, we found we could increase the diameter to an accommodating 1½ inches.

RATING INEXPENSIVE DIGITAL THERMOMETERS

In the test kitchen, we rely on an instant-read thermometer to test the doneness of a variety of foods, from poultry and steak to bread and cheesecake. Our winning instant-read thermometer is the ThermoWorks Splash-Proof Super-Fast Thermapen ($96), which has a quick response time and is incredibly accurate. But accuracy comes with a price, and we wondered if there were any digital thermometers under $35 that could hold their own in the kitchen. We tested seven models by taking the temperature of ice water, boiling water, and pan-seared chicken breasts, assessing their accuracy, response time, probe length, and design. Brands are listed in order of preference. See www.americastestkitchen.com for updates to this testing.

RECOMMENDED

THERMOWORKS Super-Fast Waterproof Pocket Thermometer (model #RT600C)
PRICE: $24
PROBE LENGTH: 4.5 inches
TEMPERATURE RANGE: -40 to 302° F
TEMPERATURE RESPONSE TIME: 14 seconds
COMMENTS: An extra-thin probe that allowed for easy tempera-ture checks and relatively fast readout times put this model at the top of the rankings. We also liked the location of the readout screen on the side (as opposed to the end) and the simplicity of its controls. Its few drawbacks are a low maximum temperature, the fact that it can't be calibrated (reset when accuracy seems off), and its lack of an automatic shutoff.

CDN ProAccurate Quick-Read Thermometer (model #DTQ450X)
PRICE: $18.99
PROBE LENGTH: 4.75 inches
TEMPERATURE RANGE: -40 to 450° F
TEMPERATURE RESPONSE TIME: 10 seconds
COMMENTS: Although this bulb-shaped thermometer felt awkward and cheaply made, and testers found it was too easy to hit the small buttons accidentally while gripping the head, it received top marks for speed, accuracy, and temperature range. An automatic shutoff preserved battery life.

THERMOWORKS Super-Fast Pocket Thermometer (model #RT301WA)
PRICE: $29
PROBE LENGTH: 4.75 inches
TEMPERATURE RANGE: -40 to 302° F
TEMPERATURE RESPONSE TIME: 14 seconds
COMMENTS: While just as fast as the ThermoWorks winner, this model lost points for its bulb-shaped head, which is awkward to handle and has a hard-to-read screen. The slightly longer probe was an advantage when reaching into the oven. Unlike the other ThermoWorks model, this one has an automatic shutoff feature.

RECOMMENDED *(cont.)*

COMARK Waterproof Digital Thermometer (model #DT400)
PRICE: $32
PROBE LENGTH: 5 inches
TEMPERATURE RANGE: -4 to 400° F
TEMPERATURE RESPONSE TIME: 15 seconds
COMMENTS: The side buttons and a screen located on the top were helpful, but the small screen was difficult to read. It also took a whopping four seconds for this thermometer to even turn on.

NOT RECOMMENDED

OXO Good Grips Digital Instant Read Meat Thermometer (model #1140500)
PRICE: $19.99
PROBE LENGTH: 4.5 inches
TEMPERATURE RANGE: -40 to 302° F
TEMPERATURE RESPONSE TIME: 22 seconds
COMMENTS: This model's large, easy-to-read screen, located on the side, was a plus, but it couldn't outweigh the minuses: an extremely slow read time, no calibration feature, and no automatic shutoff.

VWR Flip-Stick Thermometer (model #15551–002)
PRICE: $27.56
PROBE LENGTH: 4.5 inches
TEMPERATURE RANGE: -58 to 572° F
TEMPERATURE RESPONSE TIME: 24 seconds
COMMENTS: An extremely slow performer that felt flimsy in comparison with other models tested. Also, it is constantly set to Celsius, regard-less of the previous setting, so you need to press a button to switch back to Fahrenheit. It also lacks an automatic shutoff.

CDN ProAccurate Quick Read Waterproof Pocket Thermometer (model #Q2–450X)
PRICE: $18.99
PROBE LENGTH: 2.75 inches
TEMPERATURE RANGE: -40 to 450° F
TEMPERATURE RESPONSE TIME: 27 seconds
COMMENTS: The thermometer has a side screen, but that was its only advantage over other models. The incredibly short probe put our hands too close to piping hot food and the on/off button was crowded together with other buttons.

Fish IN A FLASH

Sprinkling fish fillets with a little sugar before searing them encourages browning and helps promote a flavorful, crisp crust.

RE-CREATING ELABORATE RESTAURANT DISHES AT HOME IS NO EASY matter. But even more perplexing is tackling seemingly simple recipes at home—and getting disappointing results. Take seafood like scallops and fish fillets. Quick-cooking scallops are so richly flavored they require little adornment. And what could be simpler than quickly pan-searing them until they've got a richly caramelized nut-brown crust and juicy interior? Easier said than done. With scallops, it starts with shopping. Some scallops are treated with a preservative that leaches out as the scallops cook—this inhibits browning and the preservative imparts an off-flavor. Restaurants pay dearly for untreated scallops, typically referred to as dry scallops. But what's a home cook without access to dry scallops to do? Answering this question was just one of our goals in our search for the best pan-seared scallops.

Skillet-roasted fish fillets are another popular restaurant item. Without any bread crumbs or rich sauces to hide behind, skillet-roasting shines the spotlight on the fish itself. A ripping-hot skillet creates a rich, crisp crust on the fillet while the interior of the fish remains moist and flavorful. But without the intense heat of a restaurant range and the quick-fire hands of an experienced chef, the fillets can stick and tear and dry out fast. We set out to devise a method for perfectly cooked, richly flavorful pan-roasted fish fillets that anyone can pull off.

PAN-SEARED SCALLOPS

✔ WHY THIS RECIPE WORKS: For superior pan-seared scallops with a great crust, we seared them in oil, and then basted them in butter. Waiting to add the butter ensured that it had enough time to work its browning magic on the scallops, but not enough time to burn. When using scallops treated with sodium tripolyphosphate (a common preservative), we were able to eliminate the chemical flavor by briefly brining the shellfish in a solution of water, lemon juice, and salt.

LIKE A LOT OF SEAFOOD PREPARATIONS, PAN-SEARED scallops are as easy as it gets for a restaurant chef: Slick a super-hot pan with oil, add the shellfish, flip them once, and serve. The whole process takes no more than a couple of minutes and produces golden-crusted beauties with tender, medium-rare interiors. But try the same technique at home and you're likely to run into trouble. The problem is that most home stovetops don't get nearly as hot as professional ranges, so it's difficult to properly brown the scallops without overcooking them. Moreover, restaurant chefs pay top dollar for scallops without chemical additives, which are known in the industry as "dry." The type available in most supermarkets, called "wet" scallops, are treated with a solution of water and sodium tripolyphosphate (STP) to increase shelf life and retain moisture. Unfortunately, STP lends a soapy, off-flavor to the scallops, and the extra water only compounds the problem of poor browning. We wanted to achieve superior pan-seared scallops, whether using supermarket wet scallops or the pricier dry variety. We would have to find a solution to the browning-without-overcooking conundrum and a way to get rid of the chemical taste of STP.

Our first stop was the supermarket fish counter. Scallops are available in a range of sizes: A pound of the hard-to-find large sea variety contains eight to 10 scallops, while a pound of the petite bay variety may have as many as 100 pencil eraser–sized scallops. Since small scallops are more prone to overcooking than large, we opted for the biggest commonly available size: 10 to 20 per pound.

We decided to work with wet scallops first. After all, if we could develop a good recipe for finicky wet scallops, it would surely work with premium dry scallops.

We started by seasoning 1½ pounds (the right amount for four people) with salt and pepper. We heated 1 tablespoon of vegetable oil in a 12-inch stainless steel skillet, then added the scallops in a single layer and waited for them to brown. After three minutes, they were steaming away in a ¼-inch-deep pool of liquid. At the five-minute mark, the moisture in the skillet evaporated and the flesh began to turn golden. But at this point it was too late: The scallops were already overcooked and tough, and we hadn't even flipped them. To dry out the scallops, we tried pressing them between kitchen towels. When 10 minutes didn't work, we tried a full hour—even leaving a third batch overnight in the refrigerator. The results were disheartening. While slightly drier than unblotted scallops, the pressed batches still exuded copious amounts of liquid in the skillet (and they still tasted soapy; we'd focus on that later). Our conclusion: Beyond a 10-minute blot, there's not much point in an extended drying time.

It was becoming clear that to dry out the waterlogged scallops for good browning, we'd have to get the pan as hot as possible. Without a high-output range, it was important to pay careful attention to technique. We started by waiting to add the scallops to the skillet until the oil was beginning to smoke, a clear indication of heat. We also cooked the scallops in two batches instead of one, since crowding would cool down the pan. Finally, switching to a nonstick skillet ensured that as the scallops cooked, the browned bits formed a crust on the scallops instead of sticking to the skillet. These were steps in right direction, but the scallops were still overcooked and rubbery by the time they were fully browned.

Would switching from oil to butter help our cause? Butter contains milk proteins and sugars that brown rapidly when heated, so we hoped that it would help the scallops turn golden before they overcooked. But our hopes were dashed when in our next batch, the butter that we'd swapped for oil actually made matters worse: It burned before the scallops were cooked through.

Then we recalled a method we'd used when cooking steaks and chops in restaurants: butter-basting. We gave

PAN-SEARED SCALLOPS WITH LEMON–BROWN BUTTER SAUCE

SCALLOPS AND STP

So-called wet scallops have been treated with sodium tripolyphosphate (STP), which lends a disagreeable flavor. Could we get rid of the STP by soaking the scallops in water?

THE EXPERIMENT

We prepared three batches of "wet" scallops, soaking the first in a quart of water for 30 minutes, soaking the second for an hour, and leaving the third untreated. We then cooked each batch according to our recipe and sent them to a lab to be analyzed for STP content.

THE RESULTS

The scallops soaked for 30 minutes only had about 10 percent less STP than the untreated batch, and the ones soaked for a full hour weren't much better: Only about 11 percent of the STP was removed. Tasters were still able to clearly identify an unpleasant chemical flavor in both soaked samples.

THE EXPLANATION

The phosphates in STP form chemical bonds with the proteins in scallops. The bonds are so strong that they prevent the STP from being washed away, no matter how long the scallops are soaked.

THE SOLUTION

Rather than try to remove the chemical taste from STP-treated scallops, we masked it by soaking them in a solution of lemon juice, water, and salt.

CHEMICAL COVERUP
A lemon-flavored brine camouflages the off-taste of "wet" scallops.

it a try with our scallops, searing them in oil on one side and adding a tablespoon of butter to the skillet after flipping them. We tilted the skillet to allow the butter to pool, then used a large spoon to ladle the foaming butter over the scallops. Waiting to add the butter ensured that it had just enough time to work its browning magic on the shellfish, but not enough time to burn. The scallops now achieved a deep golden brown crust in record time, and their moist interiors were preserved. They weren't quite as tender and juicy as dry scallops, but they were darn close.

Only one problem remained, and it was a big one: the soapy flavor of STP. We already knew from earlier tests that blotting removes neither excess water nor STP, but what about the opposite approach: soaking in water to wash out the STP? It was a flop. No matter how long or carefully we rinsed the scallops, the STP still remained.

We thought things over and decided that if we couldn't remove the STP, we would try to mask it. We thought maybe a saltwater brine was the answer because it would penetrate the scallops deeply. The brine did provide even seasoning, but not enough to mask the chemical flavor. We noted that the phosphate in STP is alkaline. What if we covered it up by putting acidic lemon juice in the brine? Problem solved. Only the most sensitive tasters now picked up on a hint of chemical off-flavors; most tasted only the sweet shellfish complemented by the bright flavor of citrus.

With our wet scallop approach established, it was finally time to test our recipe on dry scallops. We skipped the soaking step, which was unnecessary in the absence of STP, and proceeded with the recipe. The result? Scallops that rivaled those made on a powerful restaurant range, golden brown on the exterior and juicy and tender on the interior. We were happy to serve them with just a squeeze of lemon, but fancier occasions call for a sauce, so we developed a lemon–browned butter version.

Pan-Seared Scallops

SERVES 4

We strongly recommend purchasing dry scallops (those without chemical additives). If you can only find wet scallops, soak them in a solution of 1 quart cold water, ¼ cup lemon juice, and 2 tablespoons table salt for 30 minutes before proceeding with step 1, and season the scallops with pepper only in step 2. Prepare the sauce (if serving) while the scallops dry (between steps 1 and 2) and keep it warm while cooking them.

1½ pounds dry sea scallops (about 16 scallops), tendons removed

Table salt and ground black pepper

2 tablespoons vegetable oil

2 tablespoons unsalted butter

Lemon wedges or a butter sauce (recipes follow)

1. Place the scallops on a rimmed baking sheet lined with a clean kitchen towel. Place a second clean kitchen towel on top of the scallops and press gently on the towel to blot the liquid. Let the scallops sit at room temperature for 10 minutes while the towels absorb the moisture.

2. Remove the second towel and sprinkle the scallops on both sides with salt and pepper. Heat 1 tablespoon of the oil in a 12-inch nonstick skillet over high heat until just smoking. Add half of the scallops in a single layer, flat side down, and cook, without moving, until well browned, 1½ to 2 minutes.

3. Add 1 tablespoon of the butter to the skillet. Using tongs, flip the scallops and continue to cook, using a large spoon to baste the scallops with the melted butter, tilting the skillet so the butter runs to one side, until the sides of the scallops are firm and the centers are opaque, 30 to 90 seconds longer (remove the smaller scallops from the pan as they finish cooking). Transfer the scallops to a large plate and tent loosely with foil. Wipe out the skillet with a wad of paper towels and repeat with the remaining 1 tablespoon oil, remaining scallops, and remaining 1 tablespoon butter. Serve immediately with lemon wedges or sauce.

Lemon–Brown Butter Sauce

MAKES ABOUT ¼ CUP

We recommend using a regular saucepan, not one with a nonstick finish, so that you can easily monitor when the butter has changed color.

4 tablespoons (½ stick) unsalted butter, cut into 4 pieces

1 small shallot, minced (about 1½ tablespoons)

1 tablespoon minced fresh parsley leaves

½ teaspoon minced fresh thyme leaves

2 teaspoons juice from 1 lemon

Table salt and ground black pepper

Heat the butter in a small heavy-bottomed saucepan over medium heat and cook, swirling the pan constantly, until the butter turns dark golden brown and has a nutty aroma, 4 to 5 minutes. Add the shallot and cook until fragrant, about 30 seconds. Remove the pan from the heat and stir in the parsley, thyme, and lemon juice. Season with salt and pepper to taste. Cover to keep warm.

NOTES FROM THE TEST KITCHEN

ARE YOUR SCALLOPS WET OR DRY?
If you are unsure whether your scallops are wet (treated with chemicals) or dry (untreated), conduct this quick test: Place 1 scallop on a paper towel–lined, microwave-safe plate and microwave on high power for 15 seconds. If the scallop is dry, it will exude very little water. If it is wet, there will be a sizable ring of moisture on the paper towel. (The microwaved scallop can be cooked as is.)

REMOVING TENDONS FROM SCALLOPS

The small, crescent-shaped tendon that is sometimes attached to the scallop will be incredibly tough when cooked. Use your fingers to peel this tendon away from the side of each scallop before cooking.

PAN-ROASTED FISH FILLETS

✔ **WHY THIS RECIPE WORKS:** To come up with succulent, well-browned thick-cut fish fillets, we sprinkled them with sugar before sautéing. This simple step accelerated caramelization, so the fish could develop a good crust before its interior had a chance to dry out. Transferring the browned fillets to the oven to roast just until their centers were a touch translucent provided the perfect finish.

PAN-ROASTED FILLETS OF THICK-CUT HALIBUT, COD, and other white fish have become fixtures on restaurant menus nearly everywhere. When well executed, the cooking method yields moist, white slabs of tender, flavorful fish with a chestnut-brown crust—nothing like the stringy, overbaked fillets most of us serve at home.

Hoping to replicate the success of this method, home cooks—and those who write recipes for them—in the past have latched on to pan-roasting, but the results have been mixed. Here's the problem: To yield truly outstanding results, recipes for pan-roasted fish require keen attention and a practiced hand—that is, the skill of an experienced restaurant chef, not the busy home cook confronting an unfamiliar recipe. Our goal was a foolproof, point-and-shoot recipe for succulent, well-browned thick-cut fish fillets.

From an initial round of testing, we knew we needed fillets no less than 1 inch thick, and preferably thicker; skinnier fillets end up overcooked by the time they've achieved a serious sear. We wanted our recipe to work with popular white fish like halibut, cod, sea bass, and red snapper. Since skin-on fillets are not always available, we started our testing with skinless fillets. We carefully patted them dry to minimize sticking, then seasoned them with kosher salt (easier to distribute evenly than fine-grained table salt) and pepper. To cook four fillets at a time with ample room for flipping, a 12-inch skillet was a must, and a few quick tests confirmed a nonstick pan was also critical.

Tomato-Ginger Sauce

MAKES ABOUT ½ CUP

We recommend using a regular saucepan, not one with a nonstick finish, so that you can easily monitor when the butter has changed color.

- 6   tablespoons (¾ stick) unsalted butter
- 1   medium plum tomato, cored, seeded, and chopped small
- 1   tablespoon grated fresh ginger
- 1   tablespoon juice from 1 lemon
- ¼   teaspoon red pepper flakes
     Table salt

Heat the butter in a small heavy-bottomed saucepan over medium heat; cook, swirling the pan constantly, until the butter turns dark golden brown and has a nutty aroma, 4 to 5 minutes. Add the tomato, ginger, lemon juice, and red pepper flakes; cook, stirring constantly, until fragrant, about 1 minute. Season with salt to taste. Cover to keep warm.

PAN-ROASTED FISH FILLETS WITH ROASTED RED PEPPER, HAZELNUT, AND THYME RELISH

We started with a technique we've successfully used with skin-on salmon fillets: oven-searing. We placed the fish in a preheated skillet in a hot oven. The approach works great with a high-fat fish like salmon; if left on, the fatty skin forms a protective barrier between the meat and the hot pan. For delicate, skinless white fish fillets, however, this technique was a bust.

We moved on to a technique we'd witnessed in various restaurant kitchens: Sear the fish on one side in a blazing-hot skillet, flip it, then add a big pat of butter to the pan and repeatedly baste the fish as it cooks. A few burnt fingers later, we realized that spooning hot butter in a sizzling skillet for anything more than a minute or two is impractical at home, so we switched to a safer method: Sear in a hot pan, flip, then transfer to a hot oven to cook the fish through.

How hot, exactly, should the pan be? We seared fish at every temperature beyond a cold start, documenting texture, appearance, and flavor. No matter what we did, the results were problematic. If we added the fish to the pan just as a sheen of oil started to smoke, we could produce an attractive and flavorful sear in about three minutes, but we also got a tough, dried-out interior. On the other hand, starting in a cooler pan or cooking for less time left the fish tender but failed to develop the crust. For

now, a compromise would have to work. We scaled back the sear to a light golden brown—about 1½ minutes. It didn't look or taste nearly as good as the darker sear, but we could live with it.

As for the oven, 425 degrees was the way to go. Any hotter and the fish dried out before it cooked through, and lower temperatures did nothing for texture or flavor. In a 425-degree oven, it took seven to 10 minutes for the fillets to be just opaque. We found it best to err on the side of undercooking (just a touch translucent at the center) to preserve as much moisture as possible.

Despite testing our way through twenty-odd pounds of various fillets, we felt as though we hadn't accomplished much. Sure, the fish was tender, tasted good, and proved technically easy to prepare, but it didn't have the flavor—much less the visual appeal—of a proper restaurant sear. Temporarily putting our working recipe on hold, we focused on another experimental method. In an old recipe for seared pork chops, rather than trying—and failing—to get a good sear on both sides of the chop without drying out the meat, we'd discovered that it was better to give just one side a perfect sear, producing enough flavorful compounds to compensate for the pale second side and ensuring juicy, tender meat. Unfortunately, fish and pork are not the same. Even with just one side seared to a beautiful, crusty brown, the delicate flesh of our fish still overcooked.

To get flavor, we needed plenty of browning, but for texture, we couldn't let the fish get too hot. Part of the solution might be to increase the rate of browning. But what if we also insulated the fish at the same time, to protect it against drying out? Many recipes call for dusting the fillets with flour before searing. It sounded promising, since the proteins and sugars in the flour would contribute to browning. At first it seemed to work. The coated fish developed a flavorful crust much faster than uncoated fish, and in fact, these were the best fillets yet, but the flour lent a pasty texture to the crust. We ran into the same problem no matter what starch we tried: flour (all-purpose, pastry, and Wondra), cornmeal, cornstarch, potato starch, potato flour, rice flour, semolina, and even Cream of Wheat.

Thinking back to that pork chop recipe in which we seared only one side, we remembered an odd ingredient

SCIENCE DESK

ENCOURAGING CARAMELIZATION

Fish begins to dry out when its internal temperature reaches 120 to 135 degrees, far below the 300 degrees it takes for a good sear. Here's how we got the fish to brown at a lower temperature: When sugar is added to the fish's surface and is exposed to the pan's heat, it quickly breaks down to glucose and fructose. Fructose rapidly caramelizes at around 200 degrees—a temperature the exterior of the fish easily reaches soon after hitting the pan. A little sugar sprinkled on a fillet will lead to faster browning, helping a good crust to form quickly.

WITH SUGAR

SUGAR FREE

choice: sugar sprinkled over the chop before searing. The idea is that the sugar commingles with exuded juices from the chop, accelerating browning and giving the meat a rich color and deep flavor that's anything but sweet. Could we use the same approach for our fish? We dusted a few fillets with a touch of granulated sugar (about ⅛ teaspoon) and placed them in a hot skillet. We knew we were on the right track when just a minute later, a well-browned crust had already formed. There's no way our fish had time to dry out in that period. Tasting it after it came out of the oven less than 10 minutes later confirmed our observation: well-browned, flavorful fish that was, most important, tender. Best of all, not one taster noticed any sweetness; they just remarked on how good the fish looked and tasted, especially with a squeeze of lemon or a piquant relish. Let restaurant chefs have their recipes—this method for pan-roasted fish is a trick you really can try at home.

Pan-Roasted Thick-Cut Fish Fillets

SERVES 4

Thick white fish fillets with a meaty texture, like halibut, cod, sea bass, or red snapper, work best in this recipe. Because most fish fillets differ in thickness, some pieces may finish cooking before others—be sure to immediately remove any fillet that reaches 135 degrees. You will need an ovensafe nonstick skillet for this recipe.

4 (6 to 8-ounce) skinless white fish fillets,
   1 to 1½ inches thick
   Kosher salt and ground black pepper
½ teaspoon sugar
1 tablespoon vegetable oil
   Lemon wedges or relish (recipes follow), for serving

1. Adjust an oven rack to the middle position and heat the oven to 425 degrees. Dry the fish thoroughly with paper towels and season with salt and pepper. Sprinkle ⅛ teaspoon sugar evenly over one side of each fillet.

2. Heat the oil in a 12-inch ovensafe nonstick skillet over high heat until smoking. Place the fillets in the skillet, sugared sides down, and press down lightly to ensure

even contact with the pan. Cook until browned, 1 to 1½ minutes. Using two spatulas, flip the fillets and transfer the skillet to the oven. Roast the fillets until the centers are just opaque and the fish registers 135 degrees on an instant-read thermometer, 7 to 10 minutes. Immediately transfer the fish to individual plates and serve with lemon wedges or relish.

Green Olive, Almond, and Orange Relish

MAKES ABOUT 1½ CUPS

If your olives are marinated, rinse and drain them before chopping.

- ½ cup slivered almonds, toasted
- ½ cup green olives, chopped coarse
- 1 small garlic clove, minced (½ teaspoon)
- 1 teaspoon grated zest plus ¼ cup juice from 1 orange
- ¼ cup extra-virgin olive oil
- ¼ cup minced fresh mint
- 2 teaspoons white wine vinegar
- Salt
- Cayenne pepper

Process the almonds, olives, garlic, and zest in a food processor until the nuts and olives are finely chopped, 10 to 12 pulses. Transfer the relish to a bowl and stir in the orange juice, olive oil, mint, and vinegar. Season with salt and cayenne to taste. Spoon over the fish and serve immediately.

NOTES FROM THE TEST KITCHEN

REMOVING SKIN FROM FISH FILLETS
If you happen to buy skin-on fillets, some quick knife work can remove it.

1. With a sharp knife, separate a corner of the skin from the fish.

2. Using a paper towel to hold the skin, slide the knife between the fish and the skin to separate them.

Roasted Red Pepper, Hazelnut, and Thyme Relish

MAKES ABOUT 1½ CUPS

- ½ cup hazelnuts, toasted and skinned
- ½ cup jarred roasted red peppers, drained, patted dry, and chopped coarse
- 1 small garlic clove, minced
- ½ teaspoon grated zest plus 4 teaspoons fresh juice from 1 lemon
- ¼ cup extra-virgin olive oil
- 2 tablespoons chopped fresh parsley leaves
- 1 teaspoon chopped fresh thyme leaves
- ¼ teaspoon smoked paprika
- Salt and pepper

Process the hazelnuts, roasted peppers, garlic, and zest in a food processor until finely chopped, 10 to 12 pulses. Transfer the relish to a bowl and stir in the lemon juice, olive oil, parsley, thyme, and paprika. Season with salt and pepper to taste. Spoon over the fish and serve immediately.

RATING INEXPENSIVE NONSTICK SKILLETS

It's hard to beat a nonstick skillet when it comes to cooking—and releasing—fragile foods like thin fish fillets and eggs. Unfortunately, that nonstick coating can nick and scratch over time. Our favorite nonstick pan is the well-constructed All-Clad Stainless 12-Inch Nonstick Frying Pan. But it's $159.95—a lot to pay for something that won't last. We gathered seven nonstick skillets priced under $50 and compared them to the All-Clad and our previous Best Buy, the Calphalon Simply Nonstick 12-inch Omelette Pan ($54.95). Overall, we preferred pans with a broad cooking surface and low, flared sides (no more than 2 inches high) that helped us reach in and under food easily. We also liked pans that were substantial but still easy to maneuver (around 2½ pounds). To gauge durability of the nonstick coating, we fried eggs in new pans with no fat until the eggs stuck, keeping count of the eggs. Brands are listed in order of preference. See www.americastestkitchen.com for updates to this testing.

HIGHLY RECOMMENDED

T-FAL Professional Total Nonstick Fry Pan, 12.5 Inches (model #E9380864)
PRICE: $34.99   OVENSAFE TO: 450°F
INITIAL RELEASE: 76+ eggs   COOKING: ★★★
DESIGN: ★★½   COATING DURABILITY: ★★★
COMMENTS: At a fraction of the cost of our top-rated All-Clad nonstick fry pan, this skillet outperformed it in nearly every test. This pan had the slickest, most durable nonstick coating, releasing perfectly throughout testing. Its only flaw: During our abuse test, its handle loosened.

RECOMMENDED

ALL-CLAD Stainless 12-Inch Nonstick Frying Pan (model #5112NS)
PRICE: $159.95   OVENSAFE TO: 500°F
INITIAL RELEASE: 34 eggs   COOKING: ★★★
DESIGN: ★★★   COATING DURABILITY: ★★
COMMENTS: This is a terrific piece of cookware, but it's also the most expensive at $159.95. All-Clad offers a lifetime replacement warranty, which is why we still recommend this pan.

RECOMMENDED WITH RESERVATIONS

CALPHALON Simply Calphalon Nonstick 12-Inch Omelette Pan (model #SA1392H)
PRICE: $54.95   OVENSAFE TO: 400°F
INITIAL RELEASE: 32 eggs   COOKING: ★★★
DESIGN: ★★★   COATING DURABILITY: ★½
COMMENTS: While this pan's surface was reasonably slick in the beginning, it began to flag quickly. At the end of testing, its interior surface had become scarred.

TRAMONTINA Nonstick 12-Inch Sauté Pan (model #80132/540)
PRICE: $19.97   OVENSAFE TO: 350°F
INITIAL RELEASE: 9 eggs   COOKING: ★★★
DESIGN: ★★★   COATING DURABILITY: ★
COMMENTS: This inexpensive pan browned evenly despite a fast sauté speed. However, its surface stuck after only nine fried eggs and became visibly scratched.

RECOMMENDED WITH RESERVATIONS *(cont.)*

BIALETTI Commercial 12-Inch Sauté Pan (model #06917)
PRICE: $41.99   OVENSAFE TO: 450°F
INITIAL RELEASE: 76+ eggs   COOKING: ★★
DESIGN: ★½   COATING DURABILITY: ★★★
COMMENTS: This pan had a terrific nonstick coating that resisted scratching and maintained its slickness throughout testing, but it had the smallest cooking surface in the lineup.

PADERNO World Cuisine 12.5-Inch Nonstick Frying Pan (model #A4611732)
PRICE: $31.50   OVENSAFE TO: 500°F
INITIAL RELEASE: 49 eggs   COOKING: ★★
DESIGN: ★½   COATING DURABILITY: ★★★
COMMENTS: The flat, sharp metal handle was uncomfortable to hold, but the nonstick surface performed comparatively well. However, the pan ran hot.

NOT RECOMMENDED

CUISINART Chef's Classic Nonstick Hard-Anodized Skillet 12-Inch Skillet with Helper Handle (model #622–30H)
PRICE: $38.70   OVENSAFE TO: 500°F
INITIAL RELEASE: 6 eggs   COOKING: ★★½
DESIGN: ★★   COATING DURABILITY: ★
COMMENTS: This heavy pan was cumbersome to maneuver, and its surface scratched easily.

NORDIC WARE Restaurant Cookware 12-Inch Nonstick Skillet (model #21260)
PRICE: $49.95   OVENSAFE TO: 500°F
INITIAL RELEASE: 10 eggs   COOKING: ★★
DESIGN: ★★   COATING DURABILITY: ★
COMMENTS: This pan felt solid but heavy, and its high sides were a drawback when trying to reach under food.

FARBERWARE Premium Nonstick 12-Inch Shallow Skillet, Platinum (model #21155)
PRICE: $16.95   OVENSAFE TO: 500°F
INITIAL RELEASE: 2 eggs   COOKING: ★★
DESIGN: ★★   COATING DURABILITY: ½
COMMENTS: Despite a wide cooking surface and well-shaped handle, it never behaved like nonstick, quitting after just two fried eggs.

Shrimp IN A SKILLET

WE'RE ALWAYS ON THE LOOKOUT FOR GREAT SHRIMP RECIPES. One preparation we came across recently sounded especially intriguing: the Greek dish, shrimp *saganaki*. Here the shrimp are baked in an herb- and garlic-flavored tomato sauce and topped with tangy feta cheese. While the pairing of seafood and cheese may seem heretical, we couldn't dismiss the fact that this dish, as a Greek classic, must have merit, so we headed into the test kitchen to try our hand at a version.

Shrimp stir-fries aren't new to us, but they're not quite as easy to pull off as meat or poultry stir-fries. The reason is simple—the shrimp itself. Shrimp are especially delicate and easily dry out over the high heat of a skillet. Some recipes compensate by leaving the shell on, but picking shrimp out of our stir-fry at the table to peel them doesn't hold much appeal. We set out to find a way to give shrimp their due in a stir-fry. We wanted to preserve their sweet, delicate flavor and come up with a few light, silky sauces that complemented, but didn't overwhelm, the shrimp.

Ouzo, a Greek liqueur with a slightly sweet, anise flavor, imparts complexity and depth to our Greek-Style Shrimp with Tomatoes and Feta.

GREEK SHRIMP

✓ **WHY THIS RECIPE WORKS:** In this Greek dish, the shrimp are typically layered with the tomato sauce and feta and baked, but we found this method lacking. For better flavor and to streamline the method, we opted to cook the shrimp right in the sauce; adding the shrimp raw to the sauce helped infuse them with the sauce's bright flavor. And for even more flavor, we marinated the shrimp with olive oil, ouzo, garlic, and lemon zest first while we made the sauce. Final touches included a generous sprinkling of feta over the sauced shrimp as well as a scattering of chopped fresh dill.

THERE ARE PLENTY OF RULES IN COOKING. SOME, based on science, you ignore at your peril. Others are matters of taste. But one of these—don't combine seafood and cheese—has always seemed to us about as ironclad as it gets. So when we heard about shrimp saganaki, a classic Greek dish of shrimp baked in a tomato sauce under crumbles of feta cheese, we were not enthusiastic. (For those who are wondering, the dish takes its name from the shallow, two-handed skillet in which this recipe is traditionally made.) Still, there are exceptions to every rule, and dishes usually don't survive for hundreds of years if they're not delicious. So when we had a chance to sample this dish in a restaurant, we gave it a try. To our surprise, the triangulation of flavors worked wonderfully: The ocean essence of the shrimp echoed the brininess of the feta, the sweet-tart tomato sauce complemented the natural sweetness of the shrimp, and the feta gave the tomato sauce a rich creaminess. To add this dish to our weeknight repertoire, we set out on a saganaki marathon.

Since shrimp is incredibly easy to cook badly, our main challenge would be getting it just right—that is, tender, juicy, and just cooked through, not tough and rubbery. But before we fired up the oven, we had to choose the right size of shrimp. After sampling different sizes, we decided that jumbo or extra-large shrimp (16 to 20 to

a pound, and 21 to 25 to a pound, respectively) were best—they were appropriate for both first-course and main-dish portions, and their large size meant that peeling and deveining was a relatively quick process.

Choosing a cooking method, however, wasn't quite so easy. The modern approach—layering the tomato sauce and the shrimp into a baking dish, sprinkling the feta over the top, and slipping the dish into a hot oven, produced an unexpected problem: the shrimp around the perimeter cooked more quickly and were noticeably tougher than the ones in the center. We tried a lower oven temperature, which produced shrimp that cooked somewhat more evenly but still weren't very tender.

At this point, we decided it didn't make sense to fire up the oven for what really could be a quick and easy dish. So we threw tradition overboard and went stovetop. Taking the easiest approach first, we seared the shrimp very quickly in a hot skillet, then added the sauce and feta. Simple, for sure, but tasters remarked that there was nothing new here in terms of flavor; it was just seared shrimp topped with tomato sauce and cheese. Fair point. So next, reasoning that simmering the shrimp and tomatoes together would allow for an exchange of flavors, we added the shrimp raw to the tomato sauce and briefly simmered them over high heat until cooked through. The verdict? Richer, more unified flavor.

Unfortunately, though, the shrimp were still a little tough. What if we turned down the heat? This method might also give the flavors in the dish more time to blend. Sure enough, as we gradually decreased the heat from high to medium-high to medium and then to medium-low, the dish became better and better. Cooked gently at the barest simmer over medium-low (low was just too low), the shrimp were at their most tender and succulent, and the dish had a fuller flavor, too.

While the shrimp now were cooked just right—tender but not underdone—they still tasted a little dull. Our experience cooking stir-fries has taught us that a quick, simple, precooking marinade can do a lot to boost flavor, so as a first step, we tossed the shrimp with a minced garlic clove, some olive oil, a bit of lemon zest, and salt and pepper. The shrimp had more flavor, but they were

GREEK-STYLE SHRIMP WITH TOMATOES AND FETA

DEVEINING SHRIMP

1. After removing the shell, use a paring knife to make a shallow cut along the back of the shrimp so that the vein is exposed.

2. Use the tip of the knife to lift the vein out of the shrimp. Discard the vein by wiping the blade against a paper towel.

OUZO ALTERNATIVES

Ouzo, the popular anise-flavored spirit of Greece, lends shrimp saganaki a nuanced flavor that we like. But since ouzo is not in everyone's liquor cabinet, here are two alternatives.

PERNOD
Sweeter than ouzo, this French anise-flavored liqueur is the next best thing.

VODKA + ANISE SEEDS
This combo—1 tablespoon vodka and a large pinch of anise seeds in the marinade, and 2 tablespoons vodka and ¼ teaspoon anise seeds in the sauce—works just fine, but the whole anise seeds means that some bites will be more anise-packed than others.

not distinctively Greek-tasting. Some of the recipes we turned up in our initial research suggested ouzo. Though it required a trip to a well-stocked liquor store, the ouzo—a lightly sweet, anise-based Greek liqueur—was an undeniable improvement: Adding just a tablespoon to the marinade brought a welcome complexity of flavor and aroma.

Now it was time for the tomato sauce. We had been using a standard recipe, but a little tinkering was in order. We needed a sauce with some sweetness to balance the feta's sharpness, as well as some earthiness to complement the brininess of the cheese and shrimp. After experimenting with various forms of tomato—fresh, canned whole, canned diced, and tomato paste—we settled on canned diced, which were not only the most convenient but also had the most intense flavor. As for flavorings, garlic and onion sautéed in olive oil were naturals for this Mediterranean sauce, but we needed more. After making more than a dozen variations, we ended up with half a red bell pepper for natural sweetness, half a green bell pepper for earthy vegetal notes, red pepper flakes for a little enlivening heat, and a small measure of dry white wine for a touch of acidity. We also tried fresh and dried oregano, but both rendered the sauce pizza-like. Grassy fresh parsley was a better option. To finish with a Greek flourish, we added a couple of extra tablespoons of the ouzo we now had on the shelf.

Now, what about the feta? Supermarkets have many options, but our tasters preferred the sharper, more pungent authentic versions. We began by using a modest amount and gradually ratcheted it up to a generous 6 ounces, so that some would melt into the sauce as servings were spooned out and the rest would remain as a flavorful presence on top.

Our approach to introducing the feta was to simply scatter it over the surface of the shrimp in the tomato sauce and give it a few moments to soften, but we wondered if the added step of browning the cheese under a broiler or in an extra-hot oven would give the dish another dimension. A few tries and we had the answer: no. Feta is not a cheese that browns easily or takes on toasty notes when caramelized. Besides, the high heat overrode the gentle heat we used to cook the shrimp and toughened them up. As final touches, we drizzled on a tablespoon of extra-virgin olive oil for a rich fruitiness, then sprinkled a little dill over the top—its unique grassy, tangy notes had the big benefit of tasting distinctly Greek. Another dish successfully added to our repertoire of easy favorites.

Greek-Style Shrimp with Tomatoes and Feta

SERVES 4 TO 6

This recipe works equally well with jumbo shrimp (16 to 20 per pound) or extra-large shrimp (21 to 25 per pound). However, the cooking times in step 3 will vary slightly. If you don't have ouzo, see "Ouzo Alternatives" (page 82) for suggested alternatives. Our favorite brand of diced tomatoes is Hunt's and our favorite feta is Mt. Vikos Traditional Feta. Serve with crusty bread for soaking up the sauce.

1½ **pounds shrimp, peeled and deveined (see page 82), tails left on, if desired (see note)**
4   **tablespoons extra-virgin olive oil**
3   **tablespoons ouzo (see note)**
5   **medium garlic cloves, pressed or minced through a garlic press (about 5 teaspoons)**
1   **teaspoon grated zest from 1 lemon**
    Table salt and ground black pepper
1   **small onion, diced medium**
½   **medium red bell pepper, stemmed, seeded, and diced medium**
½   **medium green bell pepper, stemmed, seeded, and diced medium**
1   **(28-ounce) can diced tomatoes, drained, ⅓ cup juices reserved**
½   **teaspoon red pepper flakes**
¼   **cup dry white wine**
2   **tablespoons coarsely chopped fresh parsley leaves**
6   **ounces feta cheese, preferably sheep's and/or goat's milk, crumbled (about 1½ cups)**
2   **tablespoons chopped fresh dill**

1. Toss the shrimp, 1 tablespoon of the oil, 1 tablespoon of the ouzo, 1 teaspoon of the garlic, the lemon zest, ¼ teaspoon salt, and ⅛ teaspoon black pepper in a small bowl until well combined. Set aside while preparing the sauce.

2. Heat 2 tablespoons more oil in a 12-inch skillet over medium heat until shimmering. Add the onion, red and green bell peppers, and ¼ teaspoon salt and stir to combine. Cover the skillet and cook, stirring occasionally, until the vegetables release their moisture, 3 to 5 minutes. Uncover and continue to cook, stirring occasionally, until the moisture cooks off and the vegetables have softened, about 5 minutes longer. Add the remaining 4 teaspoons garlic and the red pepper flakes and cook until fragrant, about 1 minute. Add the tomatoes and reserved juices, wine, and remaining 2 tablespoons ouzo; increase the heat to medium-high and bring to a simmer. Reduce the heat to medium and simmer, stirring occasionally, until the flavors have melded and the sauce is slightly thickened (it should not be completely dry), 5 to 8 minutes. Stir in the parsley and season with salt and pepper to taste.

3. Reduce the heat to medium-low and add the shrimp along with any accumulated liquid to the pan; stir to coat and distribute evenly. Cover and cook, stirring occasionally, until the shrimp are opaque throughout, 6 to 9 minutes for extra-large shrimp or 7 to 11 minutes for jumbo shrimp, adjust the heat as needed to maintain a bare simmer. Remove the pan from the heat and sprinkle evenly with the feta. Drizzle the remaining 1 tablespoon oil evenly over the top and sprinkle with dill. Serve immediately.

SCIENCE DESK

AVOIDING MUSHY SHRIMP
Conventional wisdom dictates that shrimp cooked too slowly can turn mushy. But our shrimp, which cook over medium-low heat for up to 11 minutes (depending on the size), keep their firm texture. Here's why: The protease enzymes in shrimp that can make them mushy increase in activity as the temperature of the shrimp increases—but only up to 130 degrees to 140 degrees. After that, the heat deactivates the enzymes. Since we add the shrimp to the boiling sauce and quickly cover the pan, there's enough heat and steam to quickly dial up the temperature of the crustaceans and deactivate the enzymes—but not so much that the shrimp overcook and turn rubbery.

RATING FETA CHEESE

In Greece, salty, crumbly curds of feta are still made with methods dating back to the Trojan War, and in 2005 the European Union awarded Greece the sole right to the name. We wanted to find out if feta produced by other countries could compare. We tasted five brands—two Greek fetas, one French version, and two American cheeses—both plain and in our Greek-Style Shrimp with Tomatoes and Feta. Tasters lamented the lack of "funky," "grassy" tang in the domestic cheeses, all of which were made with 100 percent cow's milk, preferring the "barnyard" taste of the sheep's- and goat's-milk imports. In the end, true feta from Greece won out. Brands are listed in order of preference. See www.americastestkitchen.com for updates to this testing.

HIGHLY RECOMMENDED

MT. VIKOS Traditional Feta

PRICE: $6.99 for 7 oz ($15.98 per lb)
MILK: 80% sheep, 20% goat
ORIGIN: Greece
PACKAGING: In brine
SODIUM: 270 mg per oz
COMMENTS: "Floral," "funky," and "not too salty," this feta was flavorful yet mild and appealed to almost every taster with its pleasing "creamy, crumbly" texture and a "tanginess" some found similar to blue cheese. This "assertive tanginess" balanced well with the other ingredients in our Greek-style shrimp.

RECOMMENDED

VALBRESO Feta

PRICE: $5.49 for 7 oz ($12.55 per lb)
MILK: 100% sheep
ORIGIN: France
PACKAGING: In brine
SODIUM: 270 mg per oz
COMMENTS: "Really bright and tangy" with "nice fresh flavor," said tasters of this complex French cheese. Most liked its pungent "funky" flavor. (As one taster put it, "You can almost taste the barnyard.") In our Greek-style shrimp, it was pleasantly "fruity, tangy, and almost lemony" with a "goaty finish."

MT. VIKOS Barrel Aged Feta

PRICE: $15.99 per lb
MILK: 80% sheep, 20% goat
ORIGIN: Greece
PACKAGING: In brine
SODIUM: 270 mg per oz
COMMENTS: This well-balanced cheese—"fruity," "salty, but not overly so," with "nice fresh tang and rich creaminess"—is identical to our winner, except that it has been aged for four months in birch barrels. As a result, it was slightly drier, with a denser texture and a nuttier, more rounded flavor.

RECOMMENDED WITH RESERVATIONS

ALOUETTE Crumbled Feta

PRICE: $2.69 for 4 oz ($10.76 per lb)
MILK: 100% cow
ORIGIN: United States
PACKAGING: Crumbled
SODIUM: 350 mg per oz
COMMENTS: Some tasters complimented this "salty," "briny" cheese when it was sampled plain, but in the presence of the shrimp sauté's heady flavors, its character faded to one-dimensional saltiness.

NOT RECOMMENDED

PRESIDENT Natural Feta

PRICE: $3.99 for 8 oz ($7.98 per lb)
MILK: 100% cow
ORIGIN: United States
PACKAGING: In brine
SODIUM: 260 mg per oz
COMMENTS: "Dry" and "chalky" with "not much flavor other than salt," this American contender offered "subtle cheesy" flavor which some tasters praised in the plain tasting. However, it became "watery, spongy, and overwhelmed by the other flavors" in the Greek shrimp dish.

ATHENOS Natural Feta Cheese Traditional

PRICE: $8.99 per lb
MILK: 100% cow
ORIGIN: United States
PACKAGING: In brine
SODIUM: 330 mg per oz
COMMENTS: Overpoweringly salty when tasted alone, this feta "lacked the characteristic tang" tasters expected. The texture was "dry and rubbery," and though it became creamier when warmed in the shrimp dish, its flavor vanished.

SHRIMP STIR-FRIES

✔ **WHY THIS RECIPE WORKS:** For stir-fries with plump, juicy, well-seasoned shrimp in a balanced, flavorful sauce, we abandoned our usual high-heat stir-fry method in favor of cooking the shrimp over medium-low heat. Gentler, lower heat cooked the shrimp through without drying them out. Marinating the shrimp in oil, salt, and garlic boosted their flavor and helped keep them moist. Rather than heavy soy-based stir-fry sauces, we developed a few lighter sauces and reduced them to a consistency that clung tightly to the shrimp.

YEARS AGO WE PERFECTED A STIR-FRYING TECHNIQUE for the flat American stovetop: Batch-sear marinated meat and vegetables in a hot skillet (not a wok; its concave shape is designed to sit in a cylindrical pit), add aromatics, and finish with a flavorful, quick-simmered sauce. It works with just about any type of protein—beef, chicken, pork, even tofu—so how could it fail with shrimp?

That was our question—after the first tightly curled, rubbery shrimp we choked down proved that meat and shrimp are not interchangeable. To begin with, shrimp cook faster than meat. Second, marinades seem to roll right off their tightly grained flesh and end up merely burning in the hot skillet.

Chinese stir-fries often work around the problem of tough shrimp by cooking them shell-on to protect their delicate flesh, but neither crunching into shrimp shells nor peeling them at the table appealed to us. A better approach would be to modify our stir-fry technique, customizing it to produce plump, juicy, well-seasoned shrimp in a balanced, flavorful sauce.

Most stir-fry recipes suffer from a fundamental flaw: They don't account for the fact that home cooks lack high-output, restaurant-style burners. Without this blazing heat, recipes that call for cooking all the meat in a single batch turn out lackluster results; the pan can't maintain temperatures hot enough to effectively sear the food before the whole mess overcooks in a cloud of steam.

That's where our batch-cooking method comes in: To keep the pan good and hot throughout the process, we use a large, shallow nonstick skillet (which, on a Western range, heats more efficiently than a wok and provides maximum surface area for evaporation), crank up the flame to high, and cook each component separately and in small quantities so that the pieces have a chance to thoroughly brown. The meat is browned first, then set aside while vegetables are seared and aromatics such as garlic, ginger, and scallions are briefly sautéed, after which the protein goes back in, a sauce is added, and everything simmers until just cooked through.

In this case, however, we needed a buffer between the heat and the shrimp. Cooking them shell-on was out, but we wondered if the solution was as simple as fabricating an artificial "shell" to help protect the peeled shrimp's delicate meat. One such technique, a traditional Chinese method known as "velveting," coats the protein in a starch-egg-oil slurry before cooking to set up a barrier between the meat and the pan. We tried every iteration of this approach we could think of: cornstarch, flour, whole eggs, and egg whites. Some of the dishes showed slight textural improvements, but overall they were uninspiring.

If the problem was overcooking, maybe we needed to step back even further from our meat stir-fry technique to reconsider the super-hot fire. Traditionally, high heat serves two purposes: speed and flavorful browning. The time and temperature window for perfectly plump, just-firm shrimp, however, is particularly narrow. An internal temperature of 140 degrees is ideal, but even a few degrees beyond that and the shrimp turn to rubber erasers, so high heat is actually hazardous.

Substantial browning, meanwhile, doesn't occur until well above 300 degrees—a surefire path to overcooking. Since shrimp stir-fries usually call for an assertive sauce, and the vegetables could still develop deep color, we wondered what would happen if we chose not to brown the seafood.

Abandoning the high-heat method, we turned down the burner to medium-low and gently parcooked a batch of shrimp, removed them from the skillet, then turned up the heat to sear the vegetables, sauté the aromatics, and finish cooking the shrimp with the sauce. This worked beautifully. Not a single taster missed a browned exterior, instead commenting on the shrimp's supreme tenderness. Reversing the approach—cooking the veggies followed by the aromatics over high heat, then turning the heat down before adding the shrimp—made the process more efficient.

It was time to think more deeply about the marinade. The test kitchen's standard Chinese rice wine–soy sauce mixture for beef, chicken, and pork wasn't doing much for the shrimp—in fact, it merely overwhelmed their sweet taste. Instead, we tried another common Chinese texture-boosting technique that we hoped would also improve flavor: soaking the shrimp in a saltwater brine, which both seasons and hydrates the flesh. Their texture became noticeably juicier, but we still wanted more flavor in the shrimp themselves. We knew infusing the brine with aromatics—garlic, specifically—wouldn't work, since the clove's flavorful compounds are mostly oil soluble and thus don't come through in a watery solution.

So was there any need to introduce water at all? In the past when developing a garlicky shrimp sauté, we'd had luck marinating shrimp in oil, salt, and garlic. The salt not only helped the shrimp retain moisture as they cooked, but it also drew flavorful compounds out of the garlic's cells, which then dissolved in the oil and spread evenly around the shellfish. Sure enough, this method worked like a charm for our shrimp. Even better, the technique lent itself to a flavor variation with ginger.

As for an assertive sauce, the heavily soy-based brews we turn to for meat stir-fries were runny and salty. Better suited to the shrimp (and more traditional in Chinese cuisine) were sweeter or spicier sauces flavored with garlic and chiles and reduced to a consistency

that tightly adhered to the shellfish. We tweaked our vinegar-based hot and sour sauce and whipped up a spicy Sichuan-style sauce along with an intense garlic sauce, all of which complemented the shrimp perfectly. By combining Chinese traditions with new techniques, these from-the-sea stir-fries would no longer play second fiddle to their land-based counterparts.

Stir-Fried Shrimp with Snow Peas and Red Bell Pepper in Hot and Sour Sauce
SERVES 4

Serve with steamed white rice.

- 1 **pound extra-large shrimp (21 to 25 per pound), peeled, deveined (see page 82), and tails removed**
- 3 **tablespoons vegetable oil**
- 1 **tablespoon minced or grated fresh ginger**
- 2 **medium garlic cloves, 1 minced or pressed through a garlic press (about 1 teaspoon), 1 sliced thin**
- ½ **teaspoon table salt**
- 3 **tablespoons sugar**
- 3 **tablespoons white vinegar**
- 1 **tablespoon Asian chili-garlic sauce**
- 1 **tablespoon dry sherry or Chinese rice cooking wine (Shaoxing)**
- 1 **tablespoon ketchup**
- 2 **teaspoons toasted sesame oil**
- 2 **teaspoons cornstarch**
- 1 **teaspoon soy sauce**
- 1 **large shallot, sliced thin (about ⅓ cup)**
- ½ **pound snow peas or sugar snap peas, stems snapped off and strings removed**
- 1 **medium red bell pepper, stemmed, seeded, and cut into ¾-inch dice**

1. Combine the shrimp with 1 tablespoon of the vegetable oil, the ginger, minced garlic, and salt in a medium bowl. Let the shrimp marinate at room temperature for 30 minutes.

2. Meanwhile, whisk the sugar, vinegar, chili-garlic sauce, sherry, ketchup, sesame oil, cornstarch, and soy sauce in a small bowl. Combine the sliced garlic with the shallot in a second small bowl.

SCIENCE DESK

MAKING A MARINADE THAT WORKS
A 30-minute soak in a mixture of salt, oil, and aromatics is the secret to perfectly tender, deeply flavored shrimp. The salt works its magic in two ways. First, it enters the flesh of the shrimp, helping them to retain valuable juices during cooking. Second, it forces the flavors from aromatics such as garlic and ginger into the oil. The oil in the mix distributes those flavor compounds evenly over the flesh (not just in areas in direct contact with the garlic) for shrimp that taste better than ever.

STIR-FRIED SHRIMP WITH SNOW PEAS AND RED BELL PEPPER IN HOT AND SOUR SAUCE

Stir-Fried Shrimp with Garlicky Eggplant, Scallions, and Cashews

SERVES 4

Serve with steamed white rice.

- 1 pound extra-large shrimp (21 to 25 per pound), peeled, deveined (see page 82 and tails removed
- 3 tablespoons vegetable oil
- 6 medium garlic cloves, 1 minced or pressed through a garlic press (about 1 teaspoon), 5 sliced thin
- ½ teaspoon table salt
- 2 tablespoons soy sauce
- 2 tablespoons oyster-flavored sauce
- 2 tablespoons dry sherry or Chinese rice cooking wine (Shaoxing)
- 2 tablespoons sugar
- 1 tablespoon toasted sesame oil
- 1 tablespoon white vinegar
- 2 teaspoons cornstarch
- ⅛ teaspoon red pepper flakes
- 6 large scallions, greens cut into 1-inch pieces and whites sliced thin
- ½ cup unsalted cashews
- 1 medium eggplant (about ¾ pound), cut into ¾-inch dice

3. Heat 1 tablespoon more vegetable oil in a 12-inch nonstick skillet over high heat until just smoking. Add the snow peas and bell pepper and cook, stirring frequently, until the vegetables begin to brown, 1½ to 2 minutes. Transfer the vegetables to a medium bowl.

4. Add the remaining 1 tablespoon vegetable oil to the now-empty skillet and heat until just smoking. Add the garlic-shallot mixture and cook, stirring frequently, until just beginning to brown, about 30 seconds. Reduce the heat to medium-low, add the shrimp, and cook, stirring frequently, until the shrimp are light pink on both sides, 1 to 1½ minutes. Whisk the soy sauce mixture to recombine and add to the skillet; return to high heat and cook, stirring constantly, until the sauce is thickened and the shrimp are cooked through, 1 to 2 minutes. Return the vegetables to the skillet, toss to combine, and serve.

1. Combine the shrimp with 1 tablespoon of the vegetable oil, the minced garlic, and salt in a medium bowl. Let the shrimp marinate at room temperature for 30 minutes.

2. Meanwhile, whisk the soy sauce, oyster-flavored sauce, sherry, sugar, sesame oil, vinegar, cornstarch, and red pepper flakes in a small bowl; set aside. Combine the sliced garlic with the scallion whites and cashews in a small bowl.

3. Heat 1 tablespoon more vegetable oil in a 12-inch nonstick skillet over high heat until just smoking. Add the eggplant and cook, stirring frequently, until lightly browned, 3 to 6 minutes. Add the scallion greens and continue to cook until the scallion greens begin to brown and the eggplant is fully tender, 1 to 2 minutes longer. Transfer the vegetables to a medium bowl.

4. Continue with the recipe for Stir-Fried Shrimp with Snow Peas and Red Bell Pepper in Hot and Sour Sauce from step 4, replacing the garlic-shallot mixture with the garlic-scallion-cashew mixture and replacing the hot and sour sauce with the reserved sauce.

Stir-Fried Sichuan-Style Shrimp with Zucchini, Red Bell Pepper, and Peanuts

SERVES 4

This recipe is spicy. If you can find a Chinese long pepper, use it in place of the jalapeño. Broad bean chili paste is also referred to as chili bean sauce or horse bean chili paste. If you can't find it, increase the amount of Asian chili-garlic sauce by 1 teaspoon. Serve with steamed white rice.

1   pound extra-large shrimp (21 to 25 per pound), peeled, deveined (see page 82), and tails removed
3   tablespoons vegetable oil
2   medium garlic cloves, 1 minced or pressed through a garlic press (about 1 teaspoon), 1 sliced thin
½   teaspoon table salt
2   tablespoons dry sherry or Chinese rice cooking wine (Shaoxing)
1   tablespoon broad bean chili paste (see note)
1   tablespoon Asian chili-garlic sauce
1   tablespoon white vinegar or Chinese black vinegar
2   teaspoons soy sauce
2   teaspoons Chinese hot chili oil or toasted sesame oil
1   teaspoon sugar
1   teaspoon cornstarch
½   teaspoon Sichuan peppercorns, toasted and ground (optional)
1   jalapeño, halved, ribs and seeds removed, and sliced thinly on the bias (see note)
½   cup roasted unsalted peanuts

1   small zucchini, cut into ¾-inch dice (2 cups)
1   medium red bell pepper, stemmed, seeded, and cut into ¾-inch dice
½   cup lightly packed cilantro leaves

1. Combine the shrimp, 1 tablespoon of the vegetable oil, the minced garlic, and salt in a medium bowl. Let the shrimp marinate at room temperature 30 minutes.

2. Meanwhile, whisk the sherry, chili paste, chili-garlic sauce, vinegar, soy sauce, chili oil, sugar, cornstarch, and peppercorns (if using) in a small bowl; set aside. Combine the sliced garlic with the jalapeño and peanuts in a second small bowl.

3. Heat 1 tablespoon more oil in a 12-inch nonstick skillet over high heat until just smoking. Add the zucchini and bell pepper and cook, stirring frequently, until the zucchini is tender and well browned, 2 to 4 minutes. Transfer the vegetables to a medium bowl.

4. Continue with the recipe for Stir-Fried Shrimp with Snow Peas and Red Bell Pepper in Hot and Sour Sauce from step 4, replacing the garlic-shallot mixture with the garlic-jalapeño-peanut mixture, replacing the hot and sour sauce with the reserved sauce, and adding the cilantro to the skillet with the cooked vegetables.

NOTES FROM THE TEST KITCHEN

FOR TENDER SHRIMP, LOWER THE HEAT

For perfectly plump, juicy shrimp, we cook the vegetables first—and then turn the heat way down when the shrimp are added to the pan.

THANKSGIVING *Turkey*

Starting our turkey in a low oven helps keep the meat juicy, while increasing the heat later crisps and browns the skin for a bird worthy of the Thanksgiving table.

WHAT HAPPENED TO GOOD OLD-FASHIONED STUFFED TURKEY? It seems that the Thanksgiving turkey has hit a bit of an identity crisis lately between the popularity of deep-fried turkey (a recipe that requires a frightening amount of hot oil and the fire department on speed dial) to recipes that ditch the whole bird altogether in favor of a more refined centerpiece—a butterflied, stuffed, and rolled turkey breast. But if the kids can't fight over the turkey legs, where's the fun in that?

And what about bread stuffing and turkey gravy? While some eschew stuffing in favor of "healthy" sides, it's a must-have in our book. And no gravy? We can't imagine the turkey, the stuffing, or the mashed potatoes, for that matter, without big spoonfuls of gravy over the top. But gravy, which is typically made at the last-minute as guests are heading to the table can be a hassle. Could there be an easier way? We wanted it all: a holiday-worthy turkey without any pretenses—an old-fashioned stuffed bird with browned, crispy skin and moist meat; a bread stuffing moistened with the bird's juices; and plenty of rich gravy to pass at the table.

OLD-FASHIONED STUFFED TURKEY

✔ WHY THIS RECIPE WORKS: To get a roast turkey recipe with everything in one package—juicy meat, burnished skin, and rich-flavored stuffing—we discovered a few tricks. We salted the meat so it remained flavorful and moist. We started the bird in a low oven and gradually cranked up the heat for the crispiest skin. And for our perfect turkey recipe, we removed the stuffing from the turkey when the meat had reached a safe temperature, mixing it with the remaining uncooked stuffing, so we could cook it all in a baking dish without having to overcook the turkey.

NOTHING HAS IMMORTALIZED THE THANKSGIVING feast quite like Norman Rockwell's iconic painting of a perfectly bronzed turkey glistening on a serving platter. Originally splayed across the cover of *The Saturday Evening Post* as a wartime call to action, it's had the unintentional effect of raising the bar for holiday tables ever since.

But the skeptic in us has always wanted a peek beneath the surface of that mahogany-hued bird. Like anyone who's ever roasted a turkey, we know even the best recipes involve compromise. Cook a turkey long enough to get the skin immaculately burnished and the white meat is usually dry as sawdust. Brining adds moisture to the meat, but it can turn skin soggy. Salting (dry-brining) solves the crisping woes, but the drippings get too seasoned to make a proper gravy. Stuffing the cavity compounds the headaches, slowing the roasting time to a crawl and upping the chance for uneven cooking. Still, we couldn't help but wonder: Could an old-fashioned secret to a turkey with everything in one package—juicy meat, crisply burnished skin, rich-flavored stuffing that cooked inside the bird, and drippings suitable for gravy—actually exist? We went into the test kitchen to find out, once and for all.

If the key to compromise-free turkey was lost somewhere in time, we had a good idea where to find it: the old-school cookbooks in our library. But as we surveyed

bygone wisdom, disappointment set in. The oldest recipes were barely recipes at all. "Stuff the craw… spit it, and lay it down a good distance from the fire, which should be clear and brisk," advised *The Virginia Housewife* (1838). One by one, we discarded recipes for being too vague, too live-fire–specific, or too close to the basic (and unreliable) roast-and-baste method popular to this day. Only one technique, from the classic *Boston Cooking-School Cook Book* (1896) by Fannie Farmer, which promised crispier skin on roast chicken, piqued our interest enough to convince us to give it a whirl: rubbing the entire bird with a flour-butter paste. Alas, it was a bust on turkey; the skin was tough, not crisp.

It was time to return to proven techniques. First decision: salting or brining? Unwilling to compromise on skin, we opted for salting, which initially draws moisture out of the meat, but after a 24-hour rest in the fridge, all this moisture gets slowly drawn back in, seasoning the meat and helping it retain moisture. In the past we've used as many as 5 tablespoons of salt on the bird—a nonstarter for making gravy from drippings. Reducing to 3 tablespoons allowed for gravy that didn't make tasters wince, but the meat was not quite as juicy and tender.

Maybe we needed to reconsider the roasting method. We'd been using a test-kitchen favorite developed in 1994, where you start the turkey in a blazing hot oven breast-side down, flip it once, and finish at a lower, gentler pace. Since then, we've proved that, across the board, meats from pork chops to roast beef cook more evenly when you reverse the order and start out at a lower oven temperature. Why not whole turkey? We cooked the bird in a gentle 325-degree oven for a couple of hours, then cranked up the temperature to 450 to give it a final blast of skin-crisping heat and to bring the center up to temperature. It worked beautifully, yielding breast meat that was as moist and tender as we could hope for. As for the skin, some might call it crisp—but we wanted it brittle enough to crunch. We brought out a secret weapon we developed recently for chicken: massaging the skin with a baking powder and salt rub. The baking powder has a twofold effect: It helps skin dehydrate more readily and raises its pH, making it more conducive to browning. At the same time, we poked holes in the skin to help

OLD-FASHIONED STUFFED TURKEY

rendering fat escape. This technique was just the ticket, producing skin as crackling-crisp as pork rinds.

All that was left was the stuffing. We made a basic recipe (toasted cubes of sandwich bread mixed with sautéed celery, onions, herbs, broth, and eggs) and shoe-horned as much of it into the turkey as we could, placing the remainder in a baking dish to be cooked separately. For due diligence, we kept the bird in the oven until the stuffing was cooked to a safe 165 degrees—at which point the breast had reached a bone-dry 180 degrees. To get around this, some recipes have you preheat the stuff-ing in the microwave before it goes into the bird, so it cooks more or less in tandem with the white meat. We had a different idea. Since our turkey needed to rest a good 30 minutes after roasting anyway, why not remove the undercooked stuffing and finish cooking it on its own as the bird rested? As we took the stuffing out of the bird for our next go-round, we remembered the bland "poor relation" batch waiting to go in the oven. We had a new brainstorm: The parcooked stuffing was saturated with turkey juices, with plenty to spare. If we combined this with the uncooked batch, all the stuffing would get a flavor boost. But with eggs in the mix, the cooked stuffing had firmed up and wouldn't blend easily into the uncooked portion. The solution? We moistened the batch that went in the turkey with broth alone, then waited to add the eggs until we took it out of the bird and combined it with the uncooked portion.

In theory, we now had it all: moist breast meat, crisp skin, and rich stuffing in every bite. Still, today's turkeys are milder in flavor, and we couldn't get rid of the nagging feeling that the meat was bland. But short of mail-ordering a heritage bird, what could we do? For inspiration, we went back to our library. This time we grabbed a more contemporary classic: James Beard's *American Cookery* (1972). A variation on the once-popular technique of barding—wrapping lean meat with fattier meat—caught our eye. We salted another turkey, applied the baking powder–salt rub, added the stuffing, and then draped the bird with meaty salt pork. The barded bird smoked heavily in the oven, but its flavor was unbelievably intense. Not unlike the way adding a ham bone to a pot of beans can impart a meaty flavor without making them taste outright porky, the salt pork

enhanced the turkey without making its presence too clear. To fix the smoking problem, we removed the salt pork and drained the drippings from the roasting pan before cranking up the heat and returning the bird to the oven. The resulting meal was perfect—stuffing with crisp edges and a savory flavor from the turkey; tender, juicy breast meat with unparalleled richness; and crack-ling, golden-brown skin.

NOTES FROM THE TEST KITCHEN

HOW TO SALT A TURKEY

1. Rub 1 tablespoon salt inside the main cavity.

2. Use a chopstick or a thin wooden spoon handle to separate the skin from the meat over the breast, legs, thighs, and back.

3. Lift the skin and apply 1½ teaspoons salt over each breast half, massaging the salt evenly over the meat.

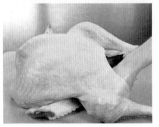

4. Apply 1½ teaspoons kosher salt under the skin of each leg.

Old-Fashioned Stuffed Turkey

SERVES 10 TO 12

Table salt is not recommended for this recipe because it is too fine. To roast a kosher or self-basting turkey (such as a frozen Butterball), do not salt it in step 1. Look for salt pork that is roughly equal parts fat and lean meat. The bread can be toasted up to 1 day in advance. Serve with Make-Ahead Turkey Gravy (recipe follows).

TURKEY

1   (12 to 14-pound turkey), giblets and neck reserved
    for gravy, if making (see note)

3   tablespoons plus 2 teaspoons kosher salt (see note)

2   teaspoons baking powder

12 ounces salt pork, cut into ¼-inch-thick slices and
    rinsed (see note)

STUFFING

1½ pounds (about 15 slices) high-quality white sandwich
    bread, cut into ½-inch cubes (about 12 cups)

4   tablespoons (½ stick) unsalted butter, plus extra for
    the baking dish

1   medium onion, minced

2   celery ribs, chopped fine
    Kosher salt and ground black pepper

2   tablespoons minced fresh thyme leaves

1   tablespoon minced fresh marjoram leaves

1   tablespoon minced fresh sage leaves

1½ cups low-sodium chicken broth

1   36-inch square cheesecloth, folded in quarters

2   large eggs

1. FOR THE TURKEY: Following the photos on page 94, use your fingers or the handle of a wooden spoon to separate the turkey skin from the meat on the breast, legs, thighs, and back; avoid breaking the skin. Rub 1 tablespoon of the salt evenly inside the cavity of the turkey, 1½ teaspoons salt under the skin of each breast half, and 1½ teaspoons salt under the skin of each leg. Wrap the turkey tightly with plastic wrap; refrigerate 24 to 48 hours.

2. FOR THE STUFFING: Adjust an oven rack to the lowest position and heat the oven to 250 degrees. Spread the bread cubes in a single layer on a rimmed baking sheet; bake until the edges have dried but the centers are slightly moist (the cubes should yield to pressure), about 45 minutes, stirring several times during baking. Transfer to a large bowl and increase the oven temperature to 325 degrees.

3. While the bread dries, heat the butter in a 12-inch skillet over medium-high heat; when the foaming subsides, add the onion, celery, 2 teaspoons salt, and 1 teaspoon pepper; cook, stirring occasionally, until the vegetables begin to soften and brown slightly, 7 to 10 minutes. Stir in the herbs; cook until fragrant, about 1 minute. Add the vegetables to the bowl with the dried bread; add 1 cup of the broth and toss until evenly moistened.

4. TO ROAST THE TURKEY: Combine the remaining 2 teaspoons kosher salt and the baking powder in a small bowl. Remove the turkey from the refrigerator and unwrap. Thoroughly dry the turkey inside and out with paper towels. Using a skewer, poke 15 to 20 holes in the fat deposits on top of the breast halves and thighs, 4 to 5 holes in each deposit. Sprinkle the surface of the turkey with the salt–baking powder mixture and rub in the mixture with your hands, coating the skin evenly. Tuck the wings underneath the turkey. Line the turkey cavity with the cheesecloth, pack with 4 to 5 cups stuffing, and tie the ends of the cheesecloth together. Cover the remaining stuffing with plastic wrap and refrigerate. Using twine, loosely tie the turkey legs together. Place the turkey breast side down in a V-rack set in a roasting pan and drape the salt pork slices over the back.

5. Roast the turkey breast side down until the thickest part of the breast registers 130 degrees on an instant-read thermometer, 2 to 2½ hours. Remove the roasting pan from the oven and increase the oven temperature to 450 degrees. Transfer the turkey in the V-rack to a rimmed baking sheet. Remove and discard the salt pork. Using clean potholders or kitchen towels, rotate the turkey breast side up. Cut the twine binding the legs and remove the stuffing bag; empty into the reserved stuffing in the bowl. Pour the drippings from the roasting pan into a fat separator and reserve for gravy, if making.

6. Once the oven has come to temperature, return the turkey in the V-rack to the roasting pan and roast until the skin is golden brown and crisp, the thickest part of the breast registers 160 degrees, and the thickest part of the thigh registers 175 degrees, about 45 minutes, rotating the pan halfway through. Transfer the turkey to a carving board and let rest, uncovered, for 30 minutes.

7. While the turkey rests, reduce the oven temperature to 400 degrees. Whisk the eggs and remaining ½ cup broth together in a small bowl. Pour the egg mixture over the stuffing and toss to combine, breaking up any large chunks; spread in a buttered 13 by 9-inch baking dish. Bake until the stuffing registers 165 degrees and the top is golden brown, about 15 minutes. Carve the turkey and serve with the stuffing and gravy.

Make-Ahead Turkey Gravy

MAKES ABOUT 2 QUARTS

Note that the optional roast turkey drippings may be quite salty—be careful when adding them to the gravy in step 4.

6	turkey thighs, trimmed, or 9 wings, separated at the joints
2	medium carrots, chopped coarse
2	medium celery ribs, chopped coarse
2	medium onions, chopped coarse
1	head garlic, halved
	Vegetable oil spray
10	cups low-sodium chicken broth, plus extra as needed
2	cups dry white wine
12	sprigs fresh thyme
	Unsalted butter, as needed
1	cup unbleached all-purpose flour
	Salt and ground black pepper
	Defatted drippings from Old-Fashioned Stuffed Turkey (page 95; optional)

1. Adjust an oven rack to the middle position and heat the oven to 450 degrees. Toss the thighs, carrots, celery, onions, and garlic together in a roasting pan and spray with vegetable oil. Roast, stirring occasionally, until well browned, 1 hour to 1 hour and 45 minutes.

2. Transfer the contents of the roasting pan to a large Dutch oven. Add the broth, wine, and thyme and bring to a boil, skimming as needed. Reduce to a gentle simmer and cook until the broth is brown and flavorful and measures about 8 cups when strained, about 1½ hours. Strain the broth through a fine-mesh strainer into a large container, pressing on the solids to extract as much liquid as possible; discard the solids. (The turkey broth can be cooled and refrigerated for up to 2 days or frozen for up to 1 month.)

3. Let the strained turkey broth settle (if necessary) then spoon off and reserve ½ cup of the fat that has risen to the top (add butter as needed if short on turkey fat). Heat the fat in a Dutch oven over medium-high heat until bubbling. Whisk in the flour and cook, whisking constantly, until well browned, 3 to 7 minutes.

4. Slowly whisk in the turkey broth and bring to a boil. Reduce to a simmer and cook until the gravy is very thick, 10 to 15 minutes. Add the defatted drippings (if using) to taste, then season with salt and pepper, and serve. (The gravy can be refrigerated for up to 2 days; reheat gently, adding additional chicken broth as needed to adjust the consistency).

RATING HYBRID CHEF'S KNIVES

The familiar all-purpose chef's knife has a thick wedge-shaped blade that can push through tough foods and a curved edge that allows the blade to rhythmically rock when chopping. It won't chip or break easily and it's simple to resharpen. By contrast, in Japan there isn't one all-purpose knife, but instead various specialized knives; all are extremely thin, with a razor-sharp cutting edge honed on just one side that allows for incredibly precise cutting. These Japanese knives have a straighter edge than the chef's knife and are typically made of very hard steel to support the thinness of the blade. Only recently have knife makers merged the two styles. Called the gyutou (ghee-YOU-toe) in Japan, this hybrid knife fuses Japanese knife making with Western knife design. The result is a feather-light, lethally sharp, and wonderfully precise knife. We tested a number of hybrid knives and our winning traditional chef's knife. For the steel hardness category in the chart below (a metal industry standard), higher numbers indicate greater hardness. Brands are listed in order of preference. See www.americastestkitchen.com for updates to this testing.

HIGHLY RECOMMENDED

MASAMOTO VG-10 Gyutou, 8.2 inches (model #VG-10)
PRICE: $136.50
ORIGIN: Japanese
MATERIAL: High-carbon stainless steel, wood composite handle
STEEL HARDNESS: 58–59 **EDGE RETENTION:** Very good
CUTTING: ★★★ **DESIGN:** ★★★
COMMENTS: "A dream" for cutting up chicken and dicing onion. With a blade more curved than most of the knives, it assisted a rocking motion that "pulverized parsley into dust."

MISONO UX-10 Chef's Knife, 8.2 inches (model #UX-10)
PRICE: $156
ORIGIN: Japanese
MATERIAL: Swedish stain-resistant steel, wood composite handle
STEEL HARDNESS: 59–60 **EDGE RETENTION:** Average
CUTTING: ★★★ **DESIGN:** ★★★
COMMENTS: "Exceptional slicing, with no effort," and "the best-feeling knife in my hand," raved some, though others disliked its squared-off collar.

VICTORINOX Fibrox 8-Inch Chef's Knife (model #40520)
PRICE: $24.95
ORIGIN: European
MATERIAL: X50 CrMoV stainless steel, Fibrox handle
STEEL HARDNESS: 55–56 **EDGE RETENTION:** Average
CUTTING: ★★★ **DESIGN:** ★★
COMMENTS: Our favorite inexpensive chef's knife rivaled fancier knives yet again. Though "clearly not as amazing," it had "no trouble going through anything," with a "good curve" for rocking.

RECOMMENDED

TOGIHARU Inox Gyutou, 8.2 inches (model #HKR-INOX-G)
PRICE: $85
ORIGIN: Japanese
MATERIAL: Inox stain-resistant steel, wood composite handle
STEEL HARDNESS: 57–58 **EDGE RETENTION:** Average
CUTTING: ★★★ **DESIGN:** ★★
COMMENTS: "Lovely, sharp, precise, light, and slim." Its straight blade won't rock, and some deemed its balance blade-heavy. Large hands found the grip too small, and knuckles knocked.

MAC Professional 8-Inch Chef's Knife with Dimples (model #MTH-80)
PRICE: $109.95
ORIGIN: Japanese
MATERIAL: High-carbon stain-resistant molybdenum alloy, Pakkawood handle (resin-impregnated)
STEEL HARDNESS: 59–60 **EDGE RETENTION:** Average
CUTTING: ★★★ **DESIGN:** ★★
COMMENTS: This knife had less taper from the spine, adding solidity, but subtracting agility. "Not as precise as I'd like."

GLOBAL G-2, 8-Inch Chef's Knife (model #G-2)
PRICE: $99.95
ORIGIN: Japanese
MATERIAL: CROMOVA 18 stainless (proprietary chromium, molybdenum, vanadium blend)
EDGE RETENTION: Very good
CUTTING: ★★★ **DESIGN:** ★★
COMMENTS: Its extreme design—the lightest, thinnest, most dramatic taper—was loved or hated. In greasy hands, the metal grip felt slippery.

AKIFUSA Gyutou, 8.2-Inch
PRICE: $168.95
ORIGIN: Japanese
MATERIAL: Powdered metallurgical stainless steel blade, "san mai" soft steel layered over harder core, Pakkawood handle
STEEL HARDNESS: 64 **EDGE RETENTION:** Very good
CUTTING: ★★ **DESIGN:** ★★
COMMENTS: "Very nice, sharp, light." Slightly rough edges made the grip less comfortable.

HORSERADISH-CRUSTED
Beef Tenderloin

SPECIAL OCCASIONS CALL FOR A SPECIAL MAIN COURSE, AND WE can think of few that rival big, beautiful beef tenderloin. Simply roasted, its rosy, tender meat is pretty great, but even better is coating it in a rich, crispy horseradish crust. But getting the crust to cook up crisp and well seasoned is one challenge. Another is keeping it stuck to the meat. There's nothing more disheartening than slicing this impressive-looking roast only to have the crust fall away in shards.

Roasted carrots make a terrific accompaniment to a host of dishes—not just beef tenderloin. Roasting brings out the natural sugars in carrots and concentrates their earthy essence, resulting in intense flavor. But roasting can also dry carrots out, turning them tough. We wanted to find a fuss-free method for roasting carrots that delivered both deep flavor and tender texture, so we could pair them with any dinner, special or not.

To prevent dried-out carrots, we cover them with foil during the first part of roasting, then remove the foil to brown them.

BEST BEEF TENDERLOIN

✔ WHY THIS RECIPE WORKS: For our horseradish-crusted beef recipe, we wanted to combine the bracing flavor of horseradish with a crisp golden crust, to contrast with the rosy, medium-rare meat. So we chose Châteaubriand, which cooks evenly, used potato chips and panko instead of regular bread crumbs to counter the moisture of the horseradish coating, and left the bottom of the roast uncoated so that meat juices had a place to escape without ruining the crust. The result is the best horseradish-crusted beef tenderloin recipe we've ever had.

COOKS GO TO ALL KINDS OF CRAZY LENGTHS TO BEEF up the taste of bland, buttery-smooth tenderloin. The most famous example is beef Wellington, in which the meat is coated in foie gras and minced mushrooms, then encrusted in pastry. More recent innovations try everything from encasing the beef in a double-truffle crust (bread crumbs, sliced truffles, and truffle oil) to saucing it with concoctions that include specialty vinegar, black cherries, and bittersweet chocolate. By comparison, simply serving tenderloin with pungent horseradish sauce, a fine but standard accompaniment, seems a little uninspired for the special dinners at which this pricey cut is typically served. But if we could combine the bracing flavor of horseradish with a crisp, golden crust that would also add textural contrast to rosy, medium-rare meat—now, that would be a different story.

When we did some research, we discovered this recipe idea wasn't a new one. But the recipes we found were disastrous. Most did nothing more than add the horseradish to a basic bread crumb mixture before spreading it over the beef and roasting it in the oven. The crust absorbed the meat's juices, causing most of it to turn mushy and fall off, while what "shell" still remained had only a trace of horseradish flavor.

Our starting point was choosing the right cut of meat and the key ingredients for our crust. A center-cut roast—also known as Châteaubriand—was a must,

because its uniform shape cooks evenly. For the crust, we figured we'd work with Japanese panko crumbs (for their ultra-crisp texture) and try a common breading technique: lightly flouring the meat, applying a thin wash of egg white, and then rolling the roast in crumbs flavored with horseradish, minced shallot, garlic, and herbs.

As for the horseradish, it seemed likely that the fresh stuff would have more pungency than the bottled variety, so we grated a couple of tablespoons of the gnarly-looking root and added it to our panko mix before breading and roasting the tenderloin. To our disappointment, the fresh horseradish turned unpleasantly bitter when cooked, and the crumb coating failed to crisp. Bottled prepared horseradish, made with grated horseradish and vinegar, proved a better choice. A good brand (see page 104) boasts a bright—not bitter—bite, even after exposure to heat. Pressing the horseradish in a strainer removed the excess moisture, but since weight for weight prepared horseradish is less potent than freshly grated we needed to use a full quarter cup to get the flavor we wanted. But even after pressing it, this amount of wet horseradish was still dampening the crust.

Perhaps we needed to reevaluate our choice of breading. Crackers and Melba toast were OK but added too much of their own flavor. On a whim, we tried crushed potato chips. These were mostly a hit, keeping their crunch and contributing a salty potato flavor that tasters loved. The only problem was their slightly processed taste. With a cut this expensive, we wanted only the best—so why not whip up our own potato crumbles? We shredded a small potato on a box grater, rinsed the shreds to remove surface starch, and then cooked them in oil until browned and crisp. A test run proved that combining them with the panko (which we pretoasted) was the best option: The panko coated the nooks in the meat that the potatoes couldn't reach, while the potato shreds jutted out, making for a craggy, golden crust full of savory flavor.

Still, our results weren't ideal. In order to keep the crust truly crisp, the most horseradish we could add to the crumb mixture was 2 tablespoons. We'd have to find another way of upping horseradish flavor.

If we couldn't add more horseradish to the crust, why not just add some to the egg wash? Unfortunately,

HORSERADISH-CRUSTED BEEF TENDERLOIN WITH HORSERADISH CREAM SAUCE

the wash was too thin to hold the horseradish, which dripped down the meat. Perhaps the answer was adding mayonnaise to create a paste, another approach we've used successfully to make breading stick. This worked well; by combining one beaten egg white, 1½ teaspoons mayonnaise, and 2 tablespoons horseradish, we were able to make a pungently flavored paste that clung firmly to the tenderloin. Adding a bit of mustard to this mix enhanced the spiciness of the horseradish. Everything seemed to be going well until we roasted the tenderloin and tried to slice it, at which point the beef came out of its shell—literally. The crust cracked into pieces that fell straight onto the cutting board.

Stumped, we consulted our science editor. He came up with a novel idea: Replace the egg white with gelatin (see "Gelatin—The Best Crust Binder," below). We added

just ½ teaspoon to the horseradish mixture, applied it to the tenderloin, and roasted the meat. Unlike the crackly egg-based paste, the gelatin mixture bound the bread crumbs firmly to the meat yet yielded slightly as we cut it. At long last, each slice delivered rosy beef topped by a cohesive horseradish crust.

Only one problem remained: Given time, the crust still became slightly soggy from meat juices released during cooking. Three final tweaks fixed this problem. First, we adjusted the oven temperature to 400 degrees (up until now, we'd been using a more moderate 300), which helped keep the crust a little more crisp. Second, we seared the meat in a hot skillet, then let it rest on a wire rack set in a baking sheet so that its juices could drain off before applying the paste and the crumbs. Finally, we coated only the top and sides of the tenderloin, leaving an "opening" on the bottom for meat juices to escape as it roasted.

Served with a horseradish cream sauce, this beef tenderloin was a standout, combining succulent meat with a crisp, salty, pungent crust. Who needs beef Wellington?

SCIENCE DESK

GELATIN—THE BEST CRUST BINDER
A simple egg wash is the usual choice for binding a bread crumb coating to meat, but it didn't work for our slippery horseradish-bread-crumb mixture. Could we do better by replacing the egg white with gelatin?

THE EXPERIMENT
We prepared two pastes, one made with egg white, horseradish, mayonnaise, and mustard and a second where we substituted ½ teaspoon of gelatin for the egg white. We applied each paste to a beef tenderloin and then cooked the roasts according to our recipe.

THE RESULTS
The gelatin paste kept the bread crumbs attached to the meat much better than the egg version. It also had a slight elasticity that allowed it to remain firmly stuck to the meat as we sliced it.

THE EXPLANATION
Meat and gelatin have a natural affinity. Both are made up of linear proteins that are able to form tight bonds with each other. The proteins in egg whites, on the other hand, are globular (wound up like balls of yarn). Although egg whites do eventually stretch into more linear shapes when heated, they still form a weaker bond with meat than gelatin.

Horseradish-Crusted Beef Tenderloin
SERVES 6

If using table salt, reduce the amount in step 1 to 1½ teaspoons. Add the gelatin to the horseradish paste at the last moment, or the mixture will become unspreadable. If desired, serve the roast with Horseradish Cream Sauce (recipe follows; you will need 2 jars of prepared horseradish for both the roast and sauce). If you choose to salt the tenderloin in advance, remove it from the refrigerator 1 hour before cooking. To make this recipe 1 day in advance, prepare it through step 3, but in step 2 do not toss the bread crumbs with the other ingredients until you are ready to sear the meat.

  1 **(2-pound) beef tenderloin center-cut Châteaubriand, trimmed of fat and silver skin**
     Kosher salt (see note)
  3 **tablespoons panko bread crumbs**
  2 **teaspoons plus 1 cup vegetable oil**
1¼ **teaspoons ground black pepper**

1 small shallot, minced (about 1 tablespoon)

2 medium garlic cloves, minced or pressed through a
   garlic press (about 2 teaspoons)

¼ cup well-drained prepared horseradish
   (see note)

2 tablespoons minced fresh parsley leaves

½ teaspoon minced fresh thyme leaves

1 small russet potato (about 6 ounces), peeled and
   grated on the large holes of a box grater

1½ teaspoons mayonnaise

1½ teaspoons Dijon mustard

½ teaspoon unflavored powdered gelatin (see note)

1. Sprinkle the roast with 1 tablespoon salt, cover with plastic wrap, and let stand at room temperature for 1 hour or refrigerate for up to 24 hours. Adjust an oven rack to the middle position and heat the oven to 400 degrees.

2. Toss the bread crumbs with 2 teaspoons of the oil, ¼ teaspoon salt, and ¼ teaspoon of the pepper in a 10-inch nonstick skillet. Cook over medium heat, stirring frequently, until deep golden brown, 3 to 5 minutes. Transfer to a rimmed baking sheet and cool to room temperature (wipe out the skillet). Once cool, toss the bread crumbs with the shallot, garlic, 2 tablespoons of the horseradish, the parsley, and thyme.

3. Rinse the grated potato under cold water, then squeeze dry in a kitchen towel. Transfer the potatoes and remaining 1 cup oil to the skillet. Cook over high heat, stirring frequently, until the potatoes are golden brown and crisp, 6 to 8 minutes. Using a slotted spoon, transfer the potatoes to a paper towel–lined plate and season lightly with salt; let cool for 5 minutes. Reserve 1 tablespoon oil from the skillet and discard the remainder. Once the potatoes are cool, transfer to a quart-size zipper-lock bag and crush until coarsely ground. Transfer the potatoes to the baking sheet with the bread crumb mixture and toss to combine.

4. Pat the exterior of the tenderloin dry with paper towels and sprinkle evenly with the remaining 1 teaspoon pepper. Heat the reserved 1 tablespoon oil in a 12-inch nonstick skillet over medium-high heat until

NOTES FROM THE TEST KITCHEN

THREE STEPS TO A CRISPIER COATING
Fried potato shreds made for a far crispier—and more flavorful—crust than the typical bread crumb coating.

1. Grate the potato on the large holes of a box grater for thin slivers that will crisp up quickly.

2. Rinse the shreds to remove surface starch, then squeeze dry in a kitchen towel.

3. Fry the potatoes in oil to create savory crumbles that keep their crunch.

just smoking. Sear the tenderloin until well browned on all sides, 5 to 7 minutes. Transfer to a wire rack set over a rimmed baking sheet and let rest 10 minutes.

5. Combine the remaining 2 tablespoons horseradish, mayonnaise, and mustard in a small bowl. Just before coating the tenderloin, add the gelatin and stir to combine. Spread the horseradish paste on the top and sides of the meat, leaving the bottom and ends bare. Roll the coated sides of the tenderloin in the bread crumb mixture, pressing gently so the crumbs adhere in an even layer that just covers the horseradish paste; pat off any excess.

6. Return the tenderloin to the wire rack. Roast until an instant-read thermometer inserted into the center of the roast registers 120 to 125 degrees for medium-rare, 25 to 30 minutes.

7. Transfer the roast to a carving board and let rest 20 minutes. Carefully cut the meat crosswise into ½-inch-thick slices and serve with Horseradish Cream Sauce, if desired.

Horseradish Cream Sauce

MAKES ABOUT 1 CUP

- ½ cup heavy cream
- ½ cup prepared horseradish
- 1 teaspoon table salt
- ⅛ teaspoon ground black pepper

Whisk the cream in a medium bowl until thickened but not yet holding soft peaks, 1 to 2 minutes. Gently fold in the horseradish, salt, and pepper. Transfer to a serving bowl and refrigerate at least 30 minutes or up to 1 hour before serving.

RATING HORSERADISH

Bottled prepared horseradish can be incredibly different from brand to brand and depending on where in the store you buy it. Refrigerated products are simply grated horseradish, vinegar, and salt. Shelf-stable ones add a laundry list of other ingredients, including sugar, eggs, citric acid, high-fructose corn syrup, soybean oil, artificial flavorings, and preservatives—and taste like chemicals as a result. The refrigerated ones deliver more natural flavor and are hot without being overpowering. We tasted four refrigerated brands, both plain from the jar and in creamy horseradish sauce. Tasters disliked samples that were "vinegary," "pickle-y," and "sweet," preferring a generous amount of heat and a finely grated texture that incorporated smoothly into the cream sauce, unlike coarser, "chunkier" horseradish that came across as "pulpy" and "chewy." Brands are listed in order of preference. See www.americastestkitchen.com for updates to this testing.

HIGHLY RECOMMENDED

BOAR'S HEAD Pure Horseradish
PRICE: $2.49 for 9 oz
COMMENTS: The kick of this "sinus-clearing" horseradish "hurt so good!" and reminded tasters of "straight wasabi." "Peppery," "complex," and "bright," this horseradish won raves for its "pure" flavor and finely grated texture that "incorporated smoothly into the sauce." "Super hot," it is "not for the faint of heart."

RECOMMENDED

BA-TAMPTE Prepared Horseradish
PRICE: $2.79 for 8 oz
COMMENTS: Tasted plain, this horseradish had "a nice balance of sweet and tart" and "good heat, but not killer." Tasted in sauce, however, tasters detected "more vinegar than heat" and a "pickle-y" flavor. Tasters reported "chewy bits" and a "slightly gritty texture" that made it less appealing than our winner.

RECOMMENDED WITH RESERVATIONS

GOLD'S Prepared Horseradish
PRICE: $2.99 for 6 oz
COMMENTS: On its own, this horseradish was "sweet and relish-y," but in sauce it tasted "very vinegary" and "bland," with "no heat at all." A "pulpy" texture made it "chewy" and a bit cottony, like "sawdust."

WOEBER'S Pure Horseradish
PRICE: $1.99 for 8 oz
COMMENTS: This "stringy," "chewy" horseradish had the texture of "wood pulp." Tasted plain, some tasters liked its "sweet, vinegary" flavor, but most agreed it had "no kick at all." Tasters likened the taste to "pickle juice." In sauce, it had "no heat, no tang," and its texture was "papery."

ROASTED CARROTS

✔ **WHY THIS RECIPE WORKS:** For roasted carrots with a pleasingly al dente chew and earthy, sweet flavor, we tossed the carrots with melted butter and roasted them, covered, on a baking sheet until softened, then we removed the foil and continued to roast them to draw out their moisture and brown them.

WHEN WE WANT TO COAX MAXIMUM FLAVOR OUT OF hardy vegetables like beets and broccoli, we pull out a roasting pan and crank the oven to high. We find the uniform blast of heat concentrates their sweet earthy notes so effectively that we can barely keep from eating them straight out of the sizzling pan. Humble carrots, however, never seem to enjoy the same popularity— even though, as roasting candidates go, they would seem like one of the best: Carrots contain about 87 percent water by weight, which, we figured, should keep their insides tender and moist as the oven's dry heat deepens their inherent sweetness.

But when we sliced a fresh bunch into coins, tossed them with oil and salt and pepper, and threw them into a hot oven, the results hardly lived up to that ideal. By the time they cooked through and developed decent browning, they were also dry and jerkylike. Maybe the problem was their shape; nickel-sized chips seemed particularly prone to shriveling up. (Plus the tapering shape of carrots made it hard to create coins that cooked evenly.) Next, we tried cutting each carrot into large matchsticks, which helped—but didn't solve—the interplay between exterior browning and interior tenderness.

It was only when we consulted our science editor for advice and he pointed out that carrots contain more pectin than any other vegetable that we had a new idea. A few years back, we developed a recipe for a deep-dish apple pie that actually capitalizes on the fruit's pectin to solve the problem of the apples shrinking so dramatically in the oven that a huge gap appears between the top crust and the filling. By gently heating them on the stove before adding them to the pie, their pectin is converted to a heat-stable form that reinforces their cell walls, keeping them from becoming mushy when cooked further in the oven.

Since carrots have even more pectin than apples, we wondered if a similar technique would work here. Blanching or steaming the carrots on the stove seemed silly—who would want to go to the trouble and dirty more pans, when so many other roasted vegetables don't require this? But maybe we could use the carrot's high moisture content to our advantage, by covering the roasting pan and steaming them in their own water, then uncovering the pan to get the browning and caramelization we wanted.

We got the oven good and hot (425 degrees), oiled and seasoned the carrots, then tightly covered the baking sheet with aluminum foil to "precook" them for about 10 to 15 minutes. When we uncovered the pan and poked a fork into one stick, it wasn't mushy, and resisted just a little. So far, so good. Then we slid the uncovered baking sheet back into the oven until the moisture had burned off and the carrots took on nut-brown caramelized streaks, about 30 minutes. Bingo. These carrots were tender-firm and particularly sweet, with minimal withering.

To add just a drop more moisture—and considerably nuttier flavor—to the pan, we swapped the oil for butter's rich flavor and slight water content. (To keep drops of butter from burning to the baking sheet, we lined the pan with foil or parchment paper.) Tender, creamy, and deeply sweet, these carrots had earned their place on our dinner table, and the simple roasting technique—which works just as well with other vegetables like parsnips, fennel, and shallots sharing the pan—a top spot in our recipe file.

ROASTED CARROTS

Roasted Carrots

SERVES 4 TO 6

Most bagged carrots come in a variety of sizes and must be cut lengthwise for evenly cooked results. After halving the carrots crosswise, leave small (less than ½ inch in diameter) pieces whole; halve medium pieces (½ to 1-inch diameter), and quarter large pieces (over 1 inch).

1½ pounds carrots, peeled, halved crosswise, and
     cut lengthwise if necessary (see note)
 2 tablespoons unsalted butter, melted
     Table salt and ground black pepper

1. Adjust an oven rack to the middle position and heat the oven to 425 degrees. In a large bowl, combine the carrots with the butter, ½ teaspoon salt, and ¼ teaspoon pepper; toss to coat. Transfer the carrots to a foil- or parchment-lined rimmed baking sheet and spread in a single layer.

2. Cover the baking sheet tightly with foil and roast for 15 minutes. Remove the foil and continue to roast, stirring twice, until well browned and tender, 30 to 35 minutes. Transfer to a serving platter, season with salt and pepper to taste, and serve.

VARIATIONS

Roasted Carrots and Fennel with Toasted Almonds and Lemon

Follow the recipe for Roasted Carrots, reducing the amount of carrots to 1 pound. Add ½ large fennel bulb, cored (see page 118) and sliced ½ inch thick, to the bowl with the carrots and roast as directed. Toss the roasted vegetables with ¼ cup toasted sliced almonds, 1 teaspoon fresh lemon juice, and 2 teaspoons chopped fresh parsley leaves before serving in step 2.

Roasted Carrots and Parsnips with Rosemary

Follow the recipe for Roasted Carrots, reducing the amount of carrots to 1 pound. Add ½ pound peeled parsnips, cut like the carrots, and 1 teaspoon chopped fresh rosemary leaves to the bowl with the carrots and roast as directed. Toss the roasted vegetables with 2 teaspoons chopped fresh parsley leaves before serving in step 2.

Roasted Carrots and Shallots with Lemon and Thyme

Follow the recipe for Roasted Carrots, reducing the amount of carrots to 1 pound. Add 6 medium shallots (about ½ pound), peeled and halved lengthwise, and 1 teaspoon chopped fresh thyme leaves to the bowl with the carrots and roast as directed. Toss the roasted vegetables with 1 teaspoon fresh lemon juice before serving in step 2.

Roasted Carrots with Chermoula Sauce

Follow the recipe for Roasted Carrots as directed. While the carrots roast, heat 1 tablespoon extra-virgin olive oil, 1 garlic clove, minced or pressed through a garlic press, ½ teaspoon sweet paprika, ¼ teaspoon ground cumin, and a pinch cayenne pepper in a small skillet over medium-low heat; cook, stirring frequently until sizzling and fragrant, about 3 minutes. Transfer the sauce to a small bowl and set aside until ready to use. Toss the carrots with the sauce, 1 tablespoon fresh chopped cilantro, and 2 teaspoons lemon juice before serving in step 2.

EQUIPMENT CORNER

JAMIE OLIVER'S FLAVOUR SHAKER

Unconventional kitchen gadgets seem that they're always either advertised by a celebrity chef, or they have a catchy, clever name. The Jamie Oliver Flavour Shaker ($29.95) has both—but unlike numerous other gadgets that get lost in the back of the kitchen drawer, we found this one to be incredibly useful. It's akin to an enclosed mortar and pestle: You open up the plastic cup, put in whole garlic cloves or spices, close it tight, and shake. Thanks to a heavy Ping-Pong-sized ceramic ball rolling around inside, the ingredients quickly break down. Without much effort, we were able to grind cumin and mustard seeds, crack lots of pepper, and create ¼ cup of salad dressing (first pulverizing garlic, then adding oil and vinegar). We recommend this tool for easy spice crushing and quick dressings, and when you're done, it can go straight into the dishwasher.

DEEP-DISH *Pizza*

Sprinkling the crust with cheese before topping the pizza with tomato sauce is Chicago tradition. In addition, the cheese forms a barrier between the sauce and dough, so the crust bakes up extra crisp.

IF YOU'RE NOT FROM CHICAGO, CHANCES ARE DEEP-DISH PIZZA IS less a gustatory delight than a guilty pleasure. Served with a pitcher of beer to wash down the bready crust, heartburn-inducing sauce, and overload of cheese, this pizza at best recalls college days when an outing to a local chain restaurant was considered a big treat. But authentic deep-dish pizza is something to savor, with a rich, buttery, almost biscuit-like crust, a bright tomato sauce, and gooey cheese. We set out to capture the Chicago ideal for great deep-dish pan pizza at home.

Chopped salads seem to have migrated onto just about every restaurant menu across the country—from fast-food joints and chain restaurants to five-star establishments. It's easy to see their appeal—bite-size pieces of vegetables, lettuce, cheese, and sometimes fruit and nuts. But too often, these salads disappoint, with watery produce and unbalanced dressings. We set out to develop a variety of chopped salads that would deliver crisp vegetables and full flavor in every forkful.

DEEP-DISH PIZZA

✓ WHY THIS RECIPE WORKS: For an authentic deep-dish pizza crust—one with an airy, flaky inside, a lightly crisp outside, and a rich taste that could hold its own under any topping, we relied on a pizza dough enriched with creamy butter and crunchy cornmeal. Rolling and folding the dough gave the crust delicious layers and refrigerating it during the second rise allowed the butter to chill, resulting in a high and flaky rise.

UNLESS YOU'VE BEEN TO CHICAGO, YOU MAY DISMISS deep-dish pizza as a doughy, tasteless pizza that's nothing more than a platform for loading on cheese and toppings. But as we discovered on a trip to Chicago, the real deal has little to do with the overwrought impostors served up in franchise pizzerias. Sure, a Chicago crust is thick, but instead of being bland and breadlike, it offers the textural contrast of a good biscuit—airy inside, lightly crisp outside, and flaky throughout, with a rich taste that can hold its own.

We began our research at Chicago's original Pizzeria Uno, the 1943 birthplace of deep-dish pizza (not to be confused with the chain Uno Chicago Grill), and continued to such legendary spots as Gino's East and Lou Malnati's. Most of the pies we sampled shared the same high sides, rich and flaky crust, and toppings that reversed the usual order—first a blanket of mozzarella, maybe some sausage, and finally tomato sauce. None of these pizzerias would give us their recipes, but taste alone told us the key rested with two unorthodox ingredients: cornmeal and butter.

Back in Boston, a little research unearthed dozens of recipes claiming to replicate authentic Chicago deep-dish pizza that proved at least part of our hunch right: Cornmeal was definitely part of the deal. But while all the recipes we found listed far more fat than what you find in classic pizza dough (which relies on just a few tablespoons of olive oil), only a handful actually called for butter. And those that did simply melted it and worked it into a recipe that, but for ½ cup cornmeal and a tiny bit of sugar, sounded an awful lot like classic pizza dough:

Combine flour, cornmeal, salt, sugar, and yeast in a bowl, add melted butter and water, transfer ingredients to a standing mixer, and knead into a dough. Allow the dough to rise, divide it in half, and let it rise again until doubled in size. Then, instead of stretching each dough ball into a circle to be baked directly on a pizza stone, press the dough into a 9-inch round pan, add some toppings, and bake it on a stone in a 500-degree oven.

First impression? Not bad. The crust was more chewy than flaky, but the buttery flavor came through, and the cornmeal added nice earthiness and crunch.

But how to transform the crust from breadlike to biscuitlike? Maybe the answer had to do with biscuit techniques. First, we swapped melted butter for cold butter: cold butter melts in the oven and then steam fills the thin spaces left behind, resulting in flaky, buttery layers. Second, we traded our standing mixer for a food processor; for biscuits, we use it to cut butter into the dry ingredients instead of kneading the dough. Third, following biscuit protocol, we waited to add our liquid—water—until after the butter and dry ingredients were combined. We were cautiously optimistic, but our hopes soon crumbled—literally. This crust was so brittle it fell apart like a cracker.

We returned to the standing mixer and melted butter. While pondering other flaky baked goods, it occurred to us: Why not try laminating? This baking term refers to the layering of butter and dough used to create baked goods like ultra-flaky croissants, Danishes, and puff pastry through a sequence of rolling and folding. After melting part of the butter, we mixed it with the dough, allowed the dough to rise, and rolled it into a 15 by 12-inch rectangle. We spread the remaining 4 tablespoons of slightly softened butter over the surface and rolled the dough into a cylinder to create layers of buttery dough. To amplify this effect, we then flattened the cylinder into a rectangle, divided it in half, and folded each half into thirds, like a business letter.

So far, so good—except all that handling caused the temperature of the dough to rise. By the time we patted each half into a ball and tried to roll the balls flat, the dough had warmed so much that the butter had practically melted, leading to a crust that was more tender and breadlike than flaky—we were right back where

CHICAGO DEEP-DISH PIZZA

we started. The solution? Moving the dough into the refrigerator for its second rise so that any butter that had melted or gotten overly soft could harden right back up again. This gave us a pizza with just the flaky texture we wanted.

Our only additional tweak was adding 2 tablespoons of oil to each pan to crisp the edges. This worked so well that we wondered if the pizza stone was still necessary. One more test and we had the answer: It wasn't.

With our crust all set, we considered the cheese and the sauce—in that order. Sliced mozzarella, common to most recipes, had been our starting point, but when we pitted it against freshly shredded mozzarella, the latter won out for its smoother texture and the way it formed a consistent barrier between dough and sauce.

As for the sauce, we decided to try our Quick Tomato Sauce, which creates surprisingly complex flavor in a mere 15 minutes from canned crushed tomatoes. For a slightly thicker rendition that was more compatible with our Chicago pizza, we simmered it for an extra 15 minutes. This bright-tasting sauce won raves.

More than 100 pizzas later, we were satisfied with our own rich and tasty homage to this distinctive Midwestern pie.

Chicago Deep-Dish Pizza
MAKES TWO 9-INCH PIZZAS

You will need a standing mixer with a dough hook for this recipe. Place a damp kitchen towel under the mixer and watch it at all times during kneading to prevent it from wobbling off the counter. Handle the dough with slightly oiled hands to prevent sticking. The test kitchen prefers Dragone Whole Milk Mozzarella; part-skim mozzarella can also be used, but avoid preshredded cheese here. Our preferred brands of crushed tomatoes are Tuttorosso and Muir Glen. Grate the onion on the large holes of a box grater.

DOUGH
3¼ cups (16¼ ounces) unbleached all-purpose flour

½ cup (2¾ ounces) yellow cornmeal

2¼ teaspoons (about 1 envelope) instant or
    rapid-rise yeast

2 teaspoons sugar

1½ teaspoons table salt

1¼ cups water, room temperature

3 tablespoons unsalted butter, melted, plus
   4 tablespoons, softened

1 teaspoon plus 4 tablespoons olive oil

SAUCE

- 2 **tablespoons unsalted butter**
- ¼ **cup grated onion (see note)**
- ¼ **teaspoon dried oregano**
  Table salt
- 2 **garlic cloves, minced**
- 1 **(28-ounce) can crushed tomatoes**
- ¼ **teaspoon sugar**
- 2 **tablespoons chopped fresh basil**
- 1 **tablespoon extra-virgin olive oil**
  Ground black pepper

TOPPINGS

- 1 **pound mozzarella, shredded (about 4 cups)**
- ¼ **cup grated Parmesan cheese**

1. FOR THE DOUGH: Mix the flour, cornmeal, yeast, sugar, and salt in the bowl of a standing mixer fitted with the dough hook on low speed until incorporated, about 1 minute. Add the water and melted butter and mix on low speed until fully combined, 1 to 2 minutes, scraping the sides and bottom of the bowl as needed. Increase the mixer speed to medium and knead until the dough is glossy and smooth and pulls away from sides of the bowl, 4 to 5 minutes. (The dough will only pull away from the sides while the mixer is on. When the mixer is off, the dough will fall back to the sides.)

2. Using your fingers, coat a large bowl with 1 teaspoon of the olive oil, rubbing excess oil from your fingers onto the blade of a rubber spatula. Using the oiled spatula, transfer the dough to the oiled bowl, turning once to oil the top. Cover the bowl tightly with plastic wrap. Let the dough rise at room temperature until nearly doubled in volume, 45 to 60 minutes.

3. FOR THE SAUCE: While the dough rises, heat the butter in a medium saucepan over medium heat until melted. Add the onion, oregano, and ½ teaspoon salt and cook, stirring occasionally, until the liquid has evaporated and the onion is golden brown, about 5 minutes. Add the garlic and cook until fragrant, about 30 seconds. Stir in the tomatoes and sugar, increase the heat to high, and bring to a simmer. Lower the heat to medium-low and simmer until the sauce has reduced to 2½ cups, 25 to

MAKING THE DEEP-DISH PIZZA CRUST

1. After rolling out the dough into a 15 by 12-inch rectangle, spread the softened butter over the dough, leaving a ½-inch border along the edges.

2. Roll the dough into a tight cylinder, starting at the short end closest to you.

3. Flatten the dough cylinder into an 18 by 4-inch rectangle, then halve the cylinder crosswise.

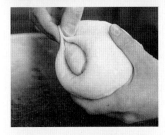

4. Fold each dough half into thirds to form a ball and pinch the seams shut; let the dough balls rise in the refrigerator for 40 to 50 minutes.

5. After rolling each ball of dough into a 13-inch disk about ¼ inch thick, transfer the dough disks to the oiled pans and lightly press the dough into the pans, pressing it into the corners and up the sides.

30 minutes. Off the heat, stir in the basil and oil, then season with salt and pepper to taste.

4. TO LAMINATE THE DOUGH: Adjust an oven rack to the lowest position and heat the oven to 425 degrees. Using a rubber spatula, turn the dough out onto a dry work surface and roll into a 15 by 12-inch rectangle. Following the photos on page 113, use an offset spatula to spread the softened butter over the surface of the dough, leaving a ½-inch border along the edges. Starting at the short end, roll the dough into a tight cylinder. With the seam side down, flatten the cylinder into an 18 by 4-inch rectangle. Cut the rectangle in half crosswise. Working with one half, fold the dough into thirds like a business letter, then pinch the seams together to form a ball. Repeat with the remaining half of dough. Return the dough balls to the oiled bowl, cover tightly with plastic wrap, and let rise in the refrigerator until nearly doubled in volume, 40 to 50 minutes.

5. Coat two 9-inch round cake pans with 2 tablespoons olive oil each. Transfer one dough ball to a dry work surface and roll out into a 13-inch disk about ¼ inch thick. Transfer the dough round to a cake pan by rolling the dough loosely around the rolling pin, then unrolling the dough into the pan. Lightly press the dough into the pan, working it into the corners and 1 inch up the sides.

If the dough resists stretching, let it relax 5 minutes before trying again. Repeat with the remaining dough ball.

6. For each pizza, sprinkle 2 cups of the mozzarella evenly over the surface of the dough. Spread 1¼ cups of the tomato sauce over the cheese and sprinkle 2 tablespoons of the Parmesan over the sauce for each pizza. Bake until the crust is golden brown, 20 to 30 minutes. Remove the pizza from the oven and let rest 10 minutes before slicing and serving.

VARIATIONS

Chicago Deep-Dish Pizza with Sausage
Remove the casings from 1 pound hot Italian sausage. Cook the sausage in a 12-inch nonstick skillet over medium-high heat, breaking it into ½-inch pieces with a wooden spoon, until browned, 3 to 5 minutes. Transfer the sausage to a paper towel–lined plate. Follow the recipe for Chicago Deep-Dish Pizza, spreading the cooked sausage evenly over the surface of the mozzarella in step 6.

Chicago Deep-Dish Pizza with Olives and Ricotta
Follow the recipe for Chicago Deep-Dish Pizza, sprinkling 2 tablespoons coarsely chopped kalamata olives evenly over the sauce in step 6. Using 2 tablespoons ricotta cheese per pizza, dot the surface with teaspoons of cheese. Bake as directed, sprinkling ¼ cup coarsely chopped arugula over the surface of each pizza after removing them from the oven.

NOTES FROM THE TEST KITCHEN

DEEP-DISH IMPERSONATORS

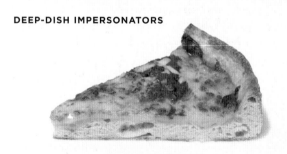

BLAND 'N' BREADY
If it's too bready, like this slice from Uno Chicago Grill, it's not the real deal.

BETTER CHOPPED SALADS

✔ WHY THIS RECIPE WORKS: To prevent the cut-up produce in our chopped salad from exuding moisture, we turned to tricks like seeding the cucumbers and quartering grape tomatoes before salting them to expose more surface area to the salt. An assertive combination of equal parts oil and vinegar delivered the bright acidic flavor we were looking for in a dressing for chopped salad. Briefly marinating other ingredients in the dressing delivered an additional flavor boost.

CHOPPED SALADS HAD THEIR HEYDAY IN THE 1950S AS a popular menu item for ladies who lunched. If you encounter a good version, it's easy to see why they're making a comeback. The best are lively, thoughtfully chosen compositions of lettuce, vegetables, and sometimes fruit cut into bite-sized pieces, with supporting players like nuts and cheese contributing hearty flavors and textures. Unfortunately, we've had more experience with the mediocre kind. These are little better than a random collection of cut-up produce from the crisper drawer, exuding moisture that turns the salad watery and bland.

Salting some of the vegetables to remove excess moisture was an obvious first step. We singled out two of the worst offenders: cucumbers and tomatoes. We halved a cucumber and scooped out its watery seeds before dicing it, tossing it with salt, and allowing it to drain over a colander. After 15 minutes, the cuke had shed a full tablespoon of water. As for the tomatoes, we had been experimenting with grape tomatoes in a Mediterranean-inspired salad. Seeding them was out of the question; much of the tomato flavor is concentrated in the seeds and surrounding jelly. But we did cut them into quarters to expose more surface area to the salt, releasing 2 tablespoons of liquid from a pint of tomatoes.

As we tried more recipes, it became clear that the dressings weren't doing anything for the chopped salads. Most recipes called for a ratio of 3 parts oil to 1 part vinegar—the same proportions as for a leafy green salad. A more assertive blend of equal parts oil and vinegar was far better at delivering the bright, acidic kick needed in salads boasting hearty flavors and chunky textures.

But could we use the dressing to even greater advantage? Tossing a green salad just before serving prevents the tender leaves from absorbing too much dressing and turning soggy. But a little flavor absorption by some of the sturdier components of a chopped salad would actually be a good thing. Marinating ingredients such as bell peppers, onions, and fruit in the dressing for just five minutes before adding cheese and other tender components brought a welcome flavor boost.

We were now ready to focus on the composition of the salads. We determined that mild, crisp romaine and firm-tender cucumber were musts in every salad, as was the bite of red onion. We also liked the crunch of nuts along with the softer texture of cheese. For a Mediterranean combo, we added chickpeas, feta, and parsley to the standard mix. Another version boasted red pepper with pear, cranberry, blue cheese, and pistachios; a third featured fennel and apples with tarragon, goat cheese, and walnuts. These vibrant, full-flavored salads are so good, they're not just for lunch—try them for dinner too.

MEDITERRANEAN CHOPPED SALAD

Mediterranean Chopped Salad

SERVES 4 TO 6

For information on our top-rated brand of feta cheese, see page 84.

- 1 cucumber, peeled, halved lengthwise, seeded, and cut into ½-inch dice (about 1¼ cups) (see page 118)
- 1 pint grape tomatoes, quartered (about 1½ cups)
  Table salt
- 3 tablespoons extra-virgin olive oil
- 3 tablespoons red wine vinegar
- 1 medium garlic clove, minced or pressed through a garlic press (about 1 teaspoon)
- 1 (15-ounce) can chickpeas, drained and rinsed
- ½ cup pitted kalamata olives, chopped
- ½ cup chopped fresh parsley leaves
- ½ small red onion, minced (about ¼ cup)
- 1 romaine heart, cut into ½-inch pieces (about 3 cups)
- 4 ounces feta cheese, crumbled (about 1 cup)
  Ground black pepper

1. Combine the cucumber, tomatoes, and 1 teaspoon salt in a colander set over a bowl and drain for 15 minutes.

2. Whisk the oil, vinegar, and garlic together in a large bowl. Add the drained cucumber and tomatoes, chickpeas, olives, parsley, and onion. Toss and let stand at room temperature to blend the flavors, 5 minutes.

3. Add the romaine and feta and toss to combine. Season with salt and pepper to taste and serve.

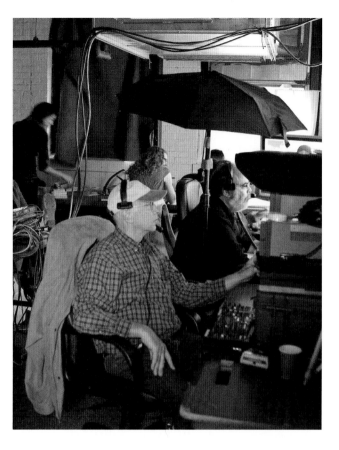

Fennel and Apple Chopped Salad

SERVES 4 TO 6

Braeburn, Jonagold, or Red Delicious apples all work well here. The cheese is sprinkled on the salads after plating because goat cheese tends to clump when tossed.

- 1 cucumber, peeled, halved lengthwise, seeded, and cut into ½-inch dice (about 1¼ cups) (see page 118)
  Table salt
- 3 tablespoons extra-virgin olive oil
- 3 tablespoons white wine vinegar
- 2 apples, cored and cut into ¼-inch dice (about 2 cups)
- ½ small red onion, minced (about ¼ cup)
- 1 fennel bulb, trimmed of stalks, halved lengthwise, cored, and cut into ¼-inch dice (about 1½ cups) (see page 118)
- ¼ cup chopped fresh tarragon leaves
- 1 romaine heart, cut into ½-inch pieces (about 3 cups)
- ½ cup chopped walnuts, toasted
  Ground back pepper
- 4 ounces crumbled goat cheese (about 1 cup)

1. Combine the cucumber and ½ teaspoon salt in a colander set over a bowl and drain for 15 minutes.

2. Whisk the oil and vinegar together in a large bowl. Add the drained cucumber, apples, onion, fennel, and tarragon. Toss and let stand at room temperature to blend the flavors, 5 minutes.

3. Add the romaine and walnuts and toss to combine. Season with salt and pepper to taste. Divide the salad among individual plates; top each with some goat cheese and serve.

Pear and Cranberry Chopped Salad

SERVES 4 TO 6

Chopped dried cherries can be substituted for the cranberries.

- 1 cucumber, peeled, halved lengthwise, seeded, and cut into ½-inch dice (about 1¼ cups) (see below)
  Table salt
- 3 tablespoons extra-virgin olive oil
- 3 tablespoons sherry vinegar
- 1 red bell pepper, stemmed, seeded, and cut into ¼-inch pieces (about 1 cup)
- 1 ripe but firm pear, cut into ¼-inch pieces (about 1 cup)
- ½ cup dried cranberries
- ½ small red onion, minced (about ¼ cup)
- 1 romaine heart, cut into ½-inch pieces (about 3 cups)
- 4 ounces blue cheese, crumbled (about 1 cup)
- ½ cup pistachios, toasted and chopped coarse
  Ground black pepper

1. Combine the cucumber and ½ teaspoon salt in a colander set over a bowl and drain for 15 minutes.

2. Whisk the oil and vinegar together in a large bowl. Add the drained cucumber, bell pepper, pear, cranberries, and onion. Toss and let stand at room temperature to blend flavors, 5 minutes.

3. Add the romaine, blue cheese, and pistachios and toss to combine. Season with salt and pepper to taste and serve.

NOTES FROM THE TEST KITCHEN

SEEDING AND CHOPPING CUCUMBERS

1. Peel the cucumber, cut it in half lengthwise, and scoop out the seeds with a spoon.

2. Cut each half crosswise into 2 to 3-inch pieces. Place the pieces cut side up on a cutting board, then slice them lengthwise into even batons.

3. Cut the batons crosswise into an even dice.

TRIMMING AND CORING FENNEL

1. Cut off the stems and feathery fronds.

2. Trim a very thin slice from the base from the bulb and remove any tough or blemished outer layers.

3. After cutting the bulb in half through the base, use a small, sharp knife to remove the pyramid-shaped core. Slice or chop the fennel as directed.

Radish and Orange Chopped Salad

SERVES 4 TO 6

Pepitas, or pumpkin seeds, are available at most super-markets and natural foods stores. Don't use an overripe avocado in the salad; it will break down and make the salad gluey.

1   cucumber, peeled, halved lengthwise, seeded, and cut into ½-inch dice (about 1¼ cups) (see page 118)
    Table salt

3   tablespoons extra-virgin olive oil

3   tablespoons juice from 2 limes

1   medium garlic clove, minced or pressed through a garlic press (about 1 teaspoon)

10   radishes, halved and sliced thin (about 1½ cups)

2   oranges, peeled, cut into ½-inch pieces, and drained (about 1 cup)

1   ripe but firm avocado, peeled, pitted, and cut into ½-inch pieces

½   cup roughly chopped fresh cilantro leaves

½   small red onion, minced (about ¼ cup)

1   romaine heart, cut into ½-inch pieces about 3 cups)

3   ounces Manchego cheese, shredded (about 1 cup)

½   cup unsalted pepitas, toasted
    Ground black pepper

1. Combine the cucumber and ½ teaspoon salt in a colander set over a bowl and drain for 15 minutes.

2. Whisk the oil, lime juice, and garlic together in a large bowl. Add the drained cucumber, radishes, oranges, avocado, cilantro, and onion. Toss and let stand at room temperature to blend the flavors, 5 minutes.

3. Add the romaine, Manchego, and pepitas and toss to combine. Season with salt and pepper to taste and serve.

STEAK *Frites*

Cooking our fries in two batches is one secret to ensuring that they will be crisp enough to stand up to a steak's rich juices.

HOW DO YOU SAY MEAT AND POTATOES IN FRENCH? *STEAK FRITES.* This bistro classic is a must-have if visiting Paris. But let's get real—most of us aren't globe-trotting types, so we need to get our fix closer to home. But that means we're out of luck because American restaurant versions often miss the mark, with steak that's just not as flavorful as the Parisian version and fries that aren't quite as thin and elegant as French batons. Even worse, the fries inevitably turn soggy under the steak's juices. We wanted rich, beefy-tasting French-style steak and fries to match—thin and supremely crisp, from first bite to last.

A salad of crisp greens dressed with a simple vinaigrette is the perfect starter to a rich steak frites dinner. But sometimes simple can turn out to be anything but. A few problems include unbalanced flavor and vinaigrettes that separate as soon as the greens are dressed so that one mouthful is bitingly acidic, while the next is oily and bland. We wanted a foolproof vinaigrette that delivered bright flavor, clung evenly to our salad, and remained emulsified until we were ready to move on to the next course.

STEAK FRITES

✔ **WHY THIS RECIPE WORKS:** To create the steak frites of our Parisian dreams, we first determined that the fries needed to be cooked in two batches, a procedure that minimizes the drop in oil temperature that naturally occurs when potatoes are added to frying oil. Our real breakthrough in our recipe, however, occurred when we coated the fries with an extra layer of starch, which added a protective sheath around each fry. For the steaks, we found that thicker rib eyes gave us more time to get a nice sear without overcooking the middle, so that the meat was juicy through and through.

IN PARISIAN BISTROS, THE STEAK IS ALWAYS PERFECTLY cooked and the fries are fluffy on the inside and crisp on the outside, even when bathed in juices from the meat. We've ordered our fair share of steak frites in American restaurants, but they often miss the mark. The fries are usually too soggy and the steak just isn't as flavorful. Great steak frites shouldn't have to require a flight across the Atlantic, so we set out to re-create authentic steak frites ourselves.

From past test kitchen work, we knew that high-starch russet potatoes make the best fries. Most recipes call for blanching the sliced potatoes in moderately hot oil to cook them through and then finishing them in hotter oil to render them golden and crispy. Following these steps was easy; achieving the desired result of a super-crisp fry that stood up to the steak and its juices was monumentally difficult. No matter what we tried, the fries were too tough, too soggy, or too greasy.

When we cooked the potatoes in a single batch, the fries were very greasy. By cooking the potatoes in two batches, we were able to increase the ratio of oil to potatoes. This also reduced the drop in oil temperature that naturally occurs when the potatoes are added.

To find out whether the type of fat played a role in crispness, we tried cooking the potatoes in vegetable oil, peanut oil, and shortening. The fries cooked in vegetable oil were bland and almost watery. The fries cooked in vegetable shortening and peanut oil were both crisp, but the shortening left a heavy aftertaste, while the fries cooked in peanut oil were light and earthy-tasting.

Following these steps resulted in better fries. However, the fries were still not crisp enough to stand up to the steak juices. Some recipes suggest soaking the potatoes in cold water before they are cooked. Compared with potatoes that were fried without presoaking, the soaked potatoes made slightly crispier fries with more even coloration. Other recipes call for "resting" the fries between the first and second frying. After 10 minutes of resting, we noticed that the starches on the exterior of the blanched fries had formed a thin film that indeed helped the fries become crisp once they were fried again. We were making progress, but we still weren't completely satisfied.

It was time to try some more unusual ideas, so we turned to the Internet. We landed on the website of a company that makes frozen fries and learned that they spray their potatoes with a thin potato starch–based coating. After more research, we realized starch was also a key ingredient in many fast-food fries. Could an extra layer of starch be the key to crispier fries?

We alternately tossed uncooked potatoes with cornstarch, potato starch, and arrowroot and fried up each batch. We saw an immediate improvement. Our science advisor explained that the starch was absorbing some of the surface moisture on the potatoes to form a gel-like coating. This coating made a super-protective sheath around each fry, helping create the shatteringly crisp crust we had been working toward. After more tests, we determined that two tablespoons of cornstarch provided a flavorless coating that guaranteed crisp fries.

In France, steak frites is usually prepared with a cut called entrecôte (literally, "between the ribs"). Although you won't find this steak in American supermarkets, it's similar to our rib-eye steak—both are cut from the same area as prime rib. The one big difference is that entrecôte steaks are quite thin, usually just ½ to ¾ inch thick. Even if your butcher will cut entrecôte steaks, we discovered that they're not the best choice for our recipe. These thin steaks work well in restaurants, where blazing hot burners reign and steaks are cooked one at a time. With a weaker home stove and four steaks in the pan, we found that thicker rib eyes gave us more time to get a nice sear on the meat without overcooking the middle.

STEAK FRITES

We had finally created a recipe that could almost rival the Parisian bistro meals we remembered. The only hitch: The steak was a little bland. Maybe French beef is better? Then we recalled that most bistros spoon a flavored butter over the steak. Spread over the steaks while they rested, the herb butter added the exclamation point to this bistro classic. We no longer have to fly across the Atlantic to enjoy great steak frites.

NOTES FROM THE TEST KITCHEN

SQUARING THE SPUD

The best way to uniformly cut fries is to start by trimming a thin slice from each side of the potato. Once the potato is "squared," you can slice it into ¼-inch planks and then cut each plank into ¼-inch fries.

ONE STEAK BECOMES TWO

In order to have four steaks that fit in a skillet at the same time, it is necessary to buy two 1-pound steaks and cut them in half according to their thickness. If your steaks are 1¼ to 1¾ inches thick, cut them in half vertically into small, thick steaks. If your steaks are thicker than 1¾ inches, cut them in half horizontally into two thinner steaks.

THIN STEAK
Cut in half vertically.

THICK STEAK
Cut in half horizontally.

Steak Frites
SERVES 4

Make sure to dry the potatoes well before tossing them with the cornstarch. For safety, use a Dutch oven with a capacity of at least 7 quarts. Use refined peanut oil (such as Planters) to fry the potatoes, not toasted peanut oil. A 12-inch skillet is essential for cooking four steaks at once. The recipe can be prepared through step 4 up to 2 hours in advance; turn off the heat under the oil, turning the heat back to medium when you start step 6. The ingredients can be halved to serve two—keep the oil amount the same and forgo blanching and frying the potatoes in batches.

HERB BUTTER

- 4 tablespoons (½ stick) unsalted butter, softened
- ½ shallot, minced (about 1 tablespoon)
- 1 garlic clove, minced or pressed through a garlic press (about 1 teaspoon)
- 1 tablespoon minced fresh parsley leaves
- 1 tablespoon minced fresh chives
- ¼ teaspoon table salt
- ¼ teaspoon ground black pepper

STEAK AND POTATOES

- 2½ pounds russet potatoes (about 4 large), sides squared off (see photo at left), cut lengthwise into ¼ by ¼-inch fries
- 2 tablespoons cornstarch
- 3 quarts peanut oil
- 1 tablespoon vegetable oil
- 2 (1-pound) boneless rib-eye steaks, cut in half (see photos at left)
  Table salt and ground pepper

1. FOR THE BUTTER: Combine all the ingredients in a medium bowl; set aside.

2. FOR THE POTATOES: Rinse the cut potatoes in a large bowl under cold running water until the water turns clear. Cover with cold water and refrigerate for at least 30 minutes or up to 12 hours.

3. Pour off the water, spread the potatoes onto kitchen towels, and dry thoroughly. Transfer the potatoes to a large bowl and toss with the cornstarch until evenly coated. Transfer the potatoes to a wire rack set over a rimmed baking sheet and let rest until a fine white coating forms, about 20 minutes.

4. Meanwhile, heat the peanut oil over medium heat to 325 degrees in a large, heavy-bottomed Dutch oven fitted with a clip-on candy thermometer.

5. Add half of the potatoes, a handful at a time, to the hot oil and increase the heat to high. Fry, stirring with a mesh spider or slotted spoon, until the potatoes start to turn from white to blond, 4 to 5 minutes. (The oil temperature will drop about 75 degrees during this frying.) Transfer the fries to a thick paper bag or paper towels. Return the oil to 325 degrees and repeat with the remaining potatoes. Reduce the heat to medium and let the fries cool while cooking the steaks, at least 10 minutes.

6. FOR THE STEAKS: Heat the vegetable oil in a 12-inch skillet over medium-high heat until smoking. Meanwhile, season the steaks with salt and pepper. Lay the steaks in the pan, leaving ¼ inch between them. Cook, without moving the steaks, until well browned, about 4 minutes. Flip the steaks and continue to cook until the center registers 120 degrees for rare to medium-rare (3 to 7 minutes) on an instant-read thermometer. Transfer the steaks to a large plate, top with the herb butter, and tent loosely with foil; let rest while finishing the fries.

7. Increase the heat under the Dutch oven to high and heat the oil to 375 degrees. Add half of the fries, a handful at a time, and fry until golden brown and puffed, 2 to 3 minutes. Transfer to a thick paper bag or paper towels. Return the oil to 375 degrees and repeat with the remaining fries. Season the fries with salt to taste and serve immediately with the steaks.

RATING SPATULAS

Spatulas are such basic kitchen tools, there shouldn't be much variation when it comes to performance across brands, right? Wrong. We picked up a number of metal and plastic spatulas—metal for use with traditional cookware and plastic for use with nonstick pots and pans—and flipped fried eggs, pancakes, and burgers; transferred cookies from baking sheets to cooling racks; and cut and served lasagna. Overall, we were disappointed with most of them; some were awkwardly shaped, making them difficult to maneuver, while others had too-thick blades that shaved the bottoms off fresh-baked cookies. A number of plastic contenders melted at lower temperatures than stipulated by the manufacturer. In the end, we identified the following traits to look for in a spatula: the front edge should be razor-thin to slip easily under food; the blade should be slightly curved to cradle food and have slots to help ease friction; and the handle should be neither too long nor too short to be manageable (about 6 inches is best). Brands are listed in order of preference. See www.americastestkitchen.com for updates to this testing.

METAL

HIGHLY RECOMMENDED

WÜSTHOF Gourmet Turner/Fish Spatula (model #4433)
PRICE: $34.95 FRONT EDGE: 0.83 mm
MATERIAL: High-carbon stainless steel with sharpened edge, polypropylene handle
PERFORMANCE: ★★★
COMMENTS: A flawless performer in all tests. It supported a 4-pound brick without the slightest slip, and its sharp, gently uptilted front edge could slip under anything—and hold it in place.

OXO Good Grips Flexible Turner—Steel (model #34491)
PRICE: $7.99 FRONT EDGE: 0.2 mm
MATERIAL: Spring-steel head, nonslip handle
PERFORMANCE: ★★★
COMMENTS: This Best Buy looked flimsy, but excelled across the board. It's slim, with a gently angled handle and a nicely proportioned head that offers moderate support.

RECOMMENDED WITH RESERVATIONS

LAMSONSHARP 2-3-Inch x 4-Inch Flexible Flared Turner (model #39546)
PRICE: $25 FRONT EDGE: 0.67 mm
MATERIAL: High-carbon stainless steel with POM (molded plastic) handle
PERFORMANCE: ★★
COMMENTS: This compact, sturdy turner hoisted a big burger and heavy lasagna. But "flexible" was a misnomer; testers found it stiff.

WMF Profi Plus 12¾-Inch Stainless Steel Slotted Turner (model #1871056030)
PRICE: $17.90 FRONT EDGE: 0.53 mm
MATERIAL: 18/10 stainless steel
PERFORMANCE: ★★
COMMENTS: We liked this model's slim front edge and sturdy construction. But the curved front corners of the head were inconvenient for getting into the corners of a pan or cutting lasagna.

PLASTIC

HIGHLY RECOMMENDED

MATFER BOURGEAT Pelton Spatula (model #112420)
PRICE: $7.50 FRONT EDGE: 0.92 mm
MATERIAL: Exoglass (polyamide plastic)
PERFORMANCE: ★★★ DURABILITY: ★★½
COMMENTS: Comfortable from any angle, this spatula boasts a thin front edge and moderately flexible head. It melted slightly at 380 degrees, despite the manufacturer's claim that it was heat resistant to 430 degrees.

RECOMMENDED WITH RESERVATIONS

OXO Good Grips Silicone Flexible Turner (model #1071536)
PRICE: $6.95 FRONT EDGE: 1.72 mm
MATERIAL: Stainless steel with silicone coating
PERFORMANCE: ★★ DURABILITY: ★★★
COMMENTS: Nicely proportioned, with a comfortable handle and angle similar to its flexible steel sibling. The soft silicone coating was impervious to even searing heat, but made the head far too thick for optimal cooking performance.

PYREX Flexible Turner (model #1083742)
PRICE: $8.95 FRONT EDGE: 1.27 mm
MATERIAL: Nylon
PERFORMANCE: ★★ DURABILITY: ★★
COMMENTS: In an 8-inch pan, this turner's super-wide, round head filled all available space. It also melted into stringy fibers at a fairly low temperature (353 degrees, though the manufacturer claimed it was good up to 400 degrees).

NOT RECOMMENDED

AMCO Houseworks Large Nylon and Stainless Steel Offset Slotted Spatula (model #8348)
PRICE: $6.50 FRONT EDGE: 1.11 mm
MATERIAL: Nylon head, stainless steel handle
PERFORMANCE: ★½ DURABILITY: ★★
COMMENTS: While this model's narrowness (3 inches across) was a plus, its nearly 8-inch-long head was too long and awkward to handle, and too thick to maneuver under cookies and burgers.

FOOLPROOF VINAIGRETTE

✔ WHY THIS RECIPE WORKS: To come up with a well-balanced vinaigrette that won't separate, we chose high-end oil and vinegar and whisked them together with a little mayonnaise, which acts as an emulsifier. Choosing the flavoring ingredients was all that was needed to finish our perfect dressing for salad greens.

A VINAIGRETTE IS ONE OF THE SIMPLEST PREPARATIONS in the sauce lexicon. At its most basic, it requires only two ingredients: oil and vinegar. However, as many accomplished cooks can attest, turning these ingredients into a dressing that transforms unadorned greens into a finished, well-balanced salad isn't simple at all. Vinaigrettes can sometimes seem a little slipshod—harsh and bristling in one bite, dull and oily in the next. The best ones do the job quietly, complementing the greens without dominating them or engaging in combat. We were determined to nail down a formula for the perfect vinaigrette, one that would consistently yield a homogeneous, harmonious blend of bright vinegar and rich oil in every forkful.

We began by brushing up on form—unearthing texts from culinary school, perusing classic French culinary tomes, even contacting noted French chefs like Eric Ripert and Jacques Pépin. The books and the experts agreed on one thing: The ingredient selection and the ratio of oil to vinegar depend on what's being dressed. To our chagrin, that was it. What method, which oil or vinegar to use, whether shallots are advised over garlic, and even what herbs and other seasonings to add were all in dispute. In fact, what we thought of as the "classic" method of mixing, the one taught in many culinary schools (combine the vinegar and seasonings, then gradually whisk in oil to create a temporary emulsion), didn't seem so widespread after all. Neither *Larousse Gastronomique* nor Escoffier's *Guide Culinaire* even mention this approach (and Pépin, for one, often resorts to simply shaking the ingredients in a jar).

We wanted two styles: a vinaigrette for tender, mild greens (such as butter lettuce and mesclun) and another for assertive, spicy greens (such as arugula, radicchio, and escarole). We would have to test ingredients, proportions, and techniques until we figured out on our own what worked best.

We began by examining ingredients. With only two starring components, quality would be critical, so we

FOOLPROOF HERB VINAIGRETTE

tried the test kitchen's favorite white wine, red wine, and balsamic vinegars, each mixed with our top-rated extra-virgin olive oil as a placeholder. We also threw champagne vinegar into the mix. Tasters did not prefer one kind of vinegar to another, though balsamic tended to overpower mild lettuce and would only serve for more assertive greens. As for oil, tasters strongly preferred fruity extra-virgin olive oil to plain olive, vegetable, peanut, and grapeseed oils as an all-purpose option, and walnut oil won fans as an alternative for nuttier vinaigrettes. For due diligence, we then tested lower-end vinegars and olive oils. Not surprisingly, the results were inferior. High-quality ingredients were clearly a must.

As for ratio, Escoffier recommends 3 parts oil to 1 part vinegar in his *Guide Culinaire* (first published in 1903), yet many modern recipes employ a ratio of 4 to 1. We wondered if palates had changed—or vinaigrette ingredients? It also occurred to us that mixing methods have grown a little slack. Recipes these days routinely dump and stir, with all the ingredients added to a bowl and whisked until more or less combined; others do as Pépin does and simply shake the ingredients in a sealed jar. Since most of the dump-and-stir and dump-and-shake recipes we had collected use a 4–1 ratio, could these be related?

After mixing oil and vinegar with each method and ratio, we found out what mixing can do to flavor. The quicker, less thorough methods yielded vinaigrettes that began to separate even before they could be tossed with greens. This in turn produces salads with overly acidic bites in spots where the vinegar had settled. For vinaigrettes made with the quick methods, tasters preferred 4 parts oil to 1 part vinegar, which subdued the acidity more than the 3–1 ratio.

Overall, these easy vinaigrettes couldn't compete with those we made following culinary school protocol, whisking so gradually that our arms ached. These "classic" vinaigrettes were more stable and separated more slowly (after five to 10 minutes), pouring onto the greens intact. Tasters now switched their preference: 3 parts oil to 1 part vinegar had a pleasantly vibrant flavor, while a 4–1 ratio tasted dull. In general, the slow-whisked

vinaigrette was smoother and more even in flavor. Yet we weren't satisfied. We wanted a more forgiving vinaigrette that could sit for a while.

Some quick research revealed what was going on. Oil and vinegar don't typically mix, since vinegar is 95 percent water. Vigorous action (whisking) creates an emulsion that combines them more smoothly, though almost as soon as the action stops the vinegar droplets cluster back together, and the vinaigrette breaks apart. Using the classic whisking method, the vinegar droplets become exceedingly small, creating a vinaigrette that is even in flavor and remains stable until this profusion of tiny droplets starts to come together. We needed to introduce an emulsifying agent that would keep the vinegar and oil combined. All emulsifiers function the same way: They have molecules that include both a fat-compatible region and a water-compatible region. These regions latch onto oil and water alike, serving as a liaison that keeps those two ingredients from parting ways. Mustard is a common emulsifier in salad dressing, so we tried it. A half teaspoon of Dijon contributed a

nice tang but didn't help to stabilize the sauce. Although a whole teaspoon worked better, it turned our standard wine vinaigrette into a mustard dressing. We decided to keep a little mustard for flavor and continue searching for the right emulsifier.

Considering our options, we recalled something that Pépin had mentioned in passing: a type of vinaigrette that uses raw egg yolk to create a mayonnaise-like sauce. We weren't wild about incorporating raw egg into what we hoped would be our staple dressing, but what about trying a little mayo, which contains egg yolk but isn't overtly eggy? We added store-bought mayo in ¼-teaspoon increments and found that ½ teaspoon mayonnaise combined with ½ teaspoon mustard created a stable vinaigrette with pleasant acidity. How long could it sit without separating? As it turned out, more than an hour.

Our science editor explained why: The egg yolk in mayonnaise contains lecithin, a fatty substance that emulsifies brilliantly. Thanks to lecithin, we needed only a small amount of mayo to keep our dressing stable. The lecithin also allowed the vinaigrette to emulsify with slightly more flexibility: we could add the oil a bit more quickly, and all was not lost if a little extra spilled in. After testing three dozen vinaigrettes, we finally had one that was foolproof. Now we could make a dressing with a 3–1 ratio that would reliably produce smooth, satisfying results.

All that remained was fine-tuning the flavor. We added salt to the vinegar to ensure it dissolved fully (salt won't dissolve in oil). Then we experimented with shallots and garlic, both typical additions. (Shallots are milder than onions.) Tasters favored 1½ teaspoons of very finely minced shallot and just a hint of garlic—instead of adding it to the vinaigrette, we rubbed a clove inside a salad bowl before adding the lettuce.

With the master recipe settled, we whisked together a few variations. Mustard and balsamic vinegar matched assertive greens, while the version for mild greens omitted the shallots and used lemon juice in place of vinegar. We also created an option with rich walnut oil and another with fresh herbs. Mayonnaise was a constant, and regular and light products worked equally well to keep the mixture together.

Foolproof Vinaigrette

MAKES ABOUT ¼ CUP, ENOUGH TO DRESS 8 TO 10 CUPS

Red wine, white wine, or champagne vinegar will work in this recipe; however, it is important to use high-quality ingredients. Spectrum Naturals Organic Red Wine Vinegar, Colavita Aged White Wine Vinegar, and Columela Extra-Virgin Olive Oil are the test kitchen's top-rated brands. This vinaigrette works with nearly any type of green (as do the walnut and herb variations). For a hint of garlic flavor, rub the inside of the salad bowl with a clove of garlic before adding the lettuce.

1	tablespoon wine vinegar (see note)
1½	teaspoons very finely minced shallot
½	teaspoon regular or light mayonnaise
½	teaspoon Dijon mustard
⅛	teaspoon table salt
	Ground black pepper
3	tablespoons extra-virgin olive oil (see note)

1. Combine the vinegar, shallot, mayonnaise, mustard, salt, and pepper to taste in a small nonreactive bowl. Whisk until the mixture is milky in appearance and no lumps of mayonnaise remain.

2. Place the oil in a small measuring cup so that it is easy to pour. Whisking constantly, very slowly drizzle the oil into the vinegar mixture. If pools of oil are gathering on the surface as you whisk, stop adding the oil and whisk the mixture well to combine, then resume whisking in the oil in a slow stream. The vinaigrette should be glossy and lightly thickened, with no pools of oil on its surface.

VARIATIONS

Foolproof Walnut Vinaigrette

Follow the recipe for Foolproof Vinaigrette, substituting 1½ tablespoons roasted walnut oil and 1½ tablespoons regular olive oil for the extra-virgin olive oil.

Foolproof Herb Vinaigrette

Follow the recipe for Foolproof Vinaigrette, adding 1 tablespoon minced fresh parsley leaves or chives and ½ teaspoon minced fresh thyme, tarragon, marjoram, or oregano leaves to the vinaigrette just before use.

Foolproof Lemon Vinaigrette

This vinaigrette is best for dressing mild greens.

Follow the recipe for Foolproof Vinaigrette, substituting lemon juice for the vinegar, omitting the shallot, and adding ¼ teaspoon finely grated lemon zest and a pinch of sugar along with the salt and pepper.

Foolproof Balsamic-Mustard Vinaigrette

This vinaigrette is best for dressing assertive greens.

Follow the recipe for Foolproof Vinaigrette, substituting balsamic vinegar for the wine vinegar, increasing the mustard to 2 teaspoons, and adding ½ teaspoon chopped fresh thyme along with the salt and pepper.

NOTES FROM THE TEST KITCHEN

MINCING SHALLOTS

1. Make a number of closely spaced parallel cuts through the peeled shallot, leaving the root end intact.

2. Next, make several cuts lengthwise through the shallot.

3. Finally, thinly slice the shallot crosswise, creating a fine mince.

SIMPLY *Italian*

After shaping our focaccia loaves, we coat them in olive oil so they bake up with a crisp, flavorful crust.

IN THE STATES, ITALIAN FOOD IS BELOVED FOR ITS GUTSY FLAVORS and family-friendly abundance—think lasagna, spaghetti and meatballs, and braciole. But there are a couple of Italian classics that we love for their pure flavor, simplicity, and refinement; among them, focaccia and *cacio e pepe* or spaghetti with pecorino and black pepper.

Focaccia is everywhere these days, from sandwich shops to supermarkets—thick, pillowy slabs of bread perfumed with olive oil and topped with herbs and often a host of other items like caramelized onions, sun-dried tomatoes, grated cheese, and more. But wait—that sounds a lot like pizza. That's not the way it should be. We wanted to bring focaccia back to its simple roots. The olive oil and herbs could stay, but our goal was to shine the spotlight on the bread itself. We wanted focaccia with a crisp crust, a chewy interior, and complex flavor.

Another simple Italian classic, cacio e pepe, boasts a luxuriously silky sauce with a sharp, cheesy flavor and the heat of freshly ground black pepper—when ordered at your favorite trattoria. But at home, this dish can take more than a few wrong turns. The sauce can separate and turn clumpy and the flavor is not all it should be. We wouldn't settle for less than an exemplary version of this dish and headed into the test kitchen to uncover the secrets behind its success.

FOCACCIA

✔ **WHY THIS RECIPE WORKS:** For focaccia with a light and airy interior and crisp crust, we adapted our almost-no-knead method of breadmaking. This technique uses a high hydration level (a higher ratio of water to flour) and allows the dough to rest in order to mimic the effects of kneading, but doesn't develop the gluten to the extent that it produces a coarse loaf. To give our loaves a flavorful, crisp crust, we oiled the baking pans and added coarse salt for flavor and an extra crunchy texture. We then placed our loaves in the pans and turned them over so they were entirely coated with fruity olive oil. This focaccia was a revelation: crackly crisp on the bottom and deeply browned on top, with an interior that was open and airy.

IN THE PANTHEON OF ARTISAN BREADS, FOCACCIA HAS a looser history than most. Centuries ago, it began as a byproduct: When Italian bakers needed to gauge the heat of the wood-fired oven—"focaccia" stems from *focolare*, meaning "fireplace"—they would tear off a swatch of dough, flatten it, drizzle it with olive oil, and pop it into the hearth to bake as an edible oven thermometer. Because the technique was handy with just about any bread, there evolved countless variations on the theme. That said, it's the deep-dish Genovese interpretation that most Americans recognize: dimpled, chewy, and thick with a smattering of herbs. We're sure a slab from the mother country would do this version justice—plenty of Italian bakeries and cafés capitalize on its denser texture by slicing the bread in half to make hearty sandwiches— but most stateside breads we've tasted are leaden, oil-slicked, and strewn with pizzalike toppings. Personally, we never understood the appeal.

Before we had a chance to consider trying to improve on the Genovese adaptation, we happened upon an entirely different style of focaccia in a bakery called Annarosa's in Newburyport, Massachusetts. The crisp-crusted loaves that owner Bill Malatesta pulled from his brick oven were round instead of flat and rectangular, and more delicately scented with herbs and olive oil than any focaccia we'd ever encountered. Biting into one revealed an interior that was also lighter, airier, and slightly less chewy than other versions we'd had. In fact, the only familiar element was the flecks of salt on top. Intrigued, we asked him to walk us through his method, a series of kneading, rising, and shaping steps that we were determined to reproduce in the test kitchen. True, we didn't have a heavy brick steam-injected oven to guarantee earthy flavor and an ultra-crisp crust. But with a little research and experimentation, we hoped we could redefine our notion of focaccia with a close replica. We wanted bread that boasted a crackly exterior, a more bubbly interior than the doughier Genovese focaccia, and just enough chew throughout.

A brush of fruity olive oil and heady seasonings gave the Annarosa's breads an addictive savory edge, but that wouldn't mean a thing if the dough itself weren't full of flavor. The biggest key here is fermentation—the process by which long chains of carbohydrates with little taste convert to sugars and proteins and carbon dioxide. Like many organic processes, it's most effective over a long period of time. A slow ferment—usually several hours— not only allows the yeast to give the dough its lofty rise, but also produces a multitude of aromatic molecules that contribute to the flavor of the bread.

To get the benefits of long fermentation with minimal effort, many bakers, Malatesta included, use a "prefer-ment" (also known as a sponge, starter, or *biga* in Italian): a mixture of flour, water, and a small amount of yeast that rests (often overnight) before being incorporated into a dough either in place of or along with more yeast. Time is the main factor here. That little bit of yeast in the biga grows as the hours go by, and the flavor that slowly develops is stronger and more complex than you would get by simply adding yeast to flour and water and kneading.

Cobbling together a basic recipe, we mixed up a biga (equal parts water and flour, plus ¼ teaspoon yeast) the night before we wanted to bake the loaf, covered the bowl tightly, and let it ferment on the counter. The next

ROSEMARY FOCACCIA

HOLD THE SALT—TEMPORARILY

Instead of relying on kneading to develop gluten, our dough uses a resting process called autolysis. During this long resting period (which usually lasts several hours), enzymes in the wheat cut long, balled-up strands of gluten into smaller pieces, which then unravel and link together to form larger, well-developed gluten networks. Could adjusting when we added salt to the dough help speed things along?

THE EXPERIMENT

We prepared two doughs. In the first, we combined the flour, water, yeast, and salt with the biga all at once before resting; in the second, we withheld the salt for 15 minutes.

THE RESULTS

Briefly omitting the salt hastened gluten development by an hour. After just 15 minutes, the unsalted dough was already pliant and smooth, while the salted dough was still gluey and stiff.

THE EXPLANATION

Salt both inhibits the ability of flour to absorb water and the activity of the enzymes that break down proteins to begin the process of forming gluten. If allowed to rest without salt, the flour is able to get a jump on gluten development by absorbing as much water as it can and letting its enzymes work sooner to develop gluten networks.

15-MINUTE REST, WITH SALT
Dough is sticky and stiff.

15-MINUTE REST, WITHOUT SALT
Dough is supple and smooth.

morning, it looked bubbly, smelled faintly boozy, and boasted a ripe, slightly sour tang. We added the biga to a basic lean dough—flour, water, salt, and yeast—and went through the typical motions of kneading in a standing mixer, then rising (or "proofing"), dividing, shaping, proofing again, brushing with olive oil, and sliding the dough onto a preheated pizza stone in a blazing-hot oven. Many focaccia recipes incorporate oil into the dough, but we left it out for the moment. From personal experience, we knew that adding oil to the dough can render bread dense and greasy. What emerged 40 minutes later was already a significant improvement over other focaccias we'd sampled: flavorful, golden brown loaves perfumed—rather than saturated—with olive oil.

What we hadn't quite nailed on a first take was the tender, airy interior we were after—and we had a hunch the mixing method might be the culprit. Our fast, powerful standing mixer was developing too much gluten, the strong, elastic network of cross-linked proteins that give bread its crumb structure. Hand kneading produced loaves that were even chewier.

Figuring a gentler approach was warranted, we immediately recalled an almost no-knead bread we'd published. This system, originally developed by Sullivan Street Bakery owner Jim Lahey, relies upon the ability of gluten to assemble into large networks on its own, given enough moisture in the dough and sufficient time. Here's how it works: When water and flour are mixed, the proteins in flour initially combine to form many individual tightly balled-up units of gluten. Rather than relying on kneading to mechanically unravel each of these gluten units and link them together into larger networks, the no-knead process takes advantage of the enzymes naturally present in the wheat to produce the same effect. During the dough resting process called autolysis (or *autolyse* in French), these enzymes (known as proteases) snip the tiny nests of gluten into shorter strands, which quickly unravel and link together into the more organized sheets of gluten that exist in a well-developed dough.

The sticking point, however, is the hydration level of the dough—in other words, the weight of the water in relation to the weight of the flour. Enzymes need water to work their magic, and the more of it in the mix, the more efficient the snipping process. Thus no-knead dough is

often wetter than machine-mixed dough. Our working recipe rang in at 68 percent hydration (meaning that it had 6.8 ounces of water for every 10 ounces of flour), while no-knead breads tend to work with hydrations in the 75 to 90 percent range. Water also makes dough more capable of expanding without tearing, promoting the formation of larger air bubbles. We figured adapting our focaccia to a no-knead method should improve its texture twice over: A higher hydration—we finally settled on 75 percent—helped to open up the crumb structure, and the lack of handling kept it tender, light, and airy.

But to be effective, the standard no-knead method requires a long resting period—anywhere from 12 to 18 hours—after the dough is mixed, during which the gluten develops. And even then the loaves were squatter than we'd hoped. But from past experience baking bread, we had a trick to try: "turning" the dough while it proofs.

A standard no-knead dough develops structure gradually because the individual gluten clusters are relatively slow to combine into larger units. But gently turning the dough over itself at regular intervals accomplishes three things: It brings the wheat proteins into closer proximity with one another, keeping the process going at maximum clip; it aerates the dough, replenishing the oxygen that the yeasts consume during fermentation; and it elongates and redistributes the bubbles.

While our next batch of dough proofed, every 30 minutes we gently lifted and folded the edges of the dough toward the middle and then let it rest. Roughly three hours (and five sets of turns) later, the dough was a soft, supple, bubbly mass that had more than doubled in volume. Once baked, the results were even better than we had hoped: From the oven's heat, the dough rounds had leapt twice as tall and bronzed beautifully. Inside, a maze of bubbles punctuated the tender, moist crumb, for bread that was light as the air it contained.

Still, we hoped we could further abbreviate the three-hour proofing and gluten development stage. Some research turned up a second approach to autolysis that supposedly hastens gluten development: Here, a freshly mixed dough is allowed to rest briefly before the salt is added, since salt inhibits the ability of flour to absorb water and prevents its enzymes from breaking down proteins to help form strong gluten networks. We gave it a whirl—and were stunned by the dramatic results. When we let the dough rest for 15 minutes before stirring in the salt, it was already supple and not at all sticky. With this new approach, we not only shaved an hour off the gluten development, but also got away with just three different sets of turns (see "Hold the Salt—Temporarily" on page 136).

Still, while it had just enough rich olive oil taste, the crust lacked the crunchy, almost fried bottom of most focaccia that the oiled-dough recipes had produced. Incorporating some olive oil into our dough did crisp up the bottom, but to the detriment of the bread's interior, which turned dense and cakelike. (Just as with shortbread, fat "shortens" the dough by blocking the gluten's ability to form continuous networks.) Instead, we moved our free-form breads into round cake pans, where the few tablespoons of oil coating the exterior would be contained. After swirling the bottom in the oil and some coarse salt, we flipped the dough, gently stretched it to the pan's edges, let it proof for just a few extra minutes, and scattered a healthy dose of chopped fresh rosemary over the top before sliding it onto the hot pizza stone. This focaccia was a revelation: crackly crisp on the bottom, deeply browned on top, with an interior that was open and airy. With a loaf this good, we'll never go back to any other style of focaccia again.

MAKING FOCACCIA

1. Fold the partially risen dough over itself by gently lifting and folding the edge of the dough toward the middle. Turn the bowl 90 degrees; fold again. Turn the bowl and fold dough six more times (for a total of eight turns).

2. Cover with plastic wrap and let rise for 30 minutes. Repeat stretching, folding, and rising two more times, for a total of three 30-minute rises.

3. Dust the dough with flour and divide in half. Shape the halves into 5-inch rounds. Place in the oiled pans and slide around to coat the bottom and sides of the dough. Flip and repeat. Cover the pans with plastic wrap and rest 5 minutes.

4. Using your fingertips, press the dough out toward the edges of the pan, taking care not to tear it. (If the dough resists stretching, let it relax for 5 to 10 minutes before trying to stretch again.)

5. Using a fork, poke the surface of the dough 25 to 30 times. Deflate any large bubbles with the fork. Sprinkle the rosemary over the top of the dough and let rest until slightly bubbly, 5 to 10 minutes, before baking.

Rosemary Focaccia

MAKES TWO 9-INCH ROUND LOAVES

If you don't have a baking stone, bake the bread on an overturned, preheated rimmed baking sheet set on the upper-middle oven rack. The bread can be kept for up to 2 days well-wrapped at room temperature or frozen for several months wrapped in foil and placed in a zipper-lock bag.

BIGA

½ cup (2½ ounces) unbleached all-purpose flour
⅓ cup (2⅔ ounces) warm water (100–110 degrees)
¼ teaspoon instant or rapid-rise yeast

DOUGH

2½ cups (12½ ounces) unbleached all-purpose flour, plus extra for the work surface
1¼ cups (10 ounces) warm water (100–110 degrees)
1 teaspoon instant or rapid-rise yeast
   Kosher salt (see note)
4 tablespoons extra-virgin olive oil
2 tablespoons chopped fresh rosemary leaves

1. FOR THE BIGA: Combine the flour, water, and yeast in a large bowl and stir with a wooden spoon until a uniform mass forms and no dry flour remains, about 1 minute. Cover the bowl tightly with plastic wrap and let stand at room temperature (about 70 degrees) overnight (at least 8 hours and up to 24 hours). Use immediately or store in the refrigerator for up to 3 days (allow to stand at room temperature 30 minutes before proceeding with the recipe).

2. FOR THE DOUGH: Stir the flour, water, and yeast into the biga with a wooden spoon until a uniform mass forms and no dry flour remains, about 1 minute. Cover with plastic wrap and let rise at room temperature 15 minutes.

3. Sprinkle 2 teaspoons of the salt over the dough; stir into the dough until thoroughly incorporated, about 1 minute. Cover with plastic wrap and let rise at room temperature, 30 minutes. Spray a rubber spatula or bowl scraper with vegetable oil spray; fold the partially risen dough over itself by gently lifting and folding the edge of the dough toward the middle. Turn the bowl 90 degrees; fold again. Turn the bowl and fold the dough six more

times (for a total of eight turns). Cover with plastic wrap and let rise, 30 minutes. Repeat the folding, turning, and rising two more times, for a total of three 30-minute rises. Meanwhile, adjust an oven rack to the upper-middle position, place a baking stone on the rack, and heat the oven to 500 degrees, at least 30 minutes before baking.

4. Gently transfer the dough to a lightly floured work surface. Lightly dust the top of the dough with flour and divide it in half. Shape each piece of dough into a 5-inch round by gently tucking under the edges. Coat two 9-inch round cake pans with 2 tablespoons olive oil each. Sprinkle each pan with ½ teaspoon salt. Place a round of dough in one pan, top side down, slide the dough around the pan to coat the bottom and sides, then flip the dough over. Repeat with the second piece of dough. Cover the pans with plastic wrap and let rest for 5 minutes.

5. Using your fingertips, press the dough out toward the edges of the pan, taking care not to tear it. (If the dough resists stretching, let it relax for 5 to 10 minutes before trying to stretch it again.) Using a dinner fork, poke the entire surface of the dough 25 to 30 times. If any large bubbles remain on the surface or sides of the dough, pop with the fork to deflate. Sprinkle the rosemary evenly over the top of the dough. Let the dough rest in the pan until slightly bubbly, 5 to 10 minutes.

6. Place the pans on the baking stone and lower the oven temperature to 450 degrees. Bake until the tops are golden brown, 25 to 28 minutes, switching the pans halfway through the baking time. Transfer the pans to a wire rack and cool 5 minutes. Remove the loaves from the pan and place on the wire rack. Brush the tops with any oil remaining in the pan. Cool 30 minutes before serving.

NOTES FROM THE TEST KITCHEN

FOR BIG FLAVOR, A LONG REST IS BEST
Creating a small batch of starter dough (also known as a preferment, or a *biga* in Italian) boosts the flavor in our bread dramatically. A starter is made by combining small amounts of flour and water with a little yeast and allowing it to ferment overnight. With a lengthy rest, long carbohydrate chains that have little taste break down into a multitude of sugars and alcohol with lots of flavor.

SPAGHETTI WITH PECORINO ROMANO AND BLACK PEPPER

SPAGHETTI WITH PECORINO ROMANO AND BLACK PEPPER

✔ **WHY THIS RECIPE WORKS:** For a smooth, intensely cheesy sauce that won't separate once tossed with the pasta, we whisked together some of the pasta cooking water with the grated Romano. Real Pecorino Romano is preferred for best flavor. Swapping out butter for cream further ensured a smooth sauce. From first bite to last, the sauce will remain silky-smooth.

RECENTLY AT LUPA, MARIO BATALI AND JOE Bastianich's New York trattoria, we tried *pasta alla cacio e pepe* (pasta with cheese and pepper). Described by the waiter as a popular Roman "spaghetti party" dish often thrown together to cap off a night on the town, it combined long, thin pasta with Pecorino Romano and fresh-cracked black pepper. The strands came napped with a barely creamy sauce boasting intense cheese flavor and speckled with the pepper. We were hooked and set out to create our own version.

An Internet search turned up dozens of approaches, including one from Batali: Toss a pound of cooked pasta with ¼ cup of olive oil and 2 tablespoons of butter, add plenty of grated cheese and black pepper along with pasta water to keep it moist, toss, and serve. Maybe the chefs at his restaurant have superior skills (or Batali is withholding something); when we tried his recipe, we couldn't get it to work. Instead of emulsifying into a creamy sauce after being tossed into the hot pasta, the Pecorino merely solidified into clumps and ended up stuck to the tongs. Ditto with the other recipes we found.

Perhaps we were grating the Pecorino too coarse and it wasn't melting properly? We tried again with cheese shredded on the grater's smallest holes. Still no luck: Although the cheese melted more quickly, it formed clumps just as fast. We tinkered around with the amount of cheese and pasta water, but no matter what we did, the cheese still clumped.

A talk with our science editor revealed the likely problem. Cheese consists mainly of three basic substances: fat, protein, and water. In a hard lump of Pecorino, the three are locked into position by the solid structure of the cheese. But when the cheese is heated, its fat begins to melt and its proteins soften. The fat acts as a sort of glue, fusing the proteins together. Cornstarch, he suggested, might be useful for coating the cheese and preventing the proteins from sticking together, so we added some as we tossed the pasta. It worked, but there was a catch: By the time we used enough cornstarch to prevent clumping, it dulled the flavor of the cheese, and we weren't about to trade flavor for texture.

Was there another way to get starch into the mix? Pasta releases starch into the cooking water as it boils, so maybe we could use this to our advantage. We reduced the cooking water from 4 quarts to 2 quarts per pound of pasta. After cooking the spaghetti, we whisked some grated cheese into a cup of the semolina-infused water that remained. Our results were the best yet, but some of the cheese was still clumping.

Hitting the books again, we discovered another factor that affects how proteins and fat interact: emulsifiers. Milk, cream, and fresh cheeses have special molecules called lipoproteins that can associate with both fat and protein, acting as a sort of liaison between the two and keeping them from separating. But as cheese ages, the lipoproteins break down, losing their emulsifying power. No wonder our Pecorino Romano, which is aged for at least eight months, was clumping. How could we get an infusion of totally intact lipoproteins? The answer was simple: add milk or cream.

Since we were already using butter, why not replace it with the same amount of cream? (At the same time, we also took the olive oil down to 2 teaspoons to satisfy a few tasters who found the dish greasy.) This time, the cheese easily formed a light, perfectly smooth sauce when we tossed it with the spaghetti. Now for the real test: we placed a serving of pasta on the table and let it cool for a full five minutes. Even as it cooled, there wasn't a clump in sight. We may never learn what really goes on in Lupa's kitchen, but our innovative version is worthy of any late-night spaghetti party.

Spaghetti with Pecorino Romano and Black Pepper

SERVES 4 TO 6

High-quality ingredients are essential in this dish, most importantly, imported Pecorino Romano. For a slightly less rich dish, substitute half-and-half for the heavy cream. Do not adjust the amount of water for cooking the pasta; the amount used is critical to the success of the recipe. Make sure to stir the pasta frequently while cooking so that it doesn't stick to the pot. Draining the pasta water into the serving bowl warms the bowl and helps keeps the dish hot until it is served. Letting the dish rest briefly before serving allows the flavors to develop and the sauce to thicken.

4 ounces Pecorino Romano grated fine (about 2 cups), plus 2 ounces grated coarse (about 1 cup), for serving

1 pound spaghetti

Table salt

2 tablespoons heavy cream

2 teaspoons extra-virgin olive oil

1½ teaspoons ground black pepper

1. Place the finely grated Pecorino in a medium bowl. Set a colander in a large bowl.

2. Bring 2 quarts water to a boil in a large Dutch oven. Add the pasta and 1½ teaspoons salt and cook, stirring frequently, until the pasta is al dente. Drain the pasta into the colander set in the bowl, reserving the cooking water. Pour 1½ cups of the cooking water into a liquid measuring cup and discard the remainder and then place the pasta in the empty bowl.

3. Slowly whisk 1 cup of the reserved pasta water into the finely grated Pecorino until smooth. Whisk in the cream, oil, and pepper. Gradually pour the cheese mixture over the pasta, tossing to coat. Let the pasta rest 1 to 2 minutes, tossing frequently, adjusting the consistency with the remaining ½ cup reserved pasta cooking water as needed. Serve, passing the coarsely grated Pecorino separately.

NOTES FROM THE TEST KITCHEN

FOR AUTHENTIC TASTE, CHOOSE AUTHENTIC CHEESE

Imported Pecorino Romano is a hard, aged sheep's milk cheese with a distinctively pungent, salty flavor that bear's almost no resemblance to domestic cheeses simply labeled "Romano." (These wan stand-ins are made with cow's milk and lack the punch of the real deal.) When you pick out your cheese, check the label carefully to be sure what you are getting is the real deal.

RATING WHOLE WHEAT PASTA

Whole wheat pasta used to be awful, with mushy texture and a cardboard taste. But with so many more options on the supermarket shelves than there once was, we figured we'd be able to find at least one that would rival white pasta. We tasted 18 nationally distributed brands of whole wheat and multigrain spaghettis tossed with olive oil, marinara sauce, and pesto. Several brands were eliminated after scoring low in the preliminary test. Of the remaining pastas, three brands earned the "recommended" status, but two were whole grain imposters, with refined wheat as their first ingredient. However, Bionaturae Organic 100% Whole Wheat Spaghetti boasted a good chewy and firm texture, making it our top pick. The manufacturer's secret? Custom milling (which ensures good flavor), extrusion through a bronze, not Teflon, die (which helps build gluten in the dough), and a slower drying process at low temperatures (which yields sturdier pasta). Brands are listed in order of preference. See www.americastestkitchen.com for updates to this testing.

RECOMMENDED

BIONATURAE Organic 100% Whole Wheat Spaghetti
PRICE: $3.49 for 16 oz
PERCENTAGE OF WHOLE GRAINS: 100
COMMENTS: Tasters lauded this spaghetti for its "earthy," flavor, which was "heartier than white pasta, without being too wheaty."

HEARTLAND Perfect Balance Spaghetti
PRICE: $1.19 for 14.5 oz
PERCENTAGE OF WHOLE GRAINS: 21
COMMENTS: Only 21 percent whole grains, it tasted "the most like white pasta" of any in the lineup.

BARILLA Plus Multigrain Spaghetti
PRICE: $2.50 for 14.5 oz
PERCENTAGE OF WHOLE GRAINS: 0
COMMENTS: It's no surprise that this spaghetti "doesn't taste like whole wheat pasta," as it contains no whole grains. Tasters enjoyed the "mildly nutty, wheaty" taste along with its "firm, chewy" texture.

RECOMMENDED WITH RESERVATIONS

HEARTLAND Plus Spaghetti
PRICE: $1.29 for 14.5 oz
PERCENTAGE OF WHOLE GRAINS: 0
COMMENTS: Tasters liked the "mild nutty flavor," which had a "neutral" flavor when paired with marinara and pesto.

RECOMMENDED WITH RESERVATIONS (cont.)

GIA RUSSA 100% Whole Wheat Spaghetti
PRICE: $2.99 for 16 oz
PERCENTAGE OF WHOLE GRAINS: 100
COMMENTS: Tossed with pesto, this spaghetti was "nutty and robust"; but plain, it was likened to eating "wheat germ."

DAVINCI 100% Whole Wheat Spaghetti
PRICE: $3.99 for 12 oz
PERCENTAGE OF WHOLE GRAINS: 100
COMMENTS: This spaghetti had "good flavor" although "not much whole wheat flavor," but tasters couldn't get past the "gummy" texture.

BARILLA Whole Grain Spaghetti
PRICE: $1.39 for 13.25 oz
PERCENTAGE OF WHOLE GRAINS: 51
COMMENTS: Its heavy "bran" flavors were "not terrible," but made this "hippie-food" spaghetti taste "more like oats than wheat."

RONZONI Healthy Harvest Whole Wheat Blend
PRICE: $2 for 13.25 oz
PERCENTAGE OF WHOLE GRAINS: 63
COMMENTS: Though this spaghetti's "healthy, earthy" flavor appealed to a few, it overwhelmed most.

Easier
ITALIAN FAVORITES

Cooking risotto shouldn't feel like you're doing time. Our innovative, almost hands-free method for this classic Italian dish liberates you from constant stirring and delivers creamy, tender grains of rice.

IF YOU HAD AN ITALIAN GRANDMOTHER, SHE PROBABLY MADE FOOD around the clock—and we bet she made it all seem so easy. In her day, she probably had time on her side, so shopping for just the right ingredients and hovering over pots for hours on end was a regular part of her day. Most cooks today, however, don't have time for this kind of cooking. Here we wanted to take two Italian favorites, minestrone and risotto, and make them accessible for any home cook, no matter their schedule.

Minestrone should burst with bright vegetable flavor, but too often this soup is bland. Sure, peak-of-summer vegetables improve this soup markedly, but we wanted great-tasting soup year-round. We set out to find a way to turn supermarket pickings into truly great minestrone.

With risotto, the difficulty lies not so much in shopping for ingredients, but in the time and attention this dish requires. Traditional versions of risotto translate to standing at the stove practically from start to finish. How reasonable is that, especially if company's coming? We wanted to reengineer risotto-making for the modern cook—a recipe that turns out tender, but not mushy, grains of rice in a creamy Parmesan-enriched sauce.

HEARTY MINESTRONE

BETTER MINESTRONE

✔ **WHY THIS RECIPE WORKS:** We tried to squeeze every last ounce of flavor out of a manageable list of supermarket vegetables while creating our minestrone. Sautéing pancetta and then cooking the veggies in the rendered fat gave our soup layers of flavor. Starch from simmering beans thickened the soup. The last component we considered was the liquid, settling on the right combination of chicken broth, water, and V8 juice.

THE SIMPLEST RECIPES ARE OFTEN THE MOST DIFFICULT. Take Italian minestrone soup. This classic of *la cucina povera*—a peasant approach to cooking that uses ordinary ingredients to create rich, satisfying fare—has a basic recipe as easy as this: Chop vegetables, add water and a hearty starch (beans, pasta, or potatoes), and simmer with aromatics. But if Italian cooks understand one thing, it's that the best minestrone can be made only from the best vegetables—and that's where the difficulty lies. Unless you've got access to a sun-drenched garden in the height of summer, you're stuck with lackluster supermarket offerings.

To see how much of a handicap this would be, we embarked on a minestrone marathon, following wildly varying recipes. Perhaps to compensate for the problem of mediocre produce, some called for upward of eight different types of veggies or time-consuming home-made stocks and copious amounts of extra flavorings like pancetta, prosciutto, or bacon. Others relied heavily on some form of canned tomato product (a good brand is more reliably flavorful than fresh tomatoes). They all fell into one of two categories: those with bland, watery flavor and those with flavor overwhelmingly dominated by the tomatoes, stock, or meat. We wanted a soup that tasted first and foremost of vegetables. Our job was to squeeze every last ounce of flavor out of supermarket vegetables to create a minestrone as satisfying as the countless styles of Italian originals.

A few parameters seemed in order. First, we limited ourselves to a manageable list of six carefully selected vegetables: the aromatic trio of onions, celery, and carrots; hearty cabbage; and fresh, summery zucchini and tomato, all simmered in 10 cups of water. We kept meat to a minimum, adding only a small piece of pancetta to the simmering liquid along with a Parmesan rind, a bay leaf, minced garlic, and red pepper flakes. A single type of bean would provide the starch component. Cannellini beans—a favorite for their creamy texture and buttery flavor—were the way to go. We soaked our beans overnight in salted water (salt water helps the beans cook evenly and seasons them thoroughly) and simmered them to tenderness before adding them to our soup and cooking everything together for 45 minutes.

Not surprisingly, the broth was watery and thin, lacking body and complexity. About the only flavor was from the Parmesan rind and the pancetta. We figured increasing the cooking time might help extract more flavor, but all it did was reduce the vegetables and beans to mush. We were going to have to consider each ingredient and slowly layer flavors to create the complexity we were after.

The first step was to brown the vegetables to help them develop sweetness. We sautéed the zucchini and aromatics together in olive oil until they browned, then added the cabbage and garlic and cooked them just until the cabbage wilted and the garlic released its aroma before adding the water and diced tomato. The Parmesan rind was a keeper, adding a sharp nuttiness, as were the bay leaf and red pepper flakes, but as we tossed a piece of pancetta into the soup, we realized that here was another potential source for flavor development. We started over, this time finely dicing the pancetta and sautéing it, then using some of the rendered fat in place of the olive oil to brown our vegetables. These simple steps made improvements, but we still had a way to go.

Using only water as the liquid in the soup and allowing the flavors of the vegetables to come through unhindered was a noble goal, but in reality, our soup needed a flavor boost. Homemade broth was too much effort,

MAKING THICKER, MORE FLAVORFUL MINESTRONE

1. Brine the beans overnight in 2 quarts water and 1½ tablespoons salt.

2. Sauté the vegetables and remove them before cooking the beans to preserve their texture.

3. Cook the beans at a vigorous simmer to release their starch, which will act as a thickener.

4. Return the vegetables to the pot, along with V8 juice and chopped fresh basil leaves.

ADDING PARMESAN FLAVOR TO MINESTRONE

In the test kitchen, we save Parmesan rinds in a zipper-lock bag in the freezer to add depth to recipes like Hearty Minestrone. If you've discarded your last Parmesan rind, is there another way to infuse your soup with cheese flavor? Add a plain 2-ounce chunk of Parmesan. It will leave stringy melted cheese in the pot, but can easily be removed. Slowly pour the cooked soup into a clean pot, leaving the cheese strands stuck to the bottom of the old pot.

and canned vegetable broths often taste tinny and overly sweet. Store-bought chicken broth seemed like the way to go, but using a full 10 cups dominated the soup with chicken flavor. We slowly cut back on the broth until we arrived at a ratio of 2 cups broth to 8 cups water.

Next we turned to the beans. Simmering them in a separate pot before adding them to the vegetables was definitely time-consuming, but using canned beans was not an option—they simply did not have the flavor or creamy texture of dried beans. Perhaps we could use the beans and their simmering liquid to our advantage. Our soup could definitely use more body: What if we used the starchy bean liquid to thicken the broth? We started a new batch of soup, this time adding soaked beans to the pot with the browned vegetables and simmering everything together until the beans were tender. The broth was definitely thicker and richer, but the vegetables were shot. To remedy this, we removed the vegetables to a baking sheet right after browning, then cooked our beans at a vigorous simmer in order to help them release more starch (see "To Thicken Soup, Boil Your Beans" on page 150). Once the beans were tender, we returned the veggies to the pot and simmered everything together just until the vegetables were cooked through. It was the richest, most flavorful minestrone yet. Nearly there, we addressed the one ingredient we had yet to consider: the tomato.

The diced supermarket tomato was doing nothing for the flavor of the soup, so we switched to canned products, trying paste, diced, and crushed. All three provided brighter flavor, but tasters cried foul on texture, spurning the diced tomatoes as too thick and chunky and the crushed ones as only marginally better. Our solution: tomato juice, which also ensured consistent tomato flavor in every spoonful. Then an idea occurred to us that we hadn't come across in either traditional or contemporary recipes: Adding V8 instead of tomato juice would instantly boost the vegetable factor in a single stroke. It was a great success, creating depth through an arsenal of vegetal flavors.

As a final flavor-boosting measure, we took a cue from the minestrone of Liguria, in northern Italy, where the dish is commonly served with a swirl of pesto. We didn't want to bother making the actual sauce, but adding its flavors in the form of chopped basil, a glug of fruity olive oil, and freshly grated Parmesan did the trick. Who would have thought that it would take an American product to re-create an Italian peasant classic?

Hearty Minestrone

SERVES 6 TO 8

If you are pressed for time you can "quick-brine" your beans. In step 1, combine the salt, water, and beans in a large Dutch oven and bring to a boil over high heat. Remove the pot from the heat, cover, and let stand 1 hour. Drain and rinse the beans and proceed with the recipe. We prefer cannellini beans, but navy or great Northern beans can be used. We prefer pancetta, but bacon can be used. To make this soup vegetarian, substitute vegetable broth for the chicken broth and 2 teaspoons of olive oil for the pancetta. Parmesan rind is added for flavor, but can be replaced with a 2-inch chunk of the cheese (see "Adding Parmesan Flavor to Minestrone" on page 148). In order for the starch from the beans to thicken the soup, it is important to maintain a vigorous simmer in step 3. The soup can be cooled, covered tightly, and refrigerated for up to 2 days. Reheat it gently and add the basil just before serving.

Table salt

½ pound dried cannellini beans (about 1 cup), rinsed and picked over (see note)

3 ounces pancetta, cut into ¼-inch pieces (see note)

1 tablespoon extra-virgin olive oil, plus extra for serving

2 small onions, peeled and cut into ½-inch pieces (about 1½ cups)

1 medium zucchini, trimmed and cut into ½-inch pieces (about 1 cup)

2 medium celery ribs, cut into ½-inch pieces (about ¾ cup)

1 medium carrot, peeled and cut into ½-inch pieces (about ¾ cup)

½ small head green cabbage, halved, cored, and cut into ½-inch pieces (about 2 cups)

2 medium garlic cloves, minced or pressed through a garlic press (about 2 teaspoons)

⅛–¼ teaspoon red pepper flakes

8 cups water

2 cups low-sodium chicken broth

1 piece Parmesan cheese rind, about 5 by 2 inches (see note)

1 bay leaf

1½ cups V8 vegetable juice

½ cup chopped fresh basil leaves

Ground black pepper

Grated Parmesan cheese, for serving

1. Dissolve 1½ tablespoons salt in 2 quarts cold water in a large bowl or container. Add the beans and soak at room temperature for at least 8 hours and up to 24 hours. Drain the beans and rinse well.

2. Heat the pancetta and oil in a large Dutch oven over medium-high heat. Cook, stirring occasionally, until the pancetta is lightly browned and the fat has rendered, 3 to 5 minutes. Add the onions, zucchini, celery, and carrot; cook, stirring frequently, until the vegetables are softened and lightly browned, 5 to 9 minutes. Stir in the cabbage, garlic, ½ teaspoon salt, and red pepper flakes; continue to cook until the cabbage starts to wilt, 1 to 2 minutes longer. Transfer the vegetables to a rimmed baking sheet and set aside.

3. Add the soaked beans, water, broth, Parmesan rind, and bay leaf to the now-empty Dutch oven and bring to a boil over high heat. Reduce the heat and simmer vigorously, stirring occasionally, until the beans are fully tender and the liquid begins to thicken, 45 to 60 minutes.

4. Add the reserved vegetables and V8 juice to the pot; cook until the vegetables are soft, about 15 minutes. Discard the bay leaf and Parmesan rind, stir in the chopped basil, and season with salt and pepper to taste. Serve with olive oil and grated Parmesan.

SCIENCE DESK

TO THICKEN SOUP, BOIL YOUR BEANS

For our Hearty Minestrone recipe, we cook the dried beans in chicken broth and water before combining them with the other ingredients. We noticed that by the time the beans became tender, the cooking liquid in some batches of beans had a nice thick consistency, while others were thin and watery. Could this be due to how much heat was under the pot?

THE EXPERIMENT

To find out, we cooked two pots of beans (both soaked first overnight in a brine, according to our recipe)—one at a bare simmer and the second pot at a vigorous simmer—until the beans in each became tender. We then drained each batch of cooking liquid into a measuring cup, adding water to the vigorously simmered batch until it was level with the gently simmered cooking liquid.

THE RESULTS

Even with water added to compensate for evaporation, the cooking liquid from the boiled beans was significantly thicker than the more gently simmered liquid.

THE EXPLANATION

A higher cooking temperature causes more starch to be released from beans. As they simmer, their coats may look smooth and unbroken, but starches are continually being released into the water through a section of their seed coat called the hilum. These starches absorb the hot liquid and eventually burst, releasing the molecule amylose, which acts as a thickener. So the next time you want a thicker bean soup, remember: The more vigorous the simmer, the more starches that burst and the more viscous the broth.

ALMOST HANDS-FREE RISOTTO

✔ **WHY THIS RECIPE WORKS:** Typical recipes for risotto dictate adding the broth in small increments after the wine has been absorbed (and stirring constantly after each addition), but we added most of the broth at once. Then we covered the pan and simmered the rice until almost all the broth had been absorbed, stirring just twice during this time. After adding the second and final addition of broth, we stirred the pot for just a few minutes to ensure the bottom didn't cook more quickly than the top and turned off the heat. Without sitting over a direct flame, the sauce turned out perfectly creamy and the rice was thickened, velvety, and just barely chewy.

ACCEPTED WISDOM FOR COOKING RISOTTO DICTATES near-constant stirring to achieve the perfect texture: tender grains with a slight bite, bound together in a light, creamy sauce. As the rice cooks, it releases a starch called amylopectin. This starch absorbs liquid and expands, thickening the broth. Constant stirring jostles the rice grains, agitating them and promoting the release of amylopectin from their exterior.

But most of us have neither the time nor the patience for 30 minutes of stirring. That's why a few years ago our test kitchen came up with an easier method. It starts like a traditional recipe: Sweat aromatics, add 2 cups of Arborio rice (a short-grained rice ideal for risotto because of its high amylopectin and starch content), toast the grains in hot fat, and pour in dry white wine, stirring until the liquid is just absorbed. Then, rather than adding the broth in traditional half-cup intervals, we add roughly half the liquid—3 cups of broth and water—at once and simmer for a full 12 minutes with only a few stirs during the process. For the last nine minutes, the traditional, incremental method is resumed as we slowly add the remaining hot broth while stirring constantly. The resulting risotto

ALMOST HANDS-FREE RISOTTO WITH PARMESAN AND HERBS

turns out every bit as creamy and al dente as those stirred for 30 minutes. Why? Once it starts bubbling, all that liquid jostles the rice grains in much the same way as constant stirring, accelerating the release of starch. But, we wondered, could we take things even further? Could we eliminate the final nine-minute stir and still deliver a perfect pot of risotto?

We had only so many variables to consider, so we started with the liquid. What if we added more from the start? If we started by pouring in 5 cups of liquid, the contents of the pot would be very fluid for the first 15 to 20 minutes of cooking, allowing the rice to bob around and cook more evenly, with minimal stirring. Only when the rice released enough starch and the sauce started to thicken, impeding fluidity, would we need to resume stirring. We gave this theory a shot, anxiously dipping a spoon into the pot as soon as the rice and sauce started to take on that familiar glossy sheen. We were pleasantly surprised. More water up front helped, though quite a few crunchy bits of uncooked rice from the cooler top of the pan lingered. But we were getting somewhere.

Simply adding more liquid at the start wasn't enough; we needed to keep that moist heat evenly distributed, top to bottom, throughout cooking. That had never been a problem when we were stirring in portions of liquid every few minutes in the final stretch, but now we needed our cooking vessel to do more of the legwork—and our saucepan wasn't cutting it.

A Dutch oven has a thick, heavy bottom, deep sides, and a tight-fitting lid—all of which are meant to trap and distribute heat as evenly as possible, which seemed ideal here. We cooked up a new batch, starting it in a Dutch oven and covering it as soon as we added our liquid. Traditionally, the lid is left off, but with this no-stir method we were free to use it to our advantage, hopefully ensuring that the top of the rice would stay as hot as the bottom. The first 19 minutes of cooking were easy—we had to lift the lid only twice for a quick stir—but after that, the liquid once again turned too viscous for the rice (which was still undercooked) to move around the pot without assistance. Even over low heat, the rice still needed at least five minutes of constant stirring to turn uniformly al dente.

That's where the second half of the Dutch oven success story comes in. The heavy metal pot should retain heat long after it comes off the burner. What if we removed the Dutch oven from the burner during the final minutes of cooking? Without sitting over a direct flame, the rice should turn perfectly al dente just from the residual heat.

For our next batch, after the initial 19-minute covered cooking period we gave the risotto a quick three-minute stir to get the sauce to the right consistency, followed by a five-minute covered, off-heat rest. As we removed the lid, a big plume of steam escaped, indicating that our rice was indeed still hot. As we stirred in some butter, a handful of Parmesan, a few herbs, and a squeeze of lemon juice, we could tell we were on the right track; the risotto looked perfectly creamy, thickened (but not sticky), and velvety. A single taste confirmed it: Using the same ingredients, the proper pot, and an up-to-speed technique, we'd made risotto with just as much love as any Italian nonna—without going stir-crazy.

To turn our risotto into a simple one-dish meal, we developed a recipe incorporating chicken. Using bone-in, skin-on pieces ensured the meat wouldn't dry out, and by searing the chicken in the Dutch oven used for the risotto, we deepened its flavor and added rich fond to the pot. We then transferred the chicken pieces to the simmering broth to gently poach as the aromatics and rice cooked. Cut in half, they were cooked through right on time. We just had to remove the skin, pick the chicken off the bones, and incorporate it just before serving.

Almost Hands-Free Risotto with Parmesan and Herbs

SERVES 6

This more hands-off method does require precise timing, so we strongly recommend using a timer. The consistency of risotto is largely a matter of personal taste; if you prefer a brothy risotto, add extra broth in step 4. This makes a great side dish for braised meats.

- 5 cups low-sodium chicken broth
- 1½ cups water
- 4 tablespoons (½ stick) unsalted butter
- 1 large onion, minced
  Table salt
- 1 medium garlic clove, minced or pressed through a garlic press (about 1 teaspoon)
- 2 cups Arborio rice
- 1 cup dry white wine
- 2 ounces Parmesan cheese, grated (about 1 cup)
- 1 teaspoon juice from 1 lemon
- 2 tablespoons chopped fresh parsley leaves
- 2 tablespoons chopped fresh chives
  Ground black pepper

1. Bring the broth and water to a boil in a large saucepan over high heat. Reduce the heat to medium-low to maintain a gentle simmer.

2. Heat 2 tablespoons of the butter in a large Dutch oven over medium heat. When the butter has melted, add the onion and ¾ teaspoon salt. Cook, stirring frequently, until the onion is softened but not browned, 5 to 7 minutes. Add the garlic and stir until fragrant, about 30 seconds. Add the rice and cook, stirring frequently, until the grains are translucent around the edges, about 3 minutes.

3. Add the wine and cook, stirring constantly, until fully absorbed, 2 to 3 minutes. Stir 5 cups of the warm broth mixture into the rice, reduce the heat to medium-low, cover, and simmer until almost all the liquid has been absorbed and the rice is just al dente, 16 to 19 minutes, stirring twice during cooking.

NOTES FROM THE TEST KITCHEN

SECRETS TO ALMOST HANDS-FREE RISOTTO

In the traditional approach to risotto, near-constant stirring for 25 minutes accomplishes two things: It maximizes the release of starch from the rice, for a creamier sauce, and it ensures that the whole pot cooks evenly. Here's how we achieved the same goals, with only 3 minutes of stirring after the broth is added.

1. Add a full 5 cups of liquid at the start, which, once brought to a boil, jostles the rice grains much like stirring, accelerating the release of creamy starch.

2. Cover the pot with a lid. Coupled with the heavy-bottomed Dutch oven and low heat, it helps distribute the heat as evenly as stirring, so every grain is as tender as the next.

3. A brief stir followed by a five-minute rest provides additional insurance that the rice turns perfectly al dente, from the top of the pot to the bottom.

4. Add ¾ cup more broth mixture and stir gently and constantly until the risotto becomes creamy, about 3 minutes. Stir in the Parmesan. Remove the pot from the heat, cover, and let stand for 5 minutes. Stir in the remaining 2 tablespoons butter, the lemon juice, parsley, and chives. Season with salt and pepper to taste. If desired, add up to ½ cup remaining broth mixture to loosen the texture of the risotto. Serve immediately.

Almost Hands-Free Risotto with Chicken and Herbs

SERVES 6

Adding chicken breasts to the risotto turns a side dish into a main course. Be aware that the thinner ends of the chicken breasts may be fully cooked by the time the broth is added to the rice, with the thicker ends finishing about 5 minutes later. If you prefer a brothy risotto, add extra broth in step 6.

- 5 cups low-sodium chicken broth
- 2 cups water
- 1 tablespoon olive oil
- 2 (12-ounce) bone-in, skin-on chicken breast halves, each cut in half crosswise
- 4 tablespoons (½ stick) unsalted butter
- 1 large onion, chopped fine (about 1½ cups)
  Table salt
- 1 medium garlic clove, minced or pressed through a garlic press (about 1 teaspoon)
- 2 cups Arborio rice
- 1 cup dry white wine
- 2 ounces grated Parmesan cheese (about 1 cup)
- 1 teaspoon juice from 1 lemon
- 2 tablespoons chopped fresh parsley leaves
- 2 tablespoons chopped fresh chives
  Ground black pepper

1. Bring the broth and water to a boil in a large saucepan over high heat. Reduce the heat to medium-low to maintain a gentle simmer.

2. Heat the olive oil in a large Dutch oven over medium heat until just starting to smoke. Add the chicken, skin side down, and cook without moving until golden brown, 4 to 6 minutes. Flip the chicken and cook the second side until lightly browned, about 2 minutes. Transfer the chicken to the saucepan of simmering broth and cook until the thickest part registers 160 to 165 degrees on an instant-read thermometer, 10 to 15 minutes. Transfer to a large plate.

3. Add 2 tablespoons of the butter to the now-empty Dutch oven set over medium heat. When the butter has melted, add the onion and ¾ teaspoon salt; cook, stirring frequently, until the onion is softened but not browned, 4 to 7 minutes. Add the garlic and stir until fragrant, about 30 seconds. Add the rice and cook, stirring frequently, until the grains are translucent around the edges, about 3 minutes.

4. Add the wine and cook, stirring constantly, until fully absorbed, 2 to 3 minutes. Stir 5 cups of the hot broth mixture into the rice; reduce the heat to medium-low, cover, and simmer until almost all the liquid has been absorbed and the rice is just al dente, 16 to 19 minutes, stirring twice during cooking.

5. Add ¾ cup more broth mixture and stir gently and constantly until the risotto becomes creamy, about 3 minutes. Stir in the Parmesan. Remove the pot from the heat, cover, and let stand for 5 minutes.

6. Meanwhile, remove and discard the chicken skin and bones and shred the meat into bite-sized pieces. Gently stir the shredded chicken, remaining 2 tablespoons butter, the lemon juice, parsley, and chives into the risotto. Season with salt and pepper to taste. If desired, add up to ½ cup remaining broth mixture to loosen the texture of the risotto. Serve immediately.

ITALIAN COMFORT *Classics*

Chicken thighs become ultra-flavorful when braised in a white wine sauce enriched with prosciutto, garlic, rosemary, and sage.

IF YOU THINK OF CHICKEN PARMESAN WHEN YOUR MIND TURNS TO Italian-style chicken, think again because in the canon of Italian cooking, braises reign supreme, among them the venerable chicken *canzanese*—chicken cooked in a white wine sauce flavored with prosciutto, rosemary, sage, garlic, and red pepper flakes. This dish, from the Abruzzo region of Italy, was popularized by the *New York Times* in the late 1960s and was a favorite of restaurant menus of the time. But back then, chickens that were sold were older and tougher and braising turned the chicken tender. We wanted to bring this Italian classic back into fashion but we knew we'd have our work cut out for us with today's mass-produced younger chicken that can easily turn dry and stringy when braised. Our goal was tender braised chicken in a richly flavored wine sauce.

And what better to serve with braised chicken than polenta—creamy and rich, it is just the thing to soak up all the robust sauce. Traditional polenta, however tempting it may be, usually comes with some serious labor in the form of stirring and a hefty commitment of time—hurdles that make us think twice about serving it. Could we develop a fuss-free version with the same creamy texture? With visions of burned pots and sticky cornmeal mush in our future, we forged ahead, hoping for the best.

Join us as we reinvent two supreme Italian classics for the modern age.

ITALIAN-BRAISED CHICKEN

✔ WHY THIS RECIPE WORKS: For a modern version of chicken *canzanese,* we turned to chicken thighs, which turn meltingly tender in this Italian chicken braise. For our sauce, we browned diced prosciutto on the stovetop until enough fat was rendered to cook the garlic, which created a rich flavor base. Then we added white wine and chicken broth and simmered them to concentrate flavors and burn off the raw alcohol flavor. We returned the chicken to the skillet and put it into the oven. The result? Chicken that was crisp-skinned on top, meltingly tender and juicy within, and deeply infused with the sauce's flavors.

IN 1969, THE *NEW YORK TIMES* PRINTED A RECIPE FOR chicken *canzanese,* a venerable braised chicken dish from the Abruzzo region of Italy. With the imprimatur of the *Times* (and an appealing-sounding name), this dish—chicken cooked in white wine flavored with prosciutto, rosemary, sage, garlic, red pepper flakes, and cloves until fork-tender—became a simple and satisfying go-to in restaurants and at home. The problem? This recipe was never intended for the lean, mass-produced birds found in today's supermarkets.

Back when the average chicken was older and tougher (and raised on a real farm), braising was a great way to make a fibrous, muscular bird palatable. Braising has another advantage: It creates a sauce. Old chickens contain lots of connective tissue, which makes their meat tough. But when the bird is simmered slowly in a little liquid, the connective tissue gradually converts to gelatin, which both tenderizes the bird and adds an intense, meaty richness to the sauce.

Unfortunately, modern chicken presents a dilemma: Most supermarket birds these days are so young, lean, and tender that braising (as a technique) is almost obsolete; all that prolonged cooking gets you is dried-out, stringy meat and bland, watery sauce. On the other hand, immature chicken is also utterly tasteless and could use a good flavor boost from a well-developed sauce. So the question is: How do you get old-fashioned results with a modern-day bird?

To be fair, the *Times* recipe at least attempts to correct the problem of overcooked chicken by skipping the initial searing common to most braises and capping the cooking time at 30 minutes. When we tried this, the legs cooked through (though they ended up slightly rubbery), but the breasts were already dry, stringy, and overdone. Plus, the skin was anemic-looking and flabby, and the sauce—despite all that flavor-boosting prosciutto, garlic, sage, rosemary, cloves, bay leaves, and red pepper flakes—lacked depth. Not the most auspicious beginning.

Even more confusing, how does a chicken simmering in liquid manage to dry out? For the most part, it's a white meat problem. Like most other meats, chicken breast is made up of long muscle fibers that resemble tightly packed straws filled with liquid. As white meat approaches doneness (165 degrees), its muscle fibers have already squeezed out plenty of juices. If the meat's temperature rises much higher (all but certain in a braising environment), the result is a tough, dry texture—no matter how much liquid the bird is cooked in. But older chickens have the advantage of connective tissues that build up as the bird ages. Given enough cooking time, these tissues (the majority of which are the protein collagen) slowly break down into rich gelatin, which helps lubricate the muscle fibers and compensates for the water they lose—even if their temperature rises well above 165 degrees. Modern chicken breasts, however, contain considerably less connective tissue, making them awful candidates for long-cooked applications.

Chicken thighs, on the other hand, have great braising potential. They contain more connective tissue than breasts but are more tender than an old bird and require less time in the pot. Our first major decision: We would use thighs rather than a cut-up whole chicken. To determine the absolute minimum amount of cooking time necessary to render them fork-tender, we ran a series of tests, cooking the thighs in a 400-degree oven, a 325-degree oven, and a 200-degree oven. The 400-degree oven was out of the question: While the meat was cooked through in just 30 minutes, it didn't allow for enough connective tissue to break down, and the meat was tough and rubbery. Braised in a 200-degree oven,

CHICKEN CANZANESE

the chicken was wonderfully moist and tender—but only after three hours, another nonstarter. The best compromise between time and temperature was the 325-degree oven. At this heat level, the chicken needed to stay in the oven for about an hour and 15 minutes for meat that was tender and juicy. (For more on time, temperature, and braised chicken texture, see "Why You Should Braise Low and Slow" below).

Our next move was to punch up the sauce even more. Instead of simply dumping all the ingredients into a covered Dutch oven, we browned the diced prosciutto on the stovetop until it had rendered enough fat to cook the garlic. Here was the rich flavor base we'd been missing. Next we added the remaining liquids—white wine and chicken broth—and let the sauce simmer for about three minutes uncovered (to concentrate flavors and allow the raw alcohol flavor to burn off), then returned the chicken to the pot, covered the vessel, and pushed it into the oven. About 75 minutes later, we lifted the lid and realized that we had two liquid-related problems: The skin was soggy and waterlogged and the braising liquid itself, while improved, still lacked body and complexity.

The problem was the Dutch oven lid, which was trapping moisture inside the pot. The simple solution, we reasoned, was to remove the lid. As long as all but the top of the meat stayed submerged under the simmering liquid, we figured, it should cook properly and allow the skin to stay crisp. We figured wrong: The skin still came out flabby.

Maybe our problem was more fundamental: Could it be that we were using the wrong vessel entirely? The deep walls of the Dutch oven are designed for trapping heat and steam, but we needed something that allowed steam to escape. A wide, shallow skillet is an odd choice for a dish that's traditionally cooked covered, but we decided to give it a go anyway. That did it. Finally, our chicken was crisp-skinned on top, meltingly tender and juicy within, and deeply infused with the flavors of the wine, prosciutto, and aromatics. Even better, now that we were cooking with the lid off, the sauce was slowly reducing during its stay in the oven. Not only could we shorten the stovetop reduction, but our sauce was coming out more concentrated than ever.

Despite its great flavor, the sauce was still on the thin side, so after removing the cooked thighs from the pan, we added a touch of flour—just enough to build up some viscosity. To round out the flavors, we added a quick squeeze of lemon juice, a knob of butter, and a sprinkling

SCIENCE DESK

WHY YOU SHOULD BRAISE LOW AND SLOW

We've always heard that braising should be done "low and slow," but how much of an effect do temperature and time actually have on the finished product?

THE EXPERIMENT

We braised thighs in a 200-degree oven, a 325-degree oven, and a 400-degree oven, recording their temperature as they cooked with a remote thermometer and removing them once they reached 195 degrees (the point at which the thighs start becoming unpalatably dry). We then compared the texture of the meat in each batch.

THE RESULTS

The chicken in the 200-degree oven was by far the most supple and moist but took nearly three hours to fully tenderize. In the 400-degree oven, the meat cooked through so rapidly we had to remove it in a little over half an hour for thighs that were still moist but tough. The best compromise was the 325-degree oven, which produced chicken nearly as moist and tender as the 200-degree oven but in just half the time.

THE EXPLANATION

As chicken thighs simmer in liquid, two things happen: At 105 degrees, muscle fibers begin to contract and expel moisture. But at 140 degrees, the tough connective tissue begins to slowly break down into soft, rich gelatin, mitigating the loss of moisture and the shrinking of muscle proteins. Still, there's a limit to this effect. Once the braised thighs go much beyond 195 degrees, no amount of gelatin can make them seem moist. The key is to keep the chicken above 140 degrees but below 195 degrees for as long as necessary to fully tenderize it. In the 400-degree oven, the chicken reached the 195-degree cutoff point much too quickly for any significant connective tissue breakdown to take place. In the 325-degree oven, the meat reached 140 degrees after a relatively leisurely 20 minutes and took another 55 minutes to reach 195 degrees—plenty of time to produce moist, tender results.

of chopped rosemary leaves and poured the reduction around the crisp, tender meat.

Who says you can't teach an old bird new tricks? Our new, improved Chicken Canzanese is good enough to be making the rounds for another 40 years.

Chicken Canzanese

SERVES 4 TO 6

When seasoning the dish at the end, be mindful that the prosciutto adds a fair amount of salt. It is important to use a piece of thickly sliced prosciutto in this recipe; thin strips will become tough and stringy. An equal amount of thickly sliced pancetta or bacon can be used in place of the prosciutto. Serve the chicken with boiled potatoes, noodles, or polenta.

- 1 tablespoon olive oil
- 2 ounces prosciutto (¼ inch thick), cut into ¼-inch cubes (see note)
- 4 medium garlic cloves, sliced thin lengthwise
- 3 pounds bone-in, skin-on chicken thighs (about 8 thighs), trimmed of excess fat and skin
  Ground black pepper
- 2 teaspoons unbleached all-purpose flour
- 2 cups dry white wine
- 1 cup low-sodium chicken broth
- 4 whole cloves
- 1 (4-inch) sprig fresh rosemary, leaves removed and minced fine (about ½ teaspoon), stem reserved
- 12 whole fresh sage leaves
- 2 bay leaves
- ¼–½ teaspoon red pepper flakes
- 1 tablespoon juice from 1 lemon
- 2 tablespoons unsalted butter
  Table salt

1. Adjust an oven rack to the lower-middle position and heat the oven to 325 degrees. Heat 1 teaspoon of the oil in a 12-inch heavy-bottomed ovensafe skillet over medium heat until shimmering. Add the prosciutto and cook, stirring frequently, until just starting to brown, about 3 minutes. Add the garlic slices and cook, stirring frequently, until the garlic is golden brown, about 1½ minutes. Using a slotted spoon, transfer the garlic and prosciutto to a small bowl and set aside. Do not rinse the pan.

2. Increase the heat to medium-high; add the remaining 2 teaspoons oil and heat until just smoking. Pat the chicken dry with paper towels and season with ground black pepper. Add the chicken, skin side down, and cook without moving until well browned, 5 to 8 minutes. Using tongs, turn the chicken and brown on the second side, about 5 minutes longer. Transfer the chicken to a large plate.

3. Remove all but 2 tablespoons fat from the pan. Sprinkle the flour over the fat and cook, stirring constantly, for 1 minute. Slowly add the wine and broth; bring to a simmer, scraping the bottom of the pan with a wooden spoon to loosen the browned bits. Cook until the liquid is slightly reduced, 3 minutes. Stir in the cloves, rosemary stem, sage leaves, bay leaves, red pepper flakes, and reserved prosciutto and garlic. Nestle the chicken into the liquid, skin side up (the skin should be above the surface of the liquid), and bake, uncovered, until the meat offers no resistance when poked with a fork but is not falling off the bones, about 1 hour 15 minutes. (Check the chicken after 15 minutes; the broth should be barely bubbling. If bubbling vigorously, reduce the oven temperature to 300 degrees.)

4. Using tongs, transfer the chicken to a serving platter and tent with foil. Remove and discard the sage leaves, rosemary stem, cloves, and bay leaves. Place the skillet over high heat and bring the sauce to a boil. Cook until the sauce is reduced to 1¼ cups, 2 to 5 minutes. Off the heat, stir in the minced rosemary, lemon juice, and butter. Season with salt and pepper to taste. Pour the sauce around the chicken and serve.

NOTES FROM THE TEST KITCHEN

A BETTER WAY TO SLOW-COOK CHICKEN

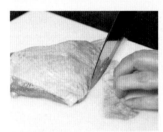

1. START WITH THIGHS: Unlike breasts, thighs have lots of connective tissue, which breaks down under heat to lubricate the meat. Trim excess fat before cooking.

2. USE A SKILLET: The straight, high walls of a Dutch oven—the typical vessel for browning and braising—trap moisture, leading to soggy skin.

3. LEAVE THE LID OFF: With no lid to trap steam and the chicken placed skin side up in the liquid, the skin can dry and crisp during its long stay in the oven.

NO-FUSS POLENTA

✔ **WHY THIS RECIPE WORKS:** For quick polenta with a creamy texture and deep corn flavor, we searched for the right type of cornmeal and a technique to hasten its cooking. Coarse-ground degerminated cornmeal gave us the soft but hearty texture and nutty flavor we were looking for. A pinch of baking soda cut cooking time in half and eliminated the need for stirring, giving us the best quick polenta.

THIS SIMPLE, HEARTY DISH OF LONG-COOKED CORN-meal dates back to 16th-century Rome, where polenta *sulla tavola* was poured onto the table to soak up flavors from previous meals. These days, polenta passes for haute restaurant cuisine. Its nutty corn flavor is equally satisfying, whether embellished simply with butter and cheese or served as a base for braised veal shanks or an exotic mushroom ragout. Today it is prepared either as a warm, porridgelike spoon food or as firmer squares that are grilled or fried. Both have their merits, but when the cold weather sets in, a bowl of the soothing, silky-textured stuff can't be beat.

The recipe sounds easy: Boil water, whisk in cornmeal, and stir until softened. But the devil is in the details: Polenta can take up to an hour to cook, and if you don't stir almost constantly, it forms intractable clumps. We wanted to find a better way. Here's what's going on in a pot of polenta: When the starchy part of the corn kernels (the endosperm) comes in contact with hot water, it eventually absorbs liquid, swells, and bursts, releasing starch in a process known as gelatinization. At the same time, the grains soften, losing their gritty texture. But the tough pieces of endosperm require plenty of time and heat for the water to break through. And the pot must be stirred constantly; if polenta heats unevenly, some of its starch gelatinizes much faster than the rest, forming little pockets of fully cooked polenta, which are nearly impossible to fully break up once formed.

NO-FUSS POLENTA WITH BROCCOLI RABE, SUN-DRIED TOMATOES, AND PINE NUTS

We tried a shortcut with parboiled "instant" brands that are ready in minutes, but tasters complained these cooked up gluey, with lackluster flavor. It was time for a tour of cornmeal options. The typical supermarket offers a bewildering assortment of products, and their labels confuse matters further. The same dried ground corn can be called anything from yellow grits to polenta to corn semolina. Labels also advertise "fine," "medium," and "coarse" grinds, but we discovered no standards exist—one manufacturer's medium grind might be another's heartiest coarse option. Then there's the choice between whole-grain and degerminated corn (which is treated before grinding to remove both the hull and germ but leaving the endosperm intact).

Our best bet was to try everything. We eventually settled on the couscous-size grains of coarse-ground degerminated cornmeal (often labeled "yellow grits"). They delivered the hearty yet soft texture we were looking for, plus plenty of nutty corn flavor. The only downside: The large, coarse grains took a full hour to cook through, during which time the mixture grew overly thick and our arms ached from stirring. We had been sticking to the typical 4–1 ratio of water to cornmeal. After experimenting, we found a 5–1 ratio (7½ cups water to 1½ cups cornmeal) produced the right loose consistency.

Now the hard part: whittling down the one-hour cooking time and decreasing the stirring. The rate at which water penetrates the corn is proportional to temperature, so raising the heat seemed logical, but even a heavy-bottomed pot couldn't protect the polenta from burning badly.

Maybe the key was in the cornmeal itself. There had to be a way to give that water a head start on penetrating the grains. Would soaking the cornmeal overnight help, the way it does with dried beans? We combined the cornmeal and water the night before, then cooked them together the next day. The results were uninspiring. While the grains did seem to absorb some of the liquid, this small improvement didn't alter the cooking time enough to make the extra step worth it.

Casting about for ideas, we came back to beans. The goal in cooking dried beans and dried corn is essentially identical. In a bean, water has to penetrate the hard outer skin to gelatinize the starch within. In a corn kernel, the water has to penetrate the endosperm. To soften bean skins and speed up cooking, some cooks advocate adding baking soda during cooking. Would this work for cornmeal?

We started up another batch, adding ¼ teaspoon baking soda to the cooking water as soon as it came to a boil. To our delight, the polenta cooked up in 20 minutes. But it was overkill. The baking soda acted so effectively that the cooked porridge turned gluey. It also added a strange flavor. We found that even ⅛ teaspoon soda was excessive. Just a pinch turned out to be plenty, producing polenta that cooked in a mere 30 minutes without any gluey texture or objectionable flavors.

As for stirring time, the solution came quite by accident. We'd just whisked the cornmeal into the boiling water when we got called away from the kitchen. Without thinking, we threw a lid on the pot (traditionally you cook polenta uncovered), turned the heat to its lowest level, and left the polenta to sputter untouched for nearly the entire 30 minutes. Rushing back to the stove, we expected to find a clumpy, burned-on-the-bottom mess, but instead we found perfectly creamy polenta.

NOTES FROM THE TEST KITCHEN

MAKING A FLAME TAMER
Our recipe for No-Fuss Creamy Parmesan Polenta relies on heat so low it barely disturbs the pot's contents. A flame tamer (or heat diffuser), a metal disk that can be fitted over an electric or gas burner to reduce the heat, can help to ensure the heat is as gentle as possible. If you don't have a flame tamer (one costs less than $10 at most kitchen supply stores), you can easily make one.

Squeeze a 3-foot length of aluminum foil into a ½-inch rope. Twist the rope into a ring the size of the burner.

The baking soda must have helped the granules break down and release their starch in a uniform way so that the bottom layer didn't cook any faster than the top. And the combination of covering the pot and adjusting the heat to low cooked the polenta so gently and evenly that the result was lump-free, even without vigorous stirring.

We eventually found that after one relatively brief whisk as soon as the ingredients went in and another, shorter one five minutes later, we didn't even have to lift the lid until it was time to add the cheese. Two cups of grated Parmesan plus a pair of butter pats gave this humble mush enough nutty tang and richness to make it a satisfying dish, with or without a topping—and with the barest amount of effort.

No-Fuss Creamy Parmesan Polenta

SERVES 6 TO 8

Coarse-ground degerminated cornmeal such as yellow grits (with grains the size of couscous) works best in this recipe. Avoid instant and quick-cooking products, as well as whole-grain, stone-ground, and regular cornmeal. Do not omit the baking soda—it reduces the cooking time and makes for a creamier polenta. The polenta should do little more than release wisps of steam. If it bubbles or sputters even slightly after the first 10 minutes, the heat is too high and you may need a flame tamer (see page 164). For a main course, serve the polenta with a topping (recipes follow) or with a wedge of rich cheese or a meat sauce. Served plain, the polenta makes a great accompaniment to stews and braises.

7½ cups water
1½ teaspoons table salt
    Pinch baking soda
1½ cups coarse-ground cornmeal (see note)
 4 ounces Parmesan cheese, grated (about 2 cups), plus extra for serving
 2 tablespoons unsalted butter
    Ground black pepper

1. Bring the water to a boil in a heavy-bottomed 4-quart saucepan over medium-high heat. Stir in the salt and baking soda. Slowly pour the cornmeal into the water in a steady stream, while stirring back and forth with a wooden spoon or rubber spatula. Bring the mixture to a boil, stirring constantly, about 1 minute. Reduce the heat to the lowest possible setting and cover.

2. After 5 minutes, whisk the polenta to smooth out any lumps that may have formed, about 15 seconds. (Make sure to scrape the sides and bottom of the pan.) Cover and continue to cook, without stirring, until the grains of polenta are tender but slightly al dente, about 25 minutes longer. (The polenta should be loose and barely hold its shape; it will continue to thicken as it cools.)

3. Remove from the heat, stir in the Parmesan and butter, and season with pepper to taste. Let stand, covered, for 5 minutes. Serve, passing extra Parmesan separately.

No-Fuss Polenta with Broccoli Rabe, Sun-Dried Tomatoes, and Pine Nuts

SERVES 4

 3 tablespoons extra-virgin olive oil
 6 medium garlic cloves, minced or pressed through a garlic press (about 2 tablespoons)
½ teaspoon red pepper flakes
½ cup sun-dried tomatoes packed in oil, rinsed, patted dry, and chopped coarse
    Table salt
 1 bunch broccoli rabe (about 1 pound), trimmed and cut into 1½-inch pieces
¼ cup low-sodium chicken broth
 1 recipe No-Fuss Creamy Parmesan Polenta
 3 tablespoons pine nuts, toasted

Heat the oil, garlic, red pepper flakes, sun-dried tomatoes, and ½ teaspoon salt in a 12-inch nonstick skillet over medium-high heat, stirring frequently, until the garlic is fragrant and slightly toasted, about 1½ minutes. Add the broccoli rabe and broth, cover, and cook until the broccoli rabe turns bright green, about 2 minutes. Uncover and cook, stirring frequently, until most of the broth has evaporated and the broccoli rabe is just tender, 2 to 3 minutes. Season with salt to taste. Serve over the polenta, sprinkling individual portions with the pine nuts.

No-Fuss Polenta with Sautéed Cherry Tomatoes and Fresh Mozzarella

SERVES 4

Don't stir the cheese into the sautéed tomatoes or it will melt prematurely and turn rubbery.

- 3   tablespoons extra-virgin olive oil
- 2   medium garlic cloves, peeled and sliced thin
     Pinch red pepper flakes
     Pinch sugar
- 2   pints cherry tomatoes, halved
     Table salt and ground black pepper
- 1   recipe No-Fuss Creamy Parmesan Polenta
- 6   ounces fresh mozzarella, cut into ½-inch cubes (about 1 cup) (see note)
- 2   tablespoons thinly sliced fresh basil leaves

Heat the oil, garlic, red pepper flakes, and sugar in a 12-inch nonstick skillet over medium-high heat until fragrant and sizzling, about 1 minute. Stir in the tomatoes and cook until they just begin to soften, about 1 minute. Season with salt and pepper to taste and remove from the heat. Serve over the polenta, topping individual portions with the mozzarella and basil.

No-Fuss Polenta with Sweet-and-Sour Onion Relish

SERVES 4

- 2   tablespoons extra-virgin olive oil
- 2   medium red onions, sliced thin
- 4   sprigs fresh thyme
     Table salt
- 2   tablespoons balsamic vinegar
- 1   tablespoon light brown sugar
- 2   tablespoons water
     Ground black pepper
- 1   recipe No-Fuss Creamy Parmesan Polenta
- 6   ounces extra-sharp cheddar cheese, shredded (about 1½ cups)
- ½   cup toasted walnuts, chopped coarse

Heat the oil in a 12-inch nonstick skillet over medium-high heat until shimmering. Add the onions, thyme sprigs, and ½ teaspoon salt; cook, stirring frequently, until the onions soften and begin to brown, 5 to 7 minutes. Reduce the heat to low, stir in the vinegar, sugar, and water; simmer until the liquid has evaporated and the onions are glossy, 5 to 7 minutes. Discard the thyme springs and season with salt and pepper to taste. Serve over the polenta, sprinkling individual portions with the cheddar and walnuts.

SCIENCE DESK

BAKING SODA'S SOFT (AND SPEEDY) TOUCH

For polenta to lose its hard, gritty texture and turn creamy, enough water must penetrate the corn's cell walls that the starch granules within swell and burst (or gelatinize). Baking soda added to the cooking liquid can reduce the time it takes for gelatinization to occur, thus shortening cooking time. Here's why: Corn cell walls are held together by pectin. When alkaline sodium bicarbonate (aka baking soda) is present, the pectin breaks down, weakening the corn's structure and allowing water to enter and gelatinize the starch in less than half the time.

KITCHEN GADGETS THAT MAKE THE GRADE

Even here in the test kitchen, we succumb to impulse buying every once in a while. After all, those gadgets and knickknacks at the cash register are meant to look like tools you just can't live without. Usually, they fall flat—useless pieces of metal, silicone, and the like that do little more than hog counter or drawer space. But occasionally, we hit on something worthwhile. Here are a number of kitchen gadgets that really deliver. See www.americastestkitchen.com for updates to this testing.

BASTING SPOON

While it might look like just another spoon, a basting spoon has a wide head that is meant to act as a platform to skim the fat off the top of soup or to scoop up a small amount of pan sauce in a skillet. In our tests, we found that models with broad, deep bowls in thicker silicone or fiberglass struggled to scoop up shallow liquids, while models with shallow, thin stainless steel heads performed with maximum efficiency. Handle angles and lengths proved to be important too: Spoons that were flat from tip to head couldn't fit into corners of pans or skim fat without forcing testers to awkwardly twist their wrists or tilt pans. The best spoons had a handle at least 9 inches long to keep hands out of the heat and a slight dip from handle to bowl. Our favorite basting spoon is the Rösle Basting Spoon with Hook Handle ($28.95), which is well shaped and easy to maneuver around every type of pan.

WINNER: RÖSLE BASTING SPOON WITH HOOK HANDLE

CHEESE WIRE

A cheese wire is an invaluable tool for cutting through large wheels of semihard cheddar or smaller rounds of soft cheeses like Camembert. But if you're not cutting into large wheels of cheese on a regular basis, does the cheese wire still deserve space in your kitchen drawer? Absolutely. We've found it also works well to cut neat, smooth slices of creamy cheesecake and other soft desserts that might get mussed when sliced with a knife. Fante's Handled Cheese Wire ($2.99) is easy to use to portion out cake pieces; you simply hold the handles and pull the wire taut, then press down through the cake. This dual-purpose tool is worth its bargain price.

WINNER: FANTE'S HANDLED CHEESE WIRE

JAR OPENER

Jar lids that stick are an incessant, annoying problem. To open both large and small jars, we reach for the Swing-A-Way Comfort Grip Jar Opener. Not only does it have a low price ($6.99), but it also adjusts quickly to any size jar. We found the Swing-A-Way could open anything from a small bottle of vanilla to a quart-sized jar of pasta sauce, and it's especially effective in breaking the vacuum seal on brand new jars. Although it takes a few tries to learn to adjust the clamp, this tool is handy in the stickiest of situations.

WINNER: SWING-A-WAY COMFORT GRIP JAR OPENER

DONERIGHT KITCHEN TIMER

While the Polder 3-in-1 Clock, Timer, and Stopwatch ($12) is our kitchen timer of choice in the test kitchen, we've found another nifty timer that comes in handy when cooking for a crowd. When you've got a pot topping each burner and food in the oven, it's hard to keep track of when each dish is done. The 5 in 1 DoneRight Kitchen Timer ($24.95) offers a clever solution: a stove-shaped device with four individual timers in the position of each burner as well as one for the oven. The timers only clock up to 99 minutes, but we found them easy to use and readable at a glance.

WINNER: 5 IN 1 DONERIGHT KITCHEN TIMER

CREAM WHIPPER

Whipping heavy cream is no big deal—all that's required is a whisk or mixer, a chilled bowl, and a few minutes. But what if you only need a dollop for a piece of leftover pie or a mug of cocoa and you don't want to waste a whole bowl of whipped cream or deal with the leftovers, which will separate as they sit? Enter cream whippers. These nitrous oxide–charged metal canisters can whip a pint of fresh cream in a matter of seconds or hold the cream for several days in the refrigerator, letting you whip it as needed, with all the convenience of Reddi-whip—minus the additives and sweeteners. Our favorite cream whipper is the Liss Professional Polished Stainless Steel Cream Whipper ($75), which is pretty enough to set out on the dining room table.

WINNER: LISS PROFESSIONAL POLISHED STAINLESS STEEL CREAM WHIPPER

Tostadas
AND EMPANADAS

We pile our spicy Mexican shredded pork onto crisp, freshly fried corn tortillas— and if you don't like frying, we provide a baked option that's just as good.

WANT TO MAKE SOMETHING DIFFERENT FOR DINNER BUT HAVING A hard time coming up with fresh options? We've got two ideas for you— pork tostadas and beef empanadas.

The pulled pork most of us are familiar with hails from down South and is made on the grill—piled high on a soft bun with pickles and coleslaw, it's one of our favorites. But another type of pulled pork and one we're equally fond of is found further south—in Mexico, called *tinga*. Tinga gets its smoky tomato flavor not from the grill, but from a chipotle chile–infused tomato sauce. It's got a wonderfully crisp texture and is typically served on crisp corn tortillas with garnishes like chopped avocado, cilantro, and crumbles of salty queso fresco. And here's a bonus: Tinga is made on the stovetop, rather than on a grill, making this version easy and accessible year-round. We set out to perfect this Mexican classic.

Empanadas, crisp pastry pockets stuffed with a spicy beef filling, are another great dinner option when you're looking for something new to add to your repertoire. But the filling is often braised, which takes more time than we'd like and once stuffed, the pockets are deep-fried. Was there an easier way to replicate this South American favorite? We set out to create hearty empanadas with tender, flaky crusts and a juicy, well-seasoned filling.

CRISP PORK TOSTADAS

✔ WHY THIS RECIPE WORKS: We wanted our pork to have a crisp texture and smoky tomato flavor characteristic of the traditional Mexican version. To get smoky, fork-tender pork on the stovetop, we simmered cubed Boston butt in water flavored with garlic, onion, and thyme, and then sautéed the drained meat in a hot frying pan to crisp it up. Finally, we used canned tomato sauce and chipotle chile powder to build a deep and complex sauce.

TRUE MEXICAN SHREDDED PORK—OR *TINGA*—IS A FAR cry from the bland burrito-joint version often found languishing in steam tables in this country. As with good barbecued pulled pork, tinga's moist, tender shreds possess an intense, sweet meatiness. Often cooked with Mexican chorizo for even more complexity, the pork is sautéed after braising until it acquires deeply browned edges that stay crisp even after a quick simmer in a chipotle-infused tomato sauce. To play against its supple texture, tinga is served on crunchy tostada shells (toasted or deep-fried corn tortillas) and garnished with avocado, sour cream, queso fresco (a Mexican fresh cheese), cilantro, and lime wedges.

While the best barbecued pulled pork is traditionally cooked for hours via indirect heat in a smoker, tinga is cooked on top of the stove and takes a fraction of the time. Another bonus: It's made entirely from ingredients found in any American supermarket. For our own homegrown version, we would simply need to perfect the methods that give the pork its characteristic crisp texture and the sauce its smoky tomato flavor.

Boston butt and picnic shoulder were the two most likely candidates for the meat; they are the test kitchen's favorites for barbecued pulled pork. Both well-marbled cuts come from the front legs of the pig and benefit from long, gentle cooking methods. But since pork butt has less sinew, we opted for it. We trimmed a 2-pound boneless butt, cubed it into 1-inch pieces, and submerged the cubes in the saucepan of plain salted water called for in most recipes. After about an hour and a half of simmering, the

pork was very tender with a clean, sweet taste. Still, we couldn't help but wonder if we could give it a bit more complexity. Replacing the water with chicken broth might do the trick, but this seemed wasteful, since the bulk of the braising liquid is discarded once the pork is cooked. Instead, we added an onion, a few smashed garlic cloves, and several sprigs of thyme (always a good complement to pork), which imparted a subtle vegetal flavor to the meat.

Now for the trait that really separates tinga from pulled pork: its overall crisp texture. Since pulled pork is smoked as a roast, only its ends have the crunchy browned bits known as bark. But because the pork in tinga is shredded before sautéing, it has far more surface area available for browning. We drained the meat, reserving a cup of cooking liquid for the sauce, then returned it to the pot to shred. The meat was so tender, it fell apart with nothing more than the pressure of a potato masher. We placed the meat in a hot frying pan with olive oil and sautéed it with the requisite additions of finely chopped onion and oregano. It took about 10 minutes for the pork to develop crackling edges that were crisp enough to survive the final step of simmering in tomato sauce.

Now we were ready to tackle the sauce. If there's one thing to be learned from American barbecue, it's that pork and smoke go hand in hand. Instead of the sweet and tangy sauce typical of American barbecue, tinga relies on a complex, smoky tomato sauce. While some all-out versions specify fresh tomatoes charred on a hot comal (a cast-iron griddle) and then pureed until smooth, most recipes call for some form of canned tomatoes. (The chipotles—dried smoked jalapeños—add plenty of charred flavor on their own.) Canned tomatoes offered a nice bright flavor, but we wondered if we could avoid hauling out our blender by using tomato puree instead. Its concentrated flavor proved too sweet. Surprisingly, the canned tomato sauce called for in many recipes worked best, contributing a supremely smooth texture and a bright taste. The cup of reserved cooking liquid diluted it to an ideal consistency, and two bay leaves added herbal complexity.

Next we considered the all-important smoky flavor. In tinga it comes not from wood chunks but from chipotles. This flavor-packed ingredient is generally available in two

SPICY MEXICAN SHREDDED PORK TOSTADAS

forms: canned in adobo sauce and ground into powder. As we made batch after batch, tasters noticed that the flavor of canned chipotles varied greatly from brand to brand. Some were more salty, sweet, and vinegary than spicy, while others offered searing heat and not much else. Ground chipotle powder, though a little harder to track down, turned out to be far more consistent, with a deeper, more complex smokiness.

There was just one more issue: the fresh Mexican chorizo included in some versions. Unlike hard, dry-cured Spanish chorizo or chunky, garlicky South American chorizo, Mexican chorizo is flavored with plenty of chili powder and vinegar. It's easy to find in the Southwest, but here in Boston there was virtually no authentic Mexican chorizo, even in specialty markets. How difficult would it be to make it ourselves? As it turned out, not very. We bought an extra pound of pork that we ground in a food processor along with spices and vinegar. We then briefly sautéed this mixture and set it aside while we crisped the shredded pork in the rendered chorizo fat before returning it to the pan along with the sauce. For those occasions when we had a little extra time, the chorizo version would be well worth the effort.

At last, we proudly served up our recipe, confident that it would win fans on both sides of the border.

Spicy Mexican Shredded Pork Tostadas

SERVES 4 TO 6

The trimmed pork should weigh about 1½ pounds. Although the shredded pork is traditionally served on tostadas (crisp fried corn tortillas), you can also use the meat in tacos or burritos or simply served over rice. Make sure to buy tortillas made only with corn, lime, and salt—preservatives will compromise quality. If you prefer not to fry your tortillas, see our recipe for baking tostadas on page 175. We prefer the complex flavor of chipotle powder, but two minced canned chipotle chiles can be used in its place. The pork can be prepared through step 1 and refrigerated in an airtight container for 2 days. The tostadas can be made up to a day in advance and stored in an airtight container.

SHREDDED PORK

- 2 pounds boneless pork butt, trimmed of excess fat and cut into 1-inch pieces (see note)
- 2 medium onions, 1 quartered and 1 chopped fine
- 5 medium garlic cloves, 3 peeled and smashed and 2 minced or pressed through a garlic press (about 2 teaspoons)
- 4 sprigs fresh thyme
  Table salt
- 2 tablespoons olive oil
- ½ teaspoon dried oregano
- 1 (14.5-ounce) can tomato sauce
- 1 tablespoon ground chipotle powder (see note)
- 2 bay leaves

TOSTADAS

- ¾ cup vegetable oil
- 12 (6-inch) corn tortillas (see note)
  Table salt
  Garnishes
  Queso fresco or feta cheese
  Fresh cilantro leaves
  Sour cream
  Diced avocado
  Lime wedges

1. FOR THE SHREDDED PORK: Bring the pork, quartered onion, smashed garlic cloves, thyme, 1 teaspoon salt, and 6 cups water to a simmer in a large saucepan over medium-high heat, skimming off any foam that rises to the surface. Reduce the heat to medium-low, partially cover, and cook until the pork is tender, 1¼ to 1½ hours. Drain the pork, reserving 1 cup cooking liquid. Discard the onion, garlic, and thyme. Return the pork to the saucepan and, using a potato masher, mash until shredded into rough ½-inch pieces; set aside.

2. Heat the olive oil in a 12-inch nonstick skillet over medium-high heat until shimmering. Add the shredded pork, chopped onion, and oregano; cook, stirring often,

until the pork is well browned and crisp, 7 to 10 minutes. Add the minced garlic and cook until fragrant, about 30 seconds.

3. Stir in the tomato sauce, chipotle powder, reserved pork cooking liquid, and bay leaves; simmer until almost all the liquid has evaporated, 5 to 7 minutes. Remove and discard the bay leaves and season with salt to taste.

4. TO FRY THE TOSTADAS: Heat the vegetable oil in an 8-inch heavy-bottomed skillet over medium heat to 350 degrees. Using a fork, poke the center of each tortilla three or four times (to prevent puffing and allow for even cooking). Fry one at a time, holding a metal potato masher in the upright position on top of the tortilla to keep it submerged, until crisp and lightly browned, 45 to 60 seconds (no flipping is necessary). Drain on a paper towel–lined plate and season with salt to taste. Repeat with the remaining tortillas.

5. TO SERVE: Spoon a small amount of shredded pork onto the center of each tostada and serve, passing the garnishes separately.

VARIATION

Spicy Mexican Shredded Pork Tostadas with Homemade Chorizo
SERVES 6 TO 8

Follow the recipe for Spicy Mexican Shredded Pork Tostadas, increasing the amount of pork to 3 pounds (2½ pounds after trimming). Using two-thirds of the trimmed pork (1½ pounds), follow the recipe as directed in step 1. To make the chorizo, place the remaining pork pieces on a large plate in a single layer and freeze until firm but still pliable, about 15 minutes. Once firm, toss the pork with 1 tablespoon red wine vinegar, 1¼ teaspoons chili powder, 1 teaspoon minced garlic, 1 teaspoon table salt, ¾ teaspoon hot paprika, ¾ teaspoon chipotle powder, ¾ teaspoon dried oregano, ¼ teaspoon ground black pepper, and ⅛ teaspoon ground cumin in a medium bowl. Place half of the chorizo mixture in a food processor and pulse until the meat is finely chopped, 8 to 10 pulses. Transfer to a bowl and repeat with the remaining chorizo mixture. In step 2, heat the oil as directed and add the chorizo mixture; cook, stirring occasionally,

---

NOTES FROM THE TEST KITCHEN

KEY STEPS TO CRISP-TENDER SHREDDED PORK

1. Simmer the pork with aromatics to infuse it with vegetal flavors. Drain, reserving 1 cup liquid.

2. Mash the pork with a potato masher to maximize the surface area for browning.

3. Cook the pork with onions and oregano until its exterior is deeply brown and crisp, then simmer in sauce.

RATING VEGETABLE OIL

With the range of vegetable oil varieties available and profusion of names like "Vegetable Plus!" and "Natural Blend," it's hard to know which one to pick—or whether it even matters. We tested 10 vegetable oils, all produced by the three companies dominant in the industry (we excluded the harder-to-find, more expensive peanut oil and olive oil) in two applications: mayonnaise and french fries. We rated the oils on greasiness (for fries), texture (in mayonnaise), presence of off-flavors (if any), and overall appeal. While tasters noticed significant differences among the oils in these tests, when we tested the top- and bottom-ranked oils again, in white cake and vinaigrette (where oil played a subordinate role) tasters could hardly differentiate between the two. Our top-ranking oil, though not a runaway favorite, performed well in every application. It has the unusual addition of sunflower oil, which we found keeps the oil fresher and more flavorful, even under high heat. Brands are listed in order of preference. See www.americastestkitchen.com for updates to this testing.

RECOMMENDED

CRISCO Natural Blend Oil (canola, sunflower, and soybean)
PRICE: $5.75 for 48 oz
MAYONNAISE: ★★★ **FRYING:** ★★★
BAKING: ★★★ **VINAIGRETTE:** ★★★
COMMENTS: In mayonnaise, the "very clean" taste of this blend outperformed the rest. Despite containing canola and soybean oils (which can contribute off-flavors), it was utterly "neutral and balanced" in fries.

MAZOLA Canola Oil
PRICE: $5.53 for 48 oz
MAYONNAISE: ★★★ **FRYING:** ★★★
COMMENTS: The "clean flavor" of this oil gave mayonnaise a "nice, light" taste. In fries, while a few sensitive tasters noticed some fishiness, the majority gave it the thumbs-up for a neutral taste that let potato flavor "shine through."

CRISCO Pure Vegetable Oil (soybean)
PRICE: $3.99 for 48 oz
MAYONNAISE: ★★★ **FRYING:** ★★★
COMMENTS: Though criticized by some for being "slightly greasy" in both the mayonnaise and the fries, overall its taste was "neutral" in both applications—just how we like our vegetable oil to be.

CRISCO Pure Corn Oil
PRICE: $5.95 for 48 oz
MAYONNAISE: ★★ **FRYING:** ★★★
COMMENTS: While tasters disliked most corn oils in mayonnaise, this brand was the exception, earning low but acceptable scores. In fries, it shone: "Great. No negatives."

CRISCO Pure Canola Oil
PRICE: $5.75 for 48 oz
MAYONNAISE: ★★★ **FRYING:** ★★
COMMENTS: This oil contributed to a "pleasant-tasting" mayonnaise with a "creamy" texture. In fries, however, some tasters detected an aftertaste "like spent oil."

RECOMMENDED (cont.)

WESSON Vegetable Oil (soybean)
PRICE: $3.99 for 48 oz
MAYONNAISE: ★★ **FRYING:** ★★
COMMENTS: Most tasters deemed this oil "inoffensive" in mayonnaise, but some noted a slight "greasy" consistency. In fries, tasters were divided: Half found it an agreeably silent partner to the potatoes; others complained of "weird," "metallic" off-flavors.

RECOMMENDED WITH RESERVATIONS

WESSON Canola Oil
PRICE: $5.99 for 48 oz
MAYONNAISE: ★★★ **FRYING:** ★
COMMENTS: This oil drew accolades for producing a mayonnaise that was "mellow" and "silky." But it finished last in the fries test; taster complaints ranged from "sour" to "disgusting fish flavor."

MAZOLA Corn Oil
PRICE: $5.49 for 48 oz
MAYONNAISE: ★ **FRYING:** ★★★
COMMENTS: Like the two bottom-ranked corn oils, this product tanked in the mayo tests, producing a sauce with "rancid," "turpentine-like" flavors. Fries were a different story altogether: "These are great; no off-flavors."

MAZOLA Corn Plus! Oil (corn and canola)
PRICE: $4.49 for 48 oz.
MAYONNAISE: ★ **FRYING:** ★★★
COMMENTS: In mayonnaise, this corn-canola blend exhibited an aftertaste so "pungent," one taster likened it to "blue cheese." But, like other corn oils, for frying it was a marvel, producing fries with "nutty," "buttery" flavor.

WESSON Corn Oil
PRICE: $5.44 for 48 oz
MAYONNAISE: ★ **FRYING:** ★★★
BAKING: ★★★ **VINAIGRETTE:** ★★★
COMMENTS: Although it was "like licking metal—funky" in mayo, french fries tasted "good."

until slightly crisp and no longer pink, 3 to 5 minutes. Transfer the meat to a paper towel–lined plate, leaving the rendered fat in the skillet. Proceed with the recipe as directed, using the rendered fat to cook the shredded pork and returning the chorizo mixture to the skillet along with the tomato sauce in step 3.

Baked Tostadas

MAKES 12 TOSTADAS

Baking tortillas to create tostadas uses much less oil than frying (the traditional approach), with very comparable results.

12 (6-inch) corn tortillas
Vegetable oil

1. Arrange the tortillas in a single layer on two rimmed baking sheets; brush both sides of each tortilla with vegetable oil (about 2 tablespoons per tray).

2. Place a wire rack upside down on top of the tortillas to keep them flat. Bake on the upper-middle and lower-middle racks of a 450-degree oven until lightly browned and crisp, 15 to 18 minutes, switching and rotating the baking sheets halfway through the baking time.

BEEF EMPANADAS

✔ WHY THIS RECIPE WORKS: To make the beef filling juicy, we enhanced packaged ground chuck with a chicken-broth-and-bread mixture. Sautéed onions, garlic, cumin, cayenne, cilantro leaves, and vinegar along with chopped hard-cooked eggs, raisins, and green olives rounded out our flavorful filling. For our crust, we made a Latin-inspired change to our pie dough by trading some of the flour for masa harina, the ground, dehydrated cornmeal used to make Mexican tortillas and tamales. Finally, a quick brush of oil on the top of the empanadas gave us a shiny, crunchy crust, and preheating the baking sheet and drizzling it with oil ensured that the underside of the empanadas got as crispy as the top.

AS ALL-IN-ONE MEALS GO, EMPANADAS—THE SOUTH American equivalent of Britain's pasties, or meat turnovers—are a difficult act to beat: a moist, savory filling encased in a tender yet sturdy crust. Though by no means tough, the crust is resilient enough to hold up to travel, making empanadas a favorite workingman's lunch in Latin America (and an ideal make-ahead candidate for us). With so much going for them, what's not to love?

For starters, all the work. Although there are endless crust and filling variations, most recipes demand more time and fuss (not to mention the deep-frying mess involved with many recipes) than the average home cook has to spare. We decided early on to make things easier for ourselves, which meant forgoing deep-frying or esoteric ingredients. Even a braised shredded beef stuffing, as many recipes suggest, would prolong our kitchen work unnecessarily. Instead, we narrowed our focus to ground beef–filled pies encased in a simple, flaky crust that would be hearty enough to stand as a main course on the dinner table.

Finding a popular flavor profile for the filling was as easy as opening a Chilean cookbook. *Empanadas de pino* combine savory-sweet spiced beef with raisins, briny olives, and hard-cooked eggs. The best pino recipes sautéed onions and garlic with a few spices, then added

BEEF EMPANADAS

tiny, hand-chopped chunks of beef before the eggs, raisins, and olives were stirred in. Starting with packaged ground beef seemed like an easy streamlining step, but even with moist 85 percent lean ground chuck, the finished pino had a rubbery, pebbly texture. For help, we turned to an Italian meatball-softening trick: blending the ground beef with a milk-and-bread mixture known as a panade. As the mixture cooks, starches in the bread absorb moisture from the milk and form a gel around the protein molecules, which lubricates the meat in much the same way as fat. Adding a slice of bread mashed with 2 tablespoons of milk to our ground chuck markedly improved the texture, but the filling really took shape when we replaced the milk with an equal amount of chicken broth, intensifying the meaty flavor.

To round out the flavor of the filling, tasters liked a hefty dose of aromatics: two onions and four cloves of garlic. The winning spice mix was a combination of cumin, cayenne, and cloves, which we sautéed in oil, or "bloomed," in the pan before adding the beef. Finally, a handful of cilantro leaves and a few teaspoons of vinegar, along with the chopped eggs, raisins, and green olives, brought freshness, sweetness, and acidity to the mix.

Until now, we'd been wrapping the filling in the test kitchen's Foolproof Pie Dough. The pastry combines butter (for flavor) and shortening (for tenderness) with water and the unusual addition of vodka. Since gluten (the protein matrix that makes pie crusts tough) doesn't form in alcohol, using the high-proof alcohol (tequila works just as well) allows you to add more liquid to the mix; the result is dough that's both more workable and more tender. (Any trace of alcohol flavor burns off during baking.)

That said, our tasters found the buttery, flaky crusts too similar to British pasties. Hoping to introduce more Latin-inspired flavors, we traded some of the flour for masa harina, the ground, dehydrated cornmeal used to make Mexican tortillas and tamales. Though unusual, the cornmeal provided welcome nutty richness and rough-hewn texture. Even better, less flour meant less protein in the dough; less protein meant we didn't need shortening (to tenderize the dough) and could switch to all butter for better flavor. Dividing the dough into a dozen smaller rounds before rolling them out into individual shells hastened the process.

For a crisp crust, we brushed the shells with a little oil. Now the tops boasted shine and crunch, but the undersides dulled in comparison. No problem; preheating the baking sheet (as you would a pizza stone) and drizzling the surface with oil helped crisp up the bottoms. The

NOTES FROM THE TEST KITCHEN

ASSEMBLING EMPANADAS

1. Divide the dough in half, then divide each half into six equal pieces.

2. Roll each piece of dough into a 6-inch round about ⅛ inch thick.

3. Place about ⅓ cup of filling on each round, then brush the edges with water.

4. Fold the dough over the filling, then crimp the edges using a fork to seal.

result was a crust so shatteringly crisp that it almost passed for fried, giving way to a filling as flavorful as those of the best hand-chopped pinos.

We'd more than succeeded in bringing this recipe home; in fact, we would put our unconventional crust up against a more authentic version any day.

Beef Empanadas

SERVES 4 TO 6

The alcohol in the dough is essential to the texture of the crust and imparts no flavor—do not omit it or substitute water. Masa harina can be found in the international aisle with other Latin foods or in the baking aisle with the flour. If you cannot find masa harina, replace it with additional all-purpose flour (for a total of 4 cups).

FILLING

- 1 slice high-quality white sandwich bread, torn into quarters
- 2 tablespoons plus ½ cup low-sodium chicken broth
- 1 pound 85 percent lean ground beef
  Table salt and ground black pepper

- 1 tablespoon olive oil
- 2 medium onions, minced
- 4 garlic cloves, minced or pressed through a garlic press (about 4 teaspoons)
- 1 teaspoon ground cumin
- ¼ teaspoon cayenne pepper
- ⅛ teaspoon ground cloves
- ½ cup fresh cilantro leaves, chopped coarse
- 2 hard-cooked eggs, chopped coarse
- ⅓ cup raisins, chopped coarse
- ¼ cup pitted green olives, chopped coarse
- 4 teaspoons cider vinegar

DOUGH

- 3 cups (15 ounces) unbleached all-purpose flour
- 1 cup (5 ounces) masa harina (see note)
- 1 tablespoon sugar
- 2 teaspoons salt
- 12 tablespoons (1½ sticks) unsalted butter, cut into ½-inch pieces and chilled
- ½ cup cold vodka or tequila
- ½ cup cold water
- 5 tablespoons olive oil

1. FOR THE FILLING: Process the bread and 2 tablespoons of the chicken broth in a food processor until a paste forms, about 5 seconds, scraping down the sides of the bowl as necessary. Add the beef, ¾ teaspoon salt, and ½ teaspoon pepper and process until the mixture is well combined, 6 to 8 pulses.

2. Heat the oil in a 12-inch nonstick skillet over medium-high heat until shimmering. Add the onions and cook, stirring frequently, until beginning to brown, about 5 minutes. Stir in the garlic, cumin, cayenne, and cloves and cook until fragrant, about 1 minute. Add the beef mixture and cook, breaking the meat into 1-inch pieces with a wooden spoon, until browned, about 7 minutes. Add the remaining ½ cup chicken broth and simmer until the mixture is moist but not wet, 3 to 5 minutes. Transfer the mixture to a bowl and cool for 10 minutes. Stir in the cilantro, eggs, raisins, olives, and vinegar. Season with salt and pepper to taste and refrigerate until cool, about 1 hour.

3. FOR THE DOUGH: Process 1 cup of the flour, the masa harina, sugar, and salt in a food processor until combined, about 2 pulses. Add the butter and process until the mixture is homogeneous and the dough resembles wet sand, about 10 seconds. Add the remaining 2 cups flour and pulse until the mixture is evenly distributed around the bowl, 4 to 6 quick pulses. Empty the mixture into a medium bowl.

4. Sprinkle the vodka and water over the mixture. Using your hands, mix the dough until it forms a tacky mass that sticks together. Following the photos on page 177, divide the dough in half, then divide each half into six equal pieces. Transfer the dough pieces to a plate, cover with plastic wrap, and refrigerate until firm, about 45 minutes.

5. TO ASSEMBLE: Adjust the oven racks to the upper-middle and lower-middle positions, place one baking sheet on each rack, and heat the oven to 425 degrees. While the baking sheets are preheating, remove the dough from the refrigerator. Roll each dough piece out on a lightly floured counter into a 6-inch circle about ⅛ inch thick, covering each rolled-out dough round with plastic wrap while rolling out the remaining dough. Place about ⅓ cup of the filling in the center of each dough round. Brush the edges of each round with water and fold the dough over the filling. Trim any ragged edges, then crimp the edges of the empanadas shut using a fork.

6. Drizzle 2 tablespoons of the oil over the surface of each hot baking sheet, then return the sheets to the oven for 2 minutes. Brush the empanadas with the remaining 1 tablespoon oil. Carefully place six empanadas on each baking sheet and cook until well browned and crisp, 25 to 30 minutes, switching and rotating the baking sheets halfway through the baking time. Cool the empanadas on a wire rack for 10 minutes before serving. (After step 5, the empanadas can be covered tightly with plastic wrap and refrigerated for up to 2 days.)

VARIATION

Beef Empanadas with Corn and Black Bean Filling
Follow the recipe for Beef Empanadas, omitting the raisins and cooking ½ cup frozen corn kernels and ½ cup rinsed canned black beans along with the onions in step 2.

NOTES FROM THE TEST KITCHEN

KEYS TO A CRISP EMPANADA CRUST

1. Drizzle oil onto the preheated baking sheets, which simulates a shallow fry, crisping up the bottom of the pies.

2. Brush the empanadas with oil rather than an egg wash before baking. This helps transfer heat more quickly and evenly, improving browning.

Asian Favorites
AT HOME

Pureeing a portion of the basil along with the aromatics distributes deep basil flavor throughout our Thai chicken stir-fry; and stirring in fresh leaves at the end of cooking delivers another layer of bright basil flavor.

TIRED OF THE SAME-OLD STIR-FRIES? TRY A THAI-STYLE STIR-FRY. IN sharp contrast to Chinese stir-fries, which are cooked over high heat to quickly sear food and where the aromatics are added toward the end of cooking to prevent scorching, Thai stir-fries are cooked over milder heat. The idea is that the aromatics are added first to infuse the cooking oil with their flavor. Once the protein and/or vegetables are added, they become coated with the infused oil and develop deep, complex flavor. We set out to master one popular Thai stir-fry—chicken and basil—for the home kitchen. Our goal was a stir-fry with juicy pieces of tender chicken coated in a spicy, bright, basil-infused sauce.

We never tire of the Chinatown dim sum staple, *shu mai,* steamed dumplings stuffed with a savory pork and shrimp filling. But does enjoying shu mai always mean a trip to Chinatown? We wanted to develop an approachable recipe so we could make these dumplings at home. Our challenge would be twofold: overcoming dry, bland fillings and forming the dumplings without resorting to kitchen origami.

THAI CHICKEN WITH BASIL

✔ **WHY THIS RECIPE WORKS:** Capturing the flavors of this classic Thai ground chicken stir-fry required learning a whole new way to stir-fry. Stir-frying at a low temperature allowed us to cook the aromatics and basil from the beginning, so they could infuse the cooking oils with their flavors. Grinding our own chicken in a food processor along with some fish sauce gave us coarse-textured meat that held on to moisture during cooking. And a combination of oyster sauce and white vinegar added rich but bright flavor to our basil chicken.

IN CHINA, THE SECRET TO A SUCCESSFUL STIR-FRY LIES not in what goes into the wok, but what's under it: an intense coal fire or a massive high-output burner. The super-high heat rapidly cooks meats and vegetables, and imparts an intense smoky flavor. But in Thailand there's more than one way to heat a wok. On nearly every street corner in Bangkok, vendors scoop hot meals out of woks set up on pushcarts. These boast only mild flames but manage to produce stir-fries every bit as complex and flavorful as those from the hottest Cantonese kitchen.

Unlike a high-heat stir-fry, in which the aromatics are added toward the end to prevent scorching, the key to the low-temperature method is to sauté the aromatics over medium-low heat at the beginning. The flavor compounds in the aromatics infuse the oil they're cooked in, which in turn coats the protein, giving the dish deep, complex flavor. It's a method pervasive in Thai cooking.

We set out to perfect a classic Thai stir-fry for the American kitchen: *gai pad krapow*, or chicken with hot basil. The Thai process is as follows: Chicken is finely chopped with a pair of cleavers, cooked with a big handful of hot basil in oil flavored with garlic, shallots, and Thai chiles, then finished with fish sauce, Thai oyster sauce, and sugar. Served with steamed jasmine rice, it has a bright, clean flavor defined by the aromatic, grassy basil and a perfect balance of heat and sweetness.

In the test kitchen, making this recipe wasn't so easy. Unevenly cooked aromatics lent a bitter burnt flavor.

Mincing a pound of chicken by hand is manageable with two cleavers, but a chore with a chef's knife. And the signature ingredient, hot basil, is nearly impossible to find in this country.

Our first task was to develop a foolproof method for infusing the oil with aromatics. We'd already burned our first attempt: a dozen finely chopped Thai chiles, three cloves of garlic, and three finely sliced shallots cooked in 2 tablespoons of oil. Adding extra oil to the skillet (we prefer a skillet to a wok for American stoves) helped them cook more evenly, but we had to use a full ¼ cup of oil to make a difference, which made the dish greasy. Turning down the heat from medium to medium-low and starting in a completely cold skillet increased our chances of success. We also dialed back the oil to 2 tablespoons. After six to eight minutes, our aromatics were a perfectly even shade of golden brown.

The dish we had in Thailand was almost unbearably spicy, so we decided to tone down the heat and reduced the chiles to six. Lowering the heat made the dish seem cloyingly sweet, so we also cut the amount of sugar in half, down from 2 tablespoons to 1.

Chopping chicken by hand was a nonstarter, so we tried store-bought ground chicken. Bad idea. It was ground too fine and cooked up into a mealy, mushy texture. Next we tried chopping meat in the food processor. Dark meat was more forgiving but contained fatty stringy bits, so we decided to stick with breast meat. Since we were pulling the processor out, we used it to chop the garlic and chiles, further streamlining this simple dish.

Getting a flavorful sear in a high-heat stir-fry requires cooking meat in batches, letting it sit undisturbed in a hot nonstick skillet. The difficulty is that lean white meat chicken can go from tender to tough in the blink of an eye. A low-temperature stir-fry, thankfully, is much more foolproof. (Since the aromatic oil and sauce provide so much complexity, the lack of browning isn't an issue.) We added all of the meat to the dish in a single batch, stirring it constantly to promote even cooking. To further guarantee moist meat, we added a tablespoon of fish sauce to the food processor as we chopped the chicken, then let the mixture rest for 15 minutes in the refrigerator. The fish sauce acted as a brine, seasoning the meat and helping it retain moisture.

THAI CHICKEN WITH BASIL

We moved on to the sauce. With no access to Thai-style oyster-flavored sauce, we'd been substituting Chinese. However, its thicker consistency and heavier flavors were weighing down the dish. Simply decreasing the amount didn't work; the dish went from overloaded to lacking complexity. Then we thought about a Thai condiment that diners often add to their dish to brighten the flavor: white vinegar. Adding a mere teaspoon balanced the heaviness of the oyster-flavored sauce and brought brightness. While we were in the business of brightening flavors, we made an unconventional move, setting aside a tablespoon of our raw garlic-chile mixture to be added to the sauce at the end of cooking. The combination of fresh and cooked aromatics was an instant hit.

Only one problem remained: incorporating the flavor of basil. Unlike sweet Italian or even Thai basil, hot basil has a robust texture that can stand up to prolonged cooking, giving it plenty of time to release its distinctive aroma into the chicken. Simply substituting Italian basil didn't work: Added any time before the last minute it became wilted and slimy. And when it only spent a short time in the skillet, it didn't offer enough flavor. We needed a way to keep the leaves bright and fresh tasting, while at the same time lending the dish a deep basil flavor.

Then it clicked: Since we were already using the oil-infusing technique to deliver garlic, chile, and shallot flavor, why not use the same method for the basil? We gave it a try, chopping a cup of basil leaves along with the chiles and garlic, then cooking them all together.

SCIENCE DESK

A HAPPY MEAL—THAI-STYLE

Nearly every dish in Thai cuisine features a combination of sweet and spicy flavors, including our Thai-Style Chicken with Basil. During testing, we noticed that adding sugar to the recipe significantly toned down the heat of the chiles. It turns out that this phenomenon is the result of complex interactions in the brain that regulate our perception of flavor, pitting pain against pleasure. Compounds in chiles (mainly capsaicin) stimulate nerves (called trigeminals) surrounding the taste buds to signal discomfort to the brain, in a process known as chemesthesis. Sugar, on the other hand, stimulates the taste buds to signal pleasure. These signals are so enjoyable, scientists believe they overshadow the "pain" caused by chiles.

The basil released its flavor into the dish, and the small pieces did not suffer from sliminess. To add fresh texture and bright green color, we stirred in an additional cup of whole basil leaves right before serving. We now had a dish infused with a deep basil flavor that could transport us back to Bangkok with about 20 minutes of work.

Thai Chicken with Basil

SERVES 4

Since tolerance for spiciness can vary, we've kept our recipe relatively mild. For a very mild version, remove the seeds and ribs from the chiles. If fresh Thai chiles are unavailable, substitute 2 serranos or 1 medium jalapeño. In Thailand, crushed red pepper and sugar are passed at the table, along with extra fish sauce and white vinegar. Serve with steamed rice and vegetables, if desired. You do not need to wash the food processor bowl after step 1.

- 2 cups tightly packed fresh basil leaves
- 3 garlic cloves, peeled
- 6 green or red Thai chiles, stemmed
- 2 tablespoons fish sauce, plus extra for serving
- 1 tablespoon oyster-flavored sauce
- 1 tablespoon sugar, plus extra for serving
- 1 teaspoon white vinegar, plus extra for serving
- 1 pound boneless, skinless chicken breasts, trimmed and cut into 2-inch pieces
- 3 shallots, peeled and sliced thin (about ¾ cup)
- 2 tablespoons vegetable oil
   Red pepper flakes, for serving

1. Pulse 1 cup of the basil leaves, the garlic, and chiles in a food processor until chopped fine, 6 to 10 pulses, scraping down the sides of the bowl once during processing. Transfer 1 tablespoon of the basil mixture to a small bowl, stir in 1 tablespoon of the fish sauce, the oyster-flavored sauce, sugar, and vinegar, and set aside. Transfer the remaining basil mixture to a 12-inch heavy-bottomed nonstick skillet.

2. Pulse the chicken and the remaining 1 tablespoon fish sauce in the food processor until the meat is chopped into ¼-inch pieces, 6 to 8 pulses. Transfer the chicken to a medium bowl and refrigerate 15 minutes.

3. Stir the shallots and oil into the basil mixture in the skillet. Heat the mixture over medium-low heat (the mixture should start to sizzle after about 1½ minutes; if it doesn't, adjust the heat accordingly), stirring constantly, until the garlic and shallots are golden brown, 5 to 8 minutes.

4. Add the chicken, increase the heat to medium, and cook, stirring and breaking up the chicken with a potato masher or rubber spatula, until only traces of pink remain, 2 to 4 minutes. Add the reserved basil–fish sauce mixture and continue to cook, stirring constantly until the chicken is no longer pink, about 1 minute. Stir in the remaining 1 cup basil leaves and cook, stirring constantly, until the basil is wilted, 30 to 60 seconds. Serve immediately, passing the extra fish sauce, sugar, vinegar, and red pepper flakes separately.

NOTES FROM THE TEST KITCHEN

A NEW WAY TO STIR-FRY

1. MINCE YOUR MEAT: Thai stir-fries often feature small pieces of chopped meat versus the larger strips or chunks in many Chinese stir-fries.

2. USE LOW HEAT: A moderately hot pan instead of a blazing hot wok means lean meats such as chicken breast won't easily overcook.

3. SAUTÉ AROMATICS FIRST: With a low temperature, aromatics can be added to the pan first, deeply flavoring the oil without risk of burning.

4. SAUTÉ MEAT LAST: At low heat, the meat won't get a flavor boost from browning. Instead, it absorbs the fully developed flavors of the oil.

5. SEASON WITH FISH SAUCE: Fish sauce, added before and after cooking, is an even more potent flavor enhancer than soy sauce.

SHU MAI

SHU MAI

✔ **WHY THIS RECIPE WORKS:** For tender steamed dumplings with a moist, flavorful filling, we chopped boneless country style ribs in a food processor rather than relying on supermarket ground pork. To prevent the meat from drying out during steaming, we mixed in a little powdered gelatin dissolved in soy sauce. As for the shrimp, we added that to the food processor, too. Dried shiitake mushrooms, minced cilantro, fresh ginger, and water chestnuts were just a few of the ingredients we relied on to round out our flavorful filling.

THE OPEN-FACED DUMPLINGS KNOWN AS *SHU MAI* ARE as ubiquitous on Cantonese menus as won ton soup and fried rice. These meaty little pouches usually satisfy; the savory-briny combo of pork and shrimp is hard to beat. But the best versions are true standouts that more than live up to their name. (Shu mai translates as "cook and sell," meaning that once they cook, they always sell.) Their filling is juicy and tender with pleasantly springy chew; their flavor is at once salty, sweet, and tangy, as well as faintly smoky from Chinese black mushrooms.

These dumplings are too good to be reserved for eating out, so we set ourselves the task of learning to make them in the test kitchen. The handful of recipes we found looked surprisingly simple—mix ground pork, shrimp, reconstituted dried mushrooms, and rice vinegar; spoon it into thin-skinned won ton wrappers; crimp; and steam. But our efforts in no way compared to the real thing. Instead of moist, tender, deeply flavorful dumplings, we got beggar's purses of one-dimensional, mealy meatballs.

The obvious move was to head to the source for a few lessons. We finagled our way into the kitchen of China Pearl, long one of our favorite dumpling destinations in Boston. After hours of watching the chef expertly turn out hundreds of shu mai, we left with new ideas for what we would do—and a few for what we wouldn't.

One idea we were definitely trying: Grind our own pork from whole cuts instead of settling for preground supermarket pork. Preground pork has a slew of issues. It's generally a hodgepodge of scraps from different parts of the animal; some batches can be lean, others riddled with fat. Furthermore, the grind is never consistent—one package can be almost pastelike while another may contain visible chunks of meat and fat. As a result, preground pork rarely cooks up exactly the same way from batch to batch.

The China Pearl chef ground pork butt into coarse ¼-inch chunks, but this fatty, flavorful cut wasn't an option for us. We needed only a pound of meat to make dumplings serving six to eight, and the butt comes in much larger sizes. Boneless country-style ribs, another widely available, well-marbled cut (which actually contains part of the butt) were the next best bet. To grind the meat, we turned to the food processor. We cut the meat into 1-inch chunks, which would help produce a more uniform grind, and pulsed it into ¼-inch bits along with ½ pound of shrimp. Though not perfect, this filling was markedly more moist and tender than the one made with preground meat.

But we had a new problem: The filling was now so chunky that it broke apart mid-bite. We found that if we divided the meat into two batches and ground one batch more finely (to ⅛ inch), the smaller pieces helped hold the larger bits together and added a pleasing textural contrast. We pulsed the shrimp with the more coarsely ground batch, which produced chunks large enough to be discernible but not distracting.

But even with this nice fatty cut, the filling was still not as juicy and tender as we wanted. The smaller bits in particular were noticeably rubbery. The culprit had to be the steam heat. Moist environments conduct heat very efficiently, and just 10 minutes of steaming cooked the pork to above 165 degrees—the point at which its proteins begin to expel water and shrink, turning the texture dry and grainy. To lubricate the meat and make it seem "juicy," the chef at China Pearl incorporates liberal amounts of lard and fatback into his filling. We don't have anything against fat, but we balked at using either of these ingredients. Neither is all that widely available and—let's be honest—it's one thing to eat a dumpling swimming in fat, no matter how richly flavored, at a restaurant and quite another to load it on yourself at home.

We tried to think of a better way to improve the meat's texture. The answer came to us when we realized that fat isn't the only thing that can improve a meat's texture—so can gelatin. It's what gives beef and veal stock their rich, unctuous quality. In past testing, we'd used powdered gelatin to prevent the meat in an all-beef meatloaf from drying out. Gelatin can hold up to 10 times its weight in water, and when added to meat, it suspends the juices in a meshlike, semisolid state that prevents them from leaching out. This also translates to a luxuriant texture similar to the suppleness contributed by fat. Using powdered gelatin seemed like a promising tack for our dumpling filling. Half a teaspoon of gelatin bloomed first in a little water proved plenty to give our dumplings just the moist, tender texture we were looking for. We got even better results dissolving the gelatin in soy sauce, which amplifies flavor. On a whim, we mixed in 2 tablespoons of cornstarch, which we've found has yet another power besides thickening: It provides a protective sheath to proteins during cooking, staving off moisture loss and shrinkage.

It was time to think about flavorings. The China Pearl chef's liberal dose of toasted sesame oil was a definite, but his use of MSG was a nonstarter. Instead, we punched up flavor with a little extra soy sauce, rice wine, and rice vinegar. We also found that the concentrated, earthy flavor of dried reconstituted shiitake mushrooms made a fine substitute for the Chinese black variety. Though not traditional, minced cilantro, fresh ginger, and the crunch of water chestnuts rounded out the filling's overall flavor and texture nicely.

For wrappers, we were using widely available square egg roll skins, which we cut into rounds with a biscuit cutter. Though we'd never achieve the speed of a practiced Cantonese chef, crimping the wrappers around the filling proved easier than we thought (see "Filling and Forming Shu Mai," on page 189). As a final touch, instead of traditional shrimp paste or roe, we garnished each dumpling's exposed center with finely grated carrot and steamed them for 10 minutes.

Served with a quick chili oil that we'd whipped up, these were the juiciest, tenderest, and most flavorful dumplings we'd tasted outside of China Pearl. Served for dim sum in a restaurant, these shu mai would definitely cook and sell.

Shu Mai (Steamed Chinese Dumplings)

MAKES ABOUT 40 DUMPLINGS

Do not trim the excess fat from the ribs, as the fat contributes flavor and moisture. Use any size shrimp except popcorn shrimp; there's no need to halve shrimp smaller than 26 to 30 per pound before processing. The dumplings may be frozen for up to 3 months; cook them straight from the freezer for about an extra 5 minutes. Shu mai are traditionally served with a spicy chili oil; you can use the recipe that follows or store-bought oil.

2 tablespoons soy sauce

½ teaspoon unflavored powdered gelatin

1 pound boneless country-style pork ribs, cut into 1-inch pieces (see note)

½ pound shrimp, peeled, deveined (see page 82), tails removed and halved lengthwise (see note)

¼ cup chopped water chestnuts

4 dried shiitake mushroom caps (about ¾ ounce), soaked in hot water 30 minutes, squeezed dry, and cut into ¼-inch dice

2 tablespoons cornstarch

2 tablespoons minced fresh cilantro leaves

1 tablespoon toasted sesame oil

1 tablespoon Chinese rice cooking wine (Shaoxing) or dry sherry

1 tablespoon rice wine vinegar

2 teaspoons sugar

2 teaspoons grated fresh ginger

½ teaspoon table salt

½ teaspoon ground black pepper

1 (1-pound) package 5½-inch square egg roll wrappers

¼ cup finely grated carrot (optional)

1. Combine the soy sauce and gelatin in a small bowl. Set aside to allow the gelatin to bloom, about 5 minutes.

2. Meanwhile, place half of the pork in a food processor and pulse until coarsely ground into pieces that are about ⅛ inch, about 10 pulses; transfer to a large bowl. Add the shrimp and remaining pork to the food processor and pulse until coarsely chopped into pieces that are about ¼ inch, about 5 pulses. Transfer to the bowl with the

FILLING AND FORMING SHU MAI

1. Brush the edges of the dumpling wrapper lightly with water. Place a heaping tablespoon of filling in the center of each wrapper.

2. Pinch two opposing sides of the wrapper with your fingers. Rotate the dumpling 90 degrees, and, again, pinch the opposing sides of the wrapper with your fingers.

3. Continue to pinch the dumpling until you have eight equidistant pinches around the circumference of the dumpling.

4. Gather up the sides of the dumpling and squeeze gently at the top to create a "waist."

5. Hold the dumpling in your hand and gently but firmly pack the filling into the dumpling with a butter knife.

TRANSLATING RESTAURANT SHU MAI

Authentic shu mai may taste great, but they contain inaccessible—and, in some cases, unappealing—ingredients. For our recipe, we kept the best of those elements and found readily available, healthier substitutes for the others.

RESTAURANT WAY | **OUR WAY**

LARD + FATBACK
Restaurant chefs pack their shu mai with fat to create rich flavor and succulent texture.

GELATIN
Gelatin mimics the luxuriant effect of fat and helps the meat retain its juices.

MSG
This flavor-boosting additive is key to the ultra-savory flavor in many Chinese dumplings.

SOY SAUCE + RICE VINEGAR + RICE WINE
Liberal doses of each season our filling without synthetic flavor enhancers.

CHINESE BLACK MUSHROOMS
These contribute rich, earthy flavor but are not available in most American supermarkets.

SHIITAKE MUSHROOMS
Dried, reconstituted shiitake mushrooms replicate the hard-to-find Chinese variety.

more finely ground pork. Stir in the soy sauce mixture, water chestnuts, mushrooms, cornstarch, cilantro, sesame oil, wine, vinegar, sugar, ginger, salt, and pepper until well combined.

3. Line a large baking sheet with parchment paper. Divide the egg roll wrappers into three stacks (six to seven per stack). Using a 3-inch biscuit cutter, cut two rounds from each stack of egg roll wrappers (you should have 40 to 42 rounds). Cover the rounds with moist paper towels to prevent drying.

4. Working with 6 rounds at a time, brush the edges of each round lightly with water. Place a heaping tablespoon of filling in the center of each round. Following the photos on page 189, form the dumplings by folding the wrapper around the sides of the filling and leaving the top exposed. Transfer to the prepared baking sheet, cover with a damp kitchen towel, and repeat with the remaining wrappers and filling. Top the center of each dumpling with a pinch of grated carrot, if using.

5. Cut a piece of parchment paper slightly smaller than the diameter of a steamer basket and place in the basket. Poke about 20 small holes in the parchment to allow steam to pass through and lightly coat with vegetable oil spray. Place batches of dumplings on the parchment, making sure they are not touching. Set the steamer basket over the simmering water and cook, covered, until cooked through, 8 to 10 minutes. Serve immediately with chili oil.

Chili Oil

MAKES ABOUT ½ CUP

- 1 tablespoon soy sauce
- 2 teaspoons sugar
- ½ teaspoon table salt
- ½ cup peanut oil
- ¼ cup red pepper flakes
- 2 medium garlic cloves, peeled

Combine the soy sauce, sugar, and salt in a small bowl; set aside. Heat the oil in a small saucepan over medium heat until it is just shimmering and registers 300 degrees on an instant-read thermometer. Remove the pan from the heat and stir in the red pepper flakes, garlic, and soy mixture. Let cool to room temperature, stirring occasionally, about 1 hour. Discard the garlic before storing.

RATING LARGE SAUCEPANS

Now that even low-cost manufacturers are offering fully clad cookware—a construction that features alternating layers of materials extending from the cooking surface up the sides, ensuring more even cooking—we wondered if we still needed to shell out $200 for our former favorite in this category, the All-Clad Stainless 4-Quart Saucepan. In our testing, we found that the real differences among large saucepans came down to design and maneuverability. Pans that were particularly heavy or had poorly designed handles did not rate well, nor did those with sharp corner angles that prevented a whisk from getting into the corners. Happily, we found that a good-quality, fully clad, easy-to-maneuver pan could be had for just $69.99, but in the end our old favorite still reigned supreme. Brands are listed in order of preference. See www.americastestkitchen.com for updates to this testing.

RECOMMENDED

ALL-CLAD Stainless 4-Quart Saucepan with Lid and Loop (model #5204LP)
PRICE: $194.99 **WEIGHT:** 3.3 lb
MATERIAL: 18/10 stainless steel interior, aluminum core, magnetic stainless steel exterior
COOKING: ★★★ **DESIGN:** ★★½
COMMENTS: Our champ held on to its title for heating slowly and evenly enough to prevent onions from scorching and pastry cream and rice from overcooking. Our only quibbles: It lacks a rounded pouring lip, and some testers complained that the handle's angle felt awkward.

CUISINART MultiClad Unlimited 4-Quart Saucepan (model #MCU194-20)
PRICE: $69.99 **WEIGHT:** 2.4 lb
MATERIAL: 18/10 stainless steel interior, hard-anodized aluminum exterior
COOKING: ★★½ **DESIGN:** ★★½
COMMENTS: This lightweight pan, which is our Best Buy, performed virtually identically to our winner (the biggest difference is that it cooks a little faster). Its biggest flaw: the interior scratches easily.

J.A. HENCKELS Classic Clad 4-Quart Saucepan with Lid (model #40316-200)
PRICE: $85.99 **WEIGHT:** 3.25 lb
MATERIAL: Stainless steel interior, aluminum core, stainless steel exterior
COOKING: ★★★ **DESIGN:** ★★
COMMENTS: This pan cooks beautifully. But when it came to design, testers were split: Some appreciated the thick, arched handle, while others dubbed it "bulky." and struggled when pouring.

RECOMMENDED WITH RESERVATIONS

TRAMONTINA Gourmet 4-Quart Tri-Ply-Clad Stainless Steel Saucepan (model #80116/514)
PRICE: $49.97 **WEIGHT:** 3.35 lb
MATERIAL: 18/10 stainless steel interior, aluminum alloy core, magnetic stainless steel exterior
COOKING: ★★½ **DESIGN:** ★★½
COMMENTS: This pan cooked a tiny bit fast. But most testers complained it felt "top-heavy" and "unbalanced," with a handle too thin to accommodate its weight.

RECOMMENDED WITH RESERVATIONS (cont.)

CUISINOX Elite 3.6-Liter (3.8-Quart) Covered Saucepan (model #POT320)
PRICE: $159.90 **WEIGHT:** 3.2 lb
MATERIAL: 18/10 stainless steel interior, aluminum core, magnetic stainless steel exterior
COOKING: ★★½ **DESIGN:** ★★
COMMENTS: This saucepan heated slightly faster than our top pans. Though it is one of the lightest pans, its shape and handle angle did little to help distribute the weight, making it nearly impossible to pour water without using the helper handle.

NOT RECOMMENDED

VIKING Professional Cookware 3-Quart Saucepan (model #DW1607)
PRICE: $199.95 **WEIGHT:** 3.5 lb
MATERIAL: 18/10 stainless steel interior, aluminum core, 18/10 magnetic stainless steel exterior
COOKING: ★★★ **DESIGN:** ★½
COMMENTS: Despite seven layers of three different types of metal, this pan performed only marginally better than pots costing a fraction of its price. Its frame was "unwieldy," with a poorly placed handle.

DEMEYERE Atlantis 3.2-Quart Saucepan with Lid (model #41420 + 41520)
PRICE: $274.95 **WEIGHT:** 3.5 lb
MATERIAL: 18/10 stainless steel interior, copper core, stainless steel exterior
COOKING: ★★½ **DESIGN:** ★
COMMENTS: This model produced perfectly browned onions and pilaf, but pastry cream stuck in this pan's sharp corners. Testers complained bottom-heaviness and the angle of the handle made pouring liquid "terribly uncomfortable."

MAUVIEL M'heritage 3.5-Quart Copper Saucepan with Cast-Iron Handle and Lid (model #6501-21)
PRICE: $384.95 **WEIGHT:** 5.5 lb.
MATERIAL: Stainless steel interior, copper alloy exterior, cast-iron handle
COOKING: ★★½ **DESIGN:** ★
COMMENTS: This heavy copper pan is better suited as kitchen décor than cooking tool. The pan's sharp corners trapped pastry cream and its cast-iron handle distributed weight poorly and became searingly hot.

Grilled PORK CHOPS AND RIBS

Thick, bone-in pork chops are great for grilling because they can roast on the grill long enough to absorb smoke flavor without drying out.

COME MEMORIAL DAY, OUR THOUGHTS TURN INVARIABLY TO THE grill and one of our favorite weeknight dishes is smoky grilled pork chops. Sure, it's easy enough to throw some pork chops on the grill, give them a good sear, and then baste them with a smoky barbecue sauce, but we were after pork chops infused throughout with deep smoke flavor. We knew we'd need to choose a thick, bone-in cut for the best flavor and also that our biggest challenge would be to figure out how to keep them on the grill for at least 30 minutes for that ultimate smoky flavor—no small feat given that even thick-cut pork chops go from juicy to tough pretty quickly on the grill. Armed with bone-in chops and a working sauce recipe, we headed outside to fire up the grill.

There are barbecued pork ribs and then there are barbecued pork ribs to write home about. We think Memphis dry-rubbed pork ribs fall into the latter category. Of course up here in Boston, it's hard to even get a taste of this regional specialty never mind duplicate the tender, smoky meat with its trademark crust (or bark as it's called in the South) without the massive smokers real Memphis pit masters use. But we were willing to give it a try. We wanted fully tender meat seasoned with a sweet-salty rub and brushed with the tangy, vinegary sauce that defines these great Tennessee ribs.

GRILL-SMOKED PORK CHOPS

GRILL-SMOKED PORK CHOPS

✔ **WHY THIS RECIPE WORKS:** For a grill-smoked pork chop recipe that had it all—charred crust, rosy-pink, ultra-moist meat, and true smoke flavor throughout, we reversed cooking by starting low and finishing with a quick sear. Bone-in chops were the best bet for our grill-smoked pork chop recipe, because bones add flavor and their connective tissue and fat boost meat tenderness as they dissolve on the grill.

TO SOME IN THE SOUTH, THE TERM "BARBECUED" doesn't mean grilled meat with some sauce brushed over it. To be worthy of the term, the meat—pork chops, for example—need to be infused to the core with deep smoke flavor. And barbecued chops should have a well-browned crust. These two goals, however, are at odds. Good smoke flavor generally requires a lengthy exposure to a slow fire to give the smoke time to penetrate, while a charred crust requires a blast of high heat to quickly sear the exterior of the meat before the interior turns dry and leathery. We wanted juicy chops covered in a crusty glaze full of real smoke flavor. We set out to find an approach that would somehow reconcile these two extremes.

Our first task was choosing the chops. Blade chops, from the shoulder end of the loin, have a lot of connective tissue and require long, moist cooking methods to render them tender. We wanted a fast weeknight dinner, so they were out of the running. We also avoided sirloin chops, which we knew from experience to be irredeemably dry and tough. That left center-cut chops and rib chops. The center-cut chops were good but the rib chops, which have slightly more fat, were even better. The size of the chop, however, proved critical. Anything less than a 1½-inch thickness and the chops turned leathery and dry before the smoke had a chance to infuse the meat. For the sauce, we kept things simple, briefly simmering ketchup, molasses, onion, Worcestershire sauce, Dijon mustard, cider vinegar, and brown sugar until thickened.

Armed with the right cut of meat and a tasty sauce, we headed outside to fire up the grill. To reap the benefits of both high and low heat, our best bet was a two-level fire, in which all the coals are banked on one side of the grill to create a hot side and cooler side. For smoke flavor, we added a handful of soaked wood chips to the coals. We placed the chops on the hot side first and cooked them uncovered for about three minutes per side to create a good sear. We then moved the chops onto the cooler side, replaced the grill lid to trap smoke, and cooked them until they reached 140 degrees, about nine minutes longer. To prevent burning, we slathered on the barbecue sauce in the last few minutes of cooking.

When we brought the chops inside, tasters deemed them good—but not great. The chops had a decent crust, but they were also dry inside, and the smoke flavor was weak. The only way we were going to get more smokiness was by extending the cooking time. But how could we do that without further overcooking the meat? A larger cut might help, so we hunted down some extra-thick 2-inch chops to try. Their greater girth allowed us to keep them on the grill for about 40 minutes longer, leading to better smoke flavor, but these Goliaths were ridiculously huge for individual servings. If we were cooking pork this thick, we might as well just put an entire roast on the fire.

We then wondered about reversing the cooking, starting low and finishing with a quick sear? After consulting with our science editor, we learned that enzymes called cathepsins break down proteins such as collagen, helping to tenderize meat, but these enzymes are only active at temperatures below 122 degrees. By cooking our pork slowly, we'd be giving these enzymes more time to work their tenderizing magic on the meat.

This time we started our chops under cover on the cooler side of the grill, allowing the smoke to do its job for about 25 minutes. We then applied a few coats of sauce and finished by searing them, uncovered, over hot coals. The result was almost everything we'd hoped for: our smokiest, most tender chops yet.

The only hitch? With four chops to cook, and only half a grill to work on at a time, things were getting pretty crowded and our chops were cooking unevenly.

Rotating the chops throughout the cooking time helped but required us to open the cover every few minutes, allowing that valuable smoke to escape. Our answer was reorganizing the coals. Banking the coals on either side of the grill with a disposable aluminum pan in the center created a cooler zone large enough for all four chops to cook more evenly. Still, the edges of the chops closest to the coals were cooking too fast. Using fewer coals was not an option—that kept the fire from getting hot enough at the end to give our chops a good sear. We had done all we could with the grill, so we turned our attention to the chops themselves.

In the test kitchen we generally opt for bone-in chops. The bones add flavor to the meat as it cooks and contain connective tissues and fat that break down to lend suppleness. What's more, the hollow structure of a bone means it acts as an insulator, slowing down heat penetration. Could we use this fact to our advantage and rest each chop on its bone instead of laying it flat? To keep the chops from toppling over on each other, we speared them together with skewers, making sure to leave a good inch between them to allow smoke to circulate, then stood them upright in the center of the grill. With bone, not meat, touching the grill, we were able to keep the chops over the fire a full 30 minutes. When the meat reached an internal temperature of 120 degrees, we removed the skewers, applied the sauce, and finished the chops, meat side down, over the hot coals. As we opened the grill, we noticed that standing the chops upright allowed the smoke to freely circulate around all their surfaces. It was easy to take this same method and apply it to a gas grill, with slight adjustments.

These chops had it all: charred crust; rosy-pink, ultra-moist meat; and true smoke flavor throughout. We may have skewered tradition, but we had perfectly barbecued pork chops on the table in about an hour.

Charcoal-Grill-Smoked Pork Chops

SERVES 4

Buy chops of the same thickness so they will cook uniformly. We prefer natural to enhanced pork (pork that has been injected with a salt solution to increase moistness and flavor) for this recipe, though enhanced pork can be used. If using enhanced pork, do not sprinkle with salt in step 3. Use the large holes on a box grater to grate the onion. Although we prefer hickory wood chips, any variety of chips will work, except mesquite. You will need a 13 by 9-inch disposable aluminum pan and skewers for this recipe.

SAUCE

½ **cup ketchup**

¼ **cup light or mild molasses**

2 **tablespoons grated onion (see note)**

2 **tablespoons Worcestershire sauce**

2 **tablespoons Dijon mustard**

2 **tablespoons cider vinegar**

1 **tablespoon brown sugar**

CHOPS

2 **cups wood chips (see note)**

4 **(12-ounce) bone-in rib loin pork chops, 1½ inches thick (see note)**

4 **teaspoons kosher salt or 2 teaspoons table salt**

2 **teaspoons ground black pepper**

1. FOR THE SAUCE: Bring all the ingredients to a simmer in a small saucepan over medium heat; cook, stirring occasionally, until the sauce reaches a ketchuplike consistency and is reduced to about 1 cup, 5 to 7 minutes. Transfer ½ cup of the sauce to a small bowl and set aside to serve with the cooked chops.

2. FOR THE CHOPS: Soak the wood chips in cold water to cover for 30 minutes; drain. Light a large chimney starter filled with charcoal (6 quarts) and allow to burn until the coals are partially covered with a layer of ash, about 20 minutes. Place a 13 by 9-inch disposable aluminum pan in the center of the grill. Empty the coals into the grill, creating equal-sized piles on each side of the pan. Sprinkle 1 cup soaked wood chips on each charcoal

pile, set the cooking grate in place, cover the grill, and heat the grate until hot and the chips are smoking, about 5 minutes. Use a grill brush to scrape the cooking grate clean.

3. While the grill is heating, pat the chops dry with paper towels. Following the photos below, use a sharp knife to cut two slits about 1 inch apart through the outer layer of fat and connective tissue to prevent buckling. Sprinkle the entire surface of each chop with 1 teaspoon salt and ½ teaspoon pepper. Place the chops side by side, facing in the same direction, on a cutting board with the curved rib bone facing down. Pass two skewers through

---

NOTES FROM THE TEST KITCHEN

PREVENTING PORK CHOPS FROM BUCKLING

Whether your pork chops are boneless or bone-in, you can use the same technique to prevent them from buckling during cooking. Simply cut two slits, about 1 inch apart, through one side of each chop.

SKEWERING PORK CHOPS FOR THE GRILL

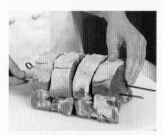

1. Pass two skewers through the loin muscle of each chop to provide stability when standing on the grill.

2. Stand the skewered chops, bone side down on the cooking grate, in the center of the grill so smoke can reach all sides.

the loin muscle of each chop, close to the bone, about 1 inch from each end. Once the chops have been threaded onto the skewers, pull them apart to create a 1-inch space between each.

4. Place the skewered chops, bone side down, in the center of the grill on the cooking grate, over the aluminum pan. Cover the grill and cook until an instant-read thermometer inserted into the center of a pork chop, but away from any bone, registers 120 degrees, 28 to 32 minutes.

5. Remove the skewers from the chops; tip the chops onto the flat side and brush the surface with 1 tablespoon sauce. Transfer the chops, sauce side down, to the hotter parts of the grill (2 on each side) and cook, uncovered, until browned, 2 to 4 minutes. Brush the top of each chop with 1 tablespoon sauce; flip and continue to cook on the second side until browned and an instant-read thermometer inserted into the center of a pork chop, but away from any bone, registers 140 to 145 degrees, 2 to 4 minutes longer. Remove the chops from the grill and allow to rest, tented with foil, 5 minutes. Serve, passing the ½ cup reserved sauce separately.

VARIATION

Gas-Grill-Smoked Pork Chops
You will need a 9-inch disposable aluminum pie plate and wooden skewers for this recipe.

Follow the recipe for Charcoal Grill-Smoked Pork Chops, through step 1. Place the soaked wood chips in a 9-inch disposable aluminum pie plate and place the plate on the primary burner (the burner that will remain on during barbecuing), then set the cooking grate(s) over the burners. Turn all the burners to high and heat the grill, with the lid down, until hot and the chips are smoking, about 15 minutes. (If the chips ignite, use a water-filled spray bottle to extinguish.) Use a grill brush to scrape the cooking grate clean. Proceed with the recipe from step 3, leaving the primary burner on high, turning off the other burner(s), and cooking with the lid down. Cook the chops on the cooler side of the grill to an internal temperature of 110 degrees, 20 to 25 minutes, and increase the browning time on the hotter side of the grill to 4 to 7 minutes per side.

MEMPHIS DRY RUB PORK RIBS

☑ **WHY THIS RECIPE WORKS:** For ribs with deep, crusty bark and satisfying chew, Memphis pit masters rely on massive smokers to cook the racks low and slow. We achieved similar results by converting a charcoal kettle into a makeshift smoker. For slow, steady, indirect heat, we banked all the coals to one side and piled lit coals on top of unlit coals to keep the fire going without opening the lid. Sprinkling soaked wood chips—rather than large chunks—over the coals introduced just enough smoke flavor, and a pan of water placed under the racks helped stabilize the air temperature and moisten the meat. These modifications were so successful that the ribs only needed to spend 90 minutes on the grill.

THE SWEET, STICKY, FALL-OFF-THE-BONE PORK SPARE-rib is the pride of more than a few U.S. cities, but only one—Memphis, Tennessee—can take credit for the dry rub rib. Unlike the sweeter, wetter version, dry rub ribs should be cooked to the precise stage at which they are fully tender and their fat has completely rendered, but the meat still clings lightly to the bone and boasts a slightly resilient chew. There's no molasses-y, finger-lickin' sauce. Instead, a thin cider- or vinegar-based "mop" is brushed across the ribs intermittently during cooking to cool down the meat and prevent the interior moisture from evaporating. The rub—a mixture of salt, sugar, and spices liberally applied to the rack up to a day before cooking—in collaboration with long, slow pit smoking, forms a crusty, deeply flavored "bark" that is the hallmark of Memphis barbecue.

The problem is, most rib joints outside the River City don't even attempt to replicate them—and those that have seldom do them justice. To get our fix, we mail-ordered a few racks from beloved hog-slinging landmarks like Charlie Vergos' Rendezvous and Central BBQ. Unfortunately, ribs that have suffered the indignity of being cooked, frozen, packaged, shipped, thawed, and warmed are hardly the truest representation of a city's culinary pride. For a close approximation of the real deal,

we were determined to re-create Memphis barbecue on our own turf. That left us with our trusty kettle grill and a tall stack of barbecue cookbooks.

Of the many backyard-friendly recipes we tried, cookbook author David Rosengarten's sweet-spicy "slow-'cued" (read: seven-hour) ribs were the clear favorite. Tasters—Southern transplants and Yankees alike—raved that these ribs were everything they should be: smoky and tender, encrusted in a thick, ample bark with gentle heat. As for us, we were too tired to eat after nearly a full day tending the grill. There had to be a faster, less fussy route to Memphis.

Before we began specific testing, we needed a proper barbecue setup. For a fire that would maintain the key amount of indirect heat (roughly 250 to 275 degrees) long enough to break down the connective tissue in the ribs, we had two choices: banking two piles of coals on either side of the grill or one pile on one side in what's known as a modified two-level fire. In tests, we've found piling the coals on one side produces steadier, more

evenly distributed heat, so we opted for that approach. To avoid the constant dance of lifting the lid to add more charcoal to keep the heat stabilized, we mounded coals we'd burned for 15 minutes in a chimney starter on top of unlit coals—a trick that would allow us to extend the life of the flame without opening the grill. In addition, we stowed a pan of water underneath the cooking grate on the cooler side of the grill, where it would absorb heat and work to keep the temperature stable, as well as help keep the meat moister.

This relatively hands-off technique kept the grill in the 250-degree range for a full hour and a half—but still nowhere near long enough for the meat to fully tenderize. Spending hours feeding the fire with coals to keep the grill at the proper temperature was out of the question. But what about moving the operation indoors? We've often had success combining the smoke of the grill with the steady heat and convenience of the oven to streamline slow-cooked barbecue recipes. The only question was the order of operations: grill to oven or oven to grill?

Since a crusty bark was one of the main goals, we figured it made sense to start the ribs in the oven and finish them on the grill, where their exterior could dry out just before serving. We applied our rub—a slight variation on Rosengarten's original, containing a sweet-hot mix of powdered spices, brown sugar, salt, and dried thyme—the day before cooking (standard procedure for these ribs). We then wrapped the rubbed ribs in foil (easier than mopping them, we figured, since they could baste in their own juices) and threw them into a 275-degree oven. In the meantime, we set up our grill with the same modified two-level fire.

Three hours later, we pulled the ribs from the oven and unwrapped them. They were undeniably tender, but we all agreed they looked a bit sweaty and steamy, too. Hoping the fire would correct this, we transferred them to the cooler side of our kettle, placed some soaked hickory chunks on the live coals to generate smoke, and replaced the lid, opening and closing vents as necessary to maintain the 250-degree temperature and occasionally mopping the ribs with a mixture of apple juice and cider vinegar. An hour later, the ribs showed no sign of a bark. In desperation, we dragged the racks to the hot side of the grill to finish, hoping that the extra heat would crisp up their exterior. Our tasters were not fooled. These overly wet, soft-textured ribs screamed "braise" rather than "barbecue," and still had no bark to speak of. A good bit of the rub had also washed away during their oven time, leaving only a hint of its spicy promise. Even worse, tasters panned the smoke flavor as "acrid" and "superficial." Where had we gone wrong?

Research revealed the first serious misstep: exposing the ribs to smoke after they cooked. Smoke contains both water-soluble and fat-soluble flavor compounds. As traditional dry rub ribs cook, the water-soluble compounds dissolve in the meat's surface moisture and get left behind as it evaporates. Fat-soluble compounds, on the other hand, dissolve in the rendering fat, which then spreads through the meat, lubricating the muscle fibers and depositing smoke flavor as it goes. The problem is, if the ribs start cooking in the oven, much of the fat renders and drips out of the meat before it even gets to the grill. Once on the coals, the parcooked ribs have less fat for the smoke compounds to dissolve in, resulting in a one-dimensional, ashtraylike essence, not the full-on smokiness we were after.

Lesson learned, we reversed the cooking order in the next batch, placing the raw, spice-rubbed rib racks over the cooler side of the grill while two hickory chunks smoldered over the coals. After 45 minutes we rotated and mopped the slabs, let them cook another 45 minutes, and finally transferred them to a wire rack set over a rimmed baking sheet to bring them indoors. The ribs then got a second vinegar-juice coat on their way into a 300-degree oven—cranking up the heat just a bit, we hoped, would expedite the cooking without compromising the meat's texture—where they stayed until tender

MEMPHIS-STYLE BARBECUED SPARERIBS

and thick-crusted. (Depending on the size and thickness of the racks, this took another one to two hours, with a third and final mopping halfway through.) We even mimicked our grill setup by pouring 1½ cups water into the rimmed baking sheet, the effect of which continued to gently humidify the cooking environment. But we'd overcompensated: The texture was fine, but now our ribs were so smoky that their flavor verged on burnt kindling. To curb the fume flavor, we downsized from wood chunks to a mere ½ cup of soaked wood chips, which smoldered just long enough (30 minutes) to give the ribs a clean, subtly wood-smoked flavor.

Up to this point, we'd been blindly following the advice of many recipes, applying our salt-spice rub to the ribs a full day before cooking them for maximum flavor. On first inspection, the approach made sense: More time with the rub means more penetration, which means a more flavorful end result, right? But the thinness of the meat on the bones meant that the rub didn't have all that far to travel. Did we really need to keep the rub on the ribs for such a long time? We set up a time check: we rubbed the spice mixture onto one batch of ribs and let them sit overnight before cooking. We then applied rub on a second batch and threw these ribs on the grill as soon as we had the fire ready, about 30 minutes later. A few hours after that, the results were in—and they were heretical. We found that applying the rub right before cooking gave us all the flavor we needed.

The last puzzle piece was figuring out when the ribs were done. Wet ribs are pretty forgiving; in fact, they're nearly impossible to overcook. But dry rub ribs are more exacting and have a very small window during which they are perfectly cooked. The foolproof solution? A thermometer. As long as we pulled our ribs out of the oven when the thickest section reached 195 degrees, the meat turned out consistently tender with a good bit of satisfying chew. Next time we're craving smoky, porky, complex barbecue, we'll leave the bottles of sweet sauce—and the mail-order forms—on the shelf.

NOTES FROM THE TEST KITCHEN

BEST RIBS FOR BBQ

BABY BACK RIBS: TOO LEAN
Cut from the top side of the animal, close to the loin, baby back ribs are tender but low in fat, which makes them prone to drying out during prolonged exposure to the heat of the grill.

SPARERIBS: PREP HEAVY
Spareribs are the entire, untrimmed rib section of the pig, cut from the underside. While good for slow-cooking, they contain portions of belly meat, plus lots of fat and gristle that require trimming once you get them home.

ST. LOUIS-STYLE RIBS: TOP CHOICE
This cut, the third option for ribs from the pig, refers to spareribs that have been trimmed of belly and skirt meat and excess cartilage. The minimal fuss involved in using them makes them our top choice for barbecue.

Memphis-Style Barbecued Spareribs on a Charcoal Grill

SERVES 4 TO 6

Pouring lit briquettes over unlit briquettes provides the low, steady heat necessary for effective smoking. To maintain a constant temperature, manipulate the upper and lower vents of your grill and do not remove the lid any more than necessary. For less spiciness, reduce the cayenne to ½ teaspoon. You will need a 13 by 9-inch disposable aluminum pan for this recipe.

RUB

- 2 tablespoons sweet paprika
- 2 tablespoons light brown sugar
- 1 tablespoon table salt
- 2 teaspoons chili powder
- 1½ teaspoons ground black pepper
- 1½ teaspoons garlic powder
- 1½ teaspoons onion powder
- 1½ teaspoons cayenne pepper (see note)
- ½ teaspoon dried thyme

RIBS

- 2 racks St. Louis–style spareribs, 2½ to 3 pounds each
- ½ cup wood chips
- ½ cup apple juice
- 3 tablespoons apple cider vinegar

1. Combine the rub ingredients in a small bowl. Place the racks on a rimmed baking sheet; sprinkle the rub on both sides of each rack, rubbing and pressing to adhere. Set the racks aside while preparing the grill.

2. Soak the wood chips in cold water to cover for 30 minutes; drain. Combine the apple juice and vinegar in a small bowl; set aside. Open the top and bottom vents halfway and arrange 15 unlit charcoal briquettes evenly on one side of the grill. Place a 13 by 9 inch disposable aluminum pan filled with 1 inch of water on the other side of the grill. Light a large chimney starter filled one-third with charcoal (about 33 briquettes) and allow to burn until the coals are partially coated with a layer of ash,

about 15 minutes. Empty the coals into the grill on top of the unlit briquettes to cover half of the grill. Sprinkle the soaked wood chips over the coals. Set the cooking grate in place, cover the grill, and heat the grate until hot and the chips are smoking, about 5 minutes. Use a grill brush to scrape the cooking grate clean.

3. Place the ribs, meat side down, on the grate over the water pan. Cover the grill, positioning the top vent over the ribs to draw smoke through the grill. Cook the ribs 45 minutes, adjusting the vents to keep the temperature inside the grill around 250 to 275 degrees. Flip the ribs meat side up, turn 180 degrees, and switch their positions so that the rack that was nearest the fire is on the outside. Brush each rack with 2 tablespoons of the apple juice mixture; cover the grill and cook another 45 minutes. About 15 minutes before removing the ribs from the grill,

---

NOTES FROM THE TEST KITCHEN

SPEEDING UP MEMPHIS-STYLE RIBS

Traditionally, Memphis dry rub ribs are a 24-hour-plus project: The racks are rubbed with spices, left to sit overnight, and then slow-smoked for the better part of a day. Here's how we mimicked the smoky, pleasantly chewy results in less than half the time.

1. A BRIEF RUBDOWN: Because the meat layer is so thin, an overnight rub is unnecessary. Applying the rub (a blend of salt, brown sugar, paprika, and other spices) just before cooking infuses plenty of sweet-spicy flavor.

2. FINISH IN THE OVEN: Thanks to our grill setup, we get great smoke flavor by grill-smoking the ribs for 1½ hours before transferring them to a low oven to cook 2 to 3 hours more. Water added to the baking sheet helps keep the meat moist.

adjust an oven rack to the middle position and heat the oven to 300 degrees.

4. Transfer the ribs, meat side up, to a wire rack set over a rimmed baking sheet; pour 1½ cups water into the bottom of the baking sheet. Brush the top of each rack with 2 tablespoons more apple juice mixture; roast 1 hour. Brush the ribs with the remaining apple juice mixture and continue to roast until the meat is tender but not falling off the bone and the thickest part of the roast registers 195 to 200 degrees on an instant-read thermometer. Transfer the ribs to a carving board, tent loosely with foil, and let rest 15 minutes. Cut the ribs between the bones to separate and serve.

VARIATION

Memphis-Style Barbecued Spareribs on a Gas Grill

If using a small two-burner gas grill, it may be necessary to cut each rack in half crosswise between the bones and use a foil shield to protect the ribs from the direct heat of the primary burner: Place a 24-inch length of heavy-duty foil down the center of the grill. Place the halved racks over the cool side of the grill, perpendicular to the cooking grates, so that they cover about half of the foil. Lift up the foil to shield the ribs. You will need two 9-inch disposable aluminum pie plates for this recipe.

Follow the recipe for Memphis-Style Barbecued Spareribs on a Charcoal Grill through step 2, increasing the amount of wood chips to ¾ cup. Place the soaked chips in a 9-inch disposable aluminum pie plate with ¼ cup water and set on the primary burner of a gas grill. Place a second 9-inch disposable aluminum pie plate filled with 1 inch of water on the other burner(s). Set the cooking grates over the burners. Turn all the burners to high and heat the grill, with the lid down, until hot, and the chips are smoking about 15 minutes. Turn the primary burner to medium-high and turn off the other burner(s). Use a grill brush to scrape the cooking grate clean. Proceed with the recipe from step 3, maintaining a grill temperature of about 250 to 275 degrees by adjusting the heat of the primary burner.

GREAT GRILLING GADGETS

When the warm weather rolls around, we grab our grill brush and tongs and head outside. While you don't really *need* any other tools for grilling (outside of a chimney starter if you have a charcoal grill), we found a few things that can make grilling easier, more fun, and more productive. See www.americastestkitchen.com for updates to this testing.

GRILL LIGHTER

As opposed to a lit match, which can singe your fingers if you're not careful or quick, grill lighters have long necks to keep your fingers at a safe distance from the flames. After firing up five models, we preferred the Zippo Flexible Neck Utility Lighter ($18.35), which has a neck that makes for easy chimney lighting, even when trying to light it from underneath. This model ignited easily, stayed lit even in windy gusts, has a refillable chamber with a large, easy-to-read fuel window, and sported a comfortable grip, while its unique adjustable flame could flare from $\frac{1}{3}$ inch to 2 inches. This model can light our fire anytime.

WINNER: ZIPPO FLEXIBLE NECK UTILITY LIGHTER

RIB RACK

If you're cooking ribs for a crowd, a rib rack might be just what you need. While a standard kettle grill can't hold more than two racks of ribs laid flat, a rib rack can hold at least four slabs upright on the cooking grate. We tested three models, all of which turned out smoky, moist ribs with good bark, so design details decided the winner. We preferred the Charcoal Companion Non-Stick Reversible Roasting/Rib Rack ($14.95), which sturdily supported six racks of ribs; the other models allowed the ribs to curl or droop or held the ribs too high off the cooking grate. Flipped upside down, our winner also doubles as a roasting rack, big enough to cook a whole chicken or even a small turkey. Its nonstick surface made cleanup a breeze—a plus, since it's not dishwasher-safe.

WINNER: CHARCOAL COMPANION NON-STICK REVERSIBLE ROASTING/RIB RACK

REMOTE THERMOMETER

So we're not stuck holding a lonely vigil at the grill, we turn to a remote thermometer. Our favorite is the Taylor Wireless Thermometer with Remote Pager Plus Timer ($21.95). We found this two-part device—a temperature probe attached to a base that rests outside the grill or oven and a pager you carry—to be incredibly accurate and easy to set. Plus, it doesn't have preset doneness temperatures that are hard to override, as with other models we've seen (a feature that often leads to overcooked meat). However, the Taylor does have a downside: Its pager does not have a temperature display. Instead it vibrates when the food is 10 degrees away from being done, then again when it's fully cooked. So while it does allow you to roam—more than 100 feet— you just can't go too far.

WINNER: TAYLOR WIRELESS THERMOMETER WITH REMOTE PAGER PLUS TIMER

DISPOSABLE GRILL

Not everyone has a portable grill, and not even a basic, no-frills charcoal grill is compact enough to travel farther than the backyard. Fortunately, there's another option for picnics and beach barbecues: the EZ Grill Disposable Instant Grill ($9.99 for large size). Inside the box is an all-in-one grill—essentially an aluminum pan (perforated for airflow) fitted with a metal grate on top and wire legs on the bottom—plus two packages of "easy to light" charcoal. We had our doubts—the whole kit looked pretty flimsy—but once we struck a match, we were cooking. The spacious cooking surface accommodated three steaks at a time with room to spare, and the heat held steady enough for us to follow up with three chicken breasts—a total of more than 45 minutes of cooking time. Once cool, the grill can be thrown away or recycled. We wouldn't use the EZ Grill for a big backyard barbecue, but it's ideal for a movable feast.

WINNER: EZ GRILL DISPOSABLE INSTANT GRILL

GREAT GRILLED
Roast Beef

*If you think roast beef is good
made indoors during cold
months, we have news for
you—it's even better on the
grill. We'll show you how to
produce a beef roast with rosy
meat and great grilled flavor.*

ROAST BEEF ON THE GRILL? IT MAY NOT BE AS POPULAR AS STEAKS, but when you've got company coming and you're not feeling as flush as you'd like, grilling an affordable beef roast is a tasty, economical alternative. But getting a bulky piece of meat like a roast to cook through without the exterior drying out can be tricky. Our goal was a rosy pink roast all the way through with great grilled flavor—a roast so good, it makes frugality fashionable.

Potatoes are a natural with roast beef and if you haven't tried crispy smashed potatoes, you should. The method is as follows: smash parcooked potatoes so that each potato forms a thick patty and then pan-fry or roast them until a crispy, craggy crust forms. The questions are which type of potato works best in this dish and which method (pan-frying or roasting), produces the crispiest potatoes while preserving their moist and creamy interior. Join us as we show you how to turn plain old potatoes into a superstar side dish.

INEXPENSIVE GRILLED ROAST BEEF

✓ **WHY THIS RECIPE WORKS:** Traditional recipes for grill-roasting sear the meat over the hot side of the grill, then move it to the cooler side, where it cooks at a slower, gentler pace. To ensure an evenly cooked, rosy pink, tender interior, we adjusted that approach in two ways: First, we minimized the overall heat output by using only half a chimney's worth of coals—just enough to give the meat a good sear. Second, we shielded the seared roast from excess heat by placing it in a disposable aluminum pan when we moved it to the grill's cooler side. Both measures help keep the roast below 122 degrees for as long as possible; past this temperature, the enzymes that tenderize meat are inactivated. And the more time meat has to break down, the more tender the results.

ROAST BEEF MAKES A TERRIFIC SUNDAY DINNER centerpiece through the cold weather, but come the sweltering days of summer, roast beef falls by the wayside. That's too bad because this bargain cut can be great on the grill. We envisioned a juicy roast with great grilled flavor and a well-seasoned garlic-rosemary crust.

Our first attempts, using inexpensive bottom round, turned out fibrous, chewy, and woefully dry in many spots—in other words, unevenly cooked. Though we used a thermometer to ensure a perfectly medium-rare center, the roast's tapered end was storm-cloud gray. Even the more uniform, thicker sections developed a wide band of overcooked meat around the edges. It left us with one question: How do you cook an uneven piece of meat evenly?

Just to see if there was something better suited to grilling than bottom round, we explored all the "cheap" ($5.99 per pound or less) roast beef options at our local market. By the end of our trip down the meat aisle, our cart was filled with top and bottom round, eye round, chuck eye, and top sirloin, all of which sat through a 24-hour salt rub—a technique we use with roasts for improved texture and seasoning—before hitting the fire. For practicality, we wanted our technique to work with any of these beef cuts, but we focused our testing on the winner of the tasting: top sirloin, a beefy, relatively tender cut from the back half of the cow.

Our technique for making thick-cut steaks with evenly cooked interiors and well-developed crusts dictates two stages of heat exposure: low and slow for a rosy interior, followed by a fast, hard sear for a nicely charred exterior—in that order. During the initial phase, the surface of the meat dries out, allowing for more efficient searing. Figuring the same method would work for our even thicker 3- to 4-pound roast, we set up a modified two-level fire, with all the coals banked to one side of the kettle. In effect, this bisected the grill into hot and cool zones for searing and gentler indirect cooking, respectively. But the slow-roast-then-sear approach didn't translate well to a charcoal grill; by the time the center of this larger cut had cooked through, there wasn't enough firepower left in the coals to sear the meat and develop a crust. Adding a second chimney of coals to the grill partway through might have worked if the timing hadn't been impossible to nail down. (Plus, it was more hassle than we were hoping for.) That left us with one chimney, meaning we needed to sear the meat first while the fire was still blazing; our roast now developed a thick, dark crust in 10 minutes.

Unfortunately, that blast of heat cycled us right back to our initial conundrum: uneven cooking and toughness, both of which are exacerbated by high temperatures. The hotter your fire, the more likely it is for the outer layers and thinner sections to overcook before the center is done. What's more, our science editor explained to us, beef contains enzymes that break down muscle fibers and act as natural tenderizers. These enzymes work faster as the temperature of the meat rises but only until it reaches 122 degrees, at which point all action by the enzymes stops. The bottom line: For more tender results, we needed to keep the meat's interior temperature below this point for as long as possible.

Our only alternative was to try tinkering with the temperature of the grill (and, in turn, the cooking time).

INEXPENSIVE GRILL-ROASTED BEEF WITH GARLIC AND ROSEMARY

A full 6-quart chimney put out too much heat too fast, cooking our roast through in under 30 minutes, before the enzymes had a chance to work effectively. We started taking away briquettes, incrementally lowering the amount until we arrived at a half chimney—the absolute minimum we could get away with while still maintaining a good sear. But even then the meat cooked too quickly. To make this technique work, we'd need to find a way to protect the meat from excess heat as soon as it came off the initial sear. In other words, we needed a meat shield.

When grilling and barbecuing, we keep a supply of disposable aluminum pans at the ready; they come in handy as vessels for marinades or water or for covering the cooking grate to concentrate the heat when cooking fish. Maybe they could also function as protective walls against the heat? We started experimenting with them: covering the coals (this time to repel their heat), shielding the meat from the top, and sandwiching the meat between two pans to deflect the heat. (We even tried cutting off the air supply to the grill, causing the coals to die, but this left a sooty taste on the meat.) The most promising method turned out to be searing the roast over the coals, then placing it directly inside the aluminum pan on the cooler side of the grill; this technique slowed the cooking time by about 20 minutes (for a total of just over an hour) and delivered meat that was as tender as any we'd tasted, not to mention uniformly rosy throughout. But it wasn't a perfect solution: As the juices exuded from the meat, they pooled around the roast and turned its underside boiled and gray, ruining any crust we'd achieved from searing. No problem—nothing a little hole-punching couldn't fix. The addition of a dozen or so small escape channels in the bottom of the pan allowed the liquid to drain away and left the meat perfectly pink with a crisp, flavorful crust. For even more flavor, we added a healthy dose of garlic and rosemary to the salt rub; the flavors made their way deep into the meat by the time we lit the grill.

As our carving knife peeled off wafer-thin slices of rosy meat (another trick for making the roast taste even more tender), we realized roast beef had made it onto the year-round rotation.

NOTES FROM THE TEST KITCHEN

THE BEST CHEAP ROASTS FOR GRILLING
Our grill-roasting method will work with any of these inexpensive cuts; however, some produced better results than others. The options are listed in order of preference, from left to right.

TOP SIRLOIN
FLAVOR: ★★★
TEXTURE: ★★★
COST: $5.99 per lb
COMMENTS: This cut was judged "buttery," with bold, beefy flavor and ample juiciness.

TOP ROUND
FLAVOR: ★★
TEXTURE: ★★
COST: $4.49 per lb
COMMENTS: Though slightly chewy, this cut boasts rich, meaty flavor.

BOTTOM ROUND
FLAVOR: ★★
TEXTURE: ★★
COST: $4.49 per lb
COMMENTS: A little tough because of its large muscle fibers, bottom round has a rich, somewhat gamy flavor.

CHUCK EYE
FLAVOR: ★★
TEXTURE: ★½
COST: $3.99 per lb
COMMENTS: This roast packs great beefy flavor, but only if it's cooked to medium so the intramuscular fat can melt.

EYE ROUND
FLAVOR: ★½
TEXTURE: ★★
COST: $4.99 per lb
COMMENTS: Though its flavor is subtle, this lean, uniform cut won fans for even cooking, tenderness, and easy slicing.

Inexpensive Charcoal-Grill-Roasted Beef with Garlic and Rosemary

SERVES 6 TO 8

A pair of kitchen shears works well for punching the holes in the aluminum pan. We prefer a top sirloin roast; see "The Best Cheap Roasts for Grilling" on page 210 for other roasts that can be used with this technique. Start this recipe the day before you plan to grill so the salt rub has time to flavor and tenderize the meat. You will need a 13 by 9-inch disposable aluminum pan for this recipe.

6   medium garlic cloves, minced or pressed through a
     garlic press (about 2 tablespoons)
2   tablespoons minced fresh rosemary leaves
1   tablespoon ground black pepper
2   teaspoons table salt
1   (3 to 4-pound) top sirloin roast (see note)
     Vegetable oil for the cooking grate

1. Combine the garlic, rosemary, pepper, and salt in a small bowl. Sprinkle all sides of the roast evenly with the salt mixture, wrap with plastic wrap, and refrigerate for 18 to 24 hours.

2. Open the bottom grill vents fully. Light a large chimney starter filled halfway with charcoal (about 3 quarts) and allow to burn until the coals are partially covered with a layer of ash, about 20 minutes. Arrange all the coals over one-third of the grill. Position the cooking grate over the coals, cover the grill, and heat the grate until hot, about 5 minutes. Use a grill brush to scrape the cooking grate clean. Dip a wad of paper towels in oil; holding the wad with tongs, oil the cooking grate.

3. Place the roast over the hot part of the grill and cook until well browned on all sides, about 10 minutes. Meanwhile, punch fifteen ¼-inch holes in the center of a 13 by 9-inch disposable aluminum pan in an area roughly the same size as the roast. Once browned, place

the beef in the pan over the holes and transfer the pan to the cool side of the grill. Open the lid vents halfway and cover the grill, positioning the vents over the meat.

4. Cook the roast, rotating the pan 180 degrees halfway through cooking and removing the lid as seldom as possible, until the thickest part of the meat registers 125 degrees for medium-rare (40 minutes) or 130 degrees for medium (60 minutes) on an instant-read thermometer. Transfer the meat to a wire rack set on a rimmed baking sheet, tent loosely with foil, and let rest for 20 minutes. Transfer the meat to a carving board and cut across the grain into thin slices. Serve immediately.

VARIATION

Inexpensive Gas-Grill-Roasted Beef with Garlic and Rosemary

Follow the recipe for Inexpensive Charcoal-Grill-Roasted Beef with Garlic and Rosemary through step 1. Turn all the burners to high and heat the grill, with the lid down, until very hot, about 15 minutes. Use a grill brush to scrape the cooking grate clean. Dip a wad of paper towels in oil; holding the wad with tongs, oil the cooking grate. Proceed with the recipe from step 3, reducing the primary burner (the burner that will remain on during grill-roasting) to medium, turning off the other burner(s), and cooking with the lid down.

RATING SMOKERS

Though it's possible to convert your charcoal grill into a makeshift smoker if you've got a hankering for ribs or brisket, proper lower-temperature smoking is best achieved with a designated outdoor appliance. Besides introducing wood to the fire, smoking is all about holding the heat at a low, steady temperature for a long time—a full day, in some cases—a process that not only bathes the meat in smoke flavor, but also helps tenderize it by breaking down its tough connective tissue. Smokers typically have the advantage of a larger fuel capacity (for a longer-burning fire), a water reservoir (to absorb and retain heat and produce moister results), and more vents (to control the air flow and temperature within a more precise range). To find the best one, we tested three "bullet" models (named for their shape): kettle grill–size vessels that feature a large cooking surface atop a charcoal pan. Brands are listed in order of preference. See www.americastestkitchen.com for updates to this testing.

HIGHLY RECOMMENDED

WEBER Smokey Mountain Cooker Smoker, 18.5-Inch (model #721001)
PRICE: $349   **WEIGHT:** 37 lb
COOKING SPACE: two 18.5-inch-diameter grates
DESIGN: ★★★   **TEMPERATURE CONSISTENCY:** ★★★
COMMENTS: Save for its lack of handles, this model literally smoked the competition: Plenty of cooking space, a water pan, and multiple vents that allowed for precise temperature control added up to meat that came off the fire consistently moist and smoky with little tending necessary.

RECOMMENDED WITH RESERVATIONS

BIG GREEN EGG (model #Large Egg)
PRICE: $750   **WEIGHT:** 150 lb
COOKING SPACE: single 18-inch-diameter grate
DESIGN: ★★   **TEMPERATURE CONSISTENCY:** ★★★
COMMENTS: This ceramic smoker's excellent heat retention and vents that opened all the way, allowing it to reach temperatures as high as 700 to 800 degrees and double as both a grill and brick oven, still couldn't make up for its cramped cooking surface or the lack of a water pan, which yielded markedly drier meats.

NOT RECOMMENDED

BRINKMANN Smoke'N Grill Charcoal Smoker & Grill (model #810-5301-C)
PRICE: $59.95   **WEIGHT:** 32 lb
COOKING SPACE: two 17-inch-diameter grates
DESIGN: ★★   **TEMPERATURE CONSISTENCY:** ★
COMMENTS: A litany of design flaws—no ash grate (meaning burnt charcoal bits smothered and eventually extinguished the fire), no air vents to control temperature, and a hard-to-reach charcoal pan—sank this cheap smoker to the bottom rung.

CRISPY SMASHED POTATOES

✔ **WHY THIS RECIPE WORKS:** For crispy smashed potatoes with creamy interiors and crisp crusts, we started by spreading the potatoes out on a baking sheet, adding a little water, covering the pan with foil, and baking them until tender. A generous dose of salt, pepper, and fresh thyme rounded out the flavor. To smash the potatoes, we used a second baking sheet, which we simply pressed evenly and firmly on top of the pan of parcooked potatoes. To crisp the potatoes we opted for olive oil over other cooking fats to coat the baking sheet (and later drizzle over the broken spuds).

WE LOVE POTATOES IN ALL FORMS, FROM MASHED, steamed, and roasted to fried and baked. We're constantly trolling through cookbooks, magazines, and (these days) food blogs to find newfangled approaches to this fundamental side dish. Our most recent discovery: crispy smashed potatoes. The basic premise—silky-smooth interior, lots of brittle, crunchy exterior—combines everything we hope for in a potato, and the technique looked simple and straightforward. Skin-on spuds are parcooked, squashed just shy of an inch thick—some sources fittingly dub them "crash potatoes"—oiled, and cooked hot enough to render the roughened edges and torn skin browned and crispy and the interior flesh creamy and sweet. These pattylike disks didn't look refined or elegant, but word had it they were as addictive as anything cooked in a deep-fryer.

Every recipe we consulted simmered the potatoes tender in seasoned water before smashing them flat with a potato masher, but from there the techniques divided. Some pan-fried them—a reasonably successful approach, provided they had plenty of close supervision and gobs of fat—while others, ourselves included, opted for the oven's more even heat and a sheet pan's roomier cooking surface. Potatoes for four cooked in one batch? No problem.

But when it came time to start smashing, some spuds cooperated more than others. Thick, oblong russets wouldn't budge under a wiry masher, let alone a towel-wrapped hand. To flatten them required the smack of a broad skillet, at which point their floury flesh crumbled into messy piles. Waxier Yukon Golds and Red Bliss potatoes held their shape nicely when they caved (although meatier, two-inch-plus tubers behaved more like russets), and their thinner skins crisped up nicely in the oven. In the end, we preferred Red Bliss for their diminutive size that smashed into neat patties.

As for cooking fat, our preferred ingredients for potatoes (butter, lard, and duck fat) didn't seem all that practical in this application. For starters, even our well-stocked supermarket doesn't carry the latter two with any regularity, and the milk solids in melted butter burned long before the potatoes fully crisped, leaving the potatoes splotched with bitter black stains. Three tablespoons of olive oil coated the baking sheet and flavored the potatoes nicely, but double that amount crisped the nooks and crannies even more—especially when we applied half the oil before smashing and drizzled the rest once the spuds were broken apart.

So far, the creamy-crispy textural interplay was panning out as planned, but somewhere along the way, the potatoes earthy-rich flavor was flattening out—or, as we eventually realized, washing away. Simmering the potatoes was standard among existing recipes but, to be honest, when does boiling improve anything's flavor? We tried spiking the cooking water with a handful of bay leaves, smashed garlic, various herbs and spices—even bacon slices—but nothing followed through to the end flavor.

Giving drier heat a try, we bundled the potatoes into a large bowl and microwaved them tender before roasting. Better—but skins turned out tough and rubbery. Meanwhile, our preheated 500-degree oven was at the ready: Why not just cook the potatoes in there from start to finish? Spreading them onto a baking sheet, we let them cook on the oven's bottom rack (closest to the heat element) until tender, then proceeded with our working recipe. The results were the best to date: Without the diluting effect of water, the creamy flesh tasted sweet,

CRISPY SMASHED POTATOES

deep, and earthy. A generous dose of salt, pepper, and fresh thyme rounded out the edges.

But roasting the potatoes took twice as long (a good hour), and by now dinnertime had come and gone. Trapping some steam would help break down their flesh faster, so we wrapped the baking sheet in foil. This cut the cooking time by 15 minutes; adding a splash of water to the pan (read: more steam) erased 15 more to just 30 minutes. After a 10-minute respite (both very hot and very cool potatoes crumbled apart when smashed), we simply pressed the potatoes right on the baking sheet and returned them to the oven for another 35–45 minutes—first on the top rack where the ambient heat would thoroughly brown their surfaces, then back to the bottom to crisp their undersides—to finish.

These were the creamy spuds encased in rough-hewn skin we'd been after, but individually smashing more than two dozen potatoes was downright fussy. We glanced around the kitchen for another, more efficient tool and spied an obvious choice: a second baking sheet. We balanced it on top of the whole cooled potatoes and then pushed down evenly and firmly. In one fell swoop, we had perfect, cracked potato patties—and, once they were brown and crunchy, a new spud to add to our starch rotation.

Crispy Smashed Potatoes
SERVES 4 TO 6

This recipe is designed to work with potatoes that are 1½ to 2 inches in diameter. Do not attempt with potatoes that are over 2 inches. Remove the potatoes from the baking sheet as soon as they are done browning—they will toughen if left on the baking sheet for too long. A potato masher can also be used to "smash" the potatoes.

    2   pounds small Red Bliss or Yukon Gold potatoes
        (about 18), scrubbed (see note)
    6   tablespoons extra-virgin olive oil
    1   teaspoon chopped fresh thyme leaves
        Kosher salt and ground black pepper

1. Adjust the oven racks to the top and bottom positions and heat the oven to 500 degrees. Spread the potatoes on a rimmed baking sheet, pour ¾ cup water into the baking sheet, and wrap tightly with aluminum foil. Cook on the bottom rack until a skewer or paring knife slips in and out of the potatoes easily, 25 to 30 minutes (poke the skewer through the foil to test). Remove the foil and cool for 10 minutes. If any water remains on the pan, blot dry with a paper towel.

2. Drizzle 3 tablespoons of the oil over the potatoes and roll to coat. Space the potatoes evenly on the baking sheet and place a second baking sheet on top; press down uniformly on the baking sheet until the potatoes are roughly ⅓ to ½ inch thick. Sprinkle with thyme leaves and season generously with salt and pepper; drizzle evenly with the remaining 3 tablespoons oil. Roast the potatoes on the top rack for 15 minutes. Transfer the potatoes to the bottom rack and continue to roast until well browned, 20 to 30 minutes longer. Serve immediately.

NOTES FROM THE TEST KITCHEN

MAKING CRISPY SMASHED POTATOES

1. After rolling the cooled, oven-steamed potatoes in olive oil, space the potatoes evenly on the baking sheet and place a second baking sheet on top; press down uniformly on the baking sheet until the potatoes are roughly ⅓ to ½ inch thick.

2. Sprinkle the smashed potatoes with the thyme leaves and season generously with salt and pepper; drizzle evenly with the remaining 3 tablespoons oil. Roast as directed.

Summertime
SUPPER FARE

MOST PEOPLE ARE COMFORTABLE TOSSING MEAT LIKE BURGERS, steak, and pork chops on the grill but fear that more delicate foods like poultry and fish will dry out. That's not an unfounded concern—but it's also one that can be overcome. Take chicken breasts. Grilling is a great way to impart flavor to chicken breasts and another is stuffing them—à la cordon bleu, with a rich ham and cheese filling. We'll show you how to overcome the challenges stuffed chicken breasts pose: cooking the chicken through so that it turns out moist and juicy, while preventing the filling from leaking onto the hot coals.

Grilled tuna is a restaurant favorite and, when done well, results in fish with a perfectly charred flavorful crust and moist, pink interior. But at home, these attributes seem to be at odds. Once the fish has achieved a charred crust, the interior has dried out. By contrast, a moist interior means no char at all. Even more vexing is getting the fish to release cleanly from the cooking grate, as fish is especially prone to sticking. Join us as we give you the know-how and confidence to grill tuna with great results every time.

When summertime hits, it's time to fire up the grill. In the test kitchen, that usually means lighting several grills to cover all of our testing.

GRILLED STUFFED CHICKEN BREASTS

✓ WHY THIS RECIPE WORKS: For juicy, tender stuffed chicken, we chose bone-in, skin-on breasts since the skin acts as a natural protector of the meat. We butterflied the breasts—cutting them horizontally nearly halfway through so the meat opened like a book. We placed prosciutto-wrapped fontina inside, folded over the breast to enclose it, and tied each breast up with kitchen twine. Encasing the fontina in prosciutto rather than layering it on top prevented the cheese from leaking. Cooking the stuffed breasts over a modified two-level fire (in which all the coals are banked on one side of the grill) allowed us to first sear the breasts over the hot coals for color and flavor, then finish cooking them over more moderate indirect heat.

FOR BETTER OR FOR WORSE, EVERY DISH THAT'S A good idea inside the kitchen seems eventually to make its way outside onto the grill. The transition is not always successful. Take the classic French dish chicken cordon bleu. Baked in the oven, it deftly solves the problem of dry, bland chicken breasts by stuffing them with sharp, nutty melted cheese and salty sliced ham, lending both moisture and flavor to this otherwise lean and insipid cut. But try bringing it out to the grill, and that same stuffing introduces more problems than it solves. The threat of leaky cheese causing flare-ups as it drips from the chicken and into the coals compounds the standard grilling difficulties: evenly cooking the meat and avoiding a tough, leathery exterior.

Of the many existing recipes we tried, all called for boneless, skinless breasts, though each had its own stuffing method. One required tediously cramming the filling into a narrow pocket. Another split the breast like a hot dog bun and heaped it with a filling that spilled from the top like a mound of sauerkraut. One notable failure sandwiched the filling between two breasts but neglected to seal it in, producing a brilliant burnt-cheese fireball on the grill. The most successful approach was to butterfly the meat by splitting the breast horizontally and leaving

it hinged like a book, but even that didn't completely manage to keep the filling in place.

Still, the prospect of moist, smoky chicken wrapped around a meaty, cheesy filling that stayed where it was put was too appealing to pass up. To make good on this dish, we decided to work from the inside out, starting with perfecting the filling.

Grilled chicken, with its smokiness, requires stronger flavors than the deli ham and Swiss cheese in most cordon bleu recipes. We opted instead for more flavorful prosciutto and fontina, a moist melting cheese with moderate tang. Butterflying seemed like our best bet, so we sliced a breast nearly in half horizontally, splayed it open, layered on prosciutto, then sprinkled it with grated fontina. We rolled the breast around the filling like a jellyroll and secured it with kitchen twine. So far, so good, but we were curious to see how it would fare on the grill.

Disaster started as a tiny drop of cheese oozing out the end and grew into a lavalike eruption, dropping onto the coals and flaring up. The result: chicken with a blackened, sooty exterior and no cheese left in the center. Adding more twine to the bundle did nothing to hold the melting cheese in place. Soaking toothpicks in water, then using them to secure the seams of the chicken, was like trying to plug a dam with chewing gum.

Then we thought that maybe the key was not to rely on the cumbersome chicken to keep the cheese in place, but to use something more flexible: the prosciutto. For our next test, we tightly wrapped the prosciutto around the cheese before we placed the whole bundle inside the chicken cavity. It worked like a charm. To make wrapping and stuffing even easier, instead of grating the fontina, we cut it into 3-inch-long, ½-inch-wide sticks.

As for the stuffing, the only thing remaining was to add a bit of moisture and flavor. A simple compound butter enlivened by shallots and tarragon did the trick: We spread it over the inside of the chicken before adding the prosciutto and cheese. We were now ready to turn our attention to the exterior, which, despite the success of the filling, was still tough to chew.

The problem was that while boneless, skinless chicken breasts are easy to butterfly and stuff, the lean, exposed meat rapidly dries out in the intense heat of a grill. Brining the chicken in a saltwater solution for 30 minutes can help it retain more moisture with any cooking method, and it certainly helped in this case. Switching from a standard one-level fire to a modified two-level fire (in which all the coals are banked on one side of the grill) was also an improvement, allowing us to first sear the breasts over the hot coals for color and flavor, then finish cooking them over more moderate indirect heat. But the fact remained that our chicken was dry and leathery, and the most flavorful stuffing in the world wasn't going to cure it.

What we needed was some kind of protective wrapping to shield the delicate meat from the direct heat of the flames. We tried wrapping the chicken with bacon, pancetta, and some of the prosciutto that we used to wrap the cheese. But on the grill, these fatty meats caused flare-ups, and they also shrank and crumbled off the chicken long before it hit the table. But hold on—why were we spending time trying to create an artificial skin for the chicken? We'd been so focused on the traditional recipe and its use of skinless breasts that the most obvious solution failed to occur to us: starting with skin-on breasts.

Skin-on breasts almost always come bone-in, but any concerns we had that the presence of the bone would make the meat difficult to butterfly proved unfounded: The only modification we needed to make was to slice from the thicker side of the meat, near the breastbone. Since bone-in breasts are larger than their boneless cousins, we anticipated a longer cooking time on the grill. Again we seared the breasts on both sides over the hot side of the grill until well colored, then moved them to the cooler side of the grill to finish cooking. To our delight, the skin protected the exterior of the chicken, releasing fat and basting the breast as it cooked. Even better, the bone also worked to our advantage, helping to prevent shrinkage and shielding the underside of the meat from the direct heat of the grill. While the cooking time had been extended from 15 minutes to about 25, the finished chicken was well worth the wait.

For serving, we opted to remove the chicken from the breastbone, which allowed us to slice it and display the stuffing. This proved remarkably easy (and didn't disturb the filling at all), requiring just the slide of a knife blade under the meat and against the ribs. Then voilà—a boneless stuffed breast that could be enjoyed straight through the grilling season.

Charcoal-Grilled Stuffed Chicken Breasts with Prosciutto and Fontina
SERVES 4

You can serve the chicken on the bone, but we prefer to carve it off and slice it before serving.

> 4 (12-ounce) bone-in, skin-on chicken breast halves, trimmed
> Table salt
> Vegetable oil for the cooking grate
> 4 tablespoons (½ stick) unsalted butter, softened
> 1 medium shallot, minced (about 3 tablespoons)
> 4 teaspoons chopped fresh tarragon leaves
> 2 ounces fontina cheese, rind removed, cut into four 3 by ½-inch sticks
> 4 thin slices prosciutto (about 2 ounces)
> Ground black pepper

1. Following the photo on page 221 and starting on the thick side of the breast, closest to the breastbone, slice each breast half horizontally, stopping ½ inch from the edge so the halves remain attached. Dissolve 3 tablespoons salt in 1 quart cold water in a large container. Add the breasts, cover with plastic wrap, and refrigerate 30 minutes.

2. Light a large chimney starter filled with charcoal (about 6 quarts) and allow to burn until the coals are partially covered with a layer of ash, about 20 minutes. Build a modified two-level fire by arranging all the coals over one half of the grill, leaving the other half empty. Set the cooking grate in place, cover, and heat the grate

NOTES FROM THE TEST KITCHEN

CARVING STUFFED CHICKEN BREASTS

Insert the tip of a boning or chef's knife into the chicken breast just above the breastbone. While gently lifting the breast meat away from the rib cage, simultaneously cut with the tip of the knife against the ribs, following the contour, to separate the meat.

GRILLED STUFFED CHICKEN BREASTS WITH PROSCIUTTO AND FONTINA

until hot, about 5 minutes. Use a grill brush to scrape the cooking grate clean. Dip a wad of paper towels in oil; holding the wad with tongs, oil the cooking grate.

3. Meanwhile, combine the butter, shallot, and tarragon in a small bowl. Roll each piece of cheese in 1 slice prosciutto. Remove the breasts from the brine, dry them thoroughly inside and out with paper towels, and season them inside and out with pepper. Spread an equal amount of the butter mixture inside each breast. Place 1 prosciutto-wrapped piece of cheese inside each breast and fold the breast over to enclose. Evenly space three pieces kitchen twine (each about 12 inches long) beneath each breast and tie, trimming any excess.

4. Place the chicken breasts, skin side down, over the hot part of the grill and cook until well browned, 3 to 5 minutes. Flip the chicken and cook until the second side is just opaque, about 2 minutes. Move the chicken, skin side up, to the cool side of the grill, with the thicker side of breasts facing the fire. Cover the grill and continue to cook until the thickest part of the stuffing registers 160 to 165 degrees on an instant-read thermometer, 25 to 30 minutes. Transfer the chicken to a carving board and let rest, tented with foil, 10 minutes. Remove the twine, then carve the breast meat from the bone following the photo on page 219. Carve into ½-inch-thick slices and serve.

VARIATION

Gas-Grilled Stuffed Chicken Breasts with Prosciutto and Fontina

Follow the recipe for Charcoal-Grilled Stuffed Chicken Breasts with Prosciutto and Fontina through step 1. Turn all the burners to high and heat the grill, with the lid down, until very hot, about 15 minutes. Use a grill brush to scrape the cooking grate clean. Dip a wad of paper towels in oil; holding the wad with tongs, oil the cooking grate. Leave the primary burner (the burner that will remain on during grilling) on high and turn off the other burner(s). Proceed with the recipe from step 3, cooking the chicken with the lid closed and increasing the cooking time on the cooler side of the grill to 30 to 40 minutes.

ASSEMBLING STUFFED CHICKEN BREASTS FOR GRILLING

1. Starting on the thick side closest to the breastbone, cut a horizontal pocket in each breast, stopping ½ inch from the edge.

2. Spread an equal portion of compound butter inside each breast.

3. Place one prosciutto-wrapped piece of cheese inside each breast and fold the breast over to enclose.

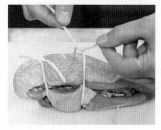

4. Tie each breast with three 12-inch pieces of kitchen twine at even intervals.

FOOLPROOF GRILLED TUNA STEAKS

✔ WHY THIS RECIPE WORKS: For moist tuna with great grilled flavor, we turned to an ingredient that can enhance browning—oil. Oil helps to distribute heat evenly over the surface of the fish, including those areas not actually touching the cooking grate, and it adds a little fat to lean tuna, which keeps the exterior from getting too dry and stringy. But oil alone didn't infuse our fish with grill flavor. We discovered that to moisten the tuna's flesh, the oil needs to penetrate the meat's tiny muscle fibers, so we incorporated it into a vinaigrette. The dressing (and its oil) clung to the fish, moistening its exterior and solving the problem of dry flesh. To improve browning we added honey to our vinaigrette. The sugars caramelized quickly on the grill, helping deliver a perfectly browned crust on our tuna steaks.

FOR MOIST TUNA WITH GREAT GRILLED FLAVOR, WE turned to an ingredient that can enhance browning—oil. Oil helps to distribute heat evenly over the surface of the fish, including those areas not actually touching the cooking grate, and it adds a little fat to lean tuna, which keeps the exterior from getting too dry and stringy. But oil alone didn't infuse our fish with grill flavor. We discovered that to moisten the tuna's flesh, the oil needs to penetrate the meat's tiny muscle fibers, so we incorporated it into a vinaigrette. The dressing (and its oil) clung to the fish, moistening its exterior and solving the problem of dry flesh. To improve browning we added honey to our vinaigrette. The sugars caramelized quickly on the grill, helping deliver a perfectly browned crust on our tuna steaks.

Grilled tuna is a study in contrasts: a thin layer of hot, grilled meat with an intense smoky char wrapped around a cool, delicately flavored, tender, and moist center that pairs with nearly any flavoring you can dream up. Grilling tuna just right might be old hat for a seasoned chef, but as a once-a-year treat in the backyard, most grilled tuna isn't quite on a par with the pros'. A few days of our testing turned out steak after steak with either a rare center and no char, or a great sear enveloping a dry, mealy interior. And in every case, a strong fishy odor dominated what we'd always regarded as a very mild fish.

The problem is, tuna is extremely lean, making it especially prone to drying out. An overcooked steak or salmon fillet, while not ideal, has enough interior fat to keep it relatively moist and palatable; overcook your tuna, and the best you've got is a nice treat for the family cat. In order to preserve its texture, it simply must be served rare or medium-rare. That's where the grill method becomes tricky. How do you char the outside of a tuna steak while leaving the interior untouched?

We began by selecting fresh, 1-inch-thick tuna steaks—any thinner, and we'd never be able to keep them on the grill long enough to achieve a decent crust without overcooking their insides. We had a hunch that a short time over an intense, direct flame was the way to go, but just to be sure, we set up two kettles: one with a moderate fire, the other with a modified two-level fire for dual-zone indirect cooking. In both cases, the tuna had to sit on the grill for nearly 10 minutes before it achieved a suitable char, by which time it was irretrievably overcooked. Using direct heat with a hot fire so we could get the tuna on and off the grill as quickly as possible was the best approach.

We followed our standard method to keep fish from sticking: we covered the grill with aluminum foil while it preheated over a modified two-level fire (with a full chimney's worth of coals under one half of the grill), allowing us to easily brush away any built-up debris. We then applied several layers of oil with paper towels to build up a nonstick surface before adding the steaks. The fish gave a promising sizzle when it hit the superheated grates, but the finished product was far from ideal: The exterior was dry and stringy with a fishy aroma, and though it bore distinct grill marks, most of the fish emerged unappetizingly gray with pallid flavor to match.

Dried herbs and spices brown much faster than meat, so we reasoned that giving our tuna a good coating of them before cooking should yield more of the charred flavor we were after. It certainly worked, but the intense flavors of the coating overwhelmed the subtle tuna. We decided to step away from spices and herbs and move on to another ingredient that can enhance browning: oil.

GRILLED TUNA STEAKS WITH RED WINE VINEGAR AND MUSTARD VINAIGRETTE

Oil doesn't brown on its own, but it does perform two important functions: First, it helps to distribute heat evenly over the surface of the fish; ideally, this would take some of the heat from the cooking grate and transfer it to those areas of the fish not actually touching the grate. Second, it adds a little fat to the lean fish, which keeps the exterior from tasting too dry and stringy. But when we pulled our olive oil–rubbed steaks off the fire, the tuna (though slightly moister) still lacked grill flavor.

With some research we discovered that in order to moisten the tuna's flesh, oil needs to be able to penetrate and coat the muscle fibers on a microscopic level. But tuna is full of water and, as we all know, oil and water don't mix. To get the oil to coat the muscle fibers, we needed it to be in a state where it wouldn't repel water. We immediately thought of a vinaigrette. In a thoroughly emulsified salad dressing, the oil is dispersed in tiny droplets in the vinegar (often with the aid of an emulsifying agent such as egg yolk, mustard, or mayonnaise), where it would be unaffected by water from the fish. As long as the flavor of the vinaigrette did not overpower the taste of the tuna itself, coating the fish in such an emulsion might be just the ticket.

For our next test, we prepared a simple dressing of olive oil, red wine vinegar, and Dijon mustard, which we brushed onto the fish before grilling it. The effect was immediate. The dressing (and its oil) clung to the fish, moistening its outer layer and solving the problem of dry, stringy flesh.

To our surprise, the vinaigrette had two other effects: It reduced fishy odor and boosted grill flavor. Our science editor explained the reason for less fishiness: The acid in the vinaigrette helps neutralize an odoriferous compound in fish called trimethylamine, created when the flesh is exposed to heat. As for the boost in smokiness, we did some more investigating and found that much of smoke flavor comes from small, oil-soluble particles coming off the burning coals. Normally, in lean foods like tuna, these compounds quickly dissipate before they can dissolve in the small amount of available fat, taking grill flavor with them. But by coating the tuna in an oily emulsion, it had more fat for the flavorful compounds to dissolve in than plain tuna, yielding smokier-tasting fish. Now only one hurdle remained: improving browning.

In the test kitchen we often add sugar to brines and marinades for pork chops or poultry to enhance browning—would the same work for fish? We whisked 2 teaspoons of sugar into a batch of vinaigrette and grilled up the fish. The sugar helped achieve the browning we wanted, but only after 8 minutes on the grill, by which time the delicate fish was overdone. We knew that before table sugar—sucrose—can brown, it has to first break down into the simpler sugars fructose and glucose, a process that takes time and energy. Larger cuts of meat that take a while to cook can accommodate that time line, but tuna is on the grill for less than five minutes. Since honey is made primarily of simple sugars, it is already primed for browning. Maybe it would be the answer for quick-cooking tuna, since it should deliver the same degree of browning faster.

Indeed, the honey's effect on browning was dramatic, and its sweetness was barely noticeable in the vinaigrette. The fish came off the grill with everything we'd hoped for: attractive grill marks, a nicely charred, pleasantly smoky crust, and a rosy, melt-in-your-mouth center. Another bonus: By making a little extra vinaigrette, we had a ready-to-go sauce built right into the recipe.

Charcoal-Grilled Tuna Steaks with Red Wine Vinegar and Mustard Vinaigrette

SERVES 6

We prefer our tuna served rare or medium-rare. If you like your fish cooked medium, observe the timing for medium-rare, then tent the steaks loosely with foil for 5 minutes before serving. To achieve a nicely grilled exterior and a rare center, it is important to use fish steaks that are at least 1 inch thick.

    Vegetable oil for the cooking grate
3   tablespoons plus 1 teaspoon red wine vinegar
    Table salt
2   tablespoons Dijon mustard
2   teaspoons honey
2   tablespoons chopped fresh thyme or rosemary leaves
¾   cup olive oil
6   (8-ounce) tuna steaks, 1 inch thick (see note)
    Ground black pepper

1. Light a large chimney starter filled with charcoal (about 6 quarts) and allow to burn until the coals are partially covered with a layer of ash, about 20 minutes. Build a modified two-level fire by arranging all the coals over one half of the grill, leaving the other half empty. Loosely cover the cooking grate with a large piece of heavy-duty aluminum foil and set the cooking grate in place. Cover the grill and heat the grate until hot, about 5 minutes. Remove the foil with tongs and discard; use a grill brush to scrape the cooking grate clean. Dip a wad of paper towels in oil; holding the wad with tongs, oil the cooking grate. Continue to wipe the grate with oiled paper towels, redipping the towels in oil between applications, until the grate is black and glossy, 5 to 10 times.

2. While the grill heats, whisk the vinegar, ½ teaspoon salt, mustard, honey, and thyme together in a large bowl. While whisking constantly, slowly drizzle the oil into the vinegar mixture until lightly thickened and emulsified. Measure out ¾ cup of the vinaigrette and set aside for cooking the fish. Reserve the remaining vinaigrette for serving.

3. Brush both sides of the fish liberally with the vinaigrette and season with salt and pepper. Grill the fish without moving until grill marks form and the underside

VINAIGRETTE—NOT JUST FOR SALAD

A simple dressing of oil, vinegar, mustard, and honey not only adds flavor but is the secret to grilled tuna with a hot smoky crust and a rosy interior (plus less fishy odor!). Each component brings its own particular benefit to the mix.

MOISTURIZER

Oil keeps the fish moist and traps the fat-soluble compounds responsible for smoke flavor, leading to richer grilled taste.

MASTER EMULSIFIER

Mustard helps hold the vinaigrette together so it properly coats the tuna steaks.

ODOR NEUTRALIZER

Vinegar neutralizes the odoriferous compound trimethylamine, created when fish is exposed to heat.

BROWNING BOOSTER

Two teaspoons of honey help the tuna brown quickly before the interior has a chance to overcook.

is opaque, about 1½ minutes. Carefully flip, cooking until grill marks form on the second side, about 1½ minutes longer for rare (opaque at the perimeter and translucent red at the center when checked with the tip of a paring knife) or 3 minutes for medium-rare (opaque at the perimeter and reddish pink at the center). Transfer to a large plate and serve immediately, passing the reserved vinaigrette.

VARIATIONS

Gas-Grilled Tuna Steaks with Red Wine Vinegar and Mustard Vinaigrette

Loosely cover the cooking grate with a large piece of heavy-duty aluminum foil. Turn all the burners to high and heat the grill, with the lid down, until very hot, about 15 minutes. Remove the foil with tongs and discard. Follow the recipe for Charcoal-Grilled Tuna Steaks with Red Wine Vinegar and Mustard Vinaigrette, oiling the cooking grate as directed in step 1. Continue with the recipe from step 2, leaving the burners on high and cooking with the lid down.

Grilled Tuna Steaks with Provençal Vinaigrette

Follow the recipe for Charcoal- or Gas-Grilled Tuna Steaks with Red Wine Vinegar and Mustard Vinaigrette, substituting ¼ cup chopped pitted oil-cured black olives, 2 tablespoons minced fresh parsley leaves, 1 tablespoon minced fresh oregano, 2 minced anchovies, and 1 minced garlic clove for the thyme or rosemary in step 2.

Grilled Tuna Steaks with Charmoula Vinaigrette

Follow the recipe for Charcoal- or Gas-Grilled Tuna Steaks with Red Wine Vinegar and Mustard Vinaigrette, substituting ¼ cup minced fresh cilantro leaves, 2 tablespoons minced fresh parsley leaves, 4 minced garlic cloves, 1 teaspoon sweet paprika, 1 teaspoon ground cumin, and ½ teaspoon ground coriander for the thyme or rosemary in step 2.

Grilled Tuna Steaks with Soy-Ginger Vinaigrette

Follow the recipe for Charcoal- or Gas-Grilled Tuna Steaks with Red Wine Vinegar and Mustard Vinaigrette, substituting rice wine vinegar for the red wine vinegar and omitting the salt. Substitute 2 thinly sliced scallions, 3 tablespoons soy sauce, 1 tablespoon toasted sesame oil, 2 teaspoons minced fresh ginger, and ½ teaspoon red pepper flakes for the thyme or rosemary in step 2.

NOTES FROM THE TEST KITCHEN

NOT-SO-GREAT GRILLED TUNA: THE INS AND OUTS

NICELY CHARRED BUT OVERCOOKED
Tuna with a smoky, well-browned crust usually features dry, overdone flesh.

PERFECT INTERIOR BUT NO CHAR
Tuna with a cool, rare center often has a pale, tasteless exterior.

COOL COCKTAIL GADGETS

When the mercury climbs, we seek relief with ice-cold drinks. Here are some useful gadgets that can help your beverages (and you) keep cool. See www.americastestkitchen.com for updates to this testing.

HAND-CRANKED ICE CRUSHERS

When you want crushed ice for just a few drinks, hand-cranked ice crushers are a convenient choice. They deliver ice that's chopped, not crushed into snow, so it melts more gradually. We like the Amco Swing-A-Way Ice Crusher ($27.99), which has a 1950s design: Load ice cubes into a top chamber fitted with rotary blades, turn the crank, and chopped ice drops into the removable bottom chamber. A lever on the model firmly vacuum-seals it to your counter and simplifies your job to merely turning the handle—and sipping drinks.

WINNER: AMCO SWING-A-WAY ICE CRUSHER

ICE TRAY/BUCKET

While it might look like something from outer space, the IceOrb by Fusionbrands ($13.99) is a functional tool that combines an ice bucket with an ice tray. Instead of lying flat (like an ice tray), its soft silicone is bent into a circular wall, creating a small bucket with protruding pockets that are filled with water for ice. To use it, you fill the bucket with about an inch of water, push in a plastic liner to force the water up and into the mold, place its lid on top, and freeze. Once the orb is frozen, wine or ice cream can be inserted in its center and kept cold for transport or serving. To free the ice, you squeeze out the cubes, producing about two cups of ice that can be stored in the bucket (which successfully keeps cubes frozen at room temperature for more than an hour). Although we found that freeing the ice can be a little tricky (we advise letting the orb thaw for a few minutes before removing the cubes), we recommend the IceOrb, especially for serving ice cream or other cold foods at summer parties and picnics.

WINNER: ICEORB BY FUSIONBRANDS

COCKTAIL SHAKER

A cocktail shaker is an essential bar tool that combines liquor, flavorings, and ice into blended suspension. It must efficiently chill its contents without leaking and easily pour into any shaped glass. We recently tested the Metrokane Fliptop Cocktail Shaker ($29.95), which has a double-walled canister that prevents any condensation from forming on the outside of the canister, for better gripping while shaking. The lid screws on tightly and doesn't leak, and its pop-up pour spout is convenient and easy to use. The Fliptop Cocktail Shaker is what we'll be using to mix up drinks at our next party.

WINNER: METROKANE FLIPTOP COCKTAIL SHAKER

SELTZER MAKERS

Home seltzer makers ensure that you don't have to lug any heavy bottles home from the grocery store. We tried three models, and by far the best was the Penguin Starter Kit by Sodastream ($199.95). While it's more expensive than its competitors, it's also a superior performer that's easy to use and turns out more crisp and cleaner-tasting seltzer (and will over time repay the initial investment). With a few pushes of a lever it's easy to control how much or how little fizz you want in your drink, and the Penguin comes with two glass carafes to store your seltzer for up to a week. Unlike the other models, which require a new CO_2 charger to make each single liter, the Penguin uses a larger charger ($15 to replace), producing about 60 liters of seltzer, depending on how fizzy you like your drinks.

WINNER: PENGUIN STARTER KIT BY SODASTREAM

Grilled Steak
AND GAZPACHO

Freezing the steaks before they're grilled gives the crust time to develop before the meat can dry out.

STEAK ON THE GRILL? HELLO, SUMMER! AS DIE-HARD CARNIVORES, we're always on the lookout for grilled steak recipes once the warm weather hits. And we thought we'd seen it all—until we came across the Argentine method. In contrast to the American technique of quickly cooking steak over an intense charcoal fire, the Argentine method relies on low and slow heat and a wood fire that imparts a deep woodsy, but not smoky, flavor to the meat. Argentine steaks are very large so that they can stay on the grill long enough to pick up that great grilled flavor without overcooking. We knew we couldn't use wood for our fire (our grill couldn't accommodate the amount needed), nor would we have access to giant Argentine steaks; nevertheless, we set out to improvise with American supermarket steaks and a standard kettle grill, so we could enjoy these great steaks all summer long.

When it feels too hot to cook and almost too hot to eat, few dishes satisfy more than a cool, refreshing bowl of gazpacho. But Spain's classic soup isn't just limited to the chunky salsalike version popular in the States. Andalusian gazpacho is particularly prized in Spain. Pureed, thickened with bread, and enriched with fruity olive and sherry vinegar, this style of gazpacho is deeply complex and creamy—yet creamless. The problem is that supermarket tomatoes—even those in summer—can vary in quality, resulting in bland soup. We wanted to bring this intriguing style of gazpacho to American shores, with all the flavor and brightness of the authentic Spanish version.

GRILLED ARGENTINE STEAK

✔ **WHY THIS RECIPE WORKS:** To mimic the woodsy flavor of Argentine steaks that are cooked over a wood fire, we added unsoaked wood chunks to the perimeter of our standard charcoal fire. To get a deep brown char on the meat without overcooking it, we used two strategies. First, we rubbed the meat with a mixture of salt and cornstarch. Then we moved the steaks into the freezer for 30 minutes to extract moisture and facilitate browning once on the grill. A traditional chimichurri sauce composed of fresh parsley, cilantro, oregano, garlic, red wine vinegar, red pepper flakes, and salt—all emulsified with fruity extra-virgin olive oil—cut through the rich, unctuous qualities of our great grilled steak.

OF ALL THE COOKING TRADITIONS INVOLVING LIVE fire and a piece of meat, none is more sacred than preparing the perfect grilled steak. In Argentina especially, where cattle farming is a major industry and the per-capita beef consumption is the highest in the world (roughly 150 pounds annually), grilling steaks over burning embers is not just a means of getting dinner on the table, but a nationwide ritual. All this we learned as we made our way to the Woodside neighborhood of Queens, New York, where the large Argentine population is served by numerous *churrascarias*, or steakhouses, serving up huge slabs of *churrasco* (which refers to both the technique and the grilled meat itself). We were intrigued by a culture that prides itself on the pleasures of a good—some would say perfect—grilled steak and curious to see how its technique would measure up to our own.

Differences were apparent not 10 minutes after we arrived at the first restaurant, La Porteña: First, this was anything but fast food. Here (and everywhere else we ate), the waiter warned us that the steak would take at least 30 minutes to prepare. In contrast to the American method of slapping meat over a blazing fire to sear hard and fast, Argentine steaks are grilled low and slow over hardwood logs, not charcoal (and never over gas), which imbues them with a smokiness that is subtler and more

complex that the typical "barbecue" flavor one comes to expect of grilled meat here in the States. The resulting steak tastes the way a roaring fireplace smells: warm (not hot) and woody (not smoky). Second, Argentines scoff at American steakhouse advertisements for "flame-broiled" meats; to them, burning the steak distracts from its prized beefy flavor. Instead, the cuts we were served boasted a mahogany-hued char that snapped with each bite, almost as if the meat were sheathed in an invisible layer of breading. And finally, there was size. Quite frankly, these extra-thick (1½- to 2-inch), nearly two-pound slabs looked monstrous by our standards, but their immensity had more to do with cooking technique than gluttony. It was simple logic: With thick steaks, the meat could remain on the grill (called a *parrilla* in Argentina) long enough to absorb smoke flavor and avoid the risk of overcooking. With the piquant parsley, garlic, and olive oil sauce known as chimichurri served alongside, they added up to some of the best eating we've ever done, and persuaded us to race back to the test kitchen, where we would try to duplicate this way of cooking steaks.

The first order of business was sorting out which cut of meat to use. In truth, there is no one cut that can be considered a "typical" Argentine steak. Instead, churrasco is a method that can be applied to just about any grill-worthy piece of meat. Still, many of the cuts popular in Argentina—including *vacio* (a type of flank steak), *bife ancho* (boneless prime rib steaks), and *tira de asado* (strips of meat and bone from the rib section similar to short ribs)—aren't available in this country. In lieu of these, the restaurants we visited in Queens offered a wide selection of the steaks Americans like, from porterhouse to T-bone. All were large (almost roastlike) and boasted either lots of marbling or a substantial layer of external fat to lubricate and moisten the beef during its long stay over the fire.

After scanning our supermarket butcher case, we selected four flavorful steaks that met our basic height and weight criteria (about 1½ inches thick, but well under 2 pounds—after all, Americans aren't quite the avid carnivores that Argentines are): strip steak, shell steak, tri-tip, and bottom round (the last an attempt to replicate rump cap steak, an oblong cut from the top round portion of the hind leg that's another favorite choice among Argentine grill cooks, or *parrilleros)*. We built a medium

fire by spreading a full chimney's worth of charcoal around the bottom of our grill (tactics for pumping up wood-grilled flavor would come later), salted each of the steaks generously, cooked them to medium-rare, let them rest briefly, and then sliced them across the grain. Tri-tip and bottom round were out. Though each offered decent flavor, tasters found them a tad tough and dry. Meanwhile, well-marbled strip steak boasted big beefy flavor, not to mention an interior that was both moist and pleasantly chewy. (Shell steak, a flavorful sirloin cut located just to the rear of the strip loin, lost a few votes for its stringier texture but makes a good bargain alternative to strip steak.)

Our steaks selected, we moved on to Meaty Matter No. 2: building up the essential wood-smoke flavor so key to Argentinean grilled steak. Cooking over actual logs was out of the question; the amount of wood required to build a hot enough fire would not fit comfortably in the average kettle grill. Instead, we tried various wood chunk and chip alternatives (soaked and unsoaked, foil-wrapped and unwrapped). In the end, we found that unsoaked chunks proved best. Four pieces nestled around the perimeter of the fire lasted long enough to tinge the steaks with a subtle essence of burning wood. (Placing the lid on the grill for the first few minutes of cooking helped to quickly trap smoke flavor.)

Unfortunately, we still hadn't nailed the requisite deep brown char without overcooking the interior. Without resorting to dry-aging our steaks for days (not even the Woodside restaurants went to that trouble), we needed to figure out a way to drive off their exterior moisture so that a deep crust could form. Salting the steaks overnight in the fridge helped—after first being drawn out by the salt, the juices gradually are pulled back in, leaving the exterior of the meat drier than before—but we hated adding this lengthy extra step. Then we thought of something else. In the test kitchen, we're always talking about how the severely dry environment of the freezer robs food of its moisture. Usually that's an effect we're trying to prevent, but could it work in our favor here? To find out, we salted the meat and then left it uncovered in the freezer for an hour. Sure enough, the meat emerged from the icebox practically bone-dry, and it browned within moments of hitting the grill. Even better, these partially frozen steaks could stand about five more minutes of fire, adding up to more char and more flavor.

Nearly satisfied with our Argentine facsimile, we focused our last few tests on that distinctive crunch we

GRILLED ARGENTINE STEAKS WITH CHIMICHURRI SAUCE

remembered from the restaurant steaks. Inspired by the "nano-breaded" quality of their crusts, we added a small amount of cornstarch to our salt rub—a trick we've used in the past to crisp up everything from turkey skin to potatoes. This twist had two results: We were able to cut the freezing time to 30 minutes, since cornstarch is another moisture-eating powerhouse, and we got steaks with all the color and snap we were looking for, because its starches enhance browning.

All our churrasco needed was the requisite chimichurri dressing, the sharp, grassy flavors of which are designed to offset the rich, unctuous qualities of the steak. Our tasters leaned toward one of the most traditional forms: fresh parsley, cilantro, oregano, garlic, red wine vinegar, red pepper flakes, and salt—all emulsified with fruity extra-virgin olive oil. As we pulled the crisp-crusted, wood-smoked steaks off the grill, splashed on a little chimichurri, and passed around plates—tasters declared them near perfect.

Charcoal-Grilled Argentine Steaks with Chimichurri Sauce
SERVES 6 TO 8

The chimichurri sauce can be made up to 3 days in advance. Our preferred steak for this recipe is strip steak, also known as New York strip. A less expensive alternative is a boneless shell sirloin steak (or top sirloin steak). We prefer oak wood chunks, but other types can be used. Flipping three times during cooking allows for even cooking and limits flare-ups.

CHIMICHURRI SAUCE
- ¼ cup hot water
- 2 teaspoons dried oregano
- 1 teaspoon table salt
- 1⅓ cups loosely packed fresh parsley leaves
- ⅔ cup loosely packed fresh cilantro leaves
- 6 medium garlic cloves, minced or pressed through a garlic press (about 2 tablespoons)
- ½ teaspoon red pepper flakes
- ¼ cup red wine vinegar
- ½ cup extra-virgin olive oil

KEY STEPS TO ARGENTINE-STYLE GRILLED STEAKS
Here's how we produced our own brand of smoky charred churrasco—without the aid of a wood-burning Argentine grill.

1. USE THE RIGHT RUB: Rubbing the steaks with cornstarch and salt seasons the meat and expedites crust formation by drying the meat's exterior; cornstarch also enhances browning.

2. FREEZE BRIEFLY: The freezer's cold, dry air drives off exterior moisture and chills the steaks' interiors, so they can stay on the grill longer, soaking up more smoke flavor.

3. ADD WOOD CHUNKS TO THE FIRE: Four large chunks of unsoaked wood added to a single-level fire infuse the meat with wood-grilled flavor.

STEAK
- 1 tablespoon cornstarch
- 1 tablespoon table salt
- 4 (1-pound) boneless strip steaks, 1½ inches thick (see note)
- 4 (2-inch) unsoaked wood chunks (see note)
- Vegetable oil for the cooking grate
- Ground black pepper

1. FOR THE SAUCE: Combine the hot water, oregano, and salt in a small bowl; let stand 5 minutes to soften the oregano. Pulse the parsley, cilantro, garlic, and red pepper flakes in a food processor until coarsely chopped, about

Build a single-level fire by arranging the coals evenly over the bottom of the grill and place the wood chunks directly on the coals, spacing them evenly around the perimeter of the grill. Set the cooking grate in place, cover, and heat the grate until hot, about 5 minutes. Use a grill brush to scrape the cooking grate clean. Dip a wad of paper towels in vegetable oil; holding the wad with tongs, oil the cooking grate.

4. Season the steaks with pepper. Place the steaks on the grill, cover, and cook until the steaks begin to char, 2 to 3 minutes. Uncover the grill, flip the steaks, and cook on the second side until beginning to char, 2 to 3 minutes. Flip again and cook the first side until well charred, 2 to 3 minutes. Flip one last time and continue to cook until the second side is well charred and the center of the steak registers 115 degrees for rare (about 2 minutes) or 120 degrees for medium-rare (about 4 minutes) on an instant-read thermometer. Transfer to a carving board and let rest, loosely tented with foil, for 10 minutes. Slice and serve, passing the chimichurri sauce separately.

VARIATION

Gas-Grilled Argentine Steaks with Chimichurri Sauce
You will need a disposable 9-inch aluminum pie plate to hold the wood chunks in this variation.

Follow the recipe for Charcoal-Grilled Argentine Steaks with Chimichurri Sauce through step 2. Turn all the burners to high and heat the grill, with the lid down, until very hot, about 15 minutes. Place wood chunks in a perforated disposable 9-inch aluminum pie plate and set on the cooking grate. Close the lid and heat until the wood chunks begin to smoke, about 5 minutes. Use a grill brush to scrape the cooking grate clean. Dip a wad of paper towels in vegetable oil; holding the wad with tongs, oil the cooking grate. Proceed with the recipe from step 4, cooking the steaks alongside the pie plate.

10 pulses. Add the water mixture and vinegar and pulse briefly to combine. Transfer the mixture to a medium bowl and slowly whisk in the oil until incorporated and the mixture is emulsified. Cover with plastic wrap and let stand at room temperature at least 1 hour (if preparing the sauce in advance, refrigerate and bring to room temperature before using).

2. FOR THE STEAK: Combine the cornstarch and salt in a small bowl. Pat the steaks dry with paper towels and place on a wire rack set over a rimmed baking sheet. Rub the entire surface of the steaks with the cornstarch mixture and place the steaks, uncovered, in a freezer until very firm, about 30 minutes.

3. Light a large chimney starter filled with charcoal (about 6 quarts) and allow to burn until the coals are partially covered with a layer of ash, about 20 minutes.

GAZPACHO ANDALUZ

✔ **WHY THIS RECIPE WORKS:** Gazpacho Andaluz starts with the same vegetables as its chunky cousin, but is blended with bread to give it some body. The result is a creamy, complex soup. But unless you have fresh, flavorful vegetables, in particular fresh, ripe tomatoes, this soup can be unremarkable and bland. We salted the tomatoes (and the other vegetables like cucumber, onion, and bell pepper) for intense vegetal flavor. We also soaked the bread in a portion of the vegetables' exuded liquid, rather than water. With a garnish of chopped vegetables, fresh herbs, and drizzles of olive oil and sherry vinegar, this Spanish classic can be enjoyed any time of the year.

YOU COULD SAY "AUTHENTIC" GAZPACHO IS MORE Old World concept than precise recipe. Centuries ago Spanish field-workers cobbled together leftover odds and ends—yesterday's bread, almonds, garlic, olive oil, water—and mashed the whole lot together into a humble potage. (Even the term's etymology is fuzzy, though most authorities suggest it derives from words for "fragments," "remainder," and "soaked bread.") Adding a bumper crop of summer produce is a relatively recent adaptation; the tomato didn't even make an appearance until explorers brought it back from the New World.

These days, just about every part of Spain prides itself on its gazpacho, but most sources still point to Andalusia, Spain's southernmost region, as the soup's home. Like the chunky, liquid-salsa interpretation popular in the States, the soup combines cucumber, bell pepper, onion, and tomatoes but adds bread (for body—and tradition), a generous glug of extra-virgin olive oil, and a bracing shot of sherry vinegar and purees the whole thing in a blender. The result? A creamy, startlingly complex soup that we were determined to add to our recipe file.

We began by preparing a typical recipe, gathering 3 pounds of tomatoes along with a cucumber, a red bell pepper, and a red onion. We finely diced a portion of each vegetable, setting the miniature cubes aside to use as a colorful garnish and then roughly chopping and pureeing the remainder in a blender along with two cloves of garlic, a slice of bread softened in water, and 2 tablespoons of sherry vinegar. With the blender still running, we slowly drizzled in ½ cup of extra-virgin olive oil until the soup was smooth and emulsified. After seasoning and chilling our concoction, we ladled out samples. As colleagues slurped away, their faces began to register the same bored expression. The consensus? The soup tasted so bland, it might as well have been made with just bread. Can't say that we were too surprised. Supermarket vegetables, particularly tomatoes, can be nearly tasteless.

Before we addressed the problematic tomatoes, we made some refinements to the other vegetables. Seedless English cucumbers seemed like the easy choice at first, but the test kitchen recently discovered that they have a higher water content than regular cucumbers. Extra water would only dilute flavor, so ordinary cukes were the way to go (and scooping out seeds takes only a few seconds anyway). And while the red pepper gave the soup an attractive, bright hue, its distinct sweetness was distracting, so we swapped it for a slightly bitter green pepper. Finally, a single serrano chile added a touch of heat.

Now the tough part: the tomatoes. Those that come still attached to the vine (often labeled "vine-ripe") fared better than the beefsteaks we'd been using, but only slightly. Expensive tomatoes packed in plastic clamshells or individual protective foam wrappers were equally unimpressive, leaving tasters cold. We even blended up a batch using canned tomatoes (which are packed when ripe), but the hallmark of the soup—bright, fresh flavor—was absent.

Why are supermarket tomatoes so consistently disappointing? To withstand the rigors of travel, the fruit is picked when still hard and green. It is then treated with ethylene gas, which accelerates ripening. These tomatoes are bright red and thus look ripe but lack the deep, sweet flavor that develops only in true vine-ripened fruit.

Looking for solutions to our tomato conundrum, we stepped out of the test kitchen and into the library for some research into the science of taste. What makes one tomato taste more tomatoey than another? It has to do with microscopic flavor molecules that stimulate taste buds. The more of these molecules exposed to your tongue, the stronger the signal to the brain, and the more intense the flavor experience. Our faux-ripened tomatoes clearly had fewer of these molecules than real vine-ripened specimens. An even bigger problem was that any flavor molecules that a hard, unripe tomato does have are trapped within its firm cell structure, bound to proteins, and can't be tasted. The key to improving the taste of an inferior supermarket tomato, it seemed, would be to burst those cells.

Our first thought: Forget coaxing and start with brute force. If flavor was bound up in the cells of the tomatoes, we would try to muscle it out. We cranked our blender to its highest setting, letting a batch of tomatoes whir for a full five minutes, then eagerly dipped our spoons in for a taste. No luck—the mixture was bland and watery with just a hint of tomato flavor. Our science editor conjectured that even after vigorous blending, most of the flavor molecules were still clinging to proteins, making them unavailable to taste and smell. He suggested a different approach: salting.

Curious about what effect something as simple as salting could have on freeing up flavor molecules, we chopped 2 pounds of tomatoes and tossed them with 1½ teaspoons of kosher salt. An hour later, the tomatoes were swimming in juice. We then pureed these salted specimens along with their exuded liquid. As a control, we also pureed unsalted tomatoes, stirring in 1½ teaspoons of salt after blending. To our surprise, the salted puree boasted a deep, full flavor while the control paled in comparison. Figuring the same process could only improve the cucumber, onion, and bell pepper, we salted them as well, yielding our finest soup yet. It turns out salt pulls out water-soluble flavor compounds as it forces the proteins to separate from the flavor molecules, releasing more flavor (see "Flavor Boosters: Salt and Time" on page 238).

Then we thought of one more way to maximize flavor. We'd been soaking the bread for the soup in water. Wouldn't it make better sense to use the exuded vegetable liquid? After salting the vegetables, we put them in a strainer set over a bowl to collect their juices, which we then reserved to soak the bread. Sure enough, this soup tasted even better, especially when we took care to properly season it with more salt before serving. In addition to the vegetable garnish, we gussied up each bowl with fresh herbs, ground black pepper, and more extra-virgin olive oil and sherry vinegar.

Who knew that with a bit of salt and time, even supermarket vegetables could create a gazpacho that would give the authentic version a run for its money?

Creamy Gazpacho Andaluz
SERVES 4 TO 6

For ideal flavor, allow the gazpacho to sit in the refrigerator overnight. Serve the soup with additional extra-virgin olive oil, sherry vinegar, ground black pepper, and the reserved diced vegetables. Red wine vinegar can be substituted for the sherry vinegar. Although we prefer kosher salt in this soup, half the amount of table salt can be used.

- 3 pounds (about 6 medium) ripe tomatoes, cored
- 1 small cucumber, peeled, halved lengthwise, and seeded
- 1 medium green bell pepper, halved, stemmed, and seeded
- 1 small red onion, peeled and halved
- 2 medium garlic cloves, peeled and quartered
- 1 small serrano chile, stemmed and halved lengthwise
  Kosher salt (see note)
- 1 slice high-quality white sandwich bread, crust removed, torn into 1-inch pieces
- ½ cup extra-virgin olive oil, plus extra for serving
- 2 tablespoons sherry vinegar, plus extra for serving (see note)
- 2 tablespoons finely minced parsley or basil leaves or chives
  Ground black pepper

CREAMY GAZPACHO ANDALUZ

using the back of a ladle or rubber spatula to press the soup through the strainer. Repeat with the remaining vegetable-bread mixture and remaining ¼ cup olive oil.

5. Stir the vinegar, parsley, and half of the diced vegetables into the soup and season to taste with salt and black pepper. Cover and refrigerate overnight or for at least 2 hours to chill completely and develop the flavors. Serve, passing the remaining diced vegetables, olive oil, sherry vinegar, and black pepper separately.

1. Roughly chop 2 pounds of the tomatoes, half of the cucumber, half of the bell pepper, and half of the onion and place in a large bowl. Add the garlic, chile, and 1½ teaspoons salt; toss until well combined. Set aside.

2. Cut the remaining tomatoes, cucumber, and pepper into ¼-inch dice; place the vegetables in a medium bowl. Mince the remaining onion and add to the diced vegetables. Toss with ½ teaspoon salt and transfer to a fine-mesh strainer set over a medium bowl. Set aside for 1 hour.

3. Transfer the drained diced vegetables to a medium bowl and set aside. Add the bread pieces to the exuded liquid (there should be about ¼ cup) and soak 1 minute. Add the soaked bread and any remaining liquid to the roughly chopped vegetables and toss thoroughly to combine.

4. Transfer half of the vegetable-bread mixture to a blender and process 30 seconds. With the blender running, slowly drizzle in ¼ cup of the oil and continue to blend until completely smooth, about 2 minutes. Strain the soup through a fine-mesh strainer into a large bowl,

SCIENCE DESK

FLAVOR BOOSTERS: SALT AND TIME

Because of salt's ability to dissolve in liquids and to draw moisture out of meat and vegetable cells, it often enhances dishes in ways that go beyond just making them taste saltier. Could the length of time we salted our vegetables affect the flavor of our soup?

THE EXPERIMENT

We made two batches of gazpacho. For the first, we salted the tomatoes, cucumber, onion, and green bell pepper in the recipe and let them sit for one hour before pureeing these ingredients with their accumulated juices in a blender. For the second batch, we skipped the salting step, but stirred in the equivalent amount of salt after we pureed the vegetables.

THE RESULTS

The vegetables that were salted for one hour before pureeing produced gazpacho with fuller, more complex flavor.

THE EXPLANATION

To experience any foodstuff's flavors, our taste buds must be exposed to its flavor molecules. But many of the flavor molecules in fruits and vegetables are not only trapped within their cell walls, they are tightly bound to proteins that also make them inaccessible to our taste buds. Vigorous blending—and chewing—release some of the flavor molecules. But for maximum flavor extraction, salting the vegetables and letting them sit for an hour works best. With time, the salt draws flavor compounds out of the cell walls while simultaneously forcing the proteins to separate from these molecules, producing a more intensely flavored soup. Simply seasoning the soup before serving will not have the same effect.

RATING DICED TOMATOES

Full, ripe tomatoes are only available a few months of the year. That's why we rely on canned diced tomatoes, which are packed at the height of ripeness, for many of our recipes. In fact, we use them in everything from soups and stews to pasta sauce and chili. But not every can packs the same bright flavor and firm texture. To find the best canned diced tomatoes, we gathered tasters to sample 16 widely available brands and styles; several were eliminated and eight moved on to the final lineup. The tomatoes were tasted plain and in tomato sauce, and rated on tomato flavor, saltiness, sweetness, texture, and overall appeal. Brands are listed in order of preference. See www.americastestkitchen.com for updates to this testing.

RECOMMENDED

HUNT'S Diced Tomatoes

PRICE: $1.99 for 28 oz
INGREDIENTS: Tomatoes, tomato juice, less than 2% of: salt, citric acid, calcium chloride
COMMENTS: Tasters deemed these tomatoes "fresh" and "bright," with a "sweet-tart" flavor and "juicy," "firm, crisp-tender chunks." In sauce, tasters liked the "concentrated," "bright," and "acidic" tomato flavor, "tender, small-to-medium-sized chunks" and "beautiful texture."

MUIR GLEN Organic Diced Tomatoes

PRICE: $2.69 for 28 oz
INGREDIENTS: Organic tomatoes and tomato juice, sea salt, naturally derived citric acid and calcium chloride
COMMENTS: These tomatoes tasted "sweet," "but in a natural way, unlike others," said tasters, with "fruity," "fresh" flavor. Tasters noted a choppy, irregular dice, though pieces were "juicy." In sauce, the tomatoes were "sweet" with a "robust," "pleasing" flavor.

RECOMMENDED WITH RESERVATIONS

DEL MONTE Diced Tomatoes

PRICE: $1.33 for 14.5 oz
INGREDIENTS: Tomatoes, tomato juice, salt, calcium chloride, citric acid
COMMENTS: Tasters said these tomatoes were "firm and meaty with lots of fresh flavor." For some, though, the dice was too big. Others found them a bit "chewy." In sauce, the tomatoes were "bright" with "rich tomato flavor," though some tasters judged them "too acidic."

CONTADINA Petite Cut Diced Tomatoes

PRICE: $1.79 for 14.5 oz
INGREDIENTS: Tomatoes, tomato juice, tomato puree, salt, calcium chloride, citric acid
COMMENTS: Many tasters liked the "sweet, clean flavor" and "nice, soft texture" of these tomatoes. But a few complained of "uber-sweetness" and felt the cut was "too small" and "stringy." The tomatoes fared better in a sauce, receiving comments such as "good chew" and "nice all around."

RECOMMENDED WITH RESERVATIONS (*cont.*)

CENTO Petite Diced Tomatoes

PRICE: $2.59 for 28 oz
INGREDIENTS: Fresh red ripe tomatoes, tomato juice, salt, calcium chloride, naturally derived citric acid
COMMENTS: When tasted plain, these tomatoes were called "mealy," "like stewed tomatoes," with "the texture of canned peaches" and a slightly "stale," "chunky-ketchup" flavor. But in sauce, they won praise for their "bright flavor," though tasters thought they broke down too much.

NOT RECOMMENDED

CONTADINA Diced Tomatoes

PRICE: $1.99 for 14.5 oz
INGREDIENTS: Tomatoes, tomato juice (tomato puree, water), salt, citric acid, calcium chloride
COMMENTS: These tomatoes were deemed "too bland" with a "very watery and artificial taste." A too-firm texture and too-acidic flavor led one taster to write: "Styrofoam city with citric acid." When describing the sauce, tasters noted "so-so" flavor and "very inconsistent" texture.

HUNT'S Petite Diced Tomatoes

PRICE: $1.99 for 28 oz
INGREDIENTS: Tomatoes, tomato juice, less than 2% of: salt, citric acid, calcium chloride
COMMENTS: These tomatoes are "unremarkable," wrote tasters, with "bright flavor at first that quickly dissipates." Tasters also disliked the "overripe texture, like too-ripe watermelon, a little slimy and pulpy." In sauce, these tomatoes looked "pre-chewed" and tasted "acidic."

REDPACK Diced Tomatoes (sold as Red Gold in some areas)

PRICE: $2.29 for 28 oz
INGREDIENTS: Tomatoes, tomato juice, salt, citric acid, calcium chloride
COMMENTS: Tasters strongly disliked these perfect-looking tomatoes, calling them "watery and bland" and "rubbery and sour." The texture was "way too mushy." In sauce, these tomatoes tasted "sour, old, and sad."

LAZY DAY
Breakfast

Thick slices of oven-dried hearty white sandwich bread or challah make the best French toast because the bread can stand up to the rich custard without turning soggy.

ON DAYS THAT YOU DON'T NEED TO REACH FOR THE OFF SWITCH ON a ringing alarm clock, skip the breakfast bars, cold cereal, or whatever on-the-go breakfast fuels your morning and savor homemade waffles or French toast.

Melted butter and warm maple syrup can mask some of the shortcomings in either breakfast favorite, but we didn't want to settle for a mediocre start to our day. Our waffles had to have a crisp, golden brown, dimpled crust surrounding a moist, fluffy interior. And we wanted a recipe that didn't require advance planning or fussy, effortful mixing.

As for French toast, we've all faced slices that tasted like sweet, soggy sponges with an overtly eggy flavor—or conversely, toast that was so dry, it seemed to have missed the requisite dunk in custard. We wanted to develop a recipe for French toast that was pleasantly crunchy on the outside with a moist, sweet, custardy interior. So brew up a pot of coffee and pour yourself some OJ as we tackle these breakfast favorites.

BUTTERMILK WAFFLES

✔ **WHY THIS RECIPE WORKS:** For crisp waffles with a moist, flavorful interior, we needed a batter with lots of leavening oomph. We found our answer in a mixture of seltzer and powdered buttermilk. The tiny bubbles of carbon dioxide released from the water inflate the batter the same way as a chemical leavener—minus the metallic taste that baking soda and powder sometimes impart. Swapping out the butter in the batter for vegetable oil also improved texture—butter contains milk solids, which can cause the waffles to become soggy seconds after they leave the waffle iron. As for flavor, no one noticed the switch, only the wonderfully crisp texture.

UNLIKE SPECIAL BREAKFAST DISHES—A QUICHE OR an omelet, say—a waffle is hard to get disastrously wrong. Sure, it may come out a little dense or a tad cottony. It may wilt too quickly. But topped with the usual gobs of butter and maple syrup, even a flawed waffle is never terrible.

The compensating effects of butter and syrup may be why so many waffle recipes settle for not-bad rather than chasing the defining balance of contrasts: a crisp, golden brown dimpled crust surrounding a moist, fluffy interior. Or "waffle" recipes, we should say, as a survey revealed that most are merely repurposed pancake recipes. Not surprisingly, a batter meant to cook on the flat, open surface of a griddle doesn't turn out the same in the enclosed, rigid environment of a waffle iron.

But even recipes designed specifically for a waffle iron had their downsides: To help ensure the proper lift, the best either involved an overnight rise or the patience to whip up egg whites just so. We wanted a recipe that didn't require day-ahead forethought—or much more effort than measuring out some flour and cracking an egg.

Waffles and pancakes have obvious structural differences, but the flavor profiles of buttermilk versions are the same. As such, it made sense to start with the test kitchen's buttermilk pancake recipe and fine-tune it for waffle duty. We made a batter with slightly less sugar and a tad more salt than our pancakes, but otherwise

the same: 2 cups flour, 1 tablespoon sugar, ¾ teaspoon salt, 1 teaspoon baking powder, ½ teaspoon baking soda, 2 cups buttermilk, ¼ cup sour cream (which we found provides far tangier flavor than buttermilk alone), 2 eggs, and 3 tablespoons melted butter and poured it into the preheated waffle iron. The result: the terrific flavor we expected but a gummy, wet interior and not much in the way of a crust.

What was causing the texture to suffer? Comparing the griddle with the waffle iron, it wasn't hard to guess. To get crisp, the exterior of a waffle must first become dry. Although a waffle iron is hardly airtight—steam escapes easily via the open sides—all that moist steam racing past the crisping waffle was slowing down the process. The waffle iron's weight bearing down while the waffle was trying to rise didn't help. We needed a drier batter with much more leavening oomph.

We first tried decreasing the amount of liquid in the batter, losing almost half of the buttermilk and adding extra sour cream (to compensate for the loss of some of the fat and tangy flavor), which yielded a net ½ cup less liquid. The resulting waffles were somewhat less wet inside, but they were still quite dense.

Shifting our focus to leaveners, we tried the technique we had hoped to outlaw: whipping the egg whites into a foam and then folding it in at the last stages of mixing. These waffles had a vastly superior texture thanks to the millions of tiny air bubbles produced in the process. (When the batter heats up in the waffle iron, these air bubbles expand, giving the waffle volume.) But getting the whites to this stage was definitely a pain—subjecting ourselves to the rigors of meringue-work before breakfast wasn't exactly the low-effort method we had in mind. There had to be an easier way. More baking soda and baking powder seemed like a good idea, but tasters complained of a metallic aftertaste when we increased them.

Then we had an idea that seemed like kind of a long shot: In Japanese tempura batters, seltzer or club soda is often used in place of still water. The idea is that the tiny bubbles of carbon dioxide released from the water will inflate the batter the same way as a chemical leavener—minus the metallic aftertaste. On a whim, we replaced the buttermilk in our recipe with a mixture of seltzer and powdered buttermilk. The resulting waffles were

EASY BUTTERMILK WAFFLES

incredibly light. In fact, they were so light that tasters claimed them to be "insubstantial" and "all surface crunch with no interior."

We wondered if the bubbly seltzer now made the baking powder and soda superfluous. When tested, waffles made without chemical leaveners had excellent texture but lacked a uniform brown exterior. That's because browning occurs best in an alkaline environment, and without the help of mildly alkaline baking soda, the buttermilk and seltzer in the recipe made the batter too acidic for browning to happen. Adding back ½ teaspoon of baking soda produced waffles that were perfect—at least when they first emerged. But after mere moments on the plate, they began to soften.

The problem is that as soon as the waffle comes away from the heat source, its interior moisture starts to migrate outward, softening the crisp crust. We needed to find a way to prevent this. A little research revealed that the key is fat. Fat and water naturally repel each other. So we thought if we could get more fat into the mix, the surface portion of the batter would be better able to stop water from softening the exterior.

After some experimentation, we found that the solution was not merely adding more fat, but also changing the type of fat we were using. We had been working with butter, which is about 20 percent water. Meanwhile, oil contributes no water at all, which translates to there being less moisture available to move to the surface of the waffle in the first place. Another test proved waffles made with oil (we ended up using ¼ cup) stayed significantly crispier than those we had made with melted butter. Additionally, when oil is swapped in, the difference in the amount of water is made up with fat. The fattier the batter, the more it repels whatever interior moisture manages to rise to the surface of the waffle. The result: The surface stays crisp and the moisture stays inside the waffle, where it belongs. We were afraid that tasters would miss the butter flavor, but in fact they didn't even notice, commenting only on how excellent the texture was. Besides, we could always add more butter at the table if we wanted to. These waffles are so good, so easy, and so foolproof, and since they practically cook themselves, we may never make any other kind of hotcakes again.

Easy Buttermilk Waffles
MAKES ABOUT EIGHT 7-INCH ROUND WAFFLES

While the waffles can be eaten directly from the waffle iron, they will have a crispier exterior if rested in a warm oven for 10 minutes. Buttermilk powder is available in most supermarkets and is generally located near the dried milk products or in the baking aisle (leftover powder can be kept in the refrigerator for up to a year). Seltzer or club soda gives these waffles their light texture; use a freshly opened container for maximum lift. Avoid Perrier, which is not bubbly enough. Serve with butter and warm maple syrup.

- 2 cups (10 ounces) unbleached all-purpose flour
- ½ cup dried buttermilk powder (see note)
- 1 tablespoon sugar
- ¾ teaspoon table salt
- ½ teaspoon baking soda
- ½ cup sour cream
- 2 large eggs
- ¼ cup vegetable oil
- ¼ teaspoon vanilla extract
- 1¼ cups unflavored seltzer water or club soda (see note)

1. Adjust an oven rack to the middle position and heat the oven to 250 degrees. Set a wire rack over a rimmed baking sheet and place the baking sheet in the oven. Whisk the flour, buttermilk powder, sugar, salt, and baking soda in a large bowl to combine. Whisk the sour cream, eggs, oil, and vanilla in a medium bowl to combine. Gently stir the seltzer into the wet ingredients. Make a well in the center of the dry ingredients and pour in the wet ingredients. Gently stir until just combined. The batter should remain slightly lumpy with streaks of flour.

2. Heat a waffle iron and bake the waffles according to the manufacturer's instructions (use about ⅓ cup for a 7-inch round iron). Transfer the waffles to the rack in the warm oven and hold for up to 10 minutes before serving.

RATING TRADITIONAL WAFFLE IRONS

Few kitchen appliances have a more specific job description than your average waffle iron—cook batter until golden brown, signal when done—yet the marketplace is still rife with machines turning out pallid, soggy results. We assessed six waffle irons (all for standard, as opposed to thicker Belgian, waffles), ranging in price from $30 to $80. Each model tested featured adjustable temperature settings for varying degrees of doneness, nonstick surfaces, and lights to indicate when the waffles were cooked. The best irons consistently produced uniformly crisped, evenly cooked waffles—and in the specific shade selected. (One of the worst performers made only lightly tanned waffles even on its darkest setting.) For the highest marks, an audible alert was a must, since it frees you from the tedium of hovering over the iron. Heat-resistant handles and casings were also important. Brands are listed in order of preference. See www.americastestkitchen.com for updates to this testing.

HIGHLY RECOMMENDED

CHEF'SCHOICE WafflePro Express
(model #840)
PRICE: $69.99
COOKING: ★★★ **DESIGN:** ★★★
SIZE AND SHAPE OF WAFFLE: 6¾-inch clover
ADJUSTABLE TEMPERATURE SETTINGS: 6
AVERAGE TIME TO COOK (ON MEDIUM SETTING):
2 minutes 56 seconds
LIGHTS WHEN DONE: Yes **SOUNDS WHEN DONE:** Yes
COMMENTS: Thick heating coils beneath most of its cooking surface helped this iron turn out even, beautifully cooked waffles, no matter the temperature setting. In addition to its six shade settings, it offers two texture settings (for a uniform bake or a crisp outside/moist inside) and a beep to indicate doneness.

RECOMMENDED

CLOER Double Waffle Maker
(model #5051329)
PRICE: $59.99
COOKING: ★★★ **DESIGN:** ★★
SIZE AND SHAPE OF WAFFLE: two 6½-inch clovers
ADJUSTABLE TEMPERATURE SETTINGS: 5
AVERAGE TIME TO COOK (ON MEDIUM SETTING):
2 minutes 36 seconds
LIGHTS WHEN DONE: Yes **SOUNDS WHEN DONE:** No
COMMENTS: This double iron speedily turned out two perfectly crisped waffles that matched the temperature setting. Its only flaw is the lack of an audible cue for doneness.

RECOMMENDED WITH RESERVATIONS

CUISINART Traditional Waffle Iron
(model #WAF-R)
PRICE: $49.95
COOKING: ★★ **DESIGN:** ★★★
SIZE AND SHAPE OF WAFFLE: 6¾-inch round
ADJUSTABLE TEMPERATURE SETTINGS: 6
AVERAGE TIME TO COOK (ON MEDIUM SETTING):
2 minutes 3 seconds
LIGHTS WHEN DONE: Yes **SOUNDS WHEN DONE:** Yes
COMMENTS: Like our winner, this iron offers indicator lights and an audible alert, and was among the fastest to heat and cook waffles. However, the heat was inconsistent—this iron almost burnt the first waffle and then turned out waffles that became progressively lighter in color (though still nicely golden) with each batch.

RECOMMENDED WITH RESERVATIONS *(cont.)*

CUISINART 6-Slice Traditional Waffle Iron
(model #WAF-6)
PRICE: $79.95
COOKING: ★★ **DESIGN:** ★★★
SIZE AND SHAPE OF WAFFLE:
8½ x 10¾-inch rectangle
ADJUSTABLE TEMPERATURE SETTINGS: 6
AVERAGE TIME TO COOK (ON MEDIUM SETTING):
2 minutes 2 seconds
LIGHTS WHEN DONE: Yes **SOUNDS WHEN DONE:** Yes
COMMENTS: This iron can cook six waffles at once. Unfortunately, except when it was on the darkest setting, it failed to create a crisp exterior on our waffles.

NOT RECOMMENDED

BLACK & DECKER 3-in-1 Wafflemaker, Grill & Griddle
(model #G48TD)
PRICE: $54.95
COOKING: ★ **DESIGN:** ★★
SIZE AND SHAPE OF WAFFLE: 8½ x 8½-inch square
ADJUSTABLE TEMPERATURE SETTINGS: Continuous Dial
AVERAGE TIME TO COOK (ON MEDIUM SETTING):
4 minutes 3 seconds
LIGHTS WHEN DONE: Yes **SOUNDS WHEN DONE:** No
COMMENTS: By the time this waffle iron had preheated, the other five irons were already cooking—and twice as fast in some cases. Additionally, once it was preheated, its cooking was inconsistent—some waffles turned out golden while others were raw and gummy.

KALORIK Waffle Maker
(model #WM 17785)
PRICE: $29.99
COOKING: ★ **DESIGN:** ★
SIZE AND SHAPE OF WAFFLE: 6¾-inch clover
ADJUSTABLE TEMPERATURE SETTINGS: 6
AVERAGE TIME TO COOK (ON MEDIUM SETTING):
3 minutes 43 seconds
LIGHTS WHEN DONE: No **SOUNDS WHEN DONE:** No
COMMENTS: This iron offers two indicator lights, but neither signals when the waffle is cooked (one is an on/off indictor, while the other tells you the appliance is warming up). Even worse, one of the plates heated more than the other, leaving us with waffles that were overdone on one side and pale on the other.

FRENCH TOAST

✔ **WHY THIS RECIPE WORKS:** For French toast that's crisp on the outside, soft on the inside, and boasts a rich custardlike flavor, we dried hearty white sandwich bread in the oven before dunking it in a yolks-only soaking liquid enriched with melted butter. Drying out the bread gave our French toast the pillowy interior we were looking for; eliminating the egg whites (which contain sulfur compounds that make eggs taste eggy) gave it richness without the scrambled egg flavor; and adding melted butter imparted a delicious, nutty flavor.

AS BREAKFAST FOODS GO, FRENCH TOAST FALLS in the same category as scrambled eggs—why bother with a recipe for something so simple? Most people merely whisk together milk and eggs, dunk in the bread, then throw the slices into the skillet. The results are rarely worth the trouble. The bread is soggy, too eggy, or just plain bland. With just a little extra effort, we figured we could solve these problems and come up with a really good French toast that's crisp on the outside, soft and puffy on the inside, with rich, custardlike flavor every time.

People all around the world soak and cook bread and have done so for centuries, all the way back to the Romans. Whatever the name or national origin, battering has always been a way to transform old bread into something new and flavorful. The French version is *pain perdu,* the Germans have *arme ritter,* and in Spain the dish is *torrijas.* American cookbooks in the 19th century typically called battered bread *arme ritter,* but after World War I the German name lost favor and the dish went Gallic—which explains why we call it French toast.

Reviewing American and European recipes, we saw many that called for rich breads such as French brioche or Jewish challah, made with eggs and butter. We would definitely test these richer styles, but first we wanted to try ordinary bread from the supermarket, the kind we would more likely have on hand on any given morning. We gathered a dozen brands of white presliced sandwich bread, along with loaves of French and Italian bread that are also widely available at grocery stores. Which would fare best in a typical batter made with 1 part milk and 3 parts eggs?

Though their tougher crust and more substantial crumb seemed promising, tasters quickly eliminated the French and Italian bread for being chewy. We then turned our attention to sandwich breads, which come in two kinds: regular and hearty. The regular bread was hopelessly gloppy both inside and out. The hearty bread crisped up nicely on the outside, but still had more mushiness inside than we wanted, even when we dipped it just long enough to soak it through.

What could we do to make that last bit of sogginess go away? Turning to a pain perdu technique, we tried soaking the bread in milk before dipping it separately in beaten eggs. This technique produced a light, puffy interior, but the exterior was overpoweringly eggy—a definite deal-breaker. Some recipes called for letting the bread go stale overnight, but these days, is such a thing even possible? Normally, exposing bread to air causes its starch molecules to bond and recrystallize, leading to a harder texture, but most breads now include stabilizers in the form of mono- and diglycerides that slow down this process. In the test kitchen, we've determined that leaving bread out to stale isn't nearly as effective as drying it in the oven, which hardens it by actually removing moisture. We checked this conclusion, testing French toast made with hearty white bread dried in a low oven side by side with the same bread left out overnight. We soaked the bread in each batch for about 20 seconds per side to help ensure thorough saturation without contributing to soggy texture. At last, success! The oven-dried version won hands-down, producing French toast that was browned and crisp on the outside and tender and velvety on the inside, with no trace of sogginess.

Though we had nailed the texture, tasters complained that the toast still tasted more like scrambled eggs than buttery fried bread. We tried reducing the eggs from three to two and increasing the milk, only to have the sogginess return. At a loss for anything else to try, we remembered a recipe that called for dipping the bread in milk mixed

with just yolks, versus whole eggs. Though we weren't sure how this would help, we decided to give it a shot. We stirred 1½ cups of milk (increased from 1 cup to compensate for the lack of whites) together with three egg yolks and dipped in the bread. To our surprise, the yolks-only soaking liquid made a huge difference, turning the taste from eggy to rich and custardlike.

So why would eliminating the whites—the bland part of the egg by anyone's standards—reduce an unpleasantly strong egg flavor? Research revealed that most of the flavor in eggs comes not from the yolk but from the sulfur compounds in the whites. These are the same compounds that lead to the offensive odors of an overdone hard-cooked egg. With French toast, the more the egg whites interact with heat, the more sulfur compounds are released, which in turn leads to eggier-tasting toast. The whites can also contribute an unappealing ropy texture, especially if they're not well combined with the milk, giving the toast a speckled white appearance.

With texture and egginess resolved, it was time to do some fine-tuning. Dunking multiple bread slices in a bowl of soaking liquid sometimes led to uneven saturation, resulting in the occasional slice that still cooked up soggy or even dry in places. The simple solution: switching to a 13 by 9-inch baking dish in which up to three slices could fit flat and soak up liquid evenly.

As for flavorings, we settled on ½ teaspoon of cinnamon and 1 tablespoon of vanilla, and a little light brown sugar for sweetness. To bump up the nutty flavor of butter throughout the toast, we borrowed a trick from pancake recipes, incorporating melted butter right into the soaking liquid, warming the milk first to prevent the butter from solidifying.

One question remained: Would our method work equally well with challah (a little more available than brioche)? We cooked up another batch to find out— and tasters polished it off faster than we could say maple syrup.

FRENCH TOAST

French Toast

SERVES 4

For best results, choose a good challah or a firm sandwich bread, such as Arnold Country Classics White or Pepperidge Farm Farmhouse Hearty White. Thomas' English Muffin Toasting Bread also works well. If you purchase an unsliced loaf, cut the bread into ½-inch-thick slices. To prevent the butter from clumping during mixing, warm the milk in a microwave or small saucepan until warm to the touch (about 80 degrees). The French toast can be cooked all at once on an electric griddle, but may take an extra 2 to 3 minutes per side. Set the griddle temperature to 350 degrees and use the entire 2 tablespoons of butter for cooking. Serve with warm maple syrup.

- 8 **large slices high-quality hearty white sandwich bread or challah (see note)**
- 1½ **cups whole milk, warmed (see note)**
- 3 **large egg yolks**
- 3 **tablespoons light brown sugar**
- ½ **teaspoon ground cinnamon**
- 2 **tablespoons unsalted butter, melted, plus 2 tablespoons for cooking**
- ¼ **teaspoon table salt**
- 1 **tablespoon vanilla extract**

1. Adjust an oven rack to the middle position and heat the oven to 300 degrees. Place the bread on a wire rack set over a rimmed baking sheet. Bake the bread until almost dry throughout (the center should remain slightly moist), about 16 minutes, flipping the slices halfway through cooking. Remove the bread from the rack and cool 5 minutes. Return the baking sheet with the wire rack to the oven and reduce the temperature to 200 degrees.

2. Whisk the milk, egg yolks, sugar, cinnamon, 2 tablespoons melted butter, salt, and vanilla in a large bowl until well blended. Transfer the mixture to a 13 by 9-inch baking pan.

3. Soak the bread in the milk mixture until saturated but not falling apart, 20 seconds per side. Using a firm slotted spatula, pick up a bread slice and allow the excess milk mixture to drip off; repeat with the remaining slices. Place the soaked bread on another baking sheet or platter.

4. Heat ½ tablespoon of the butter in a 12-inch skillet over medium-low heat. When the foaming subsides, use a slotted spatula to transfer 2 slices of the soaked bread to the skillet and cook until golden brown, 3 to 4 minutes. Flip and continue to cook until the second side is golden brown, 3 to 4 minutes longer. (If the toast is cooking too quickly, reduce the temperature slightly.) Transfer to the baking sheet in the oven. Wipe out the skillet with paper towels. Repeat cooking with the remaining bread, 2 pieces at a time, adding ½ tablespoon of butter for each batch. Serve warm.

Coffee-Time CRAVINGS

Mixing a portion of the cake batter into the cream cheese filling prevents the filling from separating so that it bakes up lush and creamy.

NEED A BAKE-AND-TAKE SWEET FOR BRUNCH, A BOOK GROUP, OR just to nibble on at home? Look no further than banana bread and coffee cake. Been there, done that, you say? We beg to differ.

We admit that banana bread can be a bit ho-hum, which is why we set out to develop a recipe for a banana bread that will knock your socks off. Sure, most loaves taste of bananas, but mostly they taste sweet. We wanted to zero in on a method for permeating this sweet, rich bread with deep, intense banana flavor, without turning its texture soggy. Most of all we wanted a banana bread so good, it would earn the "ultimate" moniker.

It's not easy improving on buttery coffee cake, but a Central European pastry called *kolachke*, which calls for swirling sweetened cream cheese through the cake, comes close. Too bad the recipes we tried produced dry, bland cakes with unremarkable cream cheese fillings. We had an ideal version of this cake in mind and set out to tackle it: a rich, moist cake with a smooth, sweetened, but-still-tangy cream cheese filling. And because we love streusel on our coffee cake, that would be there too—we envisioned a sweet topping that would lend a crackly crust to the moist cake below. Join us as we turn same-old sweets into something special.

ULTIMATE
BANANA BREAD

✓ **WHY THIS RECIPE WORKS:** To increase the banana flavor without turning the bread soggy from the extra fruit, we microwaved the bananas, drained the liquid, and added the pulp to the batter. We also reduced the flavorful banana liquid to intensify its flavor and tossed that in too; these two steps infused the bread with ripe, intensely fruity banana flavor without turning the crumb mushy. For a final layer of banana flavor, we sliced a banana and shingled it on top of the batter. A sprinkle of sugar helped the buttery slices caramelize and gave the loaf an enticingly crisp, crunchy top.

MOST RECIPES FOR BANANA BREAD ARE PASSABLE AS PTA-meeting handouts—sweet-smelling and pleasant enough to eat while warm and fresh—but their banana flavor is utterly forgettable. Simply increasing the amount of fruit results in an oversaturated batter and soggy texture. We wanted a moist, not mushy, loaf that tasted of banana through and through.

To bump up the banana flavor, we took the logical route first and simply increased the number of bananas in a standard recipe. While the flavor was fruity through and through, the bananas' moisture had oversaturated the batter. Our task was clear—figure out how to cram as many bananas as possible into the loaf without sinking its cakelike structure.

Since it was clear that simply mashing up more bananas to add to the batter compromised the crumb, we decided to limit ourselves to three bananas and try alternative avenues to ratcheting up the flavor. A few of the more inventive recipes we came across stirred crushed banana chips into the batter; presumably, the chips' toasty, concentrated flavor would pick up where the fresh fruit left off. Wrong. The loaf we made with ½ cup of ground chips had the opposite problem; it was too dry—and it had no more flavor than previous batches. Turns out, banana chips are made from

underripe bananas (because they withstand processing better than ripe fruit), and underripe bananas are largely composed of moisture-absorbing starch. We scratched them off the list.

If banana chips were too dehydrated, maybe the answer to bigger banana flavor was to start at the source—actual ripe bananas—and drain their liquid ourselves. That way, we'd get all the benefits of the fruit's creamy sweetness and be able to control the moisture level. Flipping through the test kitchen archives for ideas, we came across a recipe for low-fat banana bread, where we discovered that roasting the fruit not only helped some of the excess moisture evaporate, but also concentrated its rich brown sugar notes. Our goal was to remove enough moisture so that two more bananas (for a total of five) wouldn't overwhelm the batter. Unsure how much moisture would escape through the skin, we roasted batches of bananas three different ways—peels intact, peels split, and peels removed—and then incorporated them into the batter. No matter what the roasting method, five bananas still produced an unacceptably wet loaf, so we scaled back to four bananas. This time around, the split-peel loaf stood out for a nice, moist (but not puddinglike) crumb and a fruity flavor that was a significant step up from any three-banana loaf we'd made. But roasting tacked 45 minutes onto the recipe. And were four bananas really as high as we could go?

Our patience with this process was growing thin. Then a thrifty colleague mentioned that in lieu of throwing out bananas too ripe to eat, she saves them in the freezer, though she has seen them exude quite a lot of liquid when thawed. Armed with this promising nugget, we thawed some very ripe bananas we had stored in the freezer; sure enough, five of them yielded around ⅔ cup of liquid. We pureed the drained fruit, added it to our banana bread, and were rewarded with a flavor-packed loaf boasting a moist, fully baked crumb. Our enthusiasm was renewed—until we realized this discovery would be moot if we had no frozen ripe bananas at the ready.

We had no choice but to return to trying to cook off extra moisture. This time around, we moved our efforts out of the oven and onto the stove: we tried simmering

ULTIMATE BANANA BREAD

the mashed bananas as well as cutting them into dice and sautéing them—but the direct heat of the pan in both attempts gave the fruit an overcooked, jamlike flavor. We were stumped for what to try next, until we remembered a solution for removing moisture from waterlogged eggplant: microwaving it. We placed five bananas in a glass bowl and zapped them on high power for about five minutes, then transferred the now-pulpy fruit to a sieve to drain. Bingo! This caused them to release as much liquid as the thawed frozen bananas. Furthermore, since the bananas were heated for only a short time, they didn't take on the overly cooked flavor of the simmered puree or sautéed bananas.

But what to do about the banana liquid we'd collected? We couldn't bear the thought of pouring all that sweet flavor down the drain. (In cooking terms, it seemed as blasphemous as throwing away the fond.) We transferred this liquid to a saucepan, cooked it down to 2 ounces, and then added it back to the mashed bananas (along with another ¼ cup of flour to compensate for the extra liquid). As crazy as it sounded to extract banana liquid only to put it back (albeit in concentrated form), the result was a revelation. This step infused the bread with ripe, intensely fruity banana flavor. Furthermore, the extra moisture in the batter helped to create a crumb that was tender through and through, without being framed by overly crusty sides.

With the flavor problem solved, a few minor tweaks completed the recipe: We exchanged the granulated sugar for light brown sugar, finding that the latter's molasses notes better complemented the bananas. A teaspoon of vanilla rounded out the bananas' faintly boozy, rumlike flavor, as did swapping out the oil for the nutty richness of butter. We also added ½ cup of toasted walnuts to the batter, finding that their crunch provided a pleasing contrast to the rich, moist crumb.

This banana bread was a true showpiece, from its deep golden crust all the way through to the center's velvety crumb, yet lingering in the back of our minds was the urge to actually double the number of bananas in our original recipe. Wondering if the crust might benefit

SCIENCE DESK

BANANAS—THE RIPER THE BETTER

Don't even think of making banana bread with anything less than very ripe, heavily speckled fruit—unless you're fine with a bland loaf. As bananas ripen, their starch converts to sugar at an exponential rate. In lab tests, we found heavily speckled bananas had nearly three times the amount of fructose (the sweetest of the sugars in fruit) than less spotty bananas. (The exact percentage will vary from fruit to fruit.) But the impact of ripeness only goes so far: We found little difference in sweetness between loaves baked with completely black bananas and those made with heavily speckled ones.

1.8% FRUCTOSE = TOO SOON
A lightly speckled banana has only a little fructose, the sweetest sugar in fruit.

5.3% FRUCTOSE = JUST RIGHT
A heavily speckled banana has a lot more fructose.

from a little embellishment, we sliced a sixth banana and shingled it on top of the batter. A final sprinkle of sugar helped the buttery slices caramelize and gave the loaf an enticingly crisp, crunchy top. This banana bread is so extraordinary, we now make a point of always having a bunch of ripe bananas waiting in the wings.

Ultimate Banana Bread
MAKES ONE 8-INCH LOAF

Be sure to use very ripe, heavily speckled (or even black) bananas in this recipe. This recipe can be made using five thawed frozen bananas; since they release a lot of liquid naturally, you can bypass the microwaving in step 2 and place them directly in a fine-mesh strainer. Do not use a thawed frozen banana in step 4; it will be too soft to slice. Instead, simply sprinkle the top of the loaf with sugar. The test kitchen's preferred loaf pan measures 8½ by 4½ inches; if you use a 9 by 5-inch loaf pan, start checking for doneness 5 minutes earlier than advised in the recipe. The texture is best when the loaf is eaten fresh, but it can be stored (cool completely first), covered tightly with plastic wrap, for up to 3 days.

- 1¾ cups (8¾ ounces) unbleached all-purpose flour
- 1 teaspoon baking soda
- ½ teaspoon table salt
- 6 large very ripe bananas (about 2¼ pounds), peeled (see note)
- 8 tablespoons (1 stick) unsalted butter, melted and cooled slightly
- 2 large eggs
- ¾ cup packed (5¼ ounces) light brown sugar
- 1 teaspoon vanilla extract
- ½ cup walnuts, toasted and chopped coarse (optional)
- 2 teaspoons granulated sugar

1. Adjust an oven rack to the middle position and heat the oven to 350 degrees. Spray an 8½ by 4½-inch loaf pan with vegetable oil spray. Whisk the flour, baking soda, and salt together in a large bowl.

2. Place 5 of the bananas in a microwave-safe bowl; cover with plastic wrap and cut several steam vents in the plastic with a paring knife. Microwave on high power until the bananas are soft and have released their liquid, about 5 minutes. Transfer the bananas to a fine-mesh strainer placed over a medium bowl and allow to drain, stirring occasionally, 15 minutes (you should have ½ to ¾ cup liquid).

3. Transfer the liquid to a medium saucepan and cook over medium-high heat until reduced to ¼ cup, about 5 minutes. Remove the pan from the heat, stir the reduced liquid into the bananas, and mash them with a potato masher until fairly smooth. Whisk in the butter, eggs, brown sugar, and vanilla.

4. Pour the banana mixture into the flour mixture and stir until just combined with some streaks of flour remaining. Gently fold in the walnuts, if using. Scrape the batter into the prepared pan. Slice the remaining banana diagonally into ¼-inch-thick slices. Following the photo below, shingle the banana slices on top of either side of the loaf, leaving a 1½-inch-wide space down the center to ensure an even rise. Sprinkle the granulated sugar evenly over the loaf.

5. Bake until a toothpick inserted into the center of the loaf comes out clean, 55 to 75 minutes. Cool the bread in the pan on a wire rack 15 minutes, then remove the loaf from the pan and continue to cool on a wire rack. Serve warm or at room temperature.

NOTES FROM THE TEST KITCHEN

SHINGLING THE LOAF

Layering thin banana slices on either side of the loaf adds even more banana flavor to our bread (and brings the total number of bananas in the recipe to six). To ensure an even rise, leave a 1½-inch-wide space down the center.

CREAM CHEESE COFFEE CAKE

CREAM CHEESE COFFEE CAKE

✓ **WHY THIS RECIPE WORKS:** To develop a coffee cake with a flavor that would complement but not overpower the cream cheese filling, we used granulated sugar instead of brown sugar, along with a generous amount of vanilla and some lemon zest. To prevent the filling from becoming grainy and separating from the cake, we stirred a little bit of cake batter into it. The finishing touch to our coffee cake was a crackling-crisp topping of sliced almonds, sugar, and lemon zest.

WHEN IT COMES TO CHOOSING A BREAKFAST SWEET to nibble on with our morning coffee, some of us go for cheese Danish, while others enjoy a thick slice of coffee cake. So when we heard about a cake loosely related to a central European pastry called *kolachke* that swirls sweetened cream cheese inside coffee cake, we had to try it. Research revealed innumerable versions of this cake—even Entenmann's sells one. We seemed to be the only bakers who hadn't devised a recipe. Perusing them, we envisioned our ideal version: a silky, tangy, subtly sweet filling accenting a rich, moist cake.

We chose six of the most promising recipes and held a bake-a-thon in the test kitchen. At the end of a long day, we had produced a lineup of cakes that were mostly dry and bland, with lackluster fillings. And there was another problem: Many of the dairy swirls had sunk to the bottom. Still, the promise of a cream cheese–filled coffee cake inspired us to overcome these hurdles.

Starting with a Bundt pan (traditional for this recipe), we set out to develop a modestly sweet cake with a texture somewhere between the soft, dense crumb of yellow cake and the coarseness of quick bread that could support a substantial cheese filling. (For now, we would make cheese-free cakes—we'd address the filling later.) We assembled a batter using proportions from the best of the recipes we'd tried: 2¼ cups of all-purpose flour, 1 cup plus 2 tablespoons of granulated sugar, ½ teaspoon of salt,

one stick of butter, four eggs, 1¼ cups of whole milk, and 1 tablespoon of baking powder. We began by testing different mixing methods. The quick-bread approach was supremely easy (simply stir the dry ingredients together with the wet ingredients), but it produced a coarse crumb that was too airy. Reverse creaming (mixing the flour, sugar, and softened butter together, then adding the eggs and milk) wasn't right either—the result was an extremely tender, crumbly cake that would hardly support a heavy filling. We eventually settled on a straightforward creaming method: Beat softened butter in a standing mixer with sugar, then add the eggs, milk, and dry ingredients.

Now we had a dense batter that would surely support the cream cheese, but it baked up slightly dry. Replacing the milk with tangy (and, more importantly, richer) sour cream mostly addressed the dryness problem; 2 more tablespoons of butter completely resolved it. Our cake now had a lush texture as well as subtle acidity—a perfect backdrop for the cheese.

Speaking of which, we wanted the cake's flavor to complement, not overpower, the tangy cream cheese. We discovered right away that we should stick with granulated over brown sugar, which imparted distracting caramel-like notes. Vanilla extract was next on the list. We experimented with different amounts, finding that a generous 4 teaspoons added surprising complexity. Next, we increased the salt to a full teaspoon, sharpening the flavors of the butter and vanilla.

Finally, we considered the leavener. Now that we had sour cream in the mix, baking soda (not just baking powder, which contains an acid plus baking soda) was an option, as the soda would react with and neutralize the acidic sour cream. Since browning occurs best in an alkaline environment, adding baking soda would help our cake brown, and a more golden cake means a tastier cake. This small change—using 1⅛ teaspoons each of baking powder and baking soda—led to our best cake yet.

Now that we had a blue-ribbon cake, we moved on to the cream cheese filling. For our first attempt, we sweetened 6 ounces of softened cream cheese with ¼ cup of granulated sugar, sandwiching the mixture between equal layers of cake batter. After about 45 minutes in a 350-degree oven and an hour of cooling, the moment of truth was at hand. But unmolding the finished cake revealed a grainy, curdled filling that had settled on the bottom of the pan. As we cut into it, we noticed gaping air pockets between the filling and the cake that must have developed when the cheese shrank during baking.

Still, despite these imperfections, tasters loved the filling and wanted more. We obliged, increasing the cream cheese to 8 ounces. To prevent this greater amount from sinking, we tried spooning the filling on top of the cake batter before baking. No go: The cheese cracked and dried out in the heat of the oven. Aggressively swirling the filling into the cake batter solved the sinking problem, but it also integrated the cheese into the cake; we wanted it to remain distinct.

Unsure how to proceed, we turned our attention to the curdled cheese. We knew that if cheese is exposed to high heat, its proteins bind to each other and shrink, releasing moisture and potentially causing graininess. Recently, as we hunted down a solution for how to keep cheese sauce emulsified in our recipe for Spaghetti with Pecorino Romano and Black Pepper (page 140), we learned that cornstarch can protect and insulate cheese proteins, helping to prevent separation. A few teaspoons of cornstarch did keep the cream cheese intact, but it also made it undeniably chalky. Flour yielded the same result.

Then it hit us: Why not add just a bit of the starchy cake batter to the cheese? This might prevent curdling and help marry the filling to the cake. We gave it a shot, stirring ¼ cup of batter into the filling. Guessing that the filling would fare better if it had farther to travel to reach the bottom, this time we spooned two-thirds of the batter in the pan before adding the filling, then topped it with the rest of the batter and gently swirled it with a butter knife. Success! The filling not only stayed creamy, but it fused to the cake during baking, eliminating most of the gaps that had plagued our earlier tests. To burst any renegade bubbles, we took to tapping the pan on the counter before baking the cake. Sometimes bubbles would persist, so we tried also tapping the pan after the cake came out of the oven. Because the creamy filling was still warm and not yet fully set, the post-baking taps worked to create an entirely bubble-free cake.

Only a few minor adjustments remained. We added a little extra sugar to fully sweeten the cheese as well as fresh lemon juice to cut its richness. Finally, a teaspoon of vanilla extract added depth. And now that the filling had citrus notes, it only made sense to add a few teaspoons of lemon zest to the cake batter to make it all come together.

The combination of rich cake and cheese filling was now receiving raves, but we really wanted to make it

stand out. We started by swapping the Bundt pan for a tube pan, which would deliver a cake with a flat top that could support a topping.

A flour-and-butter-laden streusel was heavy, sinking into the batter during baking. A cinnamon-nut streusel stayed afloat, but its spicy flavor overwhelmed the delicate cheese. At last, innovation struck: We came up with a crisp, delicate coating of sliced almonds and sugar, to which we added finely grated lemon zest to accent the lemon-scented cake and filling. As it baked, the topping formed a glistening, crackly crust on the cake. Step aside, Entenmann's, this cake is the answer to all of our coffee-time cravings.

Cream Cheese Coffee Cake

SERVES 12 TO 16

Leftovers should be stored in the refrigerator, covered tightly with plastic wrap. For optimal texture, allow the cake to return to room temperature before serving.

LEMON SUGAR-ALMOND TOPPING

- ¼ cup (1¾ ounces) sugar
- 1½ teaspoons finely grated zest from 1 lemon
- ½ cup sliced almonds

CAKE

- 2¼ cups (11¼ ounces) unbleached all-purpose flour
- 1⅛ teaspoons baking powder
- 1⅛ teaspoons baking soda
- 1 teaspoon table salt
- 10 tablespoons (1 stick plus 2 tablespoons) unsalted butter, softened but still cool
- 1 cup (7 ounces) plus 7 tablespoons sugar
- 1 tablespoon finely grated zest plus 4 teaspoons juice from 1 to 2 lemons
- 4 large eggs
- 5 teaspoons vanilla extract
- 1¼ cups sour cream
- 8 ounces cream cheese, softened

MAKING CREAM CHEESE COFFEE CAKE

1. Reserve 1¼ cups batter, then fill the pan with the remaining batter; smooth the top.

2. Beat ¼ cup reserved batter with the filling ingredients; spoon the filling evenly over the batter.

3. Top the filling with the remaining 1 cup reserved batter; smooth the top.

4. Using a figure-eight motion, swirl the filling into the batter with a butter knife. Tap the pan on the counter to dislodge any air bubbles.

5. Sprinkle the lemon sugar-almond topping onto batter, then gently press to adhere.

1. FOR THE TOPPING: Adjust an oven rack to the middle position and heat the oven to 350 degrees. Stir the sugar and lemon zest in a small bowl until combined and the sugar is moistened. Stir in the almonds; set aside.

2. FOR THE CAKE: Spray a 10-inch tube pan with vegetable oil spray. Whisk the flour, baking powder, baking soda, and salt together in a medium bowl; set aside. In a standing mixer fitted with the paddle attachment, beat the butter, 1 cup plus 2 tablespoons of the sugar, and the lemon zest at medium speed until light and fluffy, about 3 minutes, scraping down the sides and bottom of the bowl with a rubber spatula. Add the eggs one at a time, beating well after each addition, about 20 seconds, and scraping down the beater and sides of the bowl as necessary. Add 4 teaspoons of the vanilla and mix to combine. Reduce the mixer speed to low and add one-third of the flour mixture, followed by half of the sour cream, mixing until incorporated after each addition, 5 to 10 seconds. Repeat, using half of the remaining flour mixture and all of the remaining sour cream. Scrape the bowl and add the remaining flour mixture; mix at low speed until the batter is thoroughly combined, about 10 seconds. Remove the bowl from the mixer and fold the batter once or twice with a rubber spatula to incorporate any remaining flour.

3. Reserve 1¼ cups batter and set aside. Spoon the remaining batter into the prepared pan and smooth the top. Return the now-empty bowl to the mixer and beat the cream cheese, remaining 5 tablespoons sugar, lemon juice, and remaining 1 teaspoon vanilla on medium speed until smooth and slightly lightened, about 1 minute. Add ¼ cup of the reserved batter and mix until incorporated. Spoon the cheese filling mixture evenly over the batter, keeping the filling about 1 inch from the edges of the pan; smooth the top. Spread the remaining 1 cup reserved batter over the filling and smooth the top. With a butter knife or offset spatula, gently swirl the filling into the batter using a figure-eight motion, being careful to not drag the filling to the bottom or edges of the pan. Firmly tap the pan on the counter two or three times to dislodge any bubbles. Sprinkle the lemon sugar–almond topping evenly over the batter and gently press into the batter to adhere.

4. Bake until the top is golden and just firm and a long skewer inserted into the cake comes out clean (the skewer will be wet if inserted into the cheese filling), 45 to 50 minutes. Remove the pan from the oven and firmly tap on the counter two or three times (the top of the cake may sink slightly). Cool the cake in the pan on a wire rack 1 hour. Gently invert the cake onto a rimmed baking sheet (the cake will be topping side down); remove the tube pan, place a wire rack on top of the cake, and invert the cake sugar side up. Cool to room temperature, about 1½ hours, before serving.

NOTES FROM THE TEST KITCHEN

TAP ONCE, TAP TWICE

Tapping the tube pan on the counter before and after baking eliminates any large air pockets in the filling.

RATING ADJUSTABLE ELECTRIC KETTLES

Coffee connoisseurs know that a good cup of java depends on a very specific water temperature (the ideal range is between 195 and 205 degrees) and ditto for those who prefer tea (the ideal range is below boiling, between 165 and 195 degrees). While you could boil water, let it cool, and check it with an instant-read thermometer before brewing your coffee or tea, a new breed of electric kettles designed to bring water quickly to a range of different temperatures (and, in some cases, to hold it there) promises to save time and effort, with precise results. We found five models; all but one boasted automatic shutoff, a separate base for cordless pouring, and a visible water level, features we like in an electric kettle. Brands are listed in order of preference. See www.americastestkitchen.com for updates to this testing.

RECOMMENDED

ZOJIRUSHI Micom Water Boiler & Warmer
(model #CD-WBC30)
PRICE: $114.95 **CAPACITY:** 13.5 cups (3 liters)
COMMENTS: Though this model took the longest to boil water, it had the greatest capacity and held water at a designated temperature for up to 10 hours. It was a breeze to fill and clean, and the dispense button made it easy to get hot water without having to lift a full kettle. The easy-to-read digital temperature display and auto shut-off safety feature were pluses, but the high price and big size gave us pause.

CHEF'SCHOICE 688 Electric Smart Kettle
(model #688)
PRICE: $99.99 **CAPACITY:** 7.25 cups
COMMENTS: User-friendly, this model has a clear display and the temperature is easy to set. It will hold the water at a set temperature for only 40 minutes before shutting off, but restarting is easy. One drawback: The kettle reached an external temperature of 185 degrees, a burn hazard.

RECOMMENDED WITH RESERVATIONS

PINO Digital Kettle Pro (model #St-8706)
PRICE: $79.95 **CAPACITY:** 6¼ cups
COMMENTS: This kettle is easy to set and boils water quickly. It holds water at the set temperature accurately. However, the level meter is inside the unit, forcing you to look inside, over the steamy hot water, to check the water level.

T-FAL Vitesse Kettle (model #BF6520004)
PRICE: $39.99 **CAPACITY:** 7.5 cups
COMMENTS: The modest price tag and speedy heating time make this a good option if you don't mind that the temperature dial is difficult to decipher. Also this kettle does not hold water at temperature and it must be restarted to reheat the water.

NOT RECOMMENDED

ADAGIO UtiliTEA Adjustable Hot Water Kettle
PRICE: $49.95 **CAPACITY:** 4.25 cups
COMMENTS: This kettle boiled water quickly, but setting the right temperature was a challenge because there are no numbers on the display, only different-colored bars on a dial. The spring-loaded lid sprayed droplets of boiling water on our hands.

Desserts
WITH AN ENGLISH ACCENT

Toasting bread cubes before soaking them in custard makes for a creamy, not soggy, bread pudding—and reserving a portion of the bread cubes to sprinkle over the pudding provides crunchy textural contrast to the silky custard below.

THE APPEAL OF MANY ENGLISH DESSERTS LIES IN THEIR THRIFT AND simplicity—and when made well, they taste good too. Here we take a look at two classics: bread pudding and shortbread.

Bread pudding was originally devised as an easy and appealing way to resurrect staled bread. Soaked in a mixture of eggs and milk or cream, the dried-out bread turns custardy and soft and the top bakes up with an appealing crunch. That's the ideal anyway. Most bread puddings we've come across are leaden specimens—or so parched from a dearth of custard that nothing, not even a dessert sauce, can rescue them. We wanted a bread pudding that played down the thrift in favor of flavor—a bread pudding with a moist, but not mushy, interior and a sweet, crisp top crust.

Admittedly, shortbread is usually not the star of the cookie plate in the U.S. Chocolate chip, oatmeal, and sugar cookies often steal the spotlight. Most of the time, shortbread is thought of as dry and bland—perhaps the tins of inferior shortbread so ubiquitous around the holidays have something to do with this sorry reputation. But in the U.K., where they know their shortbread, it is an exceptional cookie—modestly sweet, rich, and buttery—and dare we say, decadent. With loads of butter in hand, we set out to recapture the glory of traditional shortbread stateside.

BREAD PUDDING

✔ **WHY THIS RECIPE WORKS:** Toasting cubes of challah was the first step in perfecting our bread pudding. To achieve a silky but not overly eggy custard, we used equal parts milk and cream and egg-yolks only—whites imparted an overly eggy flavor. Finally, topping the pudding with extra challah cubes and sprinkling them with sugar gave our bread pudding a crunchy, buttery, sweet crust that was the perfect partner for the luscious custard below.

IN ITS ORIGINAL FORM, BREAD PUDDING WAS A HUMBLE dish whose main virtue was ingenuity: A leftover loaf of bread on its way to becoming a brick was softened with milk, sweetened with sugar, baked, and so reborn as a warm, custardy confection. During especially lean times crumbs or cracker crumbs became stand-ins for stale bread. Nothing wrong with making do with what you have, but in the years that followed, the genius of the original got lost. Bread pudding turned fancy, as the bread crumb improvisations gave way to postwar recipes dolled up with luxe ingredients like rose water, citrus rind, exotic liqueurs, and cartons of pricey eggs. No stale bread on hand? Just buy it fresh and "stale" it yourself. Meanwhile, cookbook writers held fast to the quaint notion that bread pudding recipes should retain their traditional one-size-fits-all sensibility, even as supermarkets exploded with bread options in every size and shape.

This is where the problem starts. It hardly takes a pastry whiz to recognize that baking up stale chunks of ciabatta with eggs, milk, and sugar will produce a vastly different result than doing the same with foamy cubes of Wonder Bread. It wasn't surprising, then, that the recipes we surveyed varied so widely in texture, from mushy, sweetened porridge to chewy, desiccated cousins of over-cooked holiday stuffing. If the main goal was to resurrect whatever stale bread we had on hand, a little variation would be acceptable. But for a dessert cart–worthy bread pudding as refined as any French soufflé, we were determined to nail the ideal every time: a moist, creamy (but not eggy) interior and a crisp top crust.

Freed from finding an all-purpose recipe, we headed to the supermarket to choose the best loaf for the job. Back in the test kitchen, we cut each variety into cubes, combined them with a batch of basic custard—4 cups of whole milk, 1 cup of sugar, five eggs, 1 teaspoon of vanilla extract, and ¾ teaspoon of salt—and let the cubes soak for half an hour. Once the cubes were saturated, we transferred them to 13 by 9-inch baking dishes and slid them into 325-degree ovens. (From experience, we knew that relatively low temperatures help prevent curdling: When heated, the casein in dairy products coagulates and forms clumps if the temperature surpasses 180 degrees.)

As expected, the results were as varied as the breads themselves. The pudding made with French bread was, surprisingly, too coarse and rustic to yield the refined texture we had in mind. The airy Italian loaf suffered the opposite ill of disintegrating into the custard, leaving zero distinction between bread and pudding. Meanwhile, the croissant pudding was buttery and rich to a fault; tasters bemoaned eating more than two spoonfuls, let alone an entire serving. And the plain-Jane potato and sandwich breads? Serviceable, yet hardly extraordinary.

Then there was the pudding we all fought over—the one made from challah. This soft, braided loaf swelled nicely, absorbing liquid without disintegrating, and its deep gold crust retained a satisfying chew. Best of all, its faint sweetness and rich buttery flavor aligned perfectly with the fundamental flavors of the pudding. One loaf cut into ¾-inch cubes filled out the baking dish almost perfectly; there were only a few straggler cubes left over.

There was just one problem: Bread pudding is normally made with stale bread, and our just-bought challah wasn't thirsty enough. When extending the soaking time didn't help, we let the bread stale overnight on the counter. This pudding turned out somewhat gummy, so we switched to toasting the bread in the oven. (Some bread-staling science: As bread stales slowly at room temperature, its starch molecules recrystallize in a process called retrogradation, turning the loaf hard and crumbly but not necessarily dry. Oven-staled bread hardens through the removal of moisture, not through retrogradation, ultimately leading to a drier structure.) We were careful not to let the cubes get too brown, however; overdried challah swelled into a bloated mass, eventually dissolving completely.

CLASSIC BREAD PUDDING

With the bread out of the way, we were ready to focus on the custard. Because the challah was now soaking it up so thoroughly, the dessert was emerging from the oven a little dry and bready. To fix this, we could have reduced the amount of challah, but we wanted a recipe that would use up an entire loaf. We opted instead to increase the milk by 1 cup. This extra liquid created the right balance of bread and custard.

But now we had another problem: The additional milk was preventing the custard from setting properly. Adding another egg or two would help, but tasters were already complaining that the pudding tasted somewhat eggy. Just as we felt ourselves falling into a bread-pudding catch-22, we realized we'd already cracked the egg code in our recipe for French Toast (page 249) when we discovered that eggy flavor comes from the sulfur compounds in egg whites. Perhaps we could do without the whites and just use yolks? Yes. We now had a luscious, silky custard with no trace of egginess. The richer flavor of the yolk-only custard—we ultimately needed nine for 5 cups of whole milk—was improved with extra vanilla (for a total of 4 teaspoons) and ¾ teaspoon of salt. And the pudding was even creamier and smoother when we swapped half of the milk for heavy cream.

For the topping, we knew we wanted to create a crackly crust as a foil to the custardy interior. Simply sprinkling sugar onto the pudding before baking didn't work; the granules melted into the custard before the 325-degree oven could caramelize them. When we tried broiling the sugar-topped pudding just before serving, it wound up curdling under the intense heat.

Then we noticed those extra toasted bread cubes sitting on the counter and realized we wouldn't have to waste them after all. We dotted the top of the pudding with the toasted cubes before baking it. Partial success: The topping was crisp, but terribly bland. Not a problem. Brushing the bread with melted butter and then sprinkling the dish with a flavorful mixture of brown and white sugars before transferring the pudding into the oven ushered this once-humble concoction into decadence. One bite and we knew our work was done. The crunchy, buttery, sugary crust was the perfect partner to the satiny-smooth custard that lay below. For an unnecessary but luxurious addition, we whipped up a brown sugar–bourbon sauce to drizzle over each serving. Now we had a recipe that could be the best thing since sliced bread.

Classic Bread Pudding

SERVES 8 TO 10

Challah is an egg-enriched bread that can be found in most bakeries and supermarkets. If you cannot find challah, a firm high-quality sandwich bread such as Arnold Country Classics White or Pepperidge Farm Farmhouse Hearty White may be substituted. If desired, serve this pudding with softly whipped cream or with Bourbon–Brown Sugar Sauce (recipe follows). Store leftovers tightly wrapped in the refrigerator. To retain a crisp top crust when reheating leftovers, cut the bread pudding into squares and heat, uncovered, in a 450-degree oven until warmed through, 6 to 8 minutes.

2 tablespoons light brown sugar
¾ cup (5¼ ounces) plus 1 tablespoon granulated sugar
1 (14-ounce) loaf challah bread, cut into ¾-inch cubes (about 10 cups) (see note)
9 large egg yolks
4 teaspoons vanilla extract
¾ teaspoon table salt
2½ cups heavy cream
2½ cups milk
2 tablespoons unsalted butter, melted

1. Adjust the oven racks to the middle and lower-middle positions and heat the oven to 325 degrees. Combine the brown sugar and 1 tablespoon of the granulated sugar in a small bowl; set aside.

2. Spread the bread cubes in a single layer on two rimmed baking sheets. Bake, tossing occasionally, until just dry, about 15 minutes, switching the baking sheets halfway through the baking time. Cool the bread cubes about 15 minutes; set aside 2 cups.

3. Whisk the egg yolks, remaining ¾ cup sugar, vanilla, and salt together in a large bowl. Whisk in the cream and milk until combined. Add the remaining 8 cups cooled bread cubes and toss to coat. Transfer the mixture to a 13 by 9-inch baking dish and let stand, occasionally pressing the bread cubes into the custard, until the cubes are thoroughly saturated, about 30 minutes.

4. Spread the reserved bread cubes evenly over the top of the soaked bread mixture and gently press into the custard. Using a pastry brush, dab the melted butter over the top of the unsoaked bread pieces. Sprinkle the brown sugar mixture evenly over the top. Place the bread pudding on a rimmed baking sheet and bake on the middle rack until the custard has just set, and pressing the center of the pudding with your finger reveals no runny liquid, 45 to 50 minutes. (An instant-read thermometer inserted into the center of the pudding should read 170 degrees.) Transfer to a wire rack and cool until the pudding is set and just warm, about 45 minutes. Serve.

Bourbon-Brown Sugar Sauce

MAKES ABOUT 1 CUP

Rum can be substituted for the bourbon.

- ½ cup packed (3½ ounces) light brown sugar
- 7 tablespoons heavy cream
- 2½ tablespoons unsalted butter
- 1½ tablespoons bourbon (see note)

Whisk the brown sugar and heavy cream in a small saucepan over medium heat until combined. Continue to cook, whisking frequently, until the mixture comes to a boil, about 5 minutes. Whisk in the butter and bring the mixture back to a boil, about 1 minute. Remove from the heat and whisk in the bourbon. Cool to just warm; serve with the bread pudding.

SHORTBREAD

✔ **WHY THIS RECIPE WORKS:** To produce exemplary shortbread, we found that "reverse creaming" (mixing the flour and sugar together before adding the butter) contributed an appealingly crumbly texture. Cutting back on the butter resulted in good butter flavor but without any greasiness. Adding ground oats and cornstarch to the dough cut down on gluten development and resulted in tender cookies. And baking the cookies briefly before turning off the heat and letting them dry out in the still-warm oven made our shortbread perfectly crisp.

IF YOUR EXPERIENCE WITH SHORTBREAD IS LIMITED to bland, chalky specimens from a tin, you might wonder how this plain-looking bar (which dates back at least to 12th-century Scotland) came to be one of the British Isles' most famous teacakes. But when shortbread is made well, it's easy to understand why it earned a reputation as a favorite of high-ranking palates from Mary, Queen of Scots to Elizabeth II. The best versions are an alluring tawny brown and crumble in the mouth with a pure, buttery richness. Shortbread's distinctive sandy texture distinguishes it from the simple crispness of its cousin, the American butter cookie, while its moderate sweetness makes it easy to go back for another helping— and another.

Shortbread originated as a way to turn leftover oat bread into something more special: The scraps were sprinkled with sugar and left to harden overnight in an oven still hot from the day's baking. By the 16th century, wheat flour had replaced oat bread in the recipe, and this biscuit morphed from a foodstuff of commoners into the more refined confection prized by nobility.

And yet, despite its venerable history we could find surprisingly few clues to reproducing a worthwhile version. The basics haven't changed much over the past five centuries: Combine flour, sugar, butter, and salt, then pat the dough into a round and bake. But the recipes we unearthed varied in their proportions. Some called for equal parts butter and flour, and some for only half

BEST SHORTBREAD

this ratio; several included unlikely ingredients like rice flour or cornstarch. Results were also all over the map. While some cookies crumbled in our hands before we could even take a bite, others were sturdy and crisp to a fault, and still others turned out either greasy or overly airy and cakelike. Moreover, nearly every version suffered from some degree of uneven cooking and overbrowning.

To get our bearings, we decided to limit our ingredients to the basic four before tinkering with anything extra. As for proportions, we ruled out a 1–1 ratio of butter to flour after preliminary tests proved this was just too greasy. We settled on a more moderate 4–5 ratio, with two sticks of butter, 2 cups all-purpose flour, ⅔ cup sugar, and ¼ teaspoon salt.

And what mixing method would work best? We would need to test the most traditional approach, which is akin to making pie crust: Cut the butter and dry ingredients together until they form wet crumbs, then pack the crumbs together into a dough. We also made two batches using more modern methods. In one, we creamed the butter and sugar in a standing mixer before adding the flour; in the other, we employed reverse creaming, mixing the flour and sugar before adding the butter. Next, we formed cookies from our three doughs. Shortbread traditionally takes one of three shapes: one large circle with a hole cut in the center and then scored into wedges, or "petticoat tails" (so called because the uncut cookie resembles a dressmaker's pattern); individual round cookies; or rectangular "fingers." Pursuing the petticoat shape (for no reason except that it was reportedly the shape favored by Mary, Queen of Scots), we pressed the dough into a 9-inch disk, used a biscuit cutter to remove a hole from the center, and placed the shortbread in a 450-degree oven for a few minutes. Following the usual high-low baking protocol called for in shortbread recipes, we then reduced the oven to 300 degrees and continued to bake the cookies for an hour before scoring and cooling them.

We evaluated the results. The traditional, packed-crumb method produced cookies that were crumbly in some spots and brittle in others. Regular creaming was also out. This method incorporated too much air

into the dough, making for soft, airy, cakelike cookies. Reverse creaming, which creates less aeration, yielded the most reliable results and was clearly the way to go. Tweaking the recipe, we reduced the butter even further, from 16 to 14 tablespoons, which resulted in a dough that was pliable and had plenty of buttery flavor but did not exude grease during baking. We also swapped the white sugar for confectioners' sugar to smooth out an objectionable granular texture. Although our basic ingredients and mixing technique now seemed to be in order, the shortbread cookies were somewhat tough, and they were not as crisp as we wanted.

Two factors played into this texture problem: gluten and moisture. Gluten, the protein matrix that lends baked goods structure and chew, forms naturally when liquid and all-purpose flour are combined, even without kneading. The liquid in our recipe was coming from the butter, which contains 20 percent water—just enough to make the cookies tough. In addition, cookies can only become truly crisp and crumbly if they are perfectly dry. Our goals, then, were to limit gluten development and to help the cookies dry out completely.

Intuition told us that a higher oven temperature would drive moisture from the cookies. We baked a batch entirely at 450 degrees, but the edges started overbrowning after just 10 minutes, while the inner portion remained wet. When we thought about it, we realized that baking shortbread is analogous to cooking a roast: The higher the oven temperature, the less even the cooking, and the more prone to overcooking the edges will be. We tried again, baking a second batch at 450 degrees for five minutes (to help set the dough) and then lowering the temperature to 250 degrees. This was better, but still not perfect.

Early shortbread was made by leaving the dough in a still-warm oven heated only by dying embers. What if we briefly baked the shortbread, shut off the oven, and left it inside until it was completely dry? With just 15 minutes or so of "real" baking in a hot oven—and an hour with the oven turned off—the results were striking: This batch was dry through and through, with an even, golden brown exterior.

With the moisture issue resolved, we shifted our focus to the toughness caused by excess gluten development. Various 21st-century recipes have tried to solve this problem by substituting low-protein, gluten-free rice flour for some of the all-purpose flour. We gave it a try. As we broke apart the rice-flour shortbread, its crumbly texture looked promising. But once we tasted the shortbread, we realized that reducing the all-purpose flour had also reduced the flavor; these cookies were woefully bland. Cornstarch (another gluten-free ingredient used in some modern recipes) yielded equally insipid results. We needed to curb gluten development without compromising flavor. Scanning the test kitchen's pantry shelves, we spotted a possible solution: old-fashioned oats. Oats have a nice, nutty flavor and contain few of the proteins necessary for gluten development; on top of that, they're traditional to early shortbread recipes. We ground some oats to a powder in a spice grinder and substituted ¾ cup of this home-milled oat flour for some of the all-purpose flour in our recipe. The resulting cookies had a promising crisp and crumbly texture, but the oats muted the buttery flavor. Still, we knew we were on the right track. For our next batch, we used less oat flour and supplemented it with a modest amount of cornstarch. This worked handsomely. The cookies were now perfectly crisp and flavorful, with an appealing hint of oat flavor.

We had one last problem to solve: spreading. As buttery shortbread bakes, it expands, losing its shape as the edges flatten out. We tried baking the dough in a traditional shortbread mold with ½-inch-high sides, but it still widened into an amorphous mass. Clearly, the dough needed a substantial barrier to keep its edges corralled. Our solution? A springform pan collar. We set the closed collar on a parchment-lined baking sheet, patted the dough into it, and then opened the collar to give the cookie about half an inch to spread out.

Once we removed the collar, we had a perfect circle of shortbread, ready to be scored and crisped in the oven. At last, we had produced a shortbread that was anything but plain.

Best Shortbread

MAKES 16 WEDGES

Use the collar of a springform pan to form the shortbread into an even round. Mold the shortbread with the collar in the closed position, then open the collar, but leave it in place. This allows the shortbread to expand slightly but keeps it from spreading too far. The extracted round of dough in step 2 is baked alongside the rest of the shortbread. Wrapped well and stored at room temperature, the shortbread will keep for up to 7 days.

½ cup (1½ ounces) old-fashioned oats
1½ cups (7½ ounces) unbleached all-purpose flour
⅔ cup (2⅔ ounces) confectioners' sugar
¼ cup cornstarch
½ teaspoon table salt
14 tablespoons (1¾ sticks) unsalted butter, chilled, cut into ⅛-inch-thick slices

1. Adjust an oven rack to the middle position and heat the oven to 450 degrees. Pulse the oats in a spice grinder or blender until reduced to a fine powder, about ten 5-second pulses (you should have ¼ to ⅓ cup oat flour). In the bowl of a standing mixer fitted with the paddle attachment, mix the oat flour, all-purpose flour, sugar, cornstarch, and salt on low speed until combined, about 5 seconds. Add the butter to the dry ingredients and continue to mix on low speed until the dough just forms and pulls away from the sides of the bowl, 5 to 10 minutes.

2. Place the collar of a 9- or 9½-inch springform pan on a parchment-lined rimmed baking sheet (do not use the springform pan bottom). Following the photos at right, press the dough into the collar in an even ½-inch-thick layer, smoothing the top of the dough with the back of a spoon. Place a 2-inch biscuit cutter in the center of the dough and cut out the center. Place the extracted round alongside the springform collar on the baking sheet and replace the cutter in the center of the dough. Open the springform collar, but leave it in place.

3. Bake the shortbread 5 minutes, then reduce the oven temperature to 250 degrees. Continue to bake until the edges turn pale golden, 10 to 15 minutes longer. Remove the baking sheet from the oven; turn off the oven. Remove the springform pan collar; use a chef's knife to score the surface of the shortbread into 16 even wedges, cutting halfway through the shortbread. Using a wooden skewer, poke 8 to 10 holes in each wedge. Return the shortbread to the oven and prop the door open with the handle of a wooden spoon, leaving a 1-inch gap at the top. Allow the shortbread to dry in the turned-off oven until pale golden in the center (the shortbread should be firm but giving to the touch), about 1 hour.

4. Transfer the baking sheet to a wire rack; cool the shortbread to room temperature, at least 2 hours. Cut the shortbread at the scored marks to separate and serve.

NOTES FROM THE TEST KITCHEN

FORMING AND BAKING THE SHORTBREAD

1. Press the dough into a closed springform pan collar; smooth with the back of a spoon.

2. Cut a hole in the center of the dough with a 2-inch biscuit cutter; replace the cutter in the hole.

3. Open the collar. Bake 5 minutes at 450 degrees, then 10 to 15 minutes at 250 degrees.

4. Score the partially baked shortbread into wedges, then poke 8 to 10 holes in each wedge.

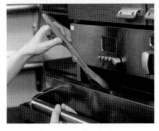

5. Return the shortbread to the turned-off oven to dry; prop the open door with a wooden spoon or stick.

BEST SMALL APPLIANCES

After nearly two decades testing small appliances, we know how to identify keepers—the most useful, durable, and high-quality equipment and brands. While a few items are not inexpensive, they're worth the investment for better cooking and baking. And although they're labeled "small" appliances, note that a few of them can take up a big chunk of counter space. Here are our recommendations for essential small appliances that we feel merit real estate in your kitchen. See www.americastestkitchen.com for updates to this testing.

FOOD PROCESSOR

We use our food processors day in and day out for all kinds of tasks that we used to do by hand, like chopping canned tomatoes, grinding fresh bread into fine crumbs, slicing vegetables, shredding cheese, and making pie dough. Our favorite food processor is the KitchenAid KFP750 12-Cup Food Processor ($179.99). Its heavy motor (this model weighs in at 12 pounds) didn't falter under especially challenging tasks, such as kneading bread dough. It has sharp, sturdy blades that chopped and sliced cleanly and evenly and a large feed tube that allows potatoes, hunks of cheese, and other big foods to slide through. Although it takes up precious counter space, we wouldn't trade our food processor for anything.

WINNER: KITCHENAID KFP750 12-CUP FOOD PROCESSOR

HAND MIXER

Although a handheld mixer isn't as powerful as a standing mixer, a good model still does a decent job whipping, creaming, and mixing. Even when faced with stiff, thick cookie dough, the metal beaters on our winning model, the Cuisinart Power Advantage 7-Speed Hand Mixer ($49.95), offered smooth, steady, and controlled mixing action. This hand mixer will sail you smoothly through most tasks, with the exception of mixing heavy bread dough. In spite of that one drawback, the hand mixer's ease of use, affordability, and compact size make it an indispensible kitchen appliance.

WINNER: CUISINART POWER ADVANTAGE 7-SPEED HAND MIXER

BLENDER

Whether you're looking to puree a pile of roasted vegetables into a creamy soup or crush ice into oblivion for a frozen cocktail, look no further—the blender is your best bet. To test the performance of 10 models, we crushed ice to produce "snow," blended smoothies, and processed chickpeas, olive oil, and tahini into hummus. Our favorite blender, the KitchenAid 5-Speed Blender ($119.95), pulverized the ice, turned out lump-free smoothies, and produced consistently smooth hummus. This blender boasts a tapered, V-shaped jar, which forces food down into the swirling vortex, and four blades, each positioned at a different angle to expertly catch and pulverize food. Our best buy, the Kalorik BL Blender ($45), performed almost as well, although slightly slower, and excelled at the core tasks.

WINNER: KITCHENAID 5-SPEED BLENDER

STANDING MIXER

With the granddaddy of all small appliances in your kitchen, you can mix, whip, beat, and knead anything from delicate egg whites to heavy bread doughs. If you are a serious baker, a standing mixer is simply something you need on your counter. The combination of its hands-free operation, numerous attachments, and strong mixing arm make it a truly significant and versatile, albeit expensive, piece of equipment. What do we look for in a standing mixer? Its bowl should have a capacity of at least 4.5 quarts and be slightly squat to keep ingredients in the mixer's range, and the mixer should operate using planetary action, meaning the bowl is stationary and the mixing arm moves around the bowl (mixers that operate with stationary beaters and a rotating bowl often bypass pockets of ingredients). Our favorite standing mixers are the Cuisinart 5.5 Quart Stand Mixer ($299) and the KitchenAid Professional 600 ($399). Both are true kitchen workhorses, and excellent across-the-board performers, although the better price of the Cuisinart puts it just a notch above the KitchenAid in our book.

WINNER: CUISINART 5.5 QUART STAND MIXER

IMMERSION BLENDER

Why bother with a smaller appliance to serve the same function as a blender? Not only is it great for small mixing jobs like blending salad dressings, whipping small measures of cream, or making smoothies, it saves time, effort, and cleanup because you can use it to puree soup right in the pot. There's no need to blend in batches and, if you have the right model, it's easy to rinse off and toss back into the drawer, where it takes up little space because it's so small. In tests of pureeing soup, making smoothies with frozen fruit, making pesto with fresh basil and nuts, and whipping cream, the Kalorik Sunny Morning Stick Mixer ($25) emerged as our top choice among eight competitors. It was comfortable to hold, it worked efficiently, and it was easy to clean because the shaft was detachable and dishwasher-safe and the cage around the blade was wide enough to clean without catching our fingers on the blade.

WINNER: KALORIK SUNNY MORNING STICK MIXER

ELECTRIC KNIFE SHARPENER

In our experience, one common mistake that home cooks make is relying on dull knives. Dull knives make cutting vegetables and hacking up chicken parts more difficult, more dangerous, and less productive, as many foods will end up incorrectly cut or sliced. Over time and with significant use, the fine point of any knife will become rounded and very dull. This is when metal must be cut away to restore the standard angle of each side of the knife's edge; for this, you need a knife sharpener. The Chef'sChoice Model 130 Professional Sharpening Station ($149.95) is our favorite model, and in tests produced the sharpest, finest, most polished edge. It has spring-loaded angle guides, large grinding wheels, and operates quietly. Also, it's exceptionally easy to use—and worth every penny.

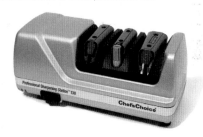

WINNER: CHEF'SCHOICE MODEL 130 PROFESSIONAL SHARPENING STATION

Chewy Brownies

AND CHOCOLATE CUPCAKES

*Our extra-chocolaty cupcakes
boast a secret in their center—
a dab of rich, chocolate ganache.*

WHEN IT COMES TO DESSERT, MOST OF US ARE KIDS AT HEART. WE'LL gladly take a pass on the latest dessert trend—French macaroons anyone?—and instead be completely satisfied with (and delighted by) brownies or chocolate cupcakes.

Growing up, most of us enjoyed the satisfying chew of a boxed mix brownie. But flavor? No gripes then, but today we definitely notice that these brownies taste more sweet than chocolaty. And some brands, with lots of artificial flavors, leave no question that the brownies are mix-made. We wanted a homemade brownie that had it all. Rich, unadulterated chocolate flavor and a soft chew just like those boxed mixes we loved so much as kids.

Chocolate cupcakes with great chocolate flavor? We thought this was a reachable goal until we started surveying the goods at cupcake bakeries as well as baking a few recipes on our own. Cupcakes with decent chocolate flavor crumbled in our hands and those that were tender, moist, and intact left us wondering where the chocolate had gone. And the frosting—don't get us started. We wanted a simple cap of creamy chocolate icing, not a hard-to-eat gargantuan glob. Heading into the test kitchen, we set out to bring these chocolate desserts back to their homemade roots.

CHEWY BROWNIES

CHEWY BROWNIES

✔ WHY THIS RECIPE WORKS: To devise a properly chewy brownie, we had to discover the perfect proportion of liquid fat to solid fat. Once we discovered the ratio of oil to butter, we combated greasiness by replacing some of the oil with egg yolks, whose emulsifiers prevent fat from separating and leaking out during baking. We found that unsweetened chocolate and cocoa powder provide the strongest chocolate flavor. Finally, folding in bittersweet chocolate chunks just before baking gave our chewy brownies gooey pockets of melted chocolate..

WHEN IT COMES TO BROWNIES, SOME PRAISE FUDGY specimens, while others go for moist, fluffy, cakey confections. But then there is the irresistible allure of the satisfyingly chewy brownie that is the hit of children's parties and bake sales—the brownie that is made from a just-add-eggs-and-oil mix. That said, box-mix brownies are all about texture, as even the best suffer from a markedly artificial, even waxy chemical sweetness. Our goal was clear: a homemade brownie with chewiness (and a shiny, crackly top) to rival the box-mix standard— but flush with a rich, all-natural chocolate flavor.

We rounded up as many recipes as we could find with "chewy" in the title. It became clear why the boxed brownie has retained its foothold: Not one recipe could actually lay claim to such a quality. All brownie recipes are composed of the same basic ingredients: fat (usually butter), eggs, salt, sugar, vanilla, flour (typically all-purpose), and of course chocolate (most often from an unsweetened bar). For fudgy brownies, use less flour and more chocolate; for cakey, do the reverse. None of the so-called chewy brownie recipes we consulted did anything different—their ratios of fat and chocolate tended to produce brownies somewhere between fudgy and cakey for a texture that was merely soft, not chewy. Their mixing techniques were also the same.

We then tried recipes with unusual techniques or ingredients, from substituting condensed milk and biscuit mix for the flour to baking brownies on a pizza stone to underbaking the brownies and then chilling them in an ice bath. All failures.

Clearly, we were on our own. We tried to think of other chewy baked goods. Brown sugar cookies came to mind. Because brown sugar and corn syrup both attract and retain water, cookie dough containing high levels of these ingredients bakes up moister and chewier than the exact same dough made with drier white sugar. Thinking a similar concept might work for our brownies, we took one of the chewier recipes we found calling for 4 ounces of unsweetened chocolate, 8 ounces of butter, 5 ounces of flour, two eggs, and 14 ounces of sugar and replaced the white sugar with a combination of brown sugar and corn syrup. Not only did it do nothing for the texture, but it also managed to lose the shiny, crackly crust. Regular sugar would have to stay.

It was time to call for reinforcements. We consulted with our science editor to see if he knew of any tricks boxed brownies use to achieve their chewiness. He responded with a phrase that completely changed the direction of our research: high-tech shortening system.

When we saw the "partially hydrogenated soybean and cottonseed oils" on the brownie-mix box, we had dismissed them as fats. But it turns out the key to the texture of a boxed brownie resides in the specific types and amounts of fat it includes. Fat can be divided into two broad types: saturated and unsaturated. Both types consist of carbon atoms strung together in long chains. In predominantly saturated fats such as shortening (aka partially hydrogenated vegetable oil), each of these carbon atoms has the maximum number of hydrogen atoms attached to it. The hydrogen acts as a buttress to keep the carbon chains rigid, so they pack together, forming a fat that is solid even at room temperature. Unsaturated fats, such as vegetable oils, have fewer hydrogen atoms, resulting in a fat that is liquid at room temperature. The right combination of rigid and flexible chains—the shortening system—is what gives boxed brownies their unique texture.

Boxed brownie mixes come with the saturated fat component. When a cook then adds unsaturated vegetable oil to this mix, the liquid fat and powdered solid fat in the mix combine in a ratio designed to deliver maximum chew. So we would have to discover the perfect proportion of liquid to solid fat—without the aid of high-tech fats used by brownie mix manufacturers.

We'd keep the butter as our saturated fat—a far more flavorful choice than vegetable shortening, which manufacturers resort to for shelf stability. To simplify our calculations, we eliminated the melted chocolate and used cocoa powder, which contains very little fat by comparison. Once we figured out the ideal fat ratios, we could put the bar chocolate back in. For an unsaturated fat, we stuck to the box-mix choice: vegetable oil.

Next we devised a series of recipes that all had roughly the same amount of total fat, but with varying ratios of butter to vegetable oil. Brownies containing mostly saturated fat baked up tender and not at all chewy, while brownies made with mostly unsaturated fat were the chewier ones. Eventually, we hit on the magic formula: 29 percent saturated fat to 71 percent unsaturated— or about a 1–3 ratio. To see how these figures compared to our gold standard Ghirardelli Chocolate Supreme box-mix brownies, we crunched the numbers on the back of the mix. Bingo! They virtually mirrored our results, with 28 percent saturated fat to 72 percent unsaturated.

But even with the 1–3 ratio, problems persisted: Our brownies left a slick of grease on the plate, and with powdered cocoa as the sole source of chocolate, their flavor was lackluster. We attacked the greasiness first. Careful to stay close to the 1–3 ratio, we decreased the fat content overall, but this gave us dry brownies. Emulsifiers can help prevent fats from separating and leaking out during baking. While recently developing a recipe for

SCIENCE DESK

IN SEARCH OF CHEWY BROWNIES

The secret to a box-mix brownie's chewy texture boils down to one thing: fat—specifically the ratio of saturated to unsaturated fat. By using both butter (a predominantly saturated fat) and unsaturated vegetable oil, we were able to approximate the same 1-3 ratio found in commercially engineered specimens to mimic their satisfying chew.

BOX FORMULA	**OUR FORMULA**	**CLASSIC FORMULA**
28% saturated fat	29% saturated fat	64% saturated fat
72% unsaturated fat	71% unsaturated fat	36% unsaturated fat
Besides containing the optimal ratio of different fat types, boxed brownies make use of highly processed powdered shortening to achieve their chewy texture.	Our brownies contain a low-tech combo of butter and vegetable oil that creates a similar chew—and imparts a far richer taste than shortening ever could.	The classic version of brownies is made with all butter (and no vegetable oil) for a high proportion of solid, saturated fat that leads to a tender texture, versus a chewy one.

vinaigrette, we found that mayonnaise—an emulsion itself—was able to keep the dressing from separating. Though it seemed an odd move, we tried replacing some of the oil in our recipe with mayo. It worked surprisingly well, but tasters were seriously taken aback when the "secret ingredient" was revealed. Delving deeper, we identified the active emulsifier in the mayonnaise as lecithin, a phospholipid that occurs naturally in egg yolks. The simple addition of two extra yolks to our recipe in exchange for a little oil made greasiness (and the mayonnaise) a thing of the past.

Now we could finally deal with the chocolate flavor. We first tried tweaks that wouldn't affect the fats. Espresso powder deepens chocolate flavor, and stirring 1½ teaspoons into the boiling water along with the cocoa helped, but we knew we could do better. A little research revealed that although the total fat in unsweetened chocolate is lower per ounce than in an equivalent amount of butter, it contains a similar ratio of saturated to unsaturated fat. This fact suggested that we could replace 2 tablespoons of butter (1 ounce) with 2 ounces of unsweetened chocolate and still stay very close to the ideal fat ratio. And with the unsweetened chocolate providing more pure chocolate flavor, we cut the powdered cocoa back to ⅓ cup.

We had just about homed in on the perfect chewy chocolaty brownie when one last thought occurred to us: Only chocolate that is melted and incorporated into the batter actually affects the ratio of fats in the mix. Theoretically, we should be able to incorporate as many chocolate chunks into the mixed batter as we wanted, and as long as they didn't melt until the batter started baking, it should have no effect on texture. We whipped up another batch, folding in a full 6 ounces of bittersweet chocolate chunks just before baking. The result: chewy, fudgy bars with gooey pockets of melted chocolate that evoked images of bake sales past, but with complex flavor and just enough adult flourish to lift them out of the realm of children's fare.

Chewy Brownies
MAKES 24 BROWNIES

For an accurate measurement of boiling water, bring a full kettle of water to a boil, then measure out the desired amount. For the chewiest texture, it is important to let the brownies cool thoroughly before cutting. If your baking dish is glass, cool the brownies 10 minutes, then remove them promptly from the pan (otherwise, the superior heat retention of glass can lead to overbaking). While any high-quality chocolate can be used, our preferred brands of bittersweet chocolate are Callebaut Intense Dark Chocolate L-60–40NV and Ghirardelli Bittersweet Chocolate Baking Bar. Our preferred brand of unsweetened chocolate is Scharffen Berger.

⅓ cup (1 ounce) Dutch-processed cocoa (see note)
1½ teaspoons instant espresso powder (optional)
½ cup plus 2 tablespoons boiling water (see note)
2 ounces unsweetened chocolate (see note), chopped fine
½ cup plus 2 tablespoons vegetable oil
4 tablespoons (½ stick) unsalted butter, melted
2 large eggs plus 2 large egg yolks
2 teaspoons vanilla extract
2½ cups (17½ ounces) sugar
1¾ cups (8¾ ounces) unbleached all-purpose flour
¾ teaspoon table salt
6 ounces bittersweet chocolate (see note), cut into ½-inch pieces

1. Adjust an oven rack to the lowest position and heat the oven to 350 degrees. Cut an 18-inch length of foil and fold lengthwise to an 8-inch width. Fit the foil into the length of a 13 by 9-inch baking pan; allow the excess to hang over the side. Cut a 14-inch length of foil and fit into the width of the pan in the same manner, perpendicular to the first sheet. Lightly coat with vegetable oil spray, and set aside.

2. Whisk the cocoa, espresso powder (if using), and boiling water together in a large bowl until smooth. Add

the unsweetened chocolate and whisk until the chocolate is melted. Whisk in the oil and melted butter. (The mixture may look curdled.) Add the eggs, egg yolks, and vanilla and continue to whisk until smooth and homogeneous. Whisk in the sugar until fully incorporated. Add the flour and salt and mix with a rubber spatula until combined. Fold in the bittersweet chocolate pieces.

3. Scrape the batter into the prepared pan and bake until a toothpick inserted halfway between the edge and center comes out with just a few moist crumbs attached, 30 to 35 minutes. Transfer the pan to a wire rack and cool 1½ hours.

4. Loosen the edges with a paring knife and lift the brownies from the pan using the foil extensions. Return the brownies to the wire rack and cool completely, about 1 hour. Cut into 2-inch squares and serve. (The brownies can be stored in an airtight container at room temperature for up to 4 days.)

NOTES FROM THE TEST KITCHEN

LOOKING FOR CHEWY TEXTURE? DON'T TRY THIS

In our efforts to create a brownie as chewy as the box-mix kind, we tried a range of unusual techniques and ingredients. None of the approaches below got us close to our goal.

MAKE A BISCUIT

Online cooks swear this strange combo creates chew; we found that these ingredients are better left on the shelf.

ADD CARAMEL

Other cooks say folding a caramel made from sugar and butter into the mix leads to chew. We didn't find it so.

BAKE ON A PIZZA STONE

The heat trapped in a pizza stone purportedly melts the sugar in brownies, contributing to chew. For us, it did nothing.

CHILL IN AN ICE BATH

Does plunging a barely baked pan of brownies into an ice bath lead to chewiness? Not when we tried it.

ULTIMATE CHOCOLATE CUPCAKES

✔ WHY THIS RECIPE WORKS: For a cupcake with intense chocolate flavor, we couldn't just cram in chocolate, or our cupcakes would crumble in hand. Instead, we built up the structure of our cupcakes by swapping in high-gluten bread flour for the all-purpose flour. The bread flour made for a sturdy, but not tough, cupcake. As for flavor, we relied on a mix of bittersweet chocolate and cocoa powder dissolved in coffee, which helped intensify the chocolate flavor. A dab of chocolate ganache inside the cupcake added more chocolate punch and a creamy chocolate buttercream provided the perfect crown.

IF CUPCAKE APPEAL IS ALL ABOUT GETTING THE BEST attributes of cake in a portable package, the irony is that most of today's highly specialized cupcake bakeries either can't deliver the goods—a moist, tender crumb capped with just enough creamy, not-too-sweet frosting—or they deviate from the classic model. To keep us interested, bakers tend to doll up the standbys with gimmicky alternatives like "Cinnamon Chai Pecan Sticky," "Mojito," and "Caramel Apple." And the core elements—cake and frosting—are barely palatable.

Call us old-fashioned, but we prefer a simple, decadent chocolate cupcake any day. To get a sense of what's on the market, we held two tastings: one for chocolate cupcakes we'd gathered from half a dozen famous bakeries around the country and another for a handful of published recipes we baked in the test kitchen. The results were grim. The bakery and homemade confections alike were fraught with a cupcake catch-22: If the cakes packed decent chocolate flavor, their structure was too crumbly. Conversely, if the cakes balanced moisture and tenderness without crumbling, the chocolate turned wimpy. We were beginning to understand the challenges ahead.

There was one recipe we hadn't tried: one for our chocolate layer cake. It features a double whammy of cocoa powder (½ cup) and melted bittersweet chocolate (3 ounces), plus the chocolate-enhancing flavor of brewed coffee (½ cup). These elements, when combined with tangy buttermilk (an appropriately less sweet alternative to regular milk), make for moist cake with unabashed chocolate intensity. Figuring a cupcake is just a pint-size version of a cake, we mixed up the batter, portioned it into a muffin pan, and popped it into the oven. About 18 minutes later, we dug in—and the swooning began. Here, tasters declared, was a chocolate cupcake that really tasted like chocolate. The only problem? Piles of ultra-tender crumbs littering the countertop. As fork food, this rich, tender cake was ideal, but eaten without utensils, it was more of a cleanup project.

We quickly fingered the cocoa and melted chocolate as culprits in the too-tender crumb. Specifically, the texture suffered from too little gluten development and too much fat. Gluten forms when proteins in flour bind together with liquid and become pliable; the more the proteins are worked into the liquid (the cake batter), the more gluten develops, and the stronger the crumb. Fat (like chocolate), meanwhile, acts as a tenderizer to create a delicate crumb.

Because all that cocoa powder contains no gluten-forming proteins, it dilutes the flour, while the extra fat from the chocolate made this cake too tender for cupcakes. To strengthen the batter we had to cut back on both chocolate components. Fifty percent less cocoa and two-thirds less bittersweet chocolate later, we had perfectly portable (if slightly dry) cupcakes—and predictably feeble chocolate flavor.

We needed to work in more chocolate without disrupting the batter's structure. On a whim, we tossed a handful of chocolate chips into the batter; unfortunately, this produced warm bits of gooey chocolate that cooled into hard, distracting lumps. Stymied, we figured our only alternative was to make do with what little chocolate we had and try to ramp up its flavor.

Thus began our experiments in eccentric chocolate flavor enhancement, gleaned from self-professed chocoholics' claims on the Internet, such as combining chocolate (which derives most of its complex taste through the Maillard reaction when the cacao beans are

ULTIMATE CHOCOLATE CUPCAKES WITH GANACHE FILLING

roasted) with other sources of Maillard-produced flavor compounds such as liquid smoke, full-bodied beers, even flour that we smoked on the grill for an hour. These ideas led to dead ends, as did stirring in glutamate-rich flavor enhancers like miso paste or soy sauce. Not only were these confections no more chocolaty, their flavor ranged from fermented to salty, sour, ashy, or bitter.

Getting back to more conventional tactics, if we had to work with less chocolate, the least we could do was take advantage of the one chocolate-enhancing ingredient we were already using: coffee. Mixing the cocoa with hot coffee eked out more chocolate flavor. Then we wondered if we could exchange the other liquid component—buttermilk—for even more coffee. The effect might benefit us twofold, since rich dairy products typically obscure other flavors. So we swapped out the buttermilk and increased the amount of coffee to ¾ cup. Bingo. The chocolate flavor was noticeably more pronounced. (To activate the baking soda without the buttermilk's acid, we added 2 teaspoons of white vinegar.) We still had another dairy ingredient to consider: butter. We had our doubts, but trying more neutral-flavored vegetable oil in place of melted butter seemed worth a shot. The result? Not a dramatic leap, but definitely a good move. In a side-by-side tasting, even the skeptics picked the oil-only cupcakes, citing fuller, unadulterated chocolate flavor. Even better, this batch was extra moist.

We'd done all we could think of to boost the existing chocolate flavor when a colleague suggested we toughen up the structure of the cupcake that we had. That way, we could add back the extra chocolate without tenderizing it too much. We tried adding an extra egg or two, but this made the texture rubbery. Next, we overmixed the batter to stimulate gluten development (as if we were kneading bread dough), but all that bought us were weary arms. However, thinking about bread baking led us to a new ingredient: bread flour. Specifically engineered for gluten development, bread flour contains more protein than all-purpose flour and turned out a cupcake that was markedly less crumble-prone, but not tough.

With newfound room for more fat, we began to add back some of the chocolate. Tablespoon by tablespoon, we traded flour for cocoa powder until the latter maxed out at ⅓ cup and worked the bar chocolate back up to 3 ounces for the most unapologetically chocolaty (and still sturdy) cake yet.

Still, chocoholics that we are, we wanted more chocolate. Thinking back to our attempt with chocolate chips, we missed those pockets of molten chocolate when the cake was still warm and wondered if there was another means to that end. Perhaps a mixture that would stay almost fluid even after it cooled—such as a chocolate ganache? We melted a standard ganache mixture of 2 ounces bittersweet chocolate and 2 tablespoons heavy cream (plus 1 tablespoon of confectioners' sugar for a hint of sweetness), let the mixture cool until slightly firm, and then spooned a teaspoon of it onto each cupcake before baking. As the cupcakes baked, the ganache sank into the batter, but a little bit too far—a problem solved by thinning the ganache with 2 more tablespoons of cream. At last, we'd hit chocolate nirvana.

Now, about that frosting. Too many of the bakery cupcakes we sampled sported swirly tufts of gritty, sickly sweet icing that cracked and disintegrated like cotton candy. We were after something more refined. A second dose of chocolate ganache took the chocolate intensity too far, but tasters thought a fluffy seven-minute meringue frosting felt insubstantial. Buttercream seemed like a reasonable compromise, but tasters vetoed the graininess of quick versions calling for simply beating butter together with confectioners' sugar.

That left us with cooked buttercreams, and we opted for the Swiss meringue variety, where egg whites and granulated sugar are heated over a double boiler, then whipped with knobs of softened butter. The result is silky and decadent, without the weight and greasiness of other rich frostings. Velvety with just enough sweetness, this buttercream crowned the cake perfectly and even lent itself to a number of easy flavor variations. After more than two months and 800 cupcakes baked, we finally had the perfect, ultimate version.

Ultimate Chocolate Cupcakes with Ganache Filling

MAKES 12 CUPCAKES

Use a high-quality bittersweet or semisweet chocolate for this recipe, such as one of the test kitchen's favorite baking chocolates, Callebaut Intense Dark Chocolate L-60–40NV or Ghirardelli Bittersweet Chocolate Baking Bar. Though we highly recommend the ganache filling, you can omit it for a more traditional cupcake.

GANACHE FILLING

- 2 ounces bittersweet chocolate, chopped fine (see note)
- ¼ cup heavy cream
- 1 tablespoon confectioners' sugar

CHOCOLATE CUPCAKES

- 3 ounces bittersweet chocolate, chopped fine (see note)
- ⅓ cup (1 ounce) Dutch-processed cocoa
- ¾ cup hot coffee
- ¾ cup (4⅛ ounces) bread flour
- ¾ cup (5¼ ounces) granulated sugar
- ½ teaspoon table salt
- ½ teaspoon baking soda
- 6 tablespoons vegetable oil
- 2 large eggs
- 2 teaspoons white vinegar
- 1 teaspoon vanilla extract
- 1 recipe frosting (recipes follow)

1. FOR THE GANACHE FILLING: Place the chocolate, cream, and confectioners' sugar in a medium microwave-safe bowl. Microwave until the mixture is warm to the touch, 20 to 30 seconds. Whisk the mixture until smooth, then refrigerate until just chilled, no longer than 30 minutes.

2. FOR THE CUPCAKES: Adjust an oven rack to the middle position and heat the oven to 350 degrees. Line a standard-sized muffin pan (cups have ½-cup capacity) with baking cup liners. Place the chocolate and cocoa in a medium bowl. Pour the hot coffee over the mixture and whisk until smooth. Refrigerate until completely cool, about 20 minutes. Whisk the flour, granulated sugar, salt, and baking soda together in a medium bowl and set aside.

3. Whisk the oil, eggs, vinegar, and vanilla into the cooled chocolate-cocoa mixture until smooth. Add the flour mixture and whisk until smooth.

4. Divide the batter evenly among the muffin pan cups. Place one slightly rounded teaspoon of the ganache filling on top of each cupcake. Bake until the cupcakes are set and just firm to the touch, 17 to 19 minutes. Cool the cupcakes in the muffin pan on a wire rack until cool enough to handle, about 10 minutes. Carefully lift each cupcake from the muffin pan and set on a wire rack. Cool to room temperature before frosting, about 1 hour.

5. TO FROST: Mound 2 to 3 tablespoons of the frosting on the center of each cupcake. Following the photos on page 285, use a small icing spatula or butter knife to ice each cupcake. (The cupcakes can be made up to 24 hours in advance and stored unfrosted in an airtight container.)

Creamy Chocolate Frosting

MAKES ABOUT 2¼ CUPS

Cool the chocolate to between 85 and 100 degrees before adding it to the frosting. If the frosting seems too soft after adding the chocolate, chill it briefly in the refrigerator and then rewhip it until creamy.

- ⅓ cup (2⅓ ounces) sugar
- 2 large egg whites
    Pinch salt
- 12 tablespoons (1½ sticks) unsalted butter, cut into 12 pieces and softened
- 6 ounces bittersweet chocolate, melted and cooled (see note)
- ½ teaspoon vanilla extract

1. Combine the sugar, egg whites, and salt in the bowl of a standing mixer, then place the bowl over a pan of simmering water. Whisking gently but constantly, heat the mixture until slightly thickened and foamy and registers 150 degrees on an instant-read thermometer, 2 to 3 minutes.

2. Using the whisk attachment, beat the mixture on medium speed in a standing mixer until it reaches the

INNER SECRET FOR SUPER-CHOCOLATY CUPCAKES

CHOCOLATE, INSIDE AND OUT

After packing lots of chocolate into the batter, we raised the bar one notch higher by filling the cupcake with a dollop of truffle-like ganache.

MAKING MERINGUE-STYLE BUTTERCREAM

Whereas uncooked frostings tend to be greasy and grainy, our Swiss meringue buttercream gets its satiny-smooth texture from whisking the egg whites and sugar in a double boiler, then whipping the mixture with softened butter.

1. Whisk the egg white mixture until foamy and it registers 150 degrees on an instant-read thermometer.

2. Beat the mixture in a standing mixer until slightly cooled, then slowly add the softened butter.

3. Add the cooled melted chocolate and vanilla, then whip until light and fluffy.

DECORATING CHOCOLATE CUPCAKES

While developing the recipe for Ultimate Chocolate Cupcakes with Ganache Filling, we experimented with countless decorating techniques. Here are our two favorites:

FLAT TOP WITH COATED SIDES

1. Place 2 to 3 tablespoons of frosting on each cupcake, forming a thick layer. Using a small offset spatula, spread to create a flat top.

2. Using the spatula, smooth the edges of the frosting so they are flush with the sides of the cupcake. Reflatten the top as necessary.

3. If desired, place a topping such as chopped nuts on a plate. Holding the cupcake at its base, gently roll the outer edges of the frosting in the topping.

PIPING THE FROSTING

Place the frosting in a pastry bag fitted with a ½-inch plain or star tip. Starting at the outside edge and working inward, pipe the frosting into a spiral. Sprinkle lightly with a topping, if desired.

consistency of shaving cream and is slightly cooled, 1 to 2 minutes. Add the butter, one piece at a time, until smooth and creamy. (The frosting may look curdled after half of the butter has been added; it will smooth with additional butter.) Once all the butter is added, add the cooled melted chocolate and the vanilla and mix until combined. Increase the mixer speed to medium-high and beat until light, fluffy, and thoroughly combined, about 30 seconds, scraping the beater and sides of the bowl with a rubber spatula as necessary. (The frosting can be made up to 24 hours in advance and refrigerated in an airtight container. When ready to frost, place the frosting in a microwave-safe container and microwave briefly until just slightly softened, 5 to 10 seconds. Once warmed, stir until creamy.)

VARIATIONS

Creamy Malted Milk Chocolate Frosting
Follow the recipe for Creamy Chocolate Frosting, reducing the sugar to ¼ cup, substituting 6 ounces milk chocolate for the bittersweet chocolate, and adding ¼ cup malted milk powder to the frosting with the vanilla in step 2.

Creamy Vanilla Frosting
Follow the recipe for Creamy Chocolate Frosting, omitting the bittersweet chocolate and increasing the sugar to ½ cup. (If the final frosting seems too thick, warm the mixer bowl briefly over a pan of simmering water. Then place the bowl back on the mixer and beat on medium-high speed until creamy.)

Creamy Peanut Butter Frosting
For an extra hit of peanut flavor, we like to garnish these cupcakes with ½ cup chopped peanuts.

Follow the recipe for Creamy Chocolate Frosting, omitting the bittersweet chocolate, increasing the sugar to ½ cup, and increasing the salt to ⅛ teaspoon. Add ⅔ cup creamy peanut butter to the frosting with the vanilla in step 2.

NOT-SO-CRAZY BAKING GADGETS

Enter just about any kitchenware store and you'll be faced with loads of gadgets among all the kitchen essentials—especially in the baking aisle. In our almost 20 years of baking in the test kitchen, we've tried out those gadgets that seemed most promising. Here are the ones that, while not mandatory, deliver the goods. See www.americastestkitchen.com for updates to this testing.

COOKIE SPATULA

Reaching between cookies on a crowded baking sheet or digging brownies out of a pan can be tricky with a full-size spatula. Enter the OXO Good Grips Cookie Spatula ($6.99), a remarkably small, maneuverable silicone spatula that's safe for nonstick cookware. In our testing, the flexible edge of its 2 by 3-inch head, attached to an angled 6.5-inch handle, glided effortlessly beneath sugar, chocolate, and oatmeal raisin cookies as well as brownies. If you're an avid baker, this spatula is an ideal addition to your kitchen.

WINNER: OXO GOOD GRIPS COOKIE SPATULA

BAKER'S COOLING RACK

When you need to cool multiple sheets of cookies, finding enough counter space can be a problem. We tested the Linden Sweden Baker's Mate Cooling Rack ($19.99), which vertically stacks cooling baking sheets. We put hot trays of cookies on the rack and removed them randomly to see if different combinations would cause it to tip—it barely wobbled. The shelves collapse to fit tall items, and the entire unit folds down to a height of 1 inch, making it easy to store. One quibble— each "shelf" is a single metal rod shaped as a 9½-inch rectangle, so it can't hold an 8-inch square baking pan, because the pan would fall through.

WINNER: LINDEN SWEDEN BAKER'S MATE COOLING RACK

CUPCAKE AND CAKE CARRIER

There's nothing more frustrating than preparing a frosted cake and having it get messed up on the way to a party. We baked chocolate layer cakes, placed them in four different cake carriers, and drove them down pothole-filled roads. Our favorite carrier is the Progressive Collapsible Cupcake and Cake Carrier ($29.99), which kept our cake in perfect shape and has comfortable handles, snap locks, and a nonskid base. It can carry either 9-inch round or square cakes and the included insert can also hold up to 24 cupcakes, plus it collapses for easy storage. Next time you're taking a cake on the road with you, take it in this sturdy carrier to ensure that it arrives looking as good as when you frosted it.

WINNER: PROGRESSIVE COLLAPSIBLE CUPCAKE AND CAKE CARRIER

ICING SPATULA

We've found that tasks like spreading batter in a cake pan or frosting cupcakes are a lot easier with an offset spatula. These moderately priced, blunt-edged metal pastry blades, which average about 4½ inches long, make it easy to tackle these messy tasks without getting your knuckles dirty. Our top pick, the 8-inch Angled Spatula by Wilton ($4.79), has a blade that's both sturdy and flexible and an easy-grip handle.

WINNER: WILTON 8-INCH ANGLED SPATULA

SLICING BROWNIE PAN

Slicing a pan of brownies isn't difficult, but we found a baking gadget that made quick work of this often-messy task. The Chicago Metallic Slice Solutions Brownie Pan ($19.99) does the cutting for you, so you don't muss the top crust of your brownies and you don't need to get out a ruler to ensure that they're the right size. The 9 by 9-inch baking pan comes with an attached cutting grid; after the batter is poured in the pan, the grid is placed into the batter so each brownie bakes up into a perfect square. After the brownies have cooled, the bottom of the pan pops up, with each brownie sliced by the grid. This easy-to-use baking gadget can be used for bar cookies, cornbread, and other baked goods too.

WINNER: CHICAGO METALLIC SLICE SOLUTIONS BROWNIE PAN

ALL-AMERICAN
Fruit Desserts

We dot our fresh cherry pie filling with pieces of sweet, creamy butter for extra richness.

WHY IS GOOD CHERRY PIE—ONE WITH DEEP CHERRY FLAVOR—so hard to come by? It turns out that sour cherries, which retain their intense berry flavor upon heating, are only available for a very short window in early summer—and only in some parts of the country. Miss that week's farmers' market and you're out of luck. It's true that sweet cherries are more widely available, but when baked into a pie, sweet cherries merely taste sweet—nothing more. Our goal was clear. We wanted to make cherry pie with easier-to-come-by sweet cherries so we could enjoy this American favorite all summer long—but we had to find a way to amplify the cherry flavor in our filling so it had the same intense cherry flavor of a pie made with prized sour cherries.

Some may scoff at using a recipe for apple crisp, a typically thrown-together dessert that requires few baking skills. But trust us, take a dump-and-bake approach to this dessert using just any apple and you'll need loads of vanilla ice cream to mask the fact that the apples aren't evenly cooked and the "crisp" is anything but. For great apple crisp any time, we set out to devise a simple recipe (yes, simple—this is a fruit crisp, after all) that guarantees perfectly cooked juicy slices of apple blanketed with a buttery, crunchy topping. Ice cream is optional.

SWEET CHERRY PIE

✔ **WHY THIS RECIPE WORKS:** To mimic the bright, tart flavor of a sour cherry pie filling, we supplemented sweet cherries with chopped plums. Cutting the cherries in half exposed their sturdy flesh, encouraging them to soften and give up their juices. A splash of bourbon and lemon juice also improved their flavor. To keep the filling juicy, rather than dry, we switched out the typical lattice crust in favor of a traditional top crust, which prevented any juices from evaporating.

WE'VE OFTEN WONDERED WHY APPLE PIE BEAT OUT cherry as our national dessert. At their best, cherry pies are juicier, more colorful, and, in our opinion, just plain tastier than apple. It all boils down to a matter of availability. You can find decent apples year-round in even the most meagerly stocked supermarket, but cherry season is cruelly short—just a brief blossoming period during the early summer. And even when cherries are available, chances are they're a sweet variety (usually crimson-colored Bing or red-yellow-blushed Rainier), not the rare, ruby-hued sour species prized for jams and pie-making.

What makes sour cherries such prime candidates for baking (most people find them too tart for snacking purposes) is their soft, juicy flesh and bright, punchy flavor that neither oven heat nor sugar can dull. Plumper sweet cherries, on the other hand, have mellower flavors and meaty, firm flesh—traits that make them ideal for eating straight off the stem but don't translate well to baking. Our challenge was obvious: Develop a recipe for sweet cherry pie with all the intense, jammy flavor and softened but still intact fruit texture of the best sour cherry pie.

Before we abandoned sour cherries altogether, we needed to get our hands on one batch to help us understand how they function in pie compared with their sweeter cousins. With help from the U.S. Postal Service, we obtained a few pounds of the tart variety from an online retailer, baked them into a pie, and tasted it side by side with one made of supermarket sweet cherries. The difference was night and day. Compared with the sour cherry pie's bracing acidity, the sweet cherry pie's taste was beyond sweet—it was downright cloying. Even more problematic, the sweet cherries' drier, relatively dense flesh failed to break down completely (even after more than an hour of baking) and resulted in a filling that called to mind slightly softened jumbo marbles, not fruit.

So we had two issues to resolve: taming the cherries' sweetness and getting them to break down to the proper juicy texture. To get our bearings, we made another pie. We combined 2 pounds of pitted fresh Bing cherries and 1 cup of sugar, stirred in 3 tablespoons of ground tapioca (our preferred thickener for juicy fruit pies), poured the filling into a shell, and wove a traditional lattice-top crust to show off the fruit's jewel-like shine. After it had baked and cooled, we offered colleagues a bite. As we expected, nobody could taste past the sweetness. Figuring all that sugar wasn't helping, we tried cutting back a few tablespoons at a time, but that only created a new problem: Since sugar draws moisture out of the cherries through osmosis, less of it made for a less juicy filling. A half-cup was as low as we could go without completely ruining the texture, but the filling still verged on candy-sweetness.

Our only other option was to add another ingredient to offset the sweetness. A couple of splashes of bourbon—a classic pairing with cherries—helped, as did the acidity of fresh lemon juice, but these were minor tweaks, and adding more of either just made the pies taste boozy or citrusy. We even tried vinegar, hoping to more closely mimic the tartness of sour cherries, but tasters objected to the sharpness of even the smallest drop. As a last-ditch effort, we tried introducing alternative fruits: super-tart fresh cranberries (too bitter), tangy red grapes (too musty), and dried sour cherries (too chewy).

None of these ideas panned out, but the concept did get us thinking about other types of fruit. Cherries fall into the stone-fruit category, along with peaches, nectarines, and plums. Sweet-fleshed peaches and nectarines wouldn't help, but the tartness of plums might be worth a shot. For our next pie, we sliced a couple of plums into the filling, but their flesh was just as dense and resilient as the cherries'. No problem, our trusty food processor could fix this. We made another pie, this time pureeing

SWEET CHERRY PIE

the plums and mixing the resulting pulp with the cherries. Perfect! The flavor, now tangy and complex, was spot on, and nobody suspected our secret.

Now that we'd crossed one challenge off our list, we were ready to tackle the sweet cherries' overly firm texture. The problem was twofold: Not only were the cherries refusing to break down, as a result they also weren't releasing enough juice to amply moisten the filling. As it turned out, the culprit was cellulose, the main structural component of fruit cells: Compared with sour cherries, the sweet variety contains a full 30 percent more cellulose, making the flesh more rigid.

Without a way to rid the cherries of that extra structure, we'd have to rely on more conventional techniques to soften the flesh. We were already macerating them in sugar before baking to help draw out some of their juices, but with their relatively thick skin, this technique wasn't effective. Halving them helped considerably, since their juice was very easily drawn out of the exposed fleshy centers. Even better, the cut cherries collapsed more readily and turned out markedly softer in the finished pie, save

for a few too many solid chunks. By tossing a portion of them (1 cup) into the food processor along with the plums (and straining the chewy skins out of the resulting pulp), we got a filling that was ideally soft, if a bit dry, and studded with a few still-intact cherry pieces. As a bonus, the pies we tested using a good brand of frozen sweet cherries—an easier alternative to pitting dozens of the fresh variety—baked up equally well, making this an any-season dessert.

We'd hoped that mashing and precooking the cherries with sugar would help release some fruit juices, but this technique actually caused moisture to evaporate through the crust's ventilated top as it baked, leading to a drier pie. Then we realized: Our problem wasn't the fruit itself, but the lattice crust. Juice-gushing sour cherry and berry pies may benefit from the extra evaporation of a woven crust, but with these cherries we needed to keep a tighter lid on the available moisture. Rolling out a traditional disk of dough, we fitted it to the bottom pastry, neatly sealed the edges, and slid the whole assembly onto a preheated baking sheet in the oven to ensure that the bottom crust crisped up before the fruit filling could seep through. An hour or so later, out came a gorgeously golden brown, perfectly juicy (but not runny) pie. When tasters began to line up for second helpings, we knew we'd finally gotten our cherry pie in apple-pie order.

Sweet Cherry Pie

SERVES 8

Vodka is essential to the texture of the crust and imparts no flavor—do not substitute. This dough will be moister and more supple than most standard pie dough and will require more flour to roll out (up to ¼ cup). The tapioca should be measured first, then ground in a coffee grinder or food processor for 30 seconds. If you are using frozen fruit, measure it frozen, but let it thaw before filling the pie. If not, you run the risk of partially cooked fruit and undissolved tapioca.

PIE DOUGH

2½ cups (12½ ounces) unbleached all-purpose flour, plus more for the work surface

1 teaspoon table salt

2 tablespoons sugar

12 tablespoons (1½ sticks) cold unsalted butter, cut into ¼-inch pieces

½ cup cold vegetable shortening, cut into 4 pieces

¼ cup cold vodka (see note)

¼ cup cold water

FILLING

2 red plums, halved and pitted

6 cups (about 2 pounds) pitted sweet cherries or 6 cups pitted frozen cherries, halved (see note)

½ cup sugar

⅛ teaspoon table salt

1 tablespoon juice from 1 lemon

2 teaspoons bourbon (optional)

2 tablespoons instant tapioca, ground (see note)

⅛ teaspoon ground cinnamon (optional)

2 tablespoons unsalted butter, cut into ¼-inch pieces

1 large egg, lightly beaten with 1 teaspoon water

1. FOR THE PIE DOUGH: Process 1½ cups of the flour, the salt, and sugar in a food processor until combined, about 2 pulses. Add the butter and shortening; process until a homogeneous dough just starts to collect in uneven clumps, about 15 seconds (the dough will resemble cottage cheese curds and there should be no uncoated flour). Scrape the bowl with a rubber spatula and redistribute the dough evenly around the processor blade. Add the remaining 1 cup flour and pulse until the mixture is evenly distributed around the bowl and the

RATING VANILLA ICE CREAM

To find the best vanilla ice cream, we put the most popular styles of the best-selling brands before our tasting panel. In the end, they strongly preferred brands containing real vanilla extract over those containing synthetic vanilla. But there were other factors at work. While a small amount of stabilizers are okay to help keep ice cream viscous and creamy as it is inevitably subjected to thawing and refreezing, an excess came across as gummy. And additives used to mimic the rich flavor traditionally provided by egg yolks couldn't hold a candle to those with the real thing. Finally, the less air incorporated into the ice cream (known as overrun), the better. Note that sugar and total fat are per ½-cup serving. Brands are listed in order of preference. See www.americastestkitchen.com for updates to this testing.

HIGHLY RECOMMENDED

BEN & JERRY'S Vanilla
PRICE: $4.39 per pint
SUGAR: 19g **TOTAL FAT:** 14g **OVERRUN:** 24%
INGREDIENTS: Cream, skim milk, liquid sugar, water, egg yolks, fair-traded certified vanilla extract with vanilla bean seeds, guar gum, carrageenan
COMMENTS: Tasters praised the "indulgent" vanilla flavor that "built in intensity" and left a "deep, creamy, hazelnut aftertaste."

RECOMMENDED

HÄAGEN-DAZS Vanilla
PRICE: $3.50 per 14-oz container ($4 per pint)
SUGAR: 21g **TOTAL FAT:** 17g **OVERRUN:** 26%
INGREDIENTS: Cream, skim milk, sugar, egg yolks, vanilla extract
COMMENTS: This brand had a "creamy, dense, and smooth" texture. While some called it "jam-packed with vanilla punch," others found the flavoring "raw and too strong."

WELLS BLUE BUNNY All Natural Vanilla
PRICE: $3.10 per 1.75-quart container ($0.89 per pint)
SUGAR: 16g **TOTAL FAT:** 9g **OVERRUN:** 78%
INGREDIENTS: Milk, cream, sugar, skim milk, grade A nonfat dry milk, egg yolks, natural vanilla extract, vanilla beans
COMMENTS: Tasters loved the "lingering" vanilla flavor, but a few complained this ice cream tasted more like milk than vanilla. Its "light and fluffy" texture was "foamy." "This reminds me of soft-serve."

BREYERS Natural Vanilla
PRICE: $5.49 per 1.5-quart container ($1.83 per pint)
SUGAR: 14g **TOTAL FAT:** 7g **OVERRUN:** 94%
INGREDIENTS: Milk, cream, sugar, natural vanilla flavor, natural tara gum
COMMENTS: While several tasters praised this ice cream's vanilla flavor as "very intense" and "clean," others pointed out that it "quickly dissipates." It lost points for having an "icy, crumbly" texture.

RECOMMENDED WITH RESERVATIONS

FRIENDLY'S Vanilla
PRICE: $5.49 per 1.5-quart container ($1.83 per pint)
SUGAR: 11g **TOTAL FAT:** 8g **OVERRUN:** 94%
INGREDIENTS: Milk, cream, corn syrup, skim milk, sugar, whey protein concentrate, whey, buttermilk, vanilla extract, guar gum, mono- and diglycerides, xanthan gum, carrageenan, annatto extract, turmeric (for color)
COMMENTS: Some tasters enjoyed the "custardy" texture of this brand. But the "muted, weak" vanilla flavor was what really knocked it down in the rankings.

BLUE BELL Homemade Vanilla
PRICE: $6.65 per 2-quart container ($1.66 per pint)
SUGAR: 21g **TOTAL FAT:** 8g **OVERRUN:** 46%
INGREDIENTS: Milk, cream, sugar, skim milk, high-fructose corn syrup, corn syrup, natural and artificial vanilla flavor, cellulose gum, vegetable gums (guar, carrageenan, carob bean), salt, annatto color
COMMENTS: Tasters disliked this ice cream's "over the top" vanilla flavor that tasted "artificial."

TURKEY HILL Vanilla Bean
PRICE: $5.29 per 1.5-quart container ($1.77 per pint)
SUGAR: 12g **TOTAL FAT:** 7g **OVERRUN:** 94%
INGREDIENTS: Milk, cream, sugar, corn syrup, whey, nonfat milk, mono- and diglycerides, vanilla, guar gum, vanilla bean, carrageenan
COMMENTS: Vanilla flavor that struck tasters as "fake" and "medicinal" helped demote this previous winner.

NOT RECOMMENDED

EDY'S GRAND Vanilla
PRICE: $5.59 per 1.5-quart container ($1.86 per pint)
SUGAR: 14g **TOTAL FAT:** 8g **OVERRUN:** 97%
INGREDIENTS: Skim milk, cream, sugar, corn syrup, cellulose gum, mono- and diglycerides, guar gum, carrageenan, annatto color, dextrose, natural flavor
COMMENTS: This brand was downgraded for its "fading vanilla flavor." It was also the most aerated ice cream in the lineup.

mass of dough has been broken up, 4 to 6 quick pulses. Empty the mixture into a medium bowl.

2. Sprinkle the vodka and water over the mixture. With a rubber spatula, use a folding motion to mix, pressing down on the dough until the dough is slightly tacky and sticks together. Divide the dough into two equal balls and flatten each into a 4-inch disk. Cover each with plastic wrap and refrigerate at least 45 minutes or up to 2 days.

3. Roll one disk of the dough into a 12-inch circle on a lightly floured work surface, then fit it into a 9-inch pie plate, letting the excess dough hang over the edge; cover with plastic wrap and refrigerate for 30 minutes. Roll the other disk of dough into a 12-inch circle on a lightly floured work surface, then transfer to a parchment-lined baking sheet; cover with plastic wrap and refrigerate for 30 minutes.

4. FOR THE FILLING: Adjust an oven rack to the lowest position, place a baking sheet on the rack, and heat the oven to 400 degrees. Process the plums and 1 cup of the halved cherries in a food processor until smooth, about 1 minute, scraping down the sides of the bowl as necessary. Strain the puree through a fine-mesh strainer into a large bowl, pressing on the solids to extract the liquid; discard the solids. Stir the remaining halved cherries, the sugar, salt, lemon juice, bourbon (if using), tapioca, and cinnamon (if using) into the puree; let stand for 15 minutes.

5. Transfer the cherry mixture, including all the juices, to the dough-lined pie plate. Scatter the butter pieces over the fruit. Loosely roll the second piece of dough around the rolling pin and gently unroll it over the pie. Trim, fold, and crimp the edges and cut eight evenly spaced vent holes in the top. Brush the dough with the egg mixture. Freeze the pie for 20 minutes.

6. Place the pie on the baking sheet and bake for 30 minutes. Reduce the oven temperature to 350 degrees and continue to bake until the juices bubble and the crust is deep golden brown, 30 to 40 minutes longer.

7. Cool the pie on a wire rack to room temperature, about 4 hours, before serving.

APPLE CRISP

✔ **WHY THIS RECIPE WORKS:** For an apple crisp with tender, not mushy, apples we sautéed Golden Delicious apples in a skillet until just softened. Reduced apple cider contributed intense sweet-tart apple flavor. As for the crisp topping, we added brown sugar to white to play up the apples' caramel notes. Swapping half of the flour for rolled oats gave the topping more character and chew. And chopped pecans not only improved the crunch factor, but added rich flavor as well. No need to use a baking dish; an ovensafe skillet makes it easy to move the whole operation from the stovetop to the oven for a quick browning.

FOR MOST, THE UNFUSSINESS OF APPLE CRISP IS ITS appeal. That said, while this dish is usually good, it's rarely great. Plus, it's not without a few issues. Instead of a tender yet intact fruit filling, the filling's texture can range from rock-hard slices to applesauce. And as for the topping, "crisp" is a rare stroke of luck. We wondered if a little more effort could deliver a lush (but not mushy) sweet-tart apple filling covered with truly crisp morsels of buttery, sugary topping.

We'd never given much thought to the best type of apple for such a humble dessert, but maybe that was the place to start. Experience with other recipes had taught us that not every variety is good for baking. For now, a basic approach—toss 3 pounds or so of peeled, sliced apples with sugar; top with a blend of melted butter, sugar, and flour; and bake in a 350-degree oven for about an hour— would do for assessing how the apples performed.

We weren't surprised when McIntosh apples turned out mushy; they have a naturally pulpy texture. Granny Smiths were another matter. Some batches made with this prized baking varietal virtually disintegrated into applesauce, while others held their shape. Baffled, we stockpiled several other varieties until a more foolproof apple emerged: Golden Delicious (Braeburns and Honeycrisps

SKILLET APPLE CRISP

measured up as well). But we were confused: What makes one type of apple more reliable than another? When we consulted our science editor, he explained that it's a storage issue. The varieties differ in their susceptibility to the ethylene, carbon dioxide, and oxygen used in storage—an important factor if you're making an apple dessert any time other than fall, since the fruits can be warehoused for up to 10 months before reaching the supermarket. In Grannies, these gases cause pectin (which holds cell walls together) to break down rapidly, accelerating disintegration when the fruit is heated. Goldens, Braeburns, and Honeycrisps are less susceptible to the gases used in long-term storage, thus their cell walls hold fast. Our soupy Granny Smith crisps were surely made with over-the-hill apples—and likely would have baked up just fine if we'd been using fresh-picked fruit. But for this year-round recipe, we'd stick with hardier Goldens.

Still, Goldens weren't a panacea: For one, their mellower, more honeyed flesh lacked the Grannies' tart punch. Another problem: While complete apple blowouts had been averted, the apples still cooked unevenly within the baking dish, with some slices remaining on the underdone side of al dente. If we baked the crisp until the center apples were fully tender, the fruit around the perimeter turned to pulp. And the topping? Burned. If patchy doneness was the problem, stirring was the obvious solution: Tossing the fruit as it transformed from crisp to softened would ensure uniformly tender slices, at which point we could add the topping. But frequently stirring an oven-baked dessert is a logistical nonstarter: Who wants to repeatedly don oven mitts, reach into a hot oven, and take a spoon to bubbling fruit? That's when we decided to move the front end of the operation to the stovetop, where we could cook (and stir) the apples in a skillet until almost fully tender before transferring them to the oven. Plus, the pan's shallow, flared shape encouraged evaporation, and we figured some direct heat and a little butter might work wonders for the Goldens' slightly flat flavor. (When cooked raw in a baking dish, the apples merely steamed in their own juices.) That's exactly what happened. Once the stovetop's heat drove away excess moisture, the Maillard reaction (a flavor-boosting process that occurs when sugars and proteins brown) kicked in,

caramelizing the fructose in the fruit and browning the proteins and lactose in the butter. This stovetop-cooked filling's sweet richness would have been impossible to achieve in the oven.

Everyone agreed that skillet crisp was a more flavorful way to go—but we also concurred that the flavor still lacked a certain depth and roundness. Because Goldens are particularly sweet, we cut the sugar from ⅓ to ¼ cup and added a few squeezes of fresh lemon juice. Again, another good move; there was the tart edge we'd missed from not using Grannies. But for full-fledged apple flavor, we ended up reaching for the essence itself: cider. Drowning our sautéed fruit in liquid would be a backward move, so we put our skillet on double-duty. Before sautéing the fruit, we reduced a full cup of cider by half. Added to the parcooked apples, this super-potent reduction contributed the intense fruity flavor we'd been looking for. We were about to transfer the fruit from the skillet to a baking dish when we realized the extra step wasn't necessary. We simply sprinkled on the topping and prepared to slide the whole assembly into a 350-degree oven, where it would only need a short stint, thanks to the parcooking. Then it occurred to us: If we cranked up the heat to, say, 450 degrees, the apples would need even less time to bake and we'd be able to achieve some quick browning on the topping. After only 15 minutes, the "crisp" was just that: crunchy and golden, an ideal contrast to the luscious, flavorful fruit that lay beneath. Well, almost ideal.

The only thing left to tweak was the topping, which was ultra-simple but a little dull. To play up the apples' caramel notes, we traded half of the white sugar for brown and added dashes of cinnamon and salt. But the biggest improvement came when we took a cue from some of the better crisps we've made, swapping part of the flour for chewy rolled oats and stirring in a handful of crunchy chopped pecans. As the topping took on a deep mahogany hue and the filling gently bubbled and thickened at the edges, we knew this more deliberate approach was worth every extra minute. Our homespun apple crisp was by no means haute cuisine (good crisp never is), but it was fail-safe, more than company-worthy—and primed for a cold, creamy scoop of vanilla ice cream.

Skillet Apple Crisp

SERVES 6 TO 8

If your skillet is not ovensafe, prepare the recipe through step 3 and then transfer the filling to a 13 by 9-inch baking dish. Top the filling as directed and bake for an additional 5 minutes. We like Golden Delicious apples for this recipe, but any sweet, crisp apple such as Honeycrisp or Braeburn can be substituted. Do not use Granny Smith apples in this recipe. While old-fashioned oats are preferable in this recipe, quick-cooking oats can be substituted. Serve the apple crisp warm or at room temperature with vanilla ice cream or whipped cream.

TOPPING

- ¾ cup (3¾ ounces) unbleached all-purpose flour
- ¾ cup (3 ounces) pecans, chopped fine
- ¾ cup (2¼ ounces) old-fashioned rolled oats (see note)
- ½ cup packed (3½ ounces) light brown sugar
- ¼ cup (1¾ ounces) granulated sugar
- ½ teaspoon ground cinnamon
- ½ teaspoon table salt
- 8 tablespoons (1 stick) unsalted butter, melted

FILLING

- 3 pounds Golden Delicious apples (about 7 medium), peeled, cored, halved, and cut into ½-inch-thick wedges (see note)
- ¼ cup (1¾ ounces) granulated sugar
- ¼ teaspoon ground cinnamon (optional)
- 1 cup apple cider
- 2 teaspoons juice from 1 lemon
- 2 tablespoons unsalted butter

1. FOR THE TOPPING: Adjust an oven rack to the middle position and heat the oven to 450 degrees. Combine the flour, pecans, oats, brown sugar, granulated sugar, cinnamon, and salt in a medium bowl. Stir in the butter until the mixture is thoroughly moistened and crumbly. Set aside while preparing the fruit filling.

2. FOR THE FILLING: Toss the apples, sugar, and cinnamon (if using) together in a large bowl; set aside. Bring the cider to a simmer in a 12-inch ovensafe skillet over medium heat; cook until reduced to ½ cup, about 5 minutes. Transfer the reduced cider to a bowl or liquid measuring cup; stir in the lemon juice and set aside.

3. Heat the butter in the now-empty skillet over medium heat. When the foaming subsides, add the apple mixture and cook, stirring frequently, until the apples are beginning to soften and become translucent, 12 to 14 minutes. (Do not fully cook the apples.) Remove the pan from the heat and gently stir in the cider mixture until the apples are coated.

4. Sprinkle the topping evenly over the fruit, breaking up any large chunks. Place the skillet on a baking sheet and bake until the fruit is tender and the topping is deep golden brown, 15 to 20 minutes. Cool on a wire rack until warm, at least 15 minutes, and serve.

RATING ICE CREAM SCOOPS

Almost every ice cream scoop can do the job—but some make you work much harder than necessary with their uncomfortable handles, thick edges that can't penetrate hard-frozen surfaces, bowls that won't release the ice cream, or scoop sizes that won't fit in an ordinary cone. To find the perfect dipper, we scooped up six models, both traditional and innovative, plus our favorite portion scoop. We quickly eliminated three models, including a stumpy, short model that stands upright. A second, untraditional model sported a comfortable, bicycle grip-style handle, but its big blunt teeth marred even hard-packed ice cream. The beak-nosed contestant rolled gawky, pointed scoops of ice cream, as did the elongated scoop on another model. The three remaining models scooped capably and easily, but the "perfect," "camera-ready" orbs made by our winner impressed us most—especially when it came to loading up a brittle sugar cone. Brands are listed in order of preference. See www.americastestkitchen.com for updates to this testing.

HIGHLY RECOMMENDED

RÖSLE Ice Cream Scoop (model #12741)
PRICE: $20.00
COMMENTS: "Easy as pie to use," admired one tester, and the thin edge made for clean, round, perfect scoops.

RECOMMENDED

ZEROLL Original Ice Cream Scoop (model #7950)
PRICE: $18.50
COMMENTS: This simple, sturdy classic packs an innovative feature in its handle: self-defrosting fluid that activates by hand warmth to melt rock-hard ice cream as you scoop. However, it's not dishwasher-safe.

FANTES Stainless Portion Scoop #16 (model #1733)
PRICE: $13.99
COMMENTS: A perfect circle divided in half, this portion scoop doubles well as a scoop for softer ice cream, though the food "pusher" activated by the squeezable handle was an obstacle when pressing down to scoop hard-frozen ice cream.

RECOMMENDED WITH RESERVATIONS

OXO Good Grips Beak Ice Cream Scoop (model #1057947)
PRICE: $14.99
COMMENTS: The handle made for comfortable scooping, but the tapered bowl turned out oblong portions.

KITCHENAID Ice Cream Scoop (model #KG117OB)
PRICE: $9.99
COMMENTS: Easy enough to use, but most found it "overbuilt," as the handle was bulky and the scoop head approached a whopping 3 inches in length.

NOT RECOMMENDED

VAN VACTER Ice Cream Knife (model #IC-103)
PRICE: $14.95
COMMENTS: Almost as flat as an ice cream paddle, this blunt-toothed tool dug into hard ice cream well, but left us with misshapen, scarred scoops.

TOVOLO Standz Ice Cream Scoop (model #80-1207-10)
PRICE: $5.99
COMMENTS: The handle on this stumpy, stand-up scoop measured only 3¼ inches, and the blue plastic head tenaciously hugged ice cream so hard that we were forced to pry it out with a second tool—otherwise, it just melted and dripped on the counter.

Simply Sweet ENDINGS

Pressing the dough balls with the bottom of a measuring cup (or drinking glass) helps produce sugar cookies of even thickness.

DESSERT? YES, PLEASE. HERE WE LOOK AT TWO OLD-FASHIONED SWEET endings that are ripe for a comeback: old-fashioned sugar cookies and a fresh spin on the classic fruit dessert, berry fool.

Everyone thinks traditional sugar cookies are easy and simple. We say, "Not so fast." Have you ever made a sugar cookie that emerged from the oven appearing soft, crackled, and puffed, but tasted hard and stale once cooled? We thought so. While sugar cookies contain few ingredients—butter, sugar, eggs, and flour—the ideal soft and chewy sugar cookie can be elusive. Properly measuring ingredients, making sure the butter is at *exactly* the right temperature for creaming, and then ensuring that you cream the butter *just* enough so it's properly aerated are just a few finicky tricks typical sugar cookie recipes require. We didn't want finicky, we wanted an approachable recipe for great sugar cookies that anyone could make anytime. And when you want something a little fancier than a simple cookie to end the meal, there's a fresh berry fool.

Heretical as it may sound, apple pie was not always the quintessential American dessert. Centuries ago, fruit fool held that honor. Brought to America by British colonists in the 1700s, this dessert was made by folding pureed stewed fruit (traditionally gooseberries) into a sweet custard. We wanted to replace hard-to-find gooseberries with berries—namely strawberries and raspberries. And the custard? We wanted an easier way to give this fruity dessert a creamy contrast. Join us as we work on putting the simple back into simple desserts.

CHAI-SPICE CHEWY SUGAR COOKIES

FOOLPROOF SUGAR COOKIES

✔️ **WHY THIS RECIPE WORKS:** We melted the butter so our sugar cookie dough could easily be mixed together with a spoon—no more fussy creaming. Replacing a portion of the butter with cream cheese gave our cookies a soft texture, while the slight tang of the cream cheese contrasted nicely with the cookies' sweet flavor. And adjusting the ratio of flour to fat guaranteed that even if the flour measures are a little off, the cookies will still come out great—soft, chewy, and sweet.

HERE'S A LITTLE INSIDE INFORMATION: THE FIRST challenge for every prospective test cook at *America's Test Kitchen* is to bake a batch of chewy sugar cookies under the watchful eye of the test kitchen director. Aspiring test cooks often underestimate the task, producing cookies that are stunted and humped or thin and brittle. Indeed, the humble sugar cookie has been the downfall of many a hopeful test kitchen applicant.

The problem is that making a traditional sugar cookie requires obsessive attention to detail because there are no nuts, oats, or chocolate chunks to distract from a less-than-ideal texture and appearance. The butter must be at precisely the right temperature, and then must be creamed to the proper degree of airiness. The baking time must be calibrated to the minute. And even if you nail the proper chew, the cookie still delivers cloying sweetness.

We were determined to engineer a recipe that would produce our ideal sugar cookie every time: crisp at the edges, soft and chewy in the center, crackly crisp on top, and richly flavorful.

Most sugar cookies share the same basic ingredients: fat (usually butter), sugar, salt, flour, eggs, vanilla, and rising agents like baking powder and/or baking soda. Whether a cookie is crisp, chewy, or tender depends on the ratios and treatments of those ingredients, specifically the fat. While developing our recipe for Chewy Brownies (page 141), we learned how a mixture of saturated and unsaturated fats—in a ratio of about 1 to 2—produces more chew.

When combined, the two types of fat molecules form a sturdier crystalline structure that requires more force to bite through than the structure formed from a high proportion of saturated fats.

Keeping that in mind, we ran the fat numbers on our traditional all-butter cookie recipe—8 ounces of butter, 8 ounces of sugar, 10 ounces of flour, one egg, ½ teaspoon baking powder, ¼ teaspoon salt, and 1½ teaspoons vanilla extract—and noticed they were way off: With 62 percent saturated and 38 percent unsaturated fat, these cookies offered a good ratio for rich flavor and tenderness, but not for the chewiness we sought. In fact, for a 1−2 ratio, we needed to almost reverse the amounts of saturated and unsaturated fat. That's when we decided to pull out our old brownie trick. In that recipe, we'd learned that butter is mostly (though not entirely) made up of saturated fat, whereas the makeup of vegetable oil is almost the opposite. Therefore, the key to chewier confections was swapping most of the butter—in this case, 5 ounces—for an equal amount of oil. At least, that was part of the solution. The switch got the numbers where we wanted them—but a whole new series of problems also unfolded as a result.

For example, we now needed to change the way we were incorporating fat into the dough. Most sugar cookie recipes cream the butter with the sugar in a standing mixer, but with only 3 ounces of butter, there was not enough solid fat to hold the air. The other common method—melting the butter and whisking it with the sugar by hand—seemed promising here. When liquefied, the small amount of water in butter mixes with the flour to form gluten, which makes for chewier cookies. Plus, from a labor standpoint, omitting the standing mixer was appealing.

The downside was that two doses of liquid fat made the dough too soft to handle, and we spent the next several tests readjusting the dry ingredients. More flour helped build up structure. But to ensure that the cookies tasted like cookies, not biscuits, we also ramped up the sugar, salt, and vanilla. Better—but the cookies still baked up chunky. We thought an extra hit of leavener—more baking powder and baking soda—would help the dough spread in the oven. But when multiple tasters detected a chemical flavor, we knew we had to cut back and deal

with the denseness some other way. We suspected a drop of liquid might help, so we added milk 1 teaspoon at a time until we hit exactly 1 tablespoon. Sure enough, this little bit went a long way.

The chewiness was spot on, and our tasters were pleased. "Shame about the taste, though," they said. The problem? Trading half the rich butter for more neutral-tasting vegetable oil had rendered the cookies very sweet—and only sweet.

We knew there was no use reducing the amount of sugar. During baking, some of the sugar granules melt and dissolve into liquid, which helps the dough spread out. Without that modicum of extra liquid, the cookies would be dry and humped. Instead, we wondered if we could add something to take the edge off all that sweetness.

Something acidic, we thought, like lemon juice or zest might work. But such assertive citrus flavor took the cookies out of the "sugar" category and dropped them squarely into the lemon family. Cream of tartar—the key to the slight tang of snickerdoodles—was too subtle. Then we remembered that we often add cultured dairy products like buttermilk, sour cream, and yogurt to muffins and cakes to round out their flavors. That same tangy richness came through in the cookies, too; unfortunately, their added liquid upset the precarious moisture balance. Once again, the dough was too soft to hold its shape.

We scanned the supermarket dairy aisle and zeroed in on cream cheese, wondering if it would enrich the dough's flavor without adding much liquid. Of course, the tradeoff would be our perfect chewiness ratio; cream cheese contains less than one third the fat of vegetable oil, but most of it is saturated. With every ounce we added, we were chipping away at our carefully calibrated ratio of fats, so we traded 1 ounce of oil for a modest 2 ounces of cream cheese. The saturated fat content increased from 25 percent to 32 percent; fortunately the mere 7 percent difference didn't markedly affect the cookies' texture. But flavorwise the effect of the cream cheese was dramatic, and our tasters' faces lit up as they bit into this latest batch.

The addition of slightly acidic cream cheese had another benefit: It allowed us to add baking soda to the mix to create the crackly top we wanted. When baking soda encounters an acidic ingredient, it immediately springs into action, releasing lots of carbon dioxide. As the cookies bake, the gas bubbles rise and burst at the surface of the dough, creating a craggy top. It also raises the pH of the dough, weakening the gluten so that rupturing happens more easily.

The recipe was in good shape: The butter-oil combination provided satisfying chew, the liquid nature of the fats made the dough easy to mix by hand, and the cream cheese provided subtle contrast to the sugar. But when we confidently passed the recipe on to a friend, touting it as "foolproof," we were dismayed to find that when she tried it, her cookies spread all over the pan to form one giant confection.

Not knowing where things had gone awry, we asked her to walk us through her process and realized we'd taken a crucial test kitchen technique for granted. When baking, we measure our ingredients by weight but, like most home cooks, our friend had measured hers by volume. In the past, we've found that weights of volume-measured ingredients can vary by as much as 20 percent, which explained the spreading. Our already-soft dough needed every bit of flour to accommodate the fat, and it was very possible that her dip-and-sweep measurement fell short of what we weighed out on a digital scale. So much for foolproof. Our recipe was in fact very unforgiving when it came to even the slightest deviations, and we were determined to provide a little more wiggle room.

The spreading occurred when there was insufficient flour in relation to fat. Marginally increasing the flour would have resulted in an awkward measurement, so we reduced the amount of vegetable oil from ½ cup to ⅓ cup. Now the recipe was flexible enough to accommodate likely discrepancies in volume measurements. Some bakers might add too much flour, but doing so would

be far less disastrous than adding too little; the cookies would just finish baking a little faster. And as for balancing saturated and unsaturated fats, the saturated now totaled 36 percent, the unsaturated 64 percent—almost the exact reverse of our original tender cookie.

The only outstanding problem? With such an easy, truly foolproof cookie recipe on record, the test kitchen director will have to find something more intimidating to spring on prospective test cooks.

Chewy Sugar Cookies
MAKES ABOUT 24 COOKIES

The final dough will be slightly softer than most cookie doughs. For best results, handle the dough as briefly and gently as possible when shaping the cookies. Overworking the dough will result in flatter cookies.

- 2¼ cups (11¼ ounces) unbleached all-purpose flour
- 1 teaspoon baking powder
- ½ teaspoon baking soda
- ½ teaspoon table salt
- 1½ cups (10½ ounces) sugar, plus ⅓ cup for rolling
- 2 ounces cream cheese, cut into 8 pieces
- 6 tablespoons (¾ stick) unsalted butter, melted and still warm
- ⅓ cup vegetable oil
- 1 large egg
- 1 tablespoon whole milk
- 2 teaspoons vanilla extract

1. Adjust an oven rack to the middle position and heat the oven to 350 degrees. Line two large rimmed baking sheets with parchment paper. Whisk the flour, baking powder, baking soda, and salt together in a medium bowl. Set aside.

2. Place 1½ cups of the sugar and the cream cheese in a large bowl. Place the remaining ⅓ cup sugar in a shallow baking dish or pie plate and set aside. Pour the warm butter over the sugar and cream cheese and whisk to combine (some small lumps of cream cheese will remain but will smooth out later). Whisk in the oil until incorporated. Add the egg, milk, and vanilla; continue to whisk until smooth. Add the flour mixture and mix with a rubber spatula until a soft homogeneous dough forms.

3. Divide the dough into 24 equal pieces, about 2 tablespoons each. Using your hands, roll each piece of dough into a ball (see note). Working in batches, roll the balls in sugar to coat and set on the prepared baking sheets, 12 dough balls per sheet. Using the bottom of a drinking glass, flatten the dough balls until 2 inches in diameter. Sprinkle the tops of the cookies evenly with the remaining sugar, using 2 teaspoons for each sheet. (Discard the remaining sugar.)

4. Bake the cookies, one sheet at a time, until the edges are set and beginning to brown, 11 to 13 minutes, rotating the sheet after 7 minutes. Cool the cookies on the baking sheets for 5 minutes; using a wide metal spatula, transfer the cookies to a wire rack and cool to room temperature.

VARIATIONS

Chai-Spice Chewy Sugar Cookies

Follow the recipe for Chewy Sugar Cookies, adding ¼ teaspoon ground cinnamon, ¼ teaspoon ground ginger, ¼ teaspoon ground cardamom, ¼ teaspoon ground cloves, and pinch ground black pepper to the sugar and cream cheese mixture in step 2 and reducing the vanilla to 1 teaspoon.

Coconut-Lime Chewy Sugar Cookies

Follow the recipe for Chewy Sugar Cookies, whisking ½ cup sweetened shredded coconut, chopped fine, into the flour mixture in step 1. Add 1 teaspoon finely grated lime zest to the sugar and cream cheese mixture and substitute 1 tablespoon lime juice for the vanilla in step 2.

Hazelnut-Brown Butter Chewy Sugar Cookies

Follow the recipe for Chewy Sugar Cookies, adding ¼ cup finely chopped toasted hazelnuts to the sugar and cream cheese mixture in step 2. Instead of melting the butter, heat it in a 10-inch skillet over medium-high heat until melted, about 2 minutes. Continue to cook, swirling the pan constantly until the butter is dark golden brown and has a nutty aroma, 1 to 3 minutes. Immediately pour the butter over the sugar and cream cheese mixture and proceed with the recipe as directed, increasing the milk to 2 tablespoons and omitting the vanilla.

RATING VACUUM ROBOTS

Long gone are the days of grabbing a broom and dustpan to sweep up spills of sugar or flour. Nowadays, cleaning robots promise to whisk away both dry and wet ingredients that have inadvertently ended up on your floor. To find out if these cleaning robots are worth the money—they can cost upward of $300—we tested three robots, two that vacuum and one that scrubs floors, trying them in the test kitchen and our homes. We gave the vacuum robots a concoction of common kitchen messes to clean up, scattering a measured amount of flour, salt, coffee grounds, minced vegetables, and garlic peels over a 3-foot square of kitchen floor. To test the capabilities of the scrubbing robot, we made a mess of corn syrup, oil, and orange juice drizzled over flour. In the end, the most expensive model (one of the two vacuum models) came out on top—proving that sometimes you do get what you pay for. Brands are listed in order of preference. See www.americastestkitchen.com for updates to this testing.

HIGHLY RECOMMENDED

iROBOT Roomba (model #560)
PRICE: $349.99
COMMENTS: This top-performing vacuum robot picked up almost everything it rolled over. It boasts user-friendly controls, a recharging dock that it returns to after cleaning, and two sensor "towers" that can be set up to contain it to a certain area. The quietest model, it's also programmable so it can clean while you're away.

iROBOT Scooba (model #330)
PRICE: $299.99
COMMENTS: While this scrubbing robot is slightly more complicated than the vacuum models, the instructions are clear and its cleaning performance was superb. One downside is that it does require cleaning solution; while the cleaning solution is inexpensive ($5.99 for 32 ounces) we liked that we could also use white vinegar or plain tap water. This model is not programmable.

RECOMMENDED WITH RESERVATIONS

P3 INTERNATIONAL V-Bot Robotic Vacuum Cleaner (model #P4960)
PRICE: $92.99
COMMENTS: This noisy, low-cost vacuum robot did an adequate job but was clearly inferior to our winner in efficiency and ease of use. Its small intake and single small brush weren't enough for a really thorough cleaning. Also, the small size of the intake made it prone to clogging. This model is not programmable.

ULTIMATE BERRY FOOL

✔ **WHY THIS RECIPE WORKS:** For a berry fool with intense fruitiness and rich body, we used gelatin to thicken our fruit and combined whipped cream with sour cream for just the right touch of richness with a tangy undertone. And crumbled sweet wheat crackers added a nutty contrast to the cream and fruit.

GOOSEBERRY FOOL WAS IMPORTANT ENOUGH TO show up in the recipes of Martha Washington. Two hundred years later, it was still enough of a classic to earn a place in *James Beard's American Cookery*. The origin of the dessert's name, however, remains a mystery. Some believe it comes from the French verb *fouler* (to crush or pound). Others think the etymology points to the idea that as a dessert, this concoction was a bit of sweet foolishness.

Traditional recipes call for gently heating milk, cream, sugar, and egg yolks until thickened and then folding in cooked, pureed fruit once the custard has cooled. The resulting dessert has a deep, fruity flavor and a wonderfully silken creaminess. But cooking custard is a fussy endeavor. Overheat the yolks and you produce scrambled eggs; neglect to bring the mixture up to a high enough temperature and you've made eggnog.

Modern recipes skip the custard and use whipped cream. But most of the whipped cream versions we tested, including one from *James Beard's American Cookery*, blunted the flavor of the fruit and seemed too light and insubstantial when compared with fool made with custard. Worse, if the recipe departed from the traditional fruit choice—gooseberries—the dessert turned soupy and loose. We knew we weren't going to be using gooseberries unless we grew them ourselves. And we definitely didn't want to cook up custard. Could we concoct a dessert with the intense fruitiness and rich body of a traditional fool just the same?

The reason fool made with gooseberries has a firmer texture is that this hard-to-find heritage fruit is naturally high in pectin. When exposed to heat, sugar, and acid, pectin breaks down and causes the fruit to thicken (see "Gelatin versus Pectin," on page 309). We wanted to use raspberries and strawberries, but they contain very little pectin and remain loose when cooked. Would adding a little commercially made pectin help? It did—but we needed to add so much extra sugar for the pectin to work that our puree turned into a supersweet jam.

Some fool recipes we found cooked low-pectin fruits such as raspberries and strawberries with egg yolks to thicken them up, in essence creating a fruit curd. Not surprisingly, a yolk-based fruit puree turned out to be just as temperamental as custard, requiring lots of attention to keep the fruit from turning lumpy. Furthermore, when we folded the curd into the whipped cream, the dessert no longer tasted fresh and fruity; it had an eggy flavor that superseded everything else. Cornstarch proved equally unhelpful in achieving the results we wanted. Though we used less than typically called for in a fruit pie filling, the cooked berries still lost some of their fresh, vibrant flavor, and the mixture had a slight chalkiness our tasters didn't like.

The idea of using gelatin had been tossed around the test kitchen—recipes for desserts such as mousse and Bavarian cream often use it to firm up texture. But adding it to fruit? Wouldn't that turn our puree into Jell-O? For gelatin to work, we would need to use a judicious hand. We added just 2 teaspoons, softening the gelatin in some uncooked berry puree and then combining the softened mixture with some heated puree to help melt and distribute the gelatin. After setting for a couple of hours in the refrigerator, the puree thickened to the consistency of a loose pie filling: perfect. Once we tasted the puree, we knew we had hit the jackpot—it had a far fresher and more intense fruit flavor than anything we'd managed to produce yet. And, unlike the other methods we'd tried, we didn't need to actually cook the fruit. We only needed to get the puree hot enough to melt the gelatin.

All that remained was to create a richer, sturdier cream base to partner with the fruit puree. Making custard was out. But why not try to make whipped cream more custardlike? We rounded up a bunch of candidates to add density to the billowy cream: whole milk yogurt, mascarpone cheese, crème fraîche, and sour cream. Whipped

ULTIMATE BERRY FOOL

together with heavy cream, each worked surprisingly well in creating a mixture that was airy yet more substantial than plain whipped cream. Sour cream won out for adding just the right degree of richness, along with a mildly tangy undertone.

Our tasters, however, were clamoring for a bit more fruit flavor, as well as contrasting fruit texture. Layering the fruit puree and cream base with fresh berries tasted great but left pools of juice in the mixture. Letting the berries stand in a sugar mixture solved the problem by drawing out excess juice that could be strained off.

We could have left the fool well enough alone, but we had encountered several recipes that sprinkled the dessert with crumbled cookies or sweet crackers. We tried a range of these, including graham crackers and gingersnaps. The tasters' favorite was sweet wheat crackers, for the pleasant contrast their nuttiness added to the cream and fruit. With its fruity flavor and creamy texture, we now had a modern, reliable recipe that kept only the best traits of this old-fashioned dessert.

SCIENCE DESK

GELATIN VERSUS PECTIN
Gelatin might be a newcomer to recipes for fruit fool, but it has long been used to impart a silken texture to desserts ranging from Bavarian cream to mousse. A pure protein derived from animal bones and connective tissues, gelatin changes liquid into a semisolid state by trapping water and slowing its movement. In contrast to other thickening agents, gelatin begins to melt at body temperature, contributing to a unique sensation in the mouth. These properties worked beautifully in our Ultimate Berry Fool, transforming a thin berry puree into a viscous mixture that lent silkiness to the enriched whipped cream.

Pectin is a carbohydrate that occurs naturally in fruits and vegetables and holds cell walls together like cement. When exposed to heat, sugar, and acid, pectin molecules loosen their grip on the cell walls and bond directly with each other, creating a matrix that traps water in much the same way gelatin molecules do. However, unlike gelatin, pectin requires high temperatures for its thickening action to be reversed. It also proved an unsuitable thickener for the fruit in our fool, requiring so much sugar to work that it turned the berries into jam.

Ultimate Berry Fool
SERVES 6

Blueberries or blackberries can be substituted for the raspberries in this recipe. You may also substitute frozen fruit for fresh, but there will be a slight compromise in texture. If using frozen fruit, reduce the amount of sugar in the puree by 1 tablespoon. The thickened fruit puree can be made up to 4 hours in advance; just make sure to whisk it well in step 4 to break up any clumps before combining it with the whipped cream. For the best results, chill your beater and bowl before whipping the cream. We like the granular texture and nutty flavor of Carr's Whole Wheat Crackers, but graham crackers or gingersnaps will also work.

2 quarts strawberries (about 2 pounds), washed, dried, and stemmed

1 pint raspberries (about 12 ounces), washed and dried (see note)

½ cup (3½ ounces) plus 4 tablespoons sugar

2 teaspoons unflavored powdered gelatin

1 cup heavy cream

¼ cup sour cream

½ teaspoon vanilla extract

4 Carr's Whole Wheat Crackers, crushed fine (about ¼ cup) (see note)

6 sprigs fresh mint (optional)

1. Process 1 quart of the strawberries, ½ pint of the raspberries, and ½ cup of the sugar in a food processor until the mixture is completely smooth, about 1 minute. Strain the berry puree through a fine-mesh strainer into a 4-cup liquid measuring cup (you should have 2½ cups puree; reserve any excess for another use). Transfer ½ cup of the puree to a small bowl and sprinkle the gelatin over the top; stir until the gelatin is incorporated and let stand at least 5 minutes. Heat the remaining 2 cups puree in a small saucepan over medium heat until it begins to bubble, 4 to 6 minutes. Remove the pan from the heat and stir in the gelatin mixture until dissolved. Transfer the gelatin-puree mixture to a medium bowl, cover with plastic wrap, and refrigerate until cold, about 2 hours.

2. Meanwhile, chop the remaining 1 quart strawberries into rough ¼-inch pieces. Toss the strawberries, remaining ½ pint raspberries, and 2 tablespoons more sugar together in a medium bowl. Set aside for 1 hour.

3. Place the cream, sour cream, vanilla, and remaining 2 tablespoons sugar in the chilled bowl of a standing mixer. Beat on low speed until bubbles form, about 30 seconds. Increase the mixer speed to medium and continue beating until the beaters leave a trail, about 30 seconds. Increase the speed to high; continue beating until the mixture has nearly doubled in volume and holds stiff peaks, about 30 seconds. Transfer ⅓ cup of the whipped cream mixture to a small bowl and set aside.

4. Remove the thickened berry puree from the refrigerator and whisk until smooth. With the mixer running at medium speed, slowly add two-thirds of the puree to the whipped cream mixture; mix until incorporated, about 15 seconds. Using a spatula, gently fold in the remaining thickened puree, leaving streaks of puree.

5. Transfer the uncooked berries to a fine-mesh strainer; shake gently to remove any excess juice. Divide two-thirds of the berries evenly among six tall parfait or sundae glasses. Divide the creamy berry mixture evenly among the glasses, followed by the remaining uncooked berries. Top each glass with the reserved plain whipped cream mixture. Sprinkle with the crushed crackers and garnish with mint sprigs, if using. Serve immediately.

RATING INNOVATIVE MIXING BOWLS

Our mixing bowls (we rely on those made of classic stainless steel or heat-resistant glass) are kitchen workhorses. Yet they have their shortcomings: They wobble as you mix, the rim can make pouring a mess, and metal bowls can't go in the microwave. Would any of the innovative new designs do better? We tested nine models in glass, plastic, metal, and silicone. The bowls had features such as silicone or rubber-lined bottoms to prevent skidding and handles and spouts to make pouring easier. All withstood the beatings of a hand mixer, whisk, spatula, and wooden spoon when we mixed cookie dough and pancake batter. We didn't like many of the plastic bowls; they scratched easily and retained odors. In the end just one bowl offered an improvement on our usual workhorses. Brands are listed in order of preference. See www.americastestkitchen.com for updates to this testing.

HIGHLY RECOMMENDED

PYREX Grip-Rite 5-Quart Teardrop Mixing Bowl (model #1078616)
PRICE: $17.09 **MICROWAVE SAFE:** Yes
STURDINESS: Good **POURING:** Good
COMMENTS: This sturdy, heavy, wide, tempered-glass bowl with silicone strips on the base gripped the counter so firmly that we didn't need to hold it when mixing cookie dough with a hand mixer. Its teardrop shape formed a spout that poured pancake batter smoothly.

RECOMMENDED

PROGRESSIVE 5-Quart Collapsible Bowl (model #10669007)
PRICE: $11.30 **MICROWAVE SAFE:** No
STURDINESS: Good **POURING:** Good
COMMENTS: This collapsible bowl made of silicone and plastic has wide curves that made it sturdy and easy to get at dry ingredients stuck at the bottom. A spout made pouring easy, but you can't use this bowl over hot water on the stove and it isn't microwave safe.

RECOMMENDED WITH RESERVATIONS

OXO Good Grips 5-Quart Plastic Mixing Bowl (model #1059701)
PRICE: $9.90 **MICROWAVE SAFE:** No
STURDINESS: Fair **POURING:** Good
COMMENTS: Though lightweight, the wide, flat, silicone-covered bottom of this plastic bowl created enough friction against the counter to keep the bowl fairly steady. But this bowl was not safe in the microwave or as part of a double boiler.

CALPHALON Mixing Bowl Set, 3 Pieces (1.5-, 3-, and 5-quart bowls) (model #BT09)
PRICE: $49.95 **MICROWAVE SAFE:** No
STURDINESS: Good **POURING:** Poor
COMMENTS: The bottom exterior of this metal bowl is covered with silicone. That feature, combined with an extra-wide and flat bottom, made it so sturdy we could mix cookie dough in it with one hand. But the short walls allowed dough to spray out of the bowl when using a hand mixer.

RECOMMENDED WITH RESERVATIONS *(cont.)*

CUISIPRO 3.5-Quart Deluxe Batter Bowl (model #74 703602)
PRICE: $16.99 **MICROWAVE SAFE:** Yes
STURDINESS: Poor **POURING:** Good
COMMENTS: This plastic bowl has a nonslip base that helps you tilt the bowl when mixing. The handle and pouring spout were useful, but the deep, curved shape trapped dry ingredients at the bottom.

KITCHENAID 3-Piece Mixing Bowl Set (2.5-, 3.5-, and 4.5-quart bowls) (model #KG175WHK)
PRICE: $18.44 **MICROWAVE SAFE:** No
STURDINESS: Poor **POURING:** Good
COMMENTS: The rubber ring around the bowl's base stopped it from skidding, and its spout neatly poured pancake batter. However, the thin plastic felt cheap and easily breakable.

ISI Basics Flex It 2-Quart Mixing Bowl (model #B25101)
PRICE: $18 **MICROWAVE SAFE:** Yes
STURDINESS: Poor **POURING:** Fair
COMMENTS: Though this 100 percent silicone bowl is both microwave- and oven-safe, it was too floppy and flimsy to be used easily with a hand mixer.

NOT RECOMMENDED

POURFECT 6- and 8-Cup Bowl Set (model #21989)
PRICE: $20 **MICROWAVE SAFE:** No
STURDINESS: Poor **POURING:** Good
COMMENTS: This plastic bowl poured out batter in a neat, even stream, but its narrow design made it difficult to reach all of the dry ingredients at the bottom.

OXO Good Grips Stainless Steel 5-Quart Mixing Bowl (White) (model #1071823)
PRICE: $22.50 **MICROWAVE SAFE:** No
STURDINESS: Poor **POURING:** Poor
COMMENTS: This bowl has double walls to keep ingredients cold or hot, but the plastic outer layer made it unusable as a double boiler. This bowl is also not microwave safe.

CONVERSIONS & EQUIVALENCIES

SOME SAY COOKING IS A SCIENCE AND AN ART. WE would say that geography has a hand in it, too. Flour milled in the United Kingdom and elsewhere will feel and taste different from flour milled in the United States. So, while we cannot promise that the loaf of bread you bake in Canada or England will taste the same as a loaf baked in the States, we can offer guidelines for converting weights and measures. We also recommend that you rely on your instincts when making our recipes. Refer to the visual cues provided. If the bread dough hasn't "come together in a ball," as described, you may need to add more flour—even if the recipe doesn't tell you so. You be the judge.

The recipes in this book were developed using standard U.S. measures following U.S. government guidelines. The charts below offer equivalents for U.S., metric, and Imperial (U.K.) measures. All conversions are approximate and have been rounded up or down to the nearest whole number. For example:

1 teaspoon = 4.929 milliliters, rounded up to 5 milliliters
1 ounce = 28.349 grams, rounded down to 28 grams

VOLUME CONVERSIONS

U.S.	METRIC
1 teaspoon	5 milliliters
2 teaspoons	10 milliliters
1 tablespoon	15 milliliters
2 tablespoons	30 milliliters
¼ cup	59 milliliters
⅓ cup	79 milliliters
½ cup	118 milliliters
¾ cup	177 milliliters
1 cup	237 milliliters
1¼ cups	296 milliliters
1½ cups	355 milliliters
2 cups	473 milliliters
2½ cups	592 milliliters
3 cups	710 milliliters
4 cups (1 quart)	0.946 liter
1.06 quarts	1 liter
4 quarts (1 gallon)	3.8 liters

WEIGHT CONVERSIONS

OUNCES	GRAMS
½	14
¾	21
1	28
1½	43
2	57
2½	71
3	85
3½	99
4	113
4½	128
5	142
6	170
7	198
8	227
9	255
10	283
12	340
16 (1 pound)	454

CONVERSIONS FOR INGREDIENTS COMMONLY USED IN BAKING

Baking is an exacting science. Because measuring by weight is far more accurate than measuring by volume, and thus more likely to achieve reliable results, in our recipes we provide ounce measures in addition to cup measures for many ingredients. Refer to the chart below to convert these measures into grams.

INGREDIENT	OUNCES	GRAMS
Flour		
1 cup all-purpose flour*	5	142
1 cup cake flour	4	113
1 cup whole wheat flour	5½	156
Sugar		
1 cup granulated (white) sugar	7	198
1 cup packed brown sugar (light or dark)	7	198
1 cup confectioners' sugar	4	113
Cocoa Powder		
1 cup cocoa powder	3	85
Butter†		
4 tablespoons (½ stick, or ¼ cup)	2	57
8 tablespoons (1 stick, or ½ cup)	4	113
16 tablespoons (2 sticks, or 1 cup)	8	227

* U.S. all-purpose flour, the most frequently used flour in this book, does not contain leaveners, as some European flours do. These leavened flours are called self-rising or self-raising. If you are using self-rising flour, take this into consideration before adding leavening to a recipe.
† In the United States, butter is sold both salted and unsalted. We generally recommend unsalted butter. If you are using salted butter, take this into consideration before adding salt to a recipe.

OVEN TEMPERATURES

FAHRENHEIT	CELSIUS	GAS MARK (imperial)
225	105	¼
250	120	½
275	130	1
300	150	2
325	165	3
350	180	4
375	190	5
400	200	6
425	220	7
450	230	8
475	245	9

CONVERTING TEMPERATURES FROM AN INSTANT-READ THERMOMETER

We include doneness temperatures in many of our recipes, such as those for poultry, meat, and bread. We recommend an instant-read thermometer for the job. Refer to the table above to convert Fahrenheit degrees to Celsius. Or, for temperatures not represented in the chart, use this simple formula:

Subtract 32 degrees from the Fahrenheit reading, then divide the result by 1.8 to find the Celsius reading.

EXAMPLE:

"Roast until the thickest part of a chicken thigh registers 175 degrees on an instant-read thermometer." To convert:

175° F − 32 = 143°
143° ÷ 1.8 = 79.44°C, rounded down to 79°C

INDEX

Cashews, Garlicky Eggplant, and
Scallions, Stir-Fried Shrimp with,
88–89
Chai-Spice Chewy Sugar Cookies,
302, 306
Charcoal-Grilled Argentine Steaks with
Chimichurri Sauce, 230–34, *232*
Charcoal-Grilled Stuffed Chicken
Breasts with Prosciutto and
Fontina, 218–21, *220*
Charcoal-Grilled Tuna Steaks with
Red Wine Vinegar and Mustard
Vinaigrette, 222–26, *223*
Charcoal–Grill-Smoked Pork Chops,
194, 195–98
Charmoula Vinaigrette, Grilled Tuna
Steaks with, 226
Cheese
Almost Hands-Free Risotto
with Chicken and Herbs, 154–55
with Parmesan and Herbs, 150–54,
151
Chicago Deep-Dish Pizza, 110–14, *111*
with Olives and Ricotta, 114
with Sausage, 114
Cream, Coffee Cake, *256,* 257–60
feta, taste tests on, 84
Greek-Style Shrimp with Tomatoes
and Feta, 80–83, *81*
Mediterranean Chopped Salad,
115–19, *116*
No-Fuss Polenta
with Broccoli Rabe, Sun-Dried
Tomatoes, and Pine Nuts, *163,*
165
Creamy Parmesan, 162–65
with Sautéed Cherry Tomato and
Fresh Mozzarella, 166
with Sweet-and-Sour Onion Relish,
166
Pecorino Romano, about, 142
Spaghetti with Pecorino Romano and
Black Pepper, *140,* 141–42
Stuffed Chicken Breasts with
Prosciutto and Fontina
Charcoal-Grilled, 218–21, *220*
Gas-Grilled, 221

Cheese wires, ratings of, 167
Chermoula Sauce, Roasted Carrots
with, 107
Cherry(ies)
Dried, and Hazelnuts, Best Baked
Apples with, 64
Pie, Sweet, 290–95, *291*
Sauce, Slow-Roasted Pork Shoulder
with, 60
Chewy Brownies, *276,* 277–80
Chewy Sugar Cookies, 303–6
Chai-Spice, *302,* 306
Coconut-Lime, 306
Hazelnut–Brown Butter, 306
Chicago Deep-Dish Pizza, 110–14, *111*
with Olives and Ricotta, 114
with Sausage, 114
Chicken
braising, low and slow, 160
Breasts, Boneless, Skinless, Pan-Seared,
4–7, *5*
Breasts, Charcoal-Grilled Stuffed,
with Prosciutto and Fontina,
218–21, *220*
Breasts, Gas-Grilled Stuffed, with
Prosciutto and Fontina, 221
buttermilk brines for, 51
Canzanese, 158–62, *159*
and Dumplings, Streamlined, 23–27, *24*
Fried, Easier, 49–52, *50*
and Herbs, Almost Hands-Free Risotto
with, 154–55
perfect coating combo for, 6
Pot Pie with Savory Crumble Topping,
35–40, *36*
Thai, with Basil, 182–85, *183*
Chiles
taming heat from, with sugar, 184
Thai Chicken with Basil, 182–85, *183*
Chili Oil, 190
Chimichurri Sauce, 233–34
Chinese Dumplings, Steamed
(Shu Mai), *186,* 187–90
Chocolate
Chewy Brownies, *276,* 277–80
Cupcakes, Ultimate, with Ganache
Filling, 281–84, *282*

Chocolate *(cont.)*
Frosting, Creamy, 284–86
Milk, Frosting, Creamy Malted, 286
Cilantro
Chimichurri Sauce, 233–34
Grilled Tuna Steaks with Charmoula
Vinaigrette, 226
Classic Bread Pudding, 264–67, *265*
Cocktail shakers, ratings of, 227
Coconut-Lime Chewy Sugar Cookies,
306
Coffee Cake, Cream Cheese, *256,*
257–60
Cookies and bars
Best Shortbread, 267–71, *268*
Chai-Spice Chewy Sugar Cookies,
302, 306
Chewy Brownies, *276,* 277–80
Chewy Sugar Cookies, 303–6
Coconut-Lime Chewy Sugar Cookies,
306
Hazelnut–Brown Butter Chewy
Sugar Cookies, 306
Cookie spatulas, ratings of, 287
Cooling racks, baker's, ratings of, 287
Corn and Black Bean Filling,
Beef Empanadas with, 179
Cornmeal. *See* Polenta
Cranberry(ies)
and Bourbon Pan Sauce, 8
Dried, and Pecans, Best Baked Apples
with, 60–64, *61*
and Pear Chopped Salad, 118
Cream Cheese Coffee Cake, *256,*
257–60
Cream Sauce, Horseradish, *101,* 104
Cream whippers, ratings of, 167
Creamy Chocolate Frosting, 284–86
Creamy Gazpacho Andaluz, 235–38,
237
Creamy Malted Milk Chocolate
Frosting, 286
Creamy Peanut Butter Frosting, 286
Creamy Vanilla Frosting, 286
Crisp, Skillet Apple, 295–98, *296*
Crispy Smashed Potatoes, 213–15,
214

Cucumbers
 Fennel and Apple Chopped Salad, 117
 Mediterranean Chopped Salad,
  115–19, *116*
 Pear and Cranberry Chopped Salad,
  118
 Radish and Orange Chopped Salad,
  119
 seeding and chopping, 118
Cupcake and cake carriers, ratings of,
 287
Cupcakes, Ultimate Chocolate, with
 Ganache Filling, 281–84, *282*

D

Desserts
 Best Baked Apples
  with Dried Apricots and Almonds,
   64
  with Dried Cherries and Hazelnuts,
   64
  with Dried Cranberries and Pecans,
   60–64, *61*
  with Dried Figs and Macadamia
   Nuts, 64
  with Raisins and Walnuts, 64
 Best Shortbread, 267–71, *268*
 Chewy Brownies, *276,* 277–80
 Chewy Sugar Cookies, 303–6
  Chai-Spice, *302,* 306
  Coconut-Lime, 306
  Hazelnut–Brown Butter, 306
 Classic Bread Pudding, 264–67, *265*
 Skillet Apple Crisp, 295–98, *296*
 Sweet Cherry Pie, 290–95, *291*
 Ultimate Berry Fool, 307–10, *308*
 Ultimate Chocolate Cupcakes with
  Ganache Filling, 281–84, *282*
Digital thermometers, ratings of, 65
Disposable grills, ratings of, 205
Dumplings, Chicken and, Streamlined,
 23–27, *24*
Dumplings, Steamed Chinese
 (Shu Mai), *186,* 187–90

E

Easier Fried Chicken, 49–52, *50*
Easy Buttermilk Waffles, 242–44, *243*
Eggplant, Garlicky, Scallions, and
 Cashews, Stir-Fried Shrimp
 with, 88–89
Electric kettles, adjustable,
 ratings of, 261
Electric knife sharpeners,
 ratings of, 273
Electric pressure cookers,
 ratings of, 53
Empanadas, Beef, 175–79, *176*
Empanadas, Beef, with Corn and
 Black Bean Filling, 179
Equipment, ratings of
 baker's cooling racks, 287
 basting spoons, 167
 blenders, immersion, 273
 blenders, upright, 272
 cheese wires, 167
 cocktail shakers, 227
 cream whippers, 167
 cupcake and cake carriers, 287
 disposable grills, 205
 electric kettles, adjustable, 261
 electric knife sharpeners, 273
 electric pressure cookers, 53
 fire extinguishers, 9
 food processors, 272
 food storage containers, plastic, 41
 grill lighters, 205
 hybrid chef's knives, 97
 ice cream scoops, 299
 ice crushers, hand-cranked, 227
 ice trays/buckets, 227
 Jamie Oliver's Flavour Shaker, 107
 jar openers, 167
 kitchen timers, 167
 meat pounders, 15
 mixers, hand, 272
 mixers, standing, 273
 mixing bowls, innovative, 311
 rib racks, 205
 saucepans, large, 191
 seltzer makers, 227
 skillets, inexpensive nonstick, 77

Equipment, ratings of *(cont.)*
 slicing brownie pans, 287
 smokers, 212
 spatulas, 126
 spatulas, cookie, 287
 spatulas, icing, 287
 thermometers, digital, 65
 thermometers, remote, 205
 vacuum robots, 306
 waffle irons, 245

F

Fennel
 and Apple Chopped Salad, 117
 and Carrots, Roasted, with Toasted
  Almonds, 107
 and Mustard Pan Sauce, 8
 trimming and coring, 118
Feta cheese
 Mediterranean Chopped Salad,
  115–19, *116*
 taste tests on, 84
 and Tomatoes, Greek-Style Shrimp
  with, 80–83, *81*
Figs, Dried, and Macadamia Nuts,
 Best Baked Apples with, 64
Fire extinguishers, ratings of, 9
Fish
 encouraging caramelization of, 74
 fillets, removing skin from, 76
 Fillets, Thick-Cut, Pan-Roasted,
  72–75, *73*
 Tuna Steaks
  Charcoal-Grilled, with Red Wine
   Vinegar and Mustard Vinaigrette,
   222–26, *223*
  Gas-Grilled, with Red Wine Vinegar
   and Mustard Vinaigrette, 226
  Grilled, with Charmoula
   Vinaigrette, 226
  Grilled, with Provençal
   Vinaigrette, 226
  Grilled, with Soy-Ginger
   Vinaigrette, 226
Flame tamer, improvising, 164
Focaccia, Rosemary, 134–39, *135*

Spatulas, ratings of
    cookie spatulas, 287
    icing spatulas, 287
    metal and plastic, 126
Spicy Mexican Shredded Pork Tostadas,
    170–73, *171*
Spicy Mexican Shredded Pork Tostadas
    with Homemade Chorizo,
    173–75
Squash. *See* Zucchini
Standing mixers, ratings of, 273
Steak Frites, 122–25, *123*
Steamed Chinese Dumplings
    (Shu Mai), *186,* 187–90
Stews
    Beef, Best, 18–21, *19*
    Streamlined Chicken and Dumplings,
        23–27, *24*
Stir-fries
    Stir-Fried Shrimp
        with Garlicky Eggplant, Scallions,
            and Cashews, 88–89
        Sichuan-Style, with Zucchini,
            Red Bell Pepper, and Peanuts, 89
        with Snow Peas and Red Bell
            Pepper in Hot and Sour Sauce,
            85–88, *87*
    Thai Chicken with Basil, 182–85, *183*
Streamlined Chicken and Dumplings,
    23–27, *24*
Stuffing, 95
Sugar Cookies, Chewy, 303–6
    Chai-Spice, *302,* 306
    Coconut-Lime, 306
    Hazelnut–Brown Butter, 306
Sweet and Tangy Barbecue Sauce,
    47–48
Sweet Cherry Pie, 290–95, *291*

T

Thai Chicken with Basil, 182–85, *183*
Thermometers, ratings of
    digital, 65
    remote, 205

Tomato(es)
    canned diced, taste tests on, 239
    Cherry, Sautéed, and Fresh Mozzarella,
        No-Fuss Polenta with, 166
    Chicago Deep-Dish Pizza, 110–14,
        111
    with Olives and Ricotta, 114
    with Sausage, 114
    Creamy Gazpacho Andaluz, 235–38,
        237
    and Feta, Greek-Style Shrimp with,
        80–83, *81*
    -Ginger Sauce, 72
    Mediterranean Chopped Salad,
        115–19, *116*
    Sun-Dried, Broccoli Rabe, and
        Pine Nuts, No-Fuss Polenta with,
        163, 165
Tortillas
    Baked Tostadas, 175
    Spicy Mexican Shredded Pork Tostadas,
        170–73, *171*
    Spicy Mexican Shredded Pork Tostadas
        with Homemade Chorizo, 173–75
Tostadas
    Baked, 175
    Spicy Mexican Shredded Pork, 170–73,
        171
    Spicy Mexican Shredded Pork, with
        Homemade Chorizo, 173–75
Tuna Steaks
    Charcoal-Grilled, with Red Wine
        Vinegar and Mustard Vinaigrette,
        222–26, *223*
    Gas-Grilled, with Red Wine Vinegar
        and Mustard Vinaigrette, 226
    Grilled, with Charmoula Vinaigrette,
        226
    Grilled, with Provençal Vinaigrette, 226
    Grilled, with Soy-Ginger Vinaigrette,
        226
Turkey
    Gravy, Make-Ahead, 96
    salting, technique for, 94
    Stuffed, Old-Fashioned, 92–96, *93*

U

Ultimate Banana Bread, 252–55, *253*
Ultimate Berry Fool, 307–10, *308*
Ultimate Chocolate Cupcakes with
    Ganache Filling, 281–84, *282*

V

Vacuum robots, ratings of, 306
Vanilla Frosting, Creamy, 286
Vanilla ice cream, ratings of, 294
Vegetable oils, taste tests on, 174
Vegetables
    Hearty Minestrone, *146,* 147–50
    Root, Old-Fashioned Pot Roast with,
        35
    salting, for soups, 238
    see also specific vegetables
Vinaigrette, Foolproof, 127–31
    Balsamic-Mustard, 131
    Herb, *128,* 131
    Lemon, 131
    Walnut, 131
Vinegar Barbecue Sauce, Lexington, 48

W

Waffle irons, ratings of, 245
Waffles, Easy Buttermilk, 242–44, *243*
Walnuts
    Fennel and Apple Chopped Salad, 117
    No-Fuss Polenta with Sweet-and-Sour
        Onion Relish, 166
    and Raisins, Best Baked Apples with,
        64
    Ultimate Banana Bread, 252–55, *253*

Z

Zucchini, Red Bell Pepper, and Peanuts,
    Stir-Fried Sichuan-Style Shrimp
    with, 89